CENSORED

"[*Censored*] should be affixed to the bulletin boards in every newsroom in America. And, perhaps read aloud to a few publishers and television executives."—Ralph Nader

"[*Censored*] offers devastating evidence of the dumbing-down of mainstream news in America.... Required reading for broadcasters, journalists and well-informed citizens."—*Los Angeles Times*

"A distant early warning system for society's problems." —*American Journalism Review*

"One of the most significant media research projects in the country." —I.F. Stone

"A terrific resource, especially for its directory of alternative media and organizations.... Recommended for media collections."—*Library Journal*

"Project Censored shines a spotlight on news that an informed public must have...a vital contribution to our democratic process." —Rhoda H. Karpatkin, President, Consumer's Union

"Buy it, read it, act on it. Our future depends on the knowledge this collection of suppressed stories allows us."—*San Diego Review*

"This volume chronicles 25 news stories about events that could affect all of us, but which we most likely did not hear or read about in the popular news media."—*Bloomsbury Review*

"*Censored* serves as a reminder that there is certainly more to the news than is easily available or willingly disclosed. To those of us who work in the newsrooms, it's an inspiration, an indictment, and an admonition to look deeper, ask more questions, then search for the truth in the answers we get."—*Creative Loafings*

"This invaluable resource deserves to be more widely known." —*Wilson Library Bulletin*

"Once again Project Censored has produced an invaluable guide to the sociopolitical landscape of the United States and the world.... A vital yearly addition to your library."—*Outposts*

CENSORED 2000

The Year's Top 25 Censored Stories

2000

PETER PHILLIPS & PROJECT CENSORED

INTRODUCTION BY MUMIA ABU-JAMAL
CARTOONS BY TOM TOMORROW

SEVEN STORIES PRESS
New York / London / Sydney / Toronto

Seven Stories Press
140 Watts Street
New York, NY 10013
www.sevenstories.com

In Canada:
Hushion House
36 Northline Road
Toronto, Ontario M4B 3E2

In the U.K.:
Turnaround Publisher Services Ltd.
Unit 3, Olympia Trading Estate
Coburg Road, Wood Green
London N22 6TZ

In Australia:
Tower Books
9/19 Rodborough Road
Frenchs Forest NSW 2086

College professors may order examination copies of Seven Stories Press titles for a
free six-month trial period. To order, visit www.sevenstories.com/textbook, or fax
on school letterhead to (212) 226-1411.

ISSN 1074-5998

9 8 7 6 5 4 3 2 1

Book design by Cindy LaBreacht

Printed in the U.S.A.

Dedication

JEFF PHILLIPS

AND

CATHY SALITA-PHILLIPS

Married November 21, 1999

Mr. B's Hello

European trains

Connecticut dreams

Dancing chairs

Maui rains

and

Trooper

Contents

THIS MODERN WORLD

by TOM TOMORROW

AND NOW -- A VERY SPECIAL OFFER FROM YOUR FRIENDS AT CNN...

NOT AVAILABLE IN ANY STORE-- IT'S "SOUND BITES: THE CNN THEME MUSIC COMPILATION"!

FROM THE POIGNANT SIX-NOTE TRIBUTE TO PRINCESS DI TO THE STIRRING EIGHT-NOTE EVOCATION OF THE KOSOVO CONFLICT-- ALL YOUR FAVORITE NEWS STORY THEMES ARE HERE!

YOU'LL RELIVE THE TENSION AND DRAMA OF THE TRIAL OF THE CENTURY WHEN YOU HEAR THE BRIEF BUT COMPELLING "THEME FROM THE O.J. TRIAL!"

AND HERE'S A BLAST FROM THE PAST: THE "THEME FROM DESERT STORM," SUMMING UP THE HEROISM AND DETERMINATION OF OUR MILITARY LEADERS IN TEN PATRIOTIC NOTES!

YOU'LL ALSO GET SUCH INSTANT CLASSICS AS "MONICA'S THEME (DID HE OR DIDN'T HE?)"-- THE "COLUMBINE MASSACRE OVERTURE"-- AND, OF COURSE, THE BITTERSWEET "JFK, JR. PLANE CRASH IN B MINOR!"

I DON'T KNOW ABOUT YOU, BERNIE, BUT I CAN'T THINK OF A BETTER GIFT FOR THAT SPECIAL SOMEONE!

BUT WAIT-- THERE'S MORE! ORDER TODAY AND YOU'LL RECEIVE THIS BONUS DANCE REMIX FEATURING THE HIP HOP STYLINGS OF OUR OWN WOLF BLITZER!

SO CALL NOW -- AND RECAPTURE THE MUSICAL MEMORIES OF A DECADE OF TRAGEDY AND SUFFERING -- AS ONLY CNN CAN COMPOSE THEM!

JAM MASTER WOLF

TOM TOMORROW©08-11-99 ... tomorrow@well.com ... www.thismodernworld.com

Preface

A common mistake in the English language is to use the word media in the singular. So my early writings often used the words "the media is" instead of "the media are." When I took over the directorship of Project Censored from the founder Carl Jensen in 1996, I quickly learned that the word media was plural. Now, after the release of our 24th annual list of the most censored news stories, we find that year by year the number of important news items that are censored increases. And I find myself wondering if media isn't singular after all: The continuation of media-merger mania is making the industry singular in action, thought, and purpose. It is singular in its methods of story editing and selection, focusing on entertainment value instead of news worthiness. News headlines today feature Tinky Winky and Jerry Falwell's Theory on this Purple Teletubby (see Chapter 3, "News Abuse"). Media is singular in its thought, through its ideological uniformity, failure to present diversified points of view, and its blind pro-American free-market-capitalism-can-do-no-wrong approach (see Chapter 6 by Michael Parenti). The media is singular in its purpose, with its simple-minded profit-maximizing greed. Media is no longer a competitive industry, but rather an oligopolic collective of like-minded rich, white, upper-class elites with shared agendas seeking to expand their power and influence globally. Elitism is what Bob McChesney refers to as "Rich Media, Poor Democracy" (Chapter 5)—and the consequences are sad for us all.

Corporate media has become so complacent as entertainer, it collectively failed to challenge NATO/Pentagon propaganda in 1999. The mainstream media in the United States were very aware that the Pentagon and NATO were releasing biased and false information regarding the war in Kosovo, yet they continued to pass on the information to the American public as if it were gospel. Senior correspondent for *Newsday*'s Washington Bureau, Patrick Sloyan states, "...the media were once more asked to sort out a few kernels of facts from a barrage of distortions and half-truths from government information manipulators...baloney-ladened military briefings in Brussels...cryptic shows at the Pentagon." Writing in the *American Journalism Review* (June 1999), Sloyan went on to describe how the elite of U.S. media complained to President Clinton, but failed to use their power to challenge the government. Little wonder that five of the top most censored stories for 1999 have to do with the U.S.'s role in Kosovo and throughout the Balkans.

With newspapers physically reducing foreign coverage (see Peter Arnett's *Censored* story #7), the American public has become the "best entertained least informed society in the world" (Neil Postman). Danny Schechter's Chapter 11 on the Falun Gong is a perfect example of the U.S. media failing to cover important foreign news.

In 1999, the U.S. government felt that foreign press coverage was such a threat to their information control ambitions that it became necessary to permanently create a new International Public Information (IPI) group. This new government group, made up of top military, diplomatic, and intelligence officials, is designed to coordinate U.S. resources to "influence the emotions, motives, objective reasoning, and ultimately, the behavior of foreign governments, organizations, groups, and individuals" (*Washington Times*, July 28, 1999). The IPI organization will attempt to squelch or limit uncomplimentary stories regarding U.S. activities and policies reported in the foreign press. IPI is *de facto* censorship as it will use governmental resources to repress foreign news stories that may reach the American public. Their ultimate desire seems to be the creation of a propaganda monopoly for the political and corporate elites in America, so that they can use their private public relations consultants to spin and distort news stories on a daily basis to favor specific ideological perspectives. Freedom of information is waning and Orwell's "1984," while a bit late, is still in the making (see Kranich, Chapter 4).

Voices of dissent in the U.S. are increasingly under attack and marginalized. The battle for KPFA's independence in Berkeley (see Chapter 10 by Dennis Bernstein) is a blatant example. The entire corporate media coverage of the WTO protests left most Americans wondering what the fuss was about, as the media focused on the minor vandalism and ignored the global socio-economic issues that drove 60,000 protesters to Seattle (see Chapter 7 by Solomon).

Project Censored, all 175 of us, are proud to present you with this volume dedicated to motivating social action and freedom of information. We have painstakingly researched and presented some 55 important under-covered news stories in Chapter 1, and completed reviews of last year's top stories in Chapter 2.

The top award-winning publications are listed in Appendix A and we encourage you to subscribe to as many of them as you can afford. Invest $25 a month in your self-education by trying out 12 new information sources this year. You can become a freedom of information/First Amendment activist by joining one or several of the media activist groups listed in Appendix B. Also visit Project Censored's Web site at www.sonoma.edu/projectcensored for weekly updates on censored news.

Only a strong system with internal checks and balances on mainstream media will protect the public's interests (see Chapter 9 by Charles Klotzer). Diversity of news sources (both foreign and domestic), ombudsmen, and reporters with tenure rights are needed in the media today to counterbalance governmental spin doctors and the media elite's self interests. Anything less means a continued deterioration of informational freedom in the United States.

Peter Phillips
Director, Project Censored
Sonoma State University

Acknowledgments

Project Censored is managed through the Department of Sociology in the School of Social Sciences at Sonoma State University. We are an investigative sociology project dedicated to freedom of information thoughout the United States.

Over 175 people were directly involved in the production of this year's *Censored 2000: The Year's Top 25 Censored Stories.* University and program staff, students, faculty, community experts, research interns, funders, and our distinguished national judges all contributed time, energy, and money to make this year's book an important resource for the promotion of freedom of information in the United States.

I want to personally thank those close friends and intimates who have counseled and supported me through another year of Project Censored. Most important, my wife Mary Lia-Phillips, who has worked long hours editing and assisting with this volume and living with Project Censored on a daily basis. The men in the Green Oaks breakfast group Noel Byrne, Bob Butler, Rick Williams, and Bill Simon have all been advisors and confidants through the socio-political trials of this past year. Thanks goes also to Carl Jensen, founder of Project Censored, and director for 20 years. His continued advice and support are very important to me and our work. Trish Boreta, intern coordinator, is an important daily associate administrator of the Project. Her dedication and enthusiasm are greatly appreciated.

A huge thanks goes to the people at Seven Stories Press. They are more than a publishing house, but rather close supportive friends who help edit our annual book in record time, and serve as the principal organizers for our annual New York awards ceremony at Fordham University. Publisher Dan

Simon is a saint, and deserves full credit for assembling an excellent support crew including: Operations director Jon Gilbert; editors Greg Ruggiero, Mei Hwei Astella Saw, Mikola De Roo, and Tania Ketenjian; and book designer Cindy LaBreacht. Thanks also to the great sales staff at Publishers Group West, who see to it that every independent bookstore, chain store, and wholesaler in the U.S. are aware of *Censored* each year. Thanks to Hushion House, our distributors in Canada as well as Turnaround Publishers Services Ltd. in Great Britian, and Tower Books in Australia.

Thank you to Mumia Abu-Jamal, who wrote the introduction this year from Death Row in Pennsylvania. He has become an international symbol of protest against censorship and the American criminal justice system. Millions stand together in support of a new trial for him. Too many questions have arisen about his case. Dozens of U.S. death row inmates have been freed because of new evidence, and Mumia's case should receive no less consideration. State-sponsored death becomes the ultimate censorship.

Thanks also to the authors of the most *Censored* stories for 2000, for without their often-unsupported efforts as investigative news reporters and writers, the stories presented in *Censored* would not be possible.

Our guest writers this year are Bob McChesney, Norman Solomon, Robin Andersen, Nancy Kranich, Carl Jensen, Dennis Bernstein, Justin Lewis, Charles Klotzer, Janine Jackson, and Michael Parenti. They each wrote an original article on an important contemporary media issue.

This year's book again features the cartoons of Tom Tomorrow. "This Modern World" appears in over 90 newspapers across the country. We are extremely pleased to learn from and enjoy Tom Tomorrow's wit and humor throughout the book.

Our national judges, some of whom have been involved with the Project for 24 years, are among the top experts in the country concerned with First Amendment freedoms and media. We are honored to have them as the final voice in ranking the top 25 most *Censored* Stories.

An important thanks goes to our major donors and funders, including: Anita Roddick and The Body Shop International, Working Assets, Office of the President & Office of the Provost at Sonoma State University, School of Social Sciences at Sonoma State University, Sonoma State University Associated Students, and several hundred donors from throughout the United States. Without their core financial support Project Censored simply could not continue.

Thanks to Steve Keller with Off The Couch Films, who was the director and producer of the documentary film *Project Censored: Is The Press Really Free?* His hard work resulted in the playing of the documentary on over 50

PBS and independent television stations throughout the country this past year stirring books sales and interest in the Project.

Members of the Organization of News Ombudsmen deserve a thank you for their continuing assistance with identifying the most superfluous stories published in our News Abuse/Junk Food News chapter.

This year we had 89 faculty/community evaluators assisting with our story assessment process. These expert volunteers read and rated the nominated stories for national importance, accuracy, and credibility. In November, they participated with the students in selecting the final top 25 stories for 2000.

Most of all, we need to recognize the Sonoma State University students in the Media Censorship, Sociology 435, class who worked long hours in the library conducting coverage reports on over 200 under-published stories. Each has become an expert in library database research. Student education is among the most important aspects of Project Censored, and we could not do this work without students' dedication and effort.

Scot Frazier served as our technical support this year, assisting with our World Wide Web site development and electronic outreach.

Lastly, I want to thank our readers, and supporters from all over the United States and the world. Hundreds of you nominated stories for consideration as the most *Censored* news stories of the year. Thank you very much!

PROJECT CENSORED STAFF AND STUDENT INTERNS
1999-2000

Peter Phillips, Ph.D.	Director
Carl Jensen, Ph.D.	Director Emeritus and Project Advisor
Trish Boreta	Intern Coordinator
Laurel Holmstrum	Fiscal Planning
Kimberly Lyman	Bookkeeping
Katie Sims	Story Management Team Leader
Scot Frazier	Webmaster
Corrie Robb	Déjà Vu Team Leader
Corey Hale	Administrative Assistant
Julieta Mancilla	Student Assistant

COMMUNITY VOLUNTEERS: Victoria Calkins, Paul Strurud, Beverly Sonoda, Jack Van Allen, Amy Danzeisen, Bonnie Faulkner, Mary Lia-Phillips, Ron Linski

TEACHING ASSISTANTS: Deb Udall, Corey Hale, Corrie Robb

FALL 1999 INTERNS: Tanya Alexander, Katie Anderson, Melissa Bonham, Brian Carlson, Lisa Desmond, Erik Hansen, Willow Lyons, Jennifer Mathis, Michael McMurtrey, Rich Orloff, Allison Surbridge, Karen Torres-Valle

SPRING 1999 INTERNS: Diane Blakney, Melissa Bonham, Craig Chapman, Neal Coats, Jason Ganz, Corey Hale, Brooke Herron, Licia Marshall, Rachel McDole, Michael McMurtrey, Suzanne Murphy, Aimee Polacci, Will Risser, Corrie Robb, Janson Sanders, Tammy Sirota, Michael Smith, Yvette Tannenbaum, Mercedes Warren-Rivendell, Amber Manfree, Eric Avery, Tom Ladegaard, Yuki Ishizaki

1999–2000 STUDENT RESEARCHERS IN MEDIA CENSORSHIP CLASS

Jennifer Acio-Peters	Marnie Goodman	Julia O'Conner
Misty Anderson	Nathan Guzik	Jeremiah Price
Rebecca Aust	Colleen Kelly	Aimee Regan
Melissa Bonham	Cassandra Larson	Doug Schiller
Fera Byrd	Jennifer Mathis	Michael Spigel
Lisa Desmond	Tanner May	Damian Uriarte
Jaime Foster	Jacob Medway	Monte Williams

The Project Censored crew (SSU Faculty, students, and PC staff), Fall 1999.

SUSAN FALUDI, Pulitzer Prize–winning journalist; author of *Backlash: The Undeclared War Against American Women*

DR. GEORGE GERBNER, dean emeritus, Annenberg School of Communications, University of Pennsylvania; founder of the Cultural Environment Movement; author of *Invisible Crises: What Conglomerate Media Control Means for America and the World,* and *Triumph and the Image: The Media's War in the Persion Gulf*

JUAN GONZALEZ, award-winning journalist and columnist for the New York *Daily News*

DR. CARL JENSEN, founder and former director of Project Censored; author, *Censored: The News That Didn't Make the News and Why, 1990 to 1996,* and *20 Years of Censored News* (1997)

SUT JHALLY, professor of communications, and executive director of The Media Education Foundation, University of Massachusetts

NICHOLAS JOHNSON,* professor, College of Law, University of Iowa; former FCC Commissioner (1966–1973); author of *How to Talk Back to Your Television Set*

RHODA H. KARPATKIN, president, Consumers Union, non-profit publisher of *Consumer Reports*

CHARLES L. KLOTZER, editor and publisher emeritus, *St. Louis Journalism Review*

NANCY KRANICH, associate dean of the New York University Libraries, and president-elect of the American Library Association

JUDITH KRUG, director of the Office for Intellectual Freedom, American Library Association; editor; *Newsletter on Intellectual Freedom; Freedom to Read Foundation News;* and the *Intellectual Freedom Action News*

FRANCES MOORE LAPPÉ, co-founder and co-director, Center for Living Democracy

WILLIAM LUTZ, professor of English, Rutgers University; former editor of *The Quarterly Review of Doublespeak;* author of *The New Doublespeak: Why No One Knows What Anyone's Saying Anymore* (1966)

JULIANNE MALVEAUX, Ph.D., economist and columnist, King Features, and Pacifica radio talk show host

ROBERT McCHESNEY, research associate professor in the Institute of Communications Research and the Graduate School of Library and Information Science, University of Illinois, Urbana-Champaign; author of *Rich Media, Poor Democracy, Telecommunications, Mass Media, and Democracy: The Battle for the Control of U.S. Broadcasting 1928-35,* and other books on media

JACK L. NELSON,* professor, Graduate School of Education, Rutgers University; author of 16 books and over 150 articles, including *Critical Issues in Education* (1996)

MICHAEL PARENTI, political analyst, lecturer, and author of several books including: *Inventing Reality; The Politics of News Media; Make Believe Media; The Politics of Entertainment;* and numerous other works

BARBARA SEAMAN, lecturer; author of *The Doctors' Case Against the Pill, Free and Female, Women and the Crisis in Sex Hormones,* and others; co-author, with Gary Null, of *For Women Only!: Your Guide to Health Empowerment;* co-founder of the National Women's Health Network

ERNA SMITH, chair of the journalism department at San Francisco State University, author of several studies on mainstream news coverage on people of color

SHEILA RABB WEIDENFELD,* president of D.C. Productions, Ltd.; former press secretary to Betty Ford

HOWARD ZINN, professor emeritus of political science at Boston University, author of *A People's History of the United States, You Can't be Neutral on a Moving Train: A Personal History of Our Times,* and *The Zinn Reader: Writings on Disobedience and Democracy*

* Indicates having been a Project Censored Judge since its founding in 1976

PROJECT CENSORED 2000 FACULTY, STAFF, AND COMMUNITY EVALUATORS

Les Adler, Ph.D.	Hutchin School, History
Julie Allen, Ph.D.	English
Ruben Armiñana, Ph.D.	President, Sonoma State University, Political Science
Byran Baker, Ph.D.	Geography
Philip Beard, Ph.D.	German Studies

Marty Bennett, M.A.	Santa Rosa Community College, Labor History
Andrew Botterell, Ph.D.	Philosophy
Maureen Buckley	Counseling
Elizabeth Burch, Ph.D.	Communications Studies
Jim Burkland	Community Expert, Geology
Barbara Butler, MLIS, MBA	Acting Director of Library
Noel Byrne, Ph.D.	Sociology
James R. Carr, Ph.D.	University of Nevada, Geology
Ray Castro, Ph.D.	Social Policy
T.K. Clarke, Ph.D.	Business
Liz Close, Ph.D.	Nursing
Lynn Cominsky, Ph.D.	Physics, Astronomy
Bill Crowley, Ph.D.	Geography
Laurie Dawson	Labor & Education
Randy Dodgen, Ph.D.	History, Asia
Peter Duffy, J.D.	Community Expert, Politics & Law
Fred Fletcher	Community Expert, Labor Issues
Dorothy Friedel, Ph.D.	Geography
Richard Gale, Ph.D.	Hutchins School
Susan Garfin, Ph.D.	Sociology
Patricia Lee Gibbs, Ph.D.	Foothill College, Sociology
Robert Girling, Ph.D.	Business, Economics
Mary Gomes, Ph.D.	Psychology
Myrna Goodman, Ph.D. Candidate	Sociology/Gender Studies
Scott Gordon, Ph.D.	Computer Science
Paula Hammett, MLIS	Information Resources in Social Sciences
Debra Hammond, Ph.D.	History of Science
Dan Haytin, Ph.D.	Sociology
Laurel Holmstrom	Sociology
Sally Hurtado, M.S.	Education
Pat Jackson, Ph.D.	Criminal Justice Administration
Thomas Jacobson, J.D.	Environmental Studies and Planning
Sherril Jaffe, M.A.	English
Mary King, M.D.	Community Volunteer
Jeanette Koshar, Ph.D.	Nursing
John Kramer, Ph.D.	Political Science
Heidi LaMoreaux, Ph.D.	Hutchins School

Virginia Lea, Ph.D.	Education
Benet Leigh, M.A.	Communication Studies
Wingham Liddell, Ph.D.	Business/Economics
Tom Lough, Ph.D.	Sociology
John Lund	Community Expert, Politics, Stock Market
Rick Luttmann, Ph.D./CFP	Economics/Budgets
Kenneth Marcus, Ph.D.	Criminal Justice
Perry Marker, Ph.D.	Education
Dan Markwyn, Ph.D.	History
Doug Martin, Ph.D.	Chemistry
Elizabeth Martinez, Ph.D.	Foreign Languages
Eric McGuckin, Ph.D.	Anthropology
Jeffrey McIllwain, Ph.D.	Criminal Justice Administration
Robert McNamara, Ph.D.	Political Science
Andy Merrifield, Ph.D.	Public Administration
Catherine Nelson, Ph.D.	Political Science
Robert Lee Nichols	Lt. General United States Marine Corps (Ret.)
Leilani Nishime, Ph.D.	American Multicultural Studies
Linda Nowak, Ph.D.	Business/Marketing
Tim Ogburn	Community Expert, International Trade
Tom Ormond, Ph.D.	Kinesiology
Ervand Peterson, Ph.D.	Environmental Studies
Jorge E. Porras, Ph.D.	Sociolinguistics
Arthur Ramirez, Ph.D.	Mexican American Studies
Jeffrey Reeder, Ph.D.	Foreign Languages
Rabi Michael Robinson	Community Expert, Social Justice
R. Thomas Rosin, Ph.D.	Anthropology
Gardner Rust, Ph.D.	Music
Richard Senghas, Ph.D.	Anthropology
Cindy Stearns, Ph.D.	Women's Studies
John Steiner, Ph.D.	Sociology
Elaine Sundberg, M.A.	Education
Velma Taylor, Ed.D.	Sociology/Women & Gender Studies
Bob Tellander, M.A.	Sociology
Laxmi G. Tewari, Ph.D.	Ethnomusicology
Suzanne Toczyski, Ph.D.	Foreign Languages
Carol Tremmel	Extended Education
David Van Nuys, Ph.D.	Psychology

Francisco H. Vazquez, Ph.D.	Hutchins School, Liberal Studies
Albert Wahrhaftig, Ph.D.	Anthropology
Sandra Walton, MLIS	Archival Management
Tim Wandling, Ph.D.	English
D. Anthony White, Ph.D.	History
R. Richard Williams, J.D.	Community Volunteer, Politics & Law
Homero Yearwood, Ph.D.	Criminal Justice
Richard Zimmer, Ph.D.	History

SONOMA STATE UNIVERSITY SUPPORTING STAFF AND OFFICES

Ruben Armiñana: President and Staff in the Office of the President
Bernard Goldstein: Chief Academic Officer and Staff
Robert Karlsrud: Dean of School of Social Sciences and Staff
William Babula: Dean of School of Arts and Humanities
Larry Furukawa-Schlereth: Chief Financial Officer and Staff
Jim Myers: Vice-President for Development and Staff
Barbara Butler and the SSU Library Staff
Tony Apolloni and the Staff in Sponsored Programs
Paula Hammett: Social Sciences Library Resources
Steve Wilson and the Staff at the SSU Academic Foundation
Jonah Raskin and Faculty in Communications Studies
Susan Kashack and Staff in SSU Public Relations Office
Colleagues in the Sociology Department: Noel Byrne, Kathy Charmaz, Susan Garfin, Dan Haytin, Robert Tellander, David Walls, and Department Secretary Laurel Holmstrom

The News that Didn't Fit

INTRODUCTION BY MUMIA ABU-JAMAL

For writers and journalists, the *New York Times,* affectionately dubbed "the Grey Old Lady," sets the standard for the practice of journalism, and its boxed motto, "All the News That's Fit to Print," signifies solid and professional, if somewhat restrained, coverage of the burning issues of the day. In the last quarter of the twentieth century, post-'60s-generation reporters, perhaps influenced by the political and psychosocial chaos wrought by Watergate, have worked to bring to public consciousness stories that have been ignored. The 1960s birthed a plethora of alternative publications, like the *Berkeley Barb,* the *Black Panther,* the *Great Speckled Bird,* the *Drummer,* and the like. Most alternative papers have passed into obsolescence, as radical political mores have changed. What were once underground political and sociopolitical positions have been sanitized and amalgamated into watered-down, safe political platitudes.

Project Censored now serves the purpose once addressed by the alternative tabloids. In many ways, it performs better than its predecessors, for while much of the alternative media served a role of giving voice to the counter-culture, much of it was also frivolous play meant to provide a pleasant diversion from the media's fascination with the Vietnam War and its permanent penchant for social conflict.

Project Censored, while sprung from these roots, is far from frivolous play. The stories covered here are indeed quite serious, and deal with public health versus profit; war and peace; the prison industrial complex; life and death. As acclaimed African-American economist and author Julianne Malveaux notes later in this text, "Capitalism and the profit motive combine, collude, and conspire to produce the lowest common denominator of news. The papers provide us with stories that are easy to digest and do not rock the boat."[1] It is within that context of capital and communications that stories get told, and others ignored. For example, consider the following:

(a) For twenty years the United States sold or gave Turkey $15 billion worth of weapons; for fifteen years a civil war raged in southeastern Turkey; and since 1990 more than 3,000 Kurdish villages have been leveled, torched, or evacuated—yet Abdullah Ocalan and the Kurdish Workers Party are the ones deemed to be terrorists.

(b) The 100-mile stretch between New Orleans and Baton Rouge, site of seven oil refineries and more than 175 heavy industrial plants, is a hotbed of cancer. This region of southeast Louisiana is called "Cancer Alley," in a state where 30 percent of the population—heavily black—straddle the poverty line; proof of environmental racism and environmental class war where the poor pay dearly for their social and class status.

(c) Journalist A. Clay Thompson reports on the caging of kids in California, so many that "the state…has no idea how many teenagers are being sentenced to life in prison."[2]

(d) Five hundred thousand to 1,000,000 people suffer from Crohn's disease in the United States alone. Crohn's is incurable, and causes severe diarrhea, excessive weight loss, rectal bleeding, bowel obstruction, and other disorders. The relatively few studies on Crohn's point to cow's milk as the culprit, and relate it to the similar Johne's disease, which has similar symptoms, and is a cattle disease.

American subsidization of a brutal "ethnic cleansing" in Turkey; "Cancer Alley" in southeast Louisiana; the caging of children; approximately 1,000,000 struck with a serious disease thought to be caused by milk that is pasteurized…these are but some of the stories that did not fit what the corporate media called "news."

As you flip through the following pages, you'll no doubt find more to engage you, more to amaze you, and more to outrage you. You'll see why these stories contained news that didn't fit. You'll see the alternative.

Mumia Abu-Jamal

January 2000

---

1. Malveaux is a judge for Censored 2000
2. See "California Convicts and Punishes Teenagers as Adults."

CHAPTER 1

The Top 25 Censored Stories of 1999

BY PETER PHILLIPS & PROJECT CENSORED

It was an international year for the United States and Project Censored. The 1999 most under-covered "censored" news stories have a strong international flavor, with an emphasis on untold stories of Kosovo (*Censored* #6, 10, 12, 20, and 22), foreign policy (*Censored* #5, 17, 21, and 23), and international corporate power abuse (*Censored* #1 and 13). Emerging this year are a number of stories on the mainstream media itself (*Censored* #7, 14, and 16). With the advancement of spin techniques, mainstream media now tends to place emphasis on particular perspectives of news stories to enhance their entertainment value. In some cases today, mainstream media may also be deliberately spinning stories for their own political/commercial purposes. Many of our old favorites are present as well, including stories on the environment (*Censored* #9 and 11), race issues (*Censored* #9 and 16), labor (*Censored* #4), U.S. military (*Censored* #8, 21, and 25), and health concerns (*Censored* #2, 3, 15, and 19).

Project Censored students and staff screened several thousand stories for 1999, and selected some 500 for evaluation by faculty and community experts. The top-ranked 200 stories were researched for national mainstream coverage by the Media Censorship class in the Fall. A final collective vote of all students, staff, and faculty occurred in early November and the top 25 stories were ranked by our national judges.

This year we have a short 200-300 word synopsis on each of the 30 runners-up. As the media consolidates, we are finding significantly more news stories are left uncovered by the corporate press, and these runners-up deserve notice as well as the top 25. In many cases only a few votes separated the two groups.

While selection of these stories each year is a subjective judgmental process, we have grown to trust this collective effort as the best possible means of fairly selecting these important news stories. Sometimes, certain groups or individuals complain about our lack of coverage of particular stories or having too many or too few stories in various categories. We do not have a quota system of selecting stories for certain categories, but rather use a holistic collective process of monitoring, researching, and decision-making that involves over 175 people. We believe this process gives us a useful annual summary of many of the most important under-covered news stories in the United States. We hope you agree.

1 CENSORED

Multinational Corporations Profit from International Brutality

Source:
DOLLARS AND SENSE,
May/June 1999
Title: "Corporation Crackdowns:
Business Backs Brutality"
Author: Arvind Ganesan

Faculty Evaluator:
Albert Wahrhafitig Ph.D.
Student Researchers:
Cassandra Larson & Melissa Bonham

In the name of commerce, huge multi-national corporations collaborate with repressive governments and, in the process, support significant human rights violations. The U.S. government knows about these human rights abuses, but continues to provide support and funding. In countries with a history of repression, corporations often argue that their presence and investment will improve human rights. This practice is referred to as "constructive engagement." A look at the actions of multinational corporations over the last five years shows that constructive engagement with undemocratic governments is basically a myth.

In March 1998, the U.S. State Department ignored its own report on human rights abuses in Turkmenistan by providing a $96 million award from the Export-Import Bank to four U.S. companies selling natural gas and other equipment to the country. Any Export-Import loan of over $10 million requires the State Department to conduct a human rights impact assessment to determine if it may give rise to significant human rights concerns.

Turkmenistan, a major human rights

violator, also possesses some of the largest oil and gas reserves in central Asia. President Saparmurad Niyazov rules the country with an iron fist, suppressing independent media and political opposition. Yet, companies such as Mobil, Exxon, and Royal Dutch Shell operate openly there. When Turkmenistan President Niyazov was visiting President Clinton in April of 1998, the U.S. government's Trade and Development Administration awarded the Houston-based Enron a $750,000 grant to conduct a pipeline feasibility study for a proposed $2.8 billion pipeline in Turkmenistan. After the deal was signed, the White House issued a press release stating that Turkmenistan is committed to free and fair elections, strengthening the rule of law, and political pluralism in accordance with international standards. Yet, when reporters asked Niyazov about the government's attitude toward opposition parties, he replied, "We do not have any opposition parties—you are ill-informed." The U.S. officials stated that they had discussed human rights issues privately with Niyazov and the State Department secured the release of 10 political prisoners, citing both instances as examples of improvement in human rights.

The government of India and Enron Corporation have partnered to protect Enron by suppressing and silencing its opponents. Enron paid local police and provided them with the means to imprison and assault over 3,000 people because they demonstrated against Enron's Dabhol power project, the largest power plant in the world. Enron faced opposition because it seized villagers' lands and polluted and diverted the local water supply.

Unocal claims its Yadana gas project in Burma "is bringing sustainable, long-term economic and social benefits to the 35,000 villagers living in the immediate pipeline region, and lasting benefits" to the Burmese people. In reality, Burma's military stands accused of killing, torturing, and raping villagers, and forcing them to work along the pipelines.

Human rights violations become framed as a "necessary evil" that insures improvement in the long run. Multinational corporations, such as Mobil, attack the practice of imposing government sanctions to punish abusive governments because it curtails business objectives. The American Petroleum Institute, an industry-funded advocacy organization, proclaimed in its 1998 report, "Oil and Natural Gas Industry Promotes Human Rights Abroad," that the use of "sanctions to punish regimes that abridge their peoples' human rights" denies local people the "rights enhancements" that oil companies confer.

Still, despite the myth that promotes foreign investment as the key to improving human rights, human rights violations are being perpetrated by huge corporations with government backing.

UPDATE BY AUTHOR ARVIND GANESAN: Since the release of the story in *Dollars and Sense*, there was not much response by the mainstream news media in the United States. European and regional press are far more aware of these issues and reported on them with greater frequency than their U.S. counterparts. The U.S. media has been decent—particularly the energy industry press—at reporting about individual reports. Human Rights Watch has released reports on India and Nigeria, but so far has not followed the broader issue concerning the energy companies impact on human rights globally and has not reported on the issue of "constructive engagement." Still, other sources of pressure, such as that from the public, environmental groups, socially-responsible investment firms, and Human Rights Watch have led companies, such as Enron, to begin to address their human rights problems.

Ironically, a number of institutions are paying serious attention to the issue. The companies themselves, however, are a different story and are much more sensitive and aware of these issues than the U.S. mainstream media. Human Rights Watch has seen companies like BP Amoco and Norway's Statoil take positive steps in addressing human rights in Angola and Azerbaijan. However, the U.S. companies and their French counterparts, Exxon-Mobil or TOTAL, lag far behind on the issue of human rights.

Part of the goal at Human Rights Watch is to create greater accountability for these mammoth corporations. The World Bank, U.K. and U.S. governments, and even the U.N. are developing programs to deal with the conduct of energy companies globally and non-governmental organizations (NGOs) are devoting their energies towards insuring reform of the industry. With all of these institutions involved, the absence of the U.S. mainstream media is glaring.

This article is reflective of detailed on-the-ground research the corporations program has conducted on the energy industry in Angola, Colombia, India, Nigeria, and Sudan and we expect to further this work on the industry as the year progresses. It is too important an issue to ignore, particularly as the world is seen more and more as a global marketplace. In this context, corporations and human rights are at the center of many of these issues. As the person at Human Rights Watch who focuses on corporations, I will continue to work to try to influence companies, governments, financial institutions, and others to insure that companies pay attention to human rights and create greater public awareness of the issue. For more information on the subject of corporations and human rights contact: Arvind Ganesan, Human Rights Watch, 1630 Connecticut Avenue, NW, Suite 500, Washington, DC 20009, Tel: (202) 612-4329, Fax: (202) 612-4333, E-mail: ganesaa@hrw.org, Web site: www.hrw.org

2 CENSORED

Pharmaceutical Companies Put Profits Before Need

Source:
THE NATION, July 19, 1999
Title: "Millions for Viagra,
Pennies for the Poor"
Author: Ken Silverstein

Faculty Evaluator: Liz Close
Student Researcher: Monte Williams

Multinational pharmaceutical companies focus their research and development on high profile profit-making drugs like Viagra instead of developing cures for life-threatening diseases in poorer countries. The market for drugs curing such ailments as impotence and male-pattern baldness is worth billions of dollars a year, and still growing. For instance, in its first year, Viagra earned more than one billion dollars while Propecia and Rogaine earned $180 million in 1998. In contrast, though representatives of the Pharmaceutical Research and Manufacturers of America (PhRMA) claim that some funds are directed towards eliminating tropical diseases, neither they nor individual firms are willing to provide statistics.

Of the medicines introduced from 1975 to 1997 by the world's biggest pharmaceutical companies, only 1 percent were created to combat such tropical diseases as tuberculosis, malaria, and acute lower-respiratory infections. In Third World countries, nearly three times as many people die of these curable diseases as from AIDS. In 1998 alone, over six million lives were lost while multinational pharmaceutical companies catered to the vanity of Americans with lifestyle drugs such as Viagra and anti-wrinkle creams. The market is filling with cures for doggy Alzheimer's along with other remedies and perks for American pets, despite the fact that approximately 3.5 million people a year die of acute respiratory infections. Still, global funds for malaria research over 20 years barely match the cost of a single B-2 bomber.

Perhaps more alarming is the fact that of the few medications that do prevent, battle, or cure life-threatening diseases in poorer regions of the world (only 13 of every 1,223), less than a third were actually designed to do so. Most medications were simply the result of military research, newer variations of old drugs, or even the result of fluke veterinary accidents.

A 1996 study concluded that of the 41 important medicines for combating tropical diseases, not a single one was discovered this decade. Since only 2 of the 24 most prominent drug companies show an interest in malaria, surely more people will suffer.

With corporate mergers in the pharmaceutical industry growing in scale and frequency every year, focus has shifted from healing to profits. As a result, research production and advertising will only continue to ignore low-profit cures for high-profile and marketable products like Viagra.

In 1998, the pharmaceutical industry spent over $10 billion on advertising alone. During the same year it spent more than $74 million on lobbying the federal government, plus $12 million on campaign contributions.

Research for Third World tropical diseases is not given serious consideration. For instance, a recent and effective medicine to fight African sleeping sickness was pulled from production. Yet older proven remedies are no longer available because they are not needed in America, and poor countries cannot afford the now unavailable remedies.

Of diseases in the Third World, AIDS is getting the most attention and focus. Not coincidentally, it is also one of the few diseases that remain a threat to First World countries.

UPDATE BY AUTHOR KEN SILVERSTEIN: This story is important given the number of people who die daily in the Third World as a result of the drug industry's lack of interest in addressing deadly tropical diseases.

This story has continued to develop primarily because Doctors Without Borders (DWB), the lead group pressing the government and industry to address the needs of the Third World, won the Nobel Prize a few months after my story ran. DWB also announced an international campaign to increase access to key drugs at about the same time my story appeared. Beyond that, there has been a lot of attention given to an issue I raised in the story,

namely the American government's attempt to prevent Third World countries from producing generic drugs for AIDS.

There has been a fair amount of attention paid to the issue, at least in comparison to the almost total silence that was the rule for many years. I do have to credit Doctors Without Borders for that!

The best sources for information regarding this issue are: Doctors Without Borders, Tel: (212) 679-6800; Jamie Love at the Center for Study of Responsive Law, Tel: (202) 387-8030; or Amir Attaran, Tel: (604) 685-5618.

3 CENSORED

Financially Bloated American Cancer Society Fails to Prevent Cancer

Source:
INTERNATIONAL JOURNAL OF HEALTH SERVICES, Vol. 29, No. 3, 1999
Title: "American Cancer Society: The World's Wealthiest 'Non-profit' Institution"
Author: Samuel S. Epstein

Faculty Evaluator: Cindy Stearns, Ph.D.
Student Evaluators:
Jennifer Acio-Peters & Lisa Desmond

The American Cancer Society (ACS), while enjoying the status of a non-profit "charity" institution, is accumulating vast wealth. This wealth accumulates in the form of donations from unsuspecting Americans who believe they are helping to fight cancer. Furthermore, though ACS is purported to be one of the largest non-profit organizations in the world, an increasing proportion of its bloated budget comes from surgeons, top drug companies, and corporations that profit from cancer cures and have little interest in cancer prevention.

The AMS Foundation's Board of Trustees includes corporate executives from pharmaceutical, investment, banking, and media industries. For instance, David R. Bethune, president of Lederle Laboratories, comes from a division of American Cyanamid, which makes chemical fertilizers and herbicides, as well as the anti-cancer drug Novatrone. Another trustee is Gordon Binder, CEO of Amgen, the world's foremost biotechnology company, whose product Neupogen has enjoyed skyrocketing success as the cancer epidemic grows.

More than half of the funds raised by the ACS go for overhead, salaries, and fringe benefits for its executives and other employees, while most direct community services are handled by unpaid volunteers. By 1998, the cash reserves of the ACS were worth more than $1 billion. In addition, the ACS owns many millions of dollars worth of land and real estate. Nationally only 16 percent of their funds goes into direct services to cancer victims. An investigator of non-profit orga-nizations, Thomas DiLorenzo, professor of economics at Loyola College, states: "More progress in the war against cancer would be made if they would divest some of their real estate holdings and use the proceeds—as well as a portion of their cash reserves—to provide more cancer services."

Conflicts of interest affect ACS's approach to cancer prevention. The "blame-the-victim" philosophy empha-sizes faulty lifestyles rather than envi-ronmental causes. Despite public promises to "wipe out cancer," the ACS has refused to provide the scientific tes-timony needed for the regulation of occupational and environmental carcino-gens to Congressional committees and other organizations.

ACS's "Cancer Facts & Figures 1998," designed to educate the public, makes little mention of prevention. ACS asserts that since women may not be able to alter their personal risk factors, their best opportunity is through early detec-tion. Five radiologists have served as ACS presidents and their influence reflects the interests of large manufacturers of mam-mogram machines and films.

ACS works closely with Zeneca Inc., a major industrial chemical company and the makers of tamoxifen (see Chapter 2), in the management of "Breast Cancer Awareness Month" in the United States. In 1992, ACS aggressively recruited 16,000 healthy women to participate in a five-year trial of the use of tamoxifen in healthy "high-risk" women as a can-cer prevention drug, even though the numerous side effects of tamoxifen include increased risk of liver and uterine cancer as well as fatal embolisms.

UPDATE BY AUTHOR DR. SAMUEL S. EPSTEIN: On the basis of detailed documentation and supporting references, the story charges the American Cancer Society (ACS) with major responsibility for losing the winnable war against cancer. The ACS fixates on damage control—screening, diagnosis, treatment, and basic genetic research—with indifference or even hostility to cancer prevention (as illustrated by a series of specific examples). Most importantly, the ACS has failed to provide Congress, regulatory agencies, and the public with scientific evidence on a wide range of involuntary and avoidable exposures to carcinogens in the workplace, air, water, and consumer products such as food, cosmetics, toiletries, and household products.

The ACS also fails to provide well-documented information on a wide range of avoidable non-smoking cancers, such as childhood, testicular, prostate, ovarian, and breast. Furthermore, the ACS trivializes the escalating incidence of cancer that has now reached epidemic proportions, with lifetime risks now reaching 1 in 2 for men and 1 in 3 for women. Still, the ACS makes grossly misleading claims on the dramatic progress in the treatment and cure of cancer. These claims are coupled with long-standing McCarthyist blacklisting of alternative treatments and harassment of responsible practitioners of alternative or unorthodox cancer therapies. These myopic mindsets and derelict policies are compounded by interlocking conflicts of interest with the cancer drug, agrochemical, and other industries. Financial irregularities add further to the problem with excessive overhead, salaries and benefits, political lobbying, and contributions.

Based on such considerations, the *Chronicle of Philanthropy*, the nation's leading major charity watchdog, has charged that "the ACS is more interested in accumulating wealth than saving lives." The story concludes that since attempts to reform the ACS for over two decades have failed, the only recourse is an economic boycott of the ACS with diversion of charitable contributions to public interest and environmental groups directly involved in cancer prevention.

Since publication of the story, further information on the ACS budget and its allocation to cancer prevention has become available. Of a $677 million 1998 budget, some $360 million was allocated to "Supporting Services," including overhead, salaries and benefits, fundraising, and other undefined sources. No information is yet available on salaries and benefits of ACS national executives and officers. Still, salaries of some five regional division executives average $230,000 each. The balance of $307 million was allocated to all "Program Services," of which $106 million is ostensibly spent on environmental carcinogenesis, prevention, and education programs to "reduce the risk of developing cancer." However, analysis of individual grants in all these program areas reveals that actual expenditures on industrial and environmental causes of cancer total less than $1 million, and that ACS claims of extensive support of research and education on cancer prevention reflect budgetary shell games.

Based on this new information, an updated and popularized version of the original ACS story has been written and recently submitted to the *Nation*. Additional new information relates to an ongoing investigation of Canadian and U.K. cancer charities. This reveals a similar pattern of misdirected policies and conflicts of interest as with the ACS.

An abridged version of the article published in the *International Journal of Health Services* is available at my Web site.

My contact information is as follows: School of Public Health, University of Illinois at Chicago Medical Center, 2121 W. Taylor, Chicago, IL 60612-7260, Tel: (312) 996-2297 (A.M. only); Fax: (312) 996-1374; E-mail: epstein@uic.edu; Web site: http://www.preventcancer.com

4 CENSORED

American Sweatshops Sew U.S. Military Uniforms

Source:
MOTHER JONES, May/June 1999
Title: "An American Sweatshop"
Author: Mark Boal

Faculty Evaluator: Sally Hurtado
Student Researcher: Jaime Foster

American sweatshops produce U.S. military uniforms for the Defense Logistics Agency (DLA), a subdivision of the U.S. Defense Department. In 1997, the DLA spent $811.8 million on uniforms and textiles.

Lion Apparel contracts with the Department of Defense to produce military uniforms. Yet, the company's workplace conditions are dismal and remain virtually unregulated by the U.S. government while the employees of Lion are mostly women who are paid as little as $5.50 per hour.

The Department of Defense has $1 billion invested in the garment industry which makes it the country's 14th largest retail apparel outlet. It has failed to adopt the Workplace Code of Conduct, which is a promise to self-regulate workplace conditions. Without the Defense Department's voluntary adherence to this code, the responsibility of stopping public-sector sweatshops falls to the Department of Labor. Federal contractors that violate wage laws or safety and health codes can lose lucrative taxpayer-financed contracts. A deputy administrator at the Department of Labor, Suzanne Seiden, says that, to her knowledge, the agency has never applied that rule to government apparel manufacturers.

According to records obtained by *Mother Jones* through a Freedom of Information request, the Occupational Safety and Health Administration (OSHA) cited the Lion Apparel 32 times for safety and health violations in the past 12 years. A 1996 General Accounting Office report estimated that 22 percent of all federal contractors have been cited by OSHA for violating safety standards.

The Lion Apparel plant in Beattyville, Kentucky, uses formaldehyde, a suspected carcinogen, to keep fabric stiff for processing. Formaldehyde emits fumes that cling to workers' clothing and for years the plant did not have air conditioning. Workers report that these fumes have caused them shortness of breath, headaches, and skin rashes.

The Union of Needle Trades, Industrial, and Textile Employees (UNITE) tried to organize Lion in 1997 but failed. Union leaders claim that the company was able to evade federal labor laws that prohibit employers from threatening plant closures and that the company managed to instill fear in many of its workers. A memo was posted that read: "Why [is UNITE] trying to get information which they may want to use to hurt Lion's business? If that happens, that could hurt all of our jobs."

Several employees sent a letter to Al Gore and eight Kentucky congressmen and senators stating, "Some of us have been told point-blank that if we get a union, the plant will close.... They've spied on people to see who took union leaflets, and they've told individuals who work here that if we talk to the union we will be fired. Up 'til now, people here have been too afraid to file any official charges, but we'd like to talk to you or someone from your staff about what can be done." Soon after, the letter was received by Lion's management who posted it on the company's bulletin board. The union drive ended shortly thereafter. The few benefits that came out of the employees' efforts were a 30-cent raise in hourly wages, and installation of an air conditioner.

*Note: Lion Apparel challenged *Mother Jones* and demanded a retraction of this story. *Mother Jones* refused but did make two changes in its report (changes included in the above story).

UPDATE BY AUTHOR MARK BOAL: In general, sweatshop stories flash across the media landscape. Coverage tends to be intense, yet short-lived. My piece in *Mother Jones* was no exception. After the

THIS MODERN WORLD
by TOM TOMORROW

story ran, several radio and TV stations interviewed the women who had toiled in American sweatshops while making uniforms for the government. On the political front, Congressman George Miller called on the army to pass reforms, but the military has been slow to respond.

About 10,000 American women are employed sewing government uniforms, often in unsanitary, unsafe conditions. The military still contributes to the situation and profits from it by buying uniforms at low prices, and selling them to other countries. Still, the military declines to sign the administration's anti-sweatshop code of conduct. The public would learn more about these American sweatshops if contractors had to meet stricter reporting and disclosure requirements. As it stands now, most firms can camouflage their worst practices behind shell corporations. Until that changes, profits made from running a sweatshop will outweigh the risks of public exposure.

For those interested in the sweatshop activism, several groups have Web sites with more information. The National Labor Committee (www.nlcnet.org) does very compelling work chronicling abuses here and abroad. SweatshopWatch (www.sweatshopwatch.org) is a clearinghouse with links and stories on the subject. Also worth mentioning is the National Association of Apparel Manufacturers in Washington, DC, which offers an industry perspective and updated statistics. Finally, the garment-workers' union, UNITE (www.unitewnion.org) runs ongoing anti-sweatshop campaigns.

5 CENSORED

Turkey Destroys Kurdish Villages with U.S. Weapons

Source:
THE BULLETIN OF ATOMIC SCIENTISTS, March/April 1999
Title: "Turkey's War on the Kurds"
Author: Kevin McKeirnan

Faculty Evaluator: Tony White, Ph.D.
Student Researchers:
Doug Schiller & Tanner May

In the past decade, Turkey has forcibly evacuated, leveled, and burned more than 3,000 Kurdish villages. Over 40,000 lives have been lost in this war. Most of the atrocities against the Kurds took place during President Clinton's first term, when the United States sold or gave Turkey billions of dollars worth of military weapons and supplies.

In 1995, the Clinton Administration recognized that the Turkish government used American arms in domestic military operations where human rights abuses occurred. Some members of Congress strongly disagree with the way the U.S. has dealt with the situation. Congresswoman Cynthia McKinney (D-GA) believes that human rights, democracy, and non-aggression criteria should be applied before American weapons are sold or given away. McKinney tried to get a code of conduct passed in 1997 but it died in a Senate conference committee. The U.S. has yet to pass an adequate code of conduct to protest the ethnic conflict in Turkey.

The Kurds remain the largest ethnic group in the world to not have their own state. Fifteen million of the 25 million Kurdish people live in Turkey, the rest are spread out over areas of Iraq, Iran, Syria, and the former Soviet Union. Intensified aggression started 15 years ago in Turkey when a Marxist-led group called the Kurdish Workers Party (PKK) began to protest the Turkish government.

Until 1991, the Turkish government banned Kurdish music, language, dress, and newspapers.

As an ally of the United States through NATO, Turkey receives U.S. weapons. Turkey's war on the Kurds relies on weaponry from dozens of American companies including Mc Donnell Douglas, General Dynamics, Hughes, Boeing, Raytheon, and Bell Textron. Most Kurdish people would not know a word of English but recounting the rocketing of their settlements, they regularly use the words "Cobra" and "Sikorsky," the U.S.-made helicopters used to clear Kurdish villages. Turkey has placed orders with Bell Textron for more helicopters and AV Technologies for U.S.-made armored personnel carriers (APCs).

Amnesty International wrote a report on the Turkish "anti-terrorist" group designated to use the APCs with the hope of blocking the sale. The report included details of the "anti-terror" units torturing children, sexually assaulting prisoners, and beating, burning, and nearly drowning suspects. Regardless of this horrifying report, the State Department passed the arms deal.

Turkey is a strategic foothold that the United States does not want to lose. Today the United States has several intelligence-gathering posts in Turkey, including a radar installation in Mardin, a largely Kurdish city, which the U.S. uses to spy deep into Iraq. NATO also has several installations in Turkey from which U.S. intelligence planes take off daily to patrol the no-fly zone in northern Iraq. The U.S. chooses to ignore human rights abuses in Turkey in order to maintain a military alliance.

UPDATE BY AUTHOR KEVIN MCKIERNAN: This story was virtually unreported in the U.S. media. The war between the U.S.-equipped Turkish army and the Kurds in Turkey represents the greatest use of U.S. weapons in combat anywhere in the world today. The ethnic cleansing of the Kurds, one of the worst human rights disasters of the century, receives little attention in the American press. That tragedy is compounded by the strategic and long-standing involvement of U.S. arms. Over the past two decades, the U.S. has sold or given Turkey $15 billion worth of weapons. In the last decade, the war has produced two million Kurdish refugees. That figure exceeds the number of refugees in Kosovo, where U.S. arms were not a factor.

Since 1990 alone, more than 3,500 Kurdish villages in Turkey have been leveled, burned, or forcibly evacuated. That is nearly the number of Iraqi Kurdish settlements that were destroyed during Saddam Hussein's infamous "Anfal" campaign in the 1980s, when the West was trading with Iraq but turning a blind eye to wide scale violations of human rights.

While the story of destruction by the U.S.-equipped Turkish army was under-reported in the American media, the arrest and trial of Kurdish rebel leader Abdullah Ocalan earlier this year produced an avalanche of publicity. Great attention has been given to Turkey's claim that Ocalan is guilty of the 37,000 reported deaths between the Turkish army and Kurdish separatists, despite the fact that most of those killed have been Kurdish guerrillas. There is ample reason to charge Ocalan's Kurdistan Worker's Party (PKK) with human rights abuses. However, organizations like Amnesty International have for years detailed widespread human rights violations by the Turkish government, and few of these reports have been given any attention by the U.S. media, even when American weapons were involved.

There has been some mainstream press response to my investigation. I was asked to act as a consultant for CBS's *60 Minutes* and I was contacted by PBS's *News-Hour* and asked for background information on the Kurds. However, most of the interest in the overall story has focused on the sensational aspects of Ocalan's capture and trial. Even when President Clinton spent a record five days at the Istanbul Summit in November, 1999, little was said about the 15-year-old civil war that has ravaged southeast Turkey. As far as I know, no reporter asked Clinton a question about the Kurds and the President never mentioned their name.

While hot spots like East Timor and Kosovo have received intense publicity, the scorched earth campaign in Turkey is still a "blind spot" to American reporters. The *New York Times*, for example, did not open a bureau in Turkey until 1996 and has never reported a first-hand account of the destruction of a single Kurdish village. As a television producer at ABC's *Nightline* once told me, "The story is just not on our radar."

The best way for a person to get more information on this story is to read Reuters accounts on the Internet. There are daily Reuters stories out of Turkey; they are rarely reprinted in the United States. There was front-page coverage in the U.S. media when Turkey was offered admission to the European Union (EU), in mid-December 1999. Some stories made a passing reference to the Kurds and to the human rights situation but the coverage in the European media was far more detailed. The American headlines dealt primarily with the political aspects of the story, and I saw no first hand reporting about the Kurds (whose treatment over the last decade has been the primary obstacle to Turkey's admission to the EU).

Here are some additional Web resources for interested readers:

American Kurdish Information
    Network (AKIN):
    www.kurdistan.org/
Amnesty International:
    www.amnesty.org/
Center for Defense Information:
    www.cdi.org/
Center for International Policy
    (World Policy Institute):
    www.us.net/cip/index.html
The Federation of American Scientists,
    Arms Sales Monitoring Project:
    www.fas.org/asmp/
Human Rights Watch: www.hrw.org/
Mother Jones: www.motherjones.com/
Washington Kurdish Institute:
    www.clark.net/kurd/

Good Kurds, Bad Kurds, an epic documentary exposes ironic inconsistencies in America's interest in the Kurds, by Kevin McKiernan. Selected as a feature in Slamdance 2000 Film Festival: www. kevinmck@silcom.com

6 CENSORED
NATO Defends Private Economic Interests in the Balkans

Sources:
WOMEN AGAINST MILITARY
MADNESS, November 1998; and
SONOMA COUNTY PEACE PRESS,
April/May 1999
Title: "The Role of Caspian Sea Oil
in the Balkan Conflict"
Author: Diana Johnstone

BECAUSE PEOPLE MATTER,
May/June 1999 (Reprinted from
Workers World, July 30, 1998)
Title: "Kosovo: It's About the Mines"
Author: Sara Flounders

SAN FRANCISCO BAY GUARDIAN,
December 16. 1999
Title: "Caspian Pipe Dreams"
Author: Pratap Chatterjee

Faculty Evaluators: Catherine Nelson, Ph.D. & Jim Burkland
Student Researchers: Misty Anderson, Jake Medway, & Damian Uriarte

NATO and the countries it represents were fully aware of numerous economic advantages to breaking up Yugoslavia and thus pursued a war over Kosovo. Despite environmental and civilian harm, NATO promoted a war with Serbia in order to position the Western nations politically and economically, and to reestablish itself militarily.

The media often depicts Kosovo as an isolated and poor region with little or no resources. Yet huge reserves of lead, zinc, cadmium, silver, gold, and coal are in Kosovo and were held by the Serbian state-owned Trepca mining complex. The most valuable resources in the Balkans are its mines, estimated to be worth in excess of $5 billion. The huge complex of mines, oil and gas refining prospects, and power and transportation futures is thought to be the largest piece of wealth not yet in the hands of U.S. and European capitalists. Whoever ultimately controls Kosovo will determine principle interest in the 22 mines and the many processing plants of the Trepca complex for decades to come.

Natural gas pipeline routes that carry Caspian oil to foreign markets may also have been a contributing factor in NATO's war against Serbia. On average, the 1990s oil prices from the Caspian Sea amounts to approximately $5 trillion. Amoco and Chevron are two leading oil companies with interests in Caspian oil.

Numerous problems exist with various proposals for delivery of Caspian oil to the West. Options for building pipelines through Iran and Russia are, for example, opposed by the U.S. for political reasons.

The possibility of shipping the oil across the Black Sea from a pipeline on the sea's eastern coast may be the cheapest option. Still, the likelihood of environmental damage while shipping 100 million tons of oil annually through the narrow Bosporus Straits is too great. The solution favored by the U.S. is to build the pipeline from the western end of the Black Sea through the NATO-controlled Balkans.

NATO's role of protecting the vital interests of multinational corporations is perhaps its principle justification for existence after the end of the Cold War. A leaked 1992 Pentagon planning document states, "It is of fundamental importance to preserve NATO as the primary instrument of Western defense and security, as well as the channel for U.S. influence and participation in European security affairs." Without a Soviet threat, the U.S. had to find other uses for the alliance.

A senior NATO official told a reporter of the *New York Times*, "Organizations seek out action. They need to do things. That's why NATO needs the Balkans...."

UPDATE BY AUTHOR PRATAP CHATTERJEE: The Caspian region has been touted as the successor to the Arabian Gulf as a source of world oil. Various experts have estimated that the region holds a treasure chest of roughly $5 trillion worth of oil that makes the region the setting for tremendous political rivalry. Although the conflict in the region has been a major news story (such as the ongoing Russian assault on Chechnya), very few reports have focused on the possible environmental consequences of the drilling, the lack of democracy in the region, and the unequal distribution of wealth.

"Caspian Pipe Dreams" provides a road map to various pipeline options and the political rivalries and conflicts, as well as the social and environmental consequences of the drilling plans.

In mid-November, President Bill Clinton went to Istanbul, Turkey, to take part in the formal signing of pipeline agreements with the presidents of Turkey, Azerbaijan, Georgia, and Turkmenistan. Russia and Iran, both of whom are rivals to the American interests, were cut out of these agreements.

One of these pipelines will carry oil from Baku, the Azerbaijani capital, some 1,080 miles across the Caucasus and through eastern Turkey to the Mediterranean port of Ceyhan. The other pipeline, which is 1,250 miles long, will run under the Caspian to take gas from Central Asia along the same route to an export outlet in Turkey. U.S. Energy Secretary Bill Richardson summed up the American position for the press at the signing of the pipeline agreements: "This is not just another oil and gas deal, and this is not just another pipeline. It is a strategic framework that advances America's national security interests."

The mainstream media has been very interested in the conflict over Caspian oil. There has even been a James Bond movie, appropriately titled *The World Is Not Enough*, but the coverage has been mostly sensationalistic and very supportive of the "need" to tap these riches and the potential benefits for the local people without questioning the possible downside locally. Nor has the mainstream media ever covered possible alternative development models for the region or the fact that the very extraction and consumption of Caspian oil will exacerbate global warming.

To get regular updates on the subject of the mineral industries I recommend that readers subscribe to a twice-monthly electronic magazine, *Project Underground, Drillbits & Tailings*, from a non-profit organization that supports communities affected by the mineral industries. The magazine is available electronically for free (financial support is encouraged) by e-mailing project_underground@moles.org. All back issues are archived and completely searchable on the World Wide Web at www.moles. org.

UPDATE BY AUTHOR SARA FLOUNDERS: "Kosovo: It's About the Mines" examines the economic and strategic interests at stake in the Balkans. It was written before NATO's war.

In May 1999, during the 78-day NATO bombardment, I traveled through Yugoslavia with former U.S. Attorney General Ramsey Clark and videographer Gloria La Riva. It was clear that NATO overwhelmingly targeted the civilian infrastructure. In Belgrade and Novi Sad I visited bombed schools and hospitals. In Nis I saw a hospital and marketplace hit by cluster bombs.

In June, as the Yugoslav military withdrew from Kosovo Province, the media debated whether the Pentagon had destroyed three or seven Yugoslav tanks. What was not publicized was that NATO had bombed 328 schools and 33 hospitals along with heating plants, food processing and pharmaceutical plants, bridges, apartments blocs, and refugee convoys. NATO planes dropped more than 35,000 cluster bombs and fired thousands of rounds of depleted uranium shells.

Three months after the war a series of articles in the *Washington Post* by Dana Priest (September 19, 20, and 21, 1999) revealed that U.S. generals directing NATO bombing purposely struck civilian targets in Serbia to pressure the government to capitulate. The Geneva Convention of 1949 prohibits bombing not justified by military necessity. If there is any likelihood that a target has a civilian function, then bombing is prohibited by international law and considered a war crime.

Back in the spring, NATO bombardment was continually justified as a "humanitarian war." Hardly anyone mentioned the powerful economic interests that drive modern war. They assured the population that NATO intervention against the Yugoslav military was the only way to stop "genocide." On April 19, the State Department said that up to 500,000 Kosovar Albanians were missing and feared dead. On May 16, Defense Secretary William S. Cohen said that up to 100,000 Albanian men in Kosovo had vanished and may have been killed. This was an unrelenting theme during the bombing. A search of the Internet turns up more than 1,000 stories written on Kosovo massacres and mass graves.

Throughout the NATO bombing the media hardly mentioned Kosovo's many resources, except to charge that the Trepca mines were sites of mass graves. The *New York Times* on July 7, 1999, wrote a major story headlined: "Crisis in the Balkans: Atrocities, Acid and Smelting Vats Evoke Fear of Grisly Burials by Serbs." According to *NY Times* correspondent Chris Hedges, truckloads of bodies arrived each night at the Trepca mines and the unusual bittersweet smell, assumed to be burning bodies, wafted up from the chimneys that ventilate the huge bowl-shaped smelting vats. Reports claimed that more than 700 bodies were in the mine.

In June, after the cease-fire, forensic teams from 17 nations converged on Kosovo to gather evidence of war crimes committed by the Yugoslav military. On November 11 a *New York Times* article reported that after five months of investigation and exhumation of 195 most serious grave sites, reported to hold thousands of bodies, they had not found even a fraction of the reported 500,000 or 100,000 bodies. Their total count was 2,108 bodies throughout the province. They found no mass graves.

After a long NATO investigation at the Trepca Mines, but with far less publicity than the original charges, the November 11, 1999, *New York Times* article admitted that no bodies or any evidence of a crime at the Trepca mines could be found. The mines are now firmly in NATO control.

Since the cease-fire the real U.S. goals have become much clearer. The largest U.S. foreign base built from scratch since the Vietnam War is under construction in Kosovo. Unlike the tent camps of the European forces, Camp Bondsteel is already a heavily fortified base surrounded by miles of barbed wire, earthen berns, and permanently heated and air-conditioned buildings.

Behind the propaganda of a humanitarian war, U.S./NATO bases have been constructed in Albania, Croatia, Bosnia, Hungary, Macedonia, and Kosovo. The Balkans, a region of enormous strategic importance, rich natural resources and important industrial capacity is now occupied by thousands of U.S. troops. All this has happened without any informed debate or discussion.

Presently I am coordinating the Independent Commission of Inquiry to Investigate U.S./NATO War Crimes Against the People of Yugoslavia. Ramsey Clark has drafted a 19-point indictment charging U.S. and NATO leaders with Crimes Against Peace, War Crimes, and Crimes Against Humanity in violation of the Nuremberg Tribunal, the Hague Regulations, the Geneva Conventions, and the U.N. Charter. Large public hearings on these charges have been held in 10 U.S. cities and in cities throughout Europe. Many more hearings are planned. This has become a people's movement demanding truth and accountability. The most dramatic event was a People's Tribunal of over 10,000 people in Athens, Greece, where the Greek Supreme Court declared President Clinton and NATO leaders guilty of war crimes. An International Tribunal will be held in June 2000 in New York City where a jury of internationally prominent individuals will review the evidence and deliver a verdict. Student interns on this project are welcome. The 19-point indictment and research papers are available on the International Action Center (IAC) Web site: www.iacenter.org.

7 CENSORED
U.S. Media Reduces Foreign Coverage

Source:
AMERICAN JOURNALISM REVIEW,
November 1998
Title: "Good-bye World"
Author: Peter Arnett

Faculty Evaluator:
Elizabeth Burch, Ph.D.
Student Researchers:
Deb Udall & Monte Williams

Mainstream coverage:
The *Boston Globe*, November 15, 1998, D6, Editorial

Foreign news is disappearing from many of America's newspapers. Today, a foreign story that doesn't involve bombs, natural disaster, or financial calamity has little chance of entering the American consciousness. This happens at a time when the United States has become the world's lone superpower and "news" has so many venues that it seems inescapable.

So how is it that Americans are less informed than ever about what's going on in the rest of the world? Because the media have stopped telling us. In the *Indianapolis Star*, for example, in the 30 days of November 1977, there were a total of 5,100 inches of foreign news. In the same month in 1997, foreign news accounted for just under 3,900 column inches, a 23 percent drop over two decades.

Beyond quantity, the trend involves an overall reduction in prominence of foreign news. For example, even in metropolitan newspapers, a subscriber can go for days without seeing a foreign news story crack the front pages. While people told pollsters that they rely primarily on TV for national and international news, mainstream newspapers have opted to cover what national networks can't—local news and sports. Television news, during the heyday of Walter Cronkite, John Chancellor, and Frank Reynolds, contained at least 40 percent international coverage. The figure today is 7-12 percent and dropping.

International news began to fade from America's newspapers in the 1970s. When the Vietnam War ended, international news fell dramatically out of favor with editors. With the emergence of Watergate, the energy crisis, and other domestic concerns, fewer papers were willing to support foreign correspondents or subscribe to foreign news services.

Nationwide interviews indicate that most editors believe readers aren't interested in foreign news. Surveys of readers, however, show the contrary. A Harris poll showed that nearly half or even more readers were interested in international news. In a 1996 poll, the Pew Research Center for the People and the Press asked readers what kind of news stories they regularly follow. Fifteen percent said international affairs—just one point below Washington politics and slightly ahead of consumer news, and two points ahead of the celebrity stuff that gets all the coverage.

UPDATE BY AUTHOR PETER ARNETT: The United States has become the world's lone superpower, with onerous responsibilities for international order never previously faced. Yet America's mainstream media is failing in its responsibility to inform the public about what's going on in the rest of the world.

The ethnic cleansing in Kosovo that led to a serious bombing campaign with risks to American lives, the nuclear confrontations between India and Pakistan, and other international crises of the past year or so came as almost total surprises to the U.S. public.

Why? Because most of the nation's newspapers and magazines and television stations, seeking greater profits through larger audiences, fed the public a diet of crime news, celebrity gossip, and soft features, choosing to exclude more serious topics that news managers feared would not stimulate public attention.

Consequently, at a time when Americans need to know more about the world than ever because of globilization and the role of the U.S. in keeping the peace, they know less than ever.

The "Good-bye World" story was the sixth in a series of articles devoted to a critical examination of the American newspaper industry, produced by the Project on the State of the American Newspaper, an initiative of the project for Excellence in Journalism, and affiliated with the University of Maryland College of Journalism. They were all published in the *American Journalism Review* and together form an important body of information on the American news industry today.

There was some limited editorial comment agreeing that more foreign news is necessary. The story was used in a continuing campaign by the president of the American Society of Newspaper Editors (ASNE), Edward Seaton, to persuade editors to use more foreign news. The foreign editor of the Associated Press, Tom Kent, used the story as the basis for his course on media responsibility at the Columbia School of Journalism. Various academic institutions, including the University of Indiana PA, used the story for extended class discussion.

The *American Journalism Review* (AJR) ran the whole "Good-bye World" story and continues to address the situation. AJR's e-mail address is editor @ajr.umd.edu. Tel: (301) 405-8803. Address: University of Maryland, 1117 Journalism Building, College Park, MD 20742-1117.

For progress on the Project ASNE for International News, contact ASNE president Edward Seaton. He is reachable at the Manhattan Mercury Newspaper, Manhattan, Kansas.

The Freedom Forum is active in advancing journalisic excellence in all fields and maintains offices internationally to develop news interests: The Freedom Forum, 1101 Wilson Boulevard, Arlington VA, 22209; E-mail: news @freedomforum.org.

8 CENSORED

Planned Weapons in Space Violate International Treaty

Sources:
EARTH ISLAND JOURNAL,
Winter/Spring 1999
Title: "U.S. Violates World Law
to Militarize Space"
Author: Karl Grossman

TOWARD FREEDOM,
September/October 1999
Title: "Pyramids to The Heavens"
Author: Bruce K. Gagnon
Community Evaluator:
Rick Williams, Attorney At Law
Student Researcher: Julia O'Connor

Mainstream coverage: *The Huntville Times,* November 7, 1999, Editorial, D2

The United States plans to militarize space while in direct violation of international treaties. The Outer Space Treaty of 1967 bans deployment of weapons of mass destruction in space. Still, the Ballistic Missile Defense system and other space weapons programs have already been approved by Congress and are currently underway. The United States Military Space Command's "Vision for 2020" report not only speaks of controlling the Earth and the sky above our planet, it also describes plans to control the vast region beyond as NASA and aerospace corporations move toward mining the moon, Mars, and other planetary bodies for minerals.

Our military successes in the Persian Gulf War convinced the U.S. military that space dominance and space control were necessary. Using its satellite supremacy, the Pentagon pre-targeted Iraq's military installations, and hit over 90 percent of its targets within the first few hours, giving the U.S. the ability to control the entire battlefield. The Space Command's Global Positioning System constellation of 24 satellites is credited with providing navigation and timing support to coordinate the actions of allied air crews and naval forces operating in the region.

The Pentagon is so convinced that whoever controls space will control the Earth and beyond that they are feverishly working to deploy anti-satellite weapons (ASATs) within the next five years. The weapons will enable the U.S. to knock out competitors' eyes-in-the-sky during any future hostilities. General Joseph Ashy, commander-in-chief of the U.S. Space Command, stated, "It's politically sensitive but it's going to happen.... Some

people don't want to hear this, and it sure isn't in vogue but, absolutely, we're going to fight in space. We're going to fight from space and we're going to fight into space."

The aerospace industry, eagerly awaiting sub-contracts, engages in a campaign called "Declaration of Space Leadership." This campaign calls for funding of NASA and "Space Defensive Systems" at costs that guarantee American leadership in the exploration of space.

Still, one of the military's problems is providing the massive power needed to project their space-based weapons. The military believes that nuclear power is the only source powerful enough to supply military space forces with the electric power needed for these weapons to work.

The Outer Space Treaty also states that nations should avoid activities that stand to produce "harmful contamination of space and celestial bodies as well as adverse changes in the environment of Earth." Between NASA's demand for future nuclear-powered space probes and the Space Command's desire for nuclear powered space weapons, the result will be nuclear contamination problems both on land and in space. With a 12 percent failure rate in both the U.S. and Russian space programs, nuclear accidents are inevitable.

NASA has launched a program to reach every science teacher in the country. Their thoughts are that by 2020, current elementary school students will be taxpayers. The industry hopes that they'll not only believe that we should spend whatever it takes to go to Mars, but also that war in space is inevitable.

UPDATE BY AUTHOR KARL GROSSMAN: The United States is violating the Outer Space Treaty, the basic international law on space, by covering its nuclear-fueled space shots with the U.S. Price Anderson Act. The Outer Space Treaty declares that nations "shall be liable for damage caused by their space objects." The Price Anderson Act limits liability in the event of an accident involving a U.S. nuclear power system—and was originally designed for nuclear plants on Earth. But in 1991 NASA and the U.S. Department of Energy, in a Space Nuclear Power Agreement, declared it would cover U.S. nuclear-fueled space shots, too.

Thus, if there had been an accident on the most recent U.S. nuclear mission, the plutonium-fueled Cassini space probe, the U.S. would have only accepted liability for a fraction of the consequences in death and damage—$8.9 billion for impacts in the U.S. and $100 million, under the Price Anderson Act, for impacts in all foreign nations. NASA documents, meanwhile, acknowledged that if an inadvertent re-entry into the Earth's atmosphere occurred during the most risky aspect of the Cassini mission—the 1999 Earth "'flyby' or 'gravity assist maneuver'...approximately 5 billion [of the world population] could receive 99 percent or more of the radiation exposure," and the cost of de-contaminating the land could run in the trillions of dollars.

Since publication of the *Earth Island Journal* article, Cassini was successful in buzzing the Earth in a 700-mile high flyby in August 1999. Yet, the following month, an accident befell NASA's Mars Climate Observer—similar to what could have happened with Cassini. It failed in buzzing Mars because one NASA team calculated altitude in meters, the other in feet. Coming in too low, it broke apart.

Meanwhile, NASA plans eight more plutonium-fueled space probe shots in coming years—all to be covered by the Space Nuclear Power Agreement. With Cassini, the world got through one in a series of space-borne rounds of nuclear Russian Roulette. The enormous risk and illegality remains if U.S. plans are not changed. And changed they could be. The next U.S. nuclear space mission, for example, is in 2003, when NASA intends to launch its plutonium-fueled Europa space probe to Jupiter. The same year, the European Space Agency will be launching its solar-energized Rosetta space probe beyond the orbit of Jupiter to rendezvous with a comet called Wirtanen. The European Space Agency has made a point of noting that it is using solar energy rather than nuclear power to energize the instruments on board Rosetta and that Rosetta will be gathering solar power as far as 500 million miles from the sun. NASA could also use solar power as an alternative to nuclear power in space.

Meanwhile, the U.S. push to weaponize space has become more intense since the publication of the *Earth Island Journal* article. The use of nuclear power in space is closely linked to this trend. U.S. military documents declare that the U.S. is seeking to control space, and from space (which the documents call "the ultimate high ground") the Earth below. As a U.S. Air Force board report, "New World Vistas: Air and Space Power for the 2lst Century," explains, the space-based weapons such as lasers, need large amounts of power and a solution "is nuclear power in space. Setting the emotional issues of nuclear power aside, this technology offers a viable alternative for large amounts of power in space." (The Pentagon's desire to use nuclear power in space is a key reason why NASA rejects the solar option and sticks with nuclear, to better coordinate its activities with the U.S. military.)

"New World Vistas" further states that "in the next two decades, new technologies will allow space based weapons of devastating effectiveness to effect very many kills." These plans remain despite the ban on deployment of weapons of mass destruction in space by the Outer Space Treaty, initiated by the U.S., the United Kingdom, and the former Soviet Union in 1967 and ratified by most of the world's nations.

In a critical United Nations General Assembly vote in November 1999, called to deal with the U.S. plans to weaponize space, 138 nations voted to reaffirm the Outer Space Treaty and its provision that space be used for peaceful purposes. The U.S. abstained on the vote. And it drives on to make the heavens a war zone.

Although there was mainstream media coverage of the Cassini mission and its Earth flyby, there was absolutely no mention of the Space Nuclear Power Agreement aspect and the Outer Space Treaty violation it involves. The current push to weaponize space remains spottily covered by mainstream media, with whatever coverage there is stressing missile defense, despite the abundance of U.S. military documents making it clear that the U.S. military's plans are largely about domination of space.

A comprehensive source of further information is the book I have authored, *The Wrong Stuff: The Space Program's Nuclear Threat To Our Planet* (Common Courage Press, Tel: (800) 497-3207), and video documentaries I wrote and narrated, *Nukes In Space: The Nuclearization and Weaponization of the Heavens* and *Nukes In Space 2: Unacceptable Risks* (EnviroVideo, Tel: (800) ECO-TV46 and www.envirovideo.com).

Also, for more information and to get involved in challenging the U.S. plans, contact the Global Network Against Weapons & Nuclear Power In Space at (352) 337-9274 or E-mail: globalnet@ mindspring.com. Its Web site: www.globenet.free-online.co.uk/.

UPDATE BY AUTHOR BRUCE K. GAGNON: As this was written, CNN ran a non-stop promotion on TV for NASA's Mars Polar Lander (which only days later turned up lost in space wasting $123 million). While we are told that NASA is looking for life on Mars, the reality is that NASA is doing planetary mapping, and soil identification, and in future missions, the space agency will do a soil sample return mission. All of this is a prelude to "manned" missions to Mars. Manned nuclear-powered mining colonies are to be set up to "exploit" Mars for cobalt, magnesium, uranium, and other rare minerals.

Nuclear-powered rockets would blast off from Cape Canaveral to shorten the amount of time it takes to get to Mars. And the cost of all this? *Space News*, an industry publication, gave the conservative figure of $400 billion as the collective cost of the Mars mission series for the U.S. taxpayer.

Indeed, as outlined in my article, "Pyramids to the Heavens," the U.S. Space Command's job would be to create a parallel military highway between Earth and these exploited planets to ensure, as they say in their "Vision for 2020" report, "U.S. military, civil, and commercial investments in space" are protected. President Clinton is expected to make the final decision prior to June 2000 on "early deployment" of the Ballistic Missile Defense (BMD) system. This system would allow for a return of Star Wars. The Air Force is now testing space-based laser weapons and anti-satellite weapons (ASATs) that would be the follow-on technologies to the BMD Trojan horse. With this space domination established, the U.S. would not only control the Earth but also the new "shipping lanes" of space.

The corporate-dominated media is ignoring the real story about space. As hundreds of billions of tax dollars are spent on space, they offer the fluff and the hype from NASA about Mars landings, but there is no analysis of where the U.S. Space Command and the aerospace corporations are taking the space program. Critics that are interviewed are used to make the case that NASA needs more money to do the job "better." In fact, a series of Mars movies will be coming out in 2000-2001 to sell the program. Filmmaker James Cameron recently told a Mars Society conference, "I want to make humans-to-Mars real in the minds of the viewing public." He said that he hopes to create a ground swell for increased NASA funding.

The alternative media must help carry this important issue to the public. Who else will? The Global Network Against Weapons & Nuclear Power in Space (GN) is now organizing to create a worldwide democratic debate about what kind of seed should be carried into space. Should we take the bad seed of war, greed, and environmental degradation with us as we leave this planet? Just how much money should be spent on the space program? And who should be in control?

For more information about this important issue please check the Global Network's Web site: www.globenet.free-online.co.uk. On the Web site you will find links to all the major military and corporate aerospace sites so you can see for yourself what they are up to. To get directly involved please contact the GN at P.O. Box 90083, Gainesville, FL 32607, Tel: (352) 337-9274. Bruce K. Gagnon, coordinator.

9 CENSORED

Louisiana Promotes Toxic Racism

Source:
SOUTHERN EXPOSURE,
Summer/Fall 1998
Title: "Toxic Gumbo"
Author: Ron Nixon

Faculty Evaluator: James Carr, Ph.D.
Student Evaluators: Lisa Desmond,
Colleen Kelly, & Monte Williams

The Nation, in the November 8, 1999 issue, published an article by Barbara Koeppel entitled "Cancer Alley, Louisiana." While outside of Project Censored's awards cycle for 1999, the piece fully supported the *Southern Exposure* story and added numerous details.

Mainstream (partial) coverage:
PBS News, September 27, 1998
CNN Cable, September 13, 1997

Southeast Louisiana, an area heavily populated with low-income minority families, is one of the worst sites for releases of toxic substances in the country. This region, a one-hundred-mile stretch of land between Baton Rouge and New Orleans, consists of seven oil refineries and approximately 175 heavy industrial plants that represent a "Who's Who" of the petrochemical industry: Texaco, Borden, Occidental Chemical, Kaiser Aluminum, Chevron, IMC-Agrico, Dow, DuPont, and many others. Toxic releases from this region and the resulting health consequences are so severe that the area is now called "Cancer Alley."

In Louisiana, 30 percent of the population live under or just above the poverty line. The invasion of toxic industries is one of the U.S.'s worst examples of environmental racism, a phenomenon in which companies target communities of color for the location of undesirable facilities.

According to an Environmental Protection Agency (EPA) report, over 23 million pounds of toxins are released annually into Louisiana's air. The majority of these releases are in two zip code areas that are primarily inhabited by Black residents.

Nationally, a 1987 study by the United Church of Christ's Commission on Racial Justice found that Blacks were four times more likely to live in areas with toxic and hazardous waste sites than were Whites. A 1992 investigation by the *National Law Journal* found that even when the government does enforce environmental regulations and fine companies, fines are much higher in White communities than in Black ones.

These reports and increased activity by environmental justice groups across the country prompted President Clinton in 1993 to sign an executive order to investigate the petrochemical industry's disproportionate impact on people of color. However, these efforts have done little to help the people who live in Cancer Alley.

Bob Hall, author of the *Green Index*, says "everything is for sale [in the South]...including cheap resources, cheap land, and even cheap lives, especially those of minorities." The state government of Louisiana provides significant incentives in order to attract industry to the region. A recent ad in the *Wall Street Journal* supports this mode of boosterism. The ad shows a man in a suit bent over backwards with the words, "What has Louisiana done for business lately?" The ad goes on to tout the state's passage of tort reform legislation and the governor's business background.

While some small communities, such as Convent, have successfully kept new industries (Shintech) out, most communities are still fighting for their lives, and the polluting process continues. Black towns like Sunrise, Revelltown, and Morrisonville no longer exist. Contaminated and bought out by Dow, Georgia Gulf, and Polacid Oil, as well as other companies, these communities are now toxic ghost towns.

Years ago, Louisiana struck a Faustian deal with the chemical industry. Today Black residents are paying the price with their health, their communities, their very lives, and their history.

UPDATE BY AUTHOR RON NIXON: After "Toxic Gumbo" ran in *Southern Exposure*, the struggle was picked up by several mainstream news organizations including ABC News. *Life* magazine ran a cover story on one of the organizers of the protest, who went to Japan to protest Shintech's plans to build a PVC plant in St. James Parish. Following the coverage in *Southern Exposure* and other media outlets, Shintech abandoned its plans to build the polyvinyl chloride (PVC) plant in St. James Parish. The company said it would build somewhere else, but as of this moment hasn't decided on a new location.

For more information contact Damu Smith at Greenpeace in Washington, DC, Tel: (202) 462-1177.

10 CENSORED

The U.S. and NATO Deliberately Started the War with Yugoslavia

Sources:
THE VILLAGE VOICE, May 18, 1999
Title: "The Real Rambouillet"
Author: Jason Vest

EXTRA, July/August 1999
Title: "Redefining Diplomacy"
Author: Seth Ackerman

IN THESE TIMES, August 8, 1999
Title: "What Was the War For?"
Author: Seth Ackerman

COVERTACTION QUARTERLY, Spring/Summer 1999
Title: "Hawks and Eagles: 'Greater NATO' flies to Aid of 'Greater Albania'"
Author: Diana Johnstone

PACIFICA RADIO NETWORK,
April 23, 1999, www.Pacifica.org
Title: "Democracy Now"
Host: Amy Goodman

Faculty Evaluator: Phil Beard
Student Researchers: Nathan Guzik,
Jennifer Mathis, & Jennifer Acio

Mainstream coverage:
C-SPAN *Washington Journal*,
San Husseini, April 22, 1999
Washington Post, "For the Record,"
April 28, 1999, A-24
Star-Tribune Newspaper of the Twin
Cities Minneapolis–St. Paul, May 17,
1999, 6A
Harper's Magazine, July 1, 1999

The U.S. and NATO pushed for war with Yugoslavia by demanding full military occupation of the entire country as a condition of not bombing. Belgrade could not accept the U.S. drafted two-part Rambouillet ultimatum, not only because it was a thinly veiled plan to detach Kosovo from Serbia, but also because it contained provisions even worse than loss of that historic province, provisions no sovereign country in the world could possibly accept.

Appendix B of the proposed pre-war Rambouillet treaty, subsections 7 and 8, stated that: "NATO personnel shall be immune from any form of arrest, investigation, or detention by the authorities in the Federal Republic of Yugoslavia (FRY) and "shall enjoy...free and unrestricted passage and unimpeded access throughout the FRY, including associated airspace and territorial waters."

Clauses 11 and 15 granted NATO "the use of airports, roads, rails, and ports without payment [and] the right to use all of the electromagnetic spectrum." Also included were arbitrary arrest and detention powers for NATO personnel. President Milosevic, fearing the loss of sovereignty of Yugoslavia, refused to ratify the agreement—the bombing started the next day.

Robert Hayden, director of the Center for Russian and European Studies at the University of Pittsburgh, stated that, in his view, a close reading of the accords "provided for the independence of Kosovo in all but name, and the military occupation by NATO of all of Yugoslavia, not just Kosovo."

According to NATO spokesperson Jamie Shea, "There was no intention whatever of having any kind of NATO occupation regime in Yugoslavia itself. What Rambouillet refers to is simply the right to transit, nothing more." Yet NATO had carefully planned military operations several months in advance and the treaty gave the Serbs no alternative.

Dan Goure, deputy director of political and military studies at the Center of Strategic and International Studies states the following: "The administration went to Rambouillet basically to arrange a trap for Milosevic. It was a no-win situation for him and frankly, Albright was trying to find a pretext for bombing. They told the Kosovar Albanians that if they signed and Milosevic didn't, they'd bomb Serbia. Rambouillet was not a negotiation, it was a setup, a lynch party."

Unreported in the mainstream media was the fact that when Serbia rejected the treaty they also passed a resolution declaring their willingness to negotiate for Kosovo's self-management. For months, the Serbian government had offered to negotiate. High level government teams made many trips to Pristina to hold talks with Ibrahim Rugova and other nonviolent ethnic Albanians. The Albanians refused to negotiate, for fear of going against the rising armed rebel movement, the Kosovo Libertarian Army (KLA), hostile to any compromise and ready to assassinate "traitors" who dealt with the Serbs.

At Rambouillet, the older generation of nationalist leaders did not have the slightest opportunity to enter negotiations with the multi-ethnic official Serbian delegation. They were overshadowed in the ethnic Albanian delegation by the KLA, who by then were assured U.S. support. Genuine negotiations would have at least paid attention to the extensive 10-page proposal of the Serbian government. Some of the points outlined in the proposal included the following: Equality of all citizens and guaranteed human rights, facilitated return of all citizens to their homes, safe unhindered access of all international and national or non-governmental humanitarian organizations to the population for purposes of aid, and the widest possible media freedoms.

UPDATE BY AUTHOR DIANA JOHNSTONE: NATO's war against Yugoslavia was the major ongoing news story of 1999 and will continue into 2000 and beyond. Presented by NATO propagandists and most of the media as a "humanitarian" war on behalf of the ethnic Albanians of Kosovo, this war violated international law, killed thousands of people, wantonly destroyed the livelihood of millions of innocent civilians in Yugoslavia, and left the supposed beneficiary of this aggression—Kosovo province—in a shambles.

NATO's airstrikes triggered violent Serb retaliation against ethnic Albanians who by the hundreds of thousands fled to safety in neighboring countries. They have since returned to a province under foreign military occupation, with no government administration or judicial system, at the mercy of a ruthless Albanian nationalist armed group, the Kosovo Liberation Army (KLA), which, while pretending to disband, has continued to drive out Kosovo's non-Albanian citizens and to terrorize fellow ethnic Albanians. This disastrous situation has its roots in the opportunistic alliance, which I described in "Hawks and Eagles," between U.S. strategists seeking a pretext to expand NATO and a nationalist Albanian lobby with influential supporters such as former Senator Bob Dole. This alliance culminated in the Clinton Administration's promotion of KLA leader Hashim Thaqi to head the Kosovo Albanian delegation that, by signing the "Rambouillet accords"—in fact a U.S. ultimatum—gave Washington the pretext it sought to launch NATO airstrikes against Yugoslavia in time for NATO's 50th anniversary celebration in April of 1999.

This unscrupulous alliance has dire consequences for the people of Kosovo and the entire region. A few words of Serbian spoken in public can equal a death sentence. Nobody is safe. Moderate Kosovo Albanian leaders have been publicly threatened by the KLA. The only people who may be safe now in Kosovo are the U.S. soldiers for whom the United States has hastily built a huge fortified military base, Camp Bondsteel, in total illegality on the territory of a foreign state.

Meanwhile, the Clinton Administration is encouraging further disintegration of Yugoslavia itself by inciting separatists in Montenegro, Voivodina, and the Sandjak region, as well as certain opposition leaders, to resort to secession and even civil war, in order to end the sanctions that continue to punish the people of Yugoslavia.

Never has an event of such tragic dimensions been so badly reported by Western mainstream media. Except for Greece, and to some extent Italy, the NATO propaganda version dominated media reporting. To justify continued airstrikes, NATO apologists even resorted to racist stigmatization of the Serbs as a people.

NATO propaganda has gradually lost credibility thanks to its own excesses, to the reporting of a few mainstream journalists such as Paul Watson and Robert Fisk, and more than ever before to the alternative press and the Internet. Just as Seattle may mark a new phase in activism against the excesses of economic globalization, the Kosovo War marked a new phase in the role of e-mail and Web

sites in overcoming the information monopoly of the corporate media. Thanks to the Internet, my own articles have appeared on Web sites and in publications I didn't know existed. The Web site of the Transnational Foundation for Future and Peace research, www. transnational.org, has been of particular value in spreading information and stimulating debate, as have ZNet and emperors-clothes.com.

Diana Johnstone
65 rue Marcadet
75018 Paris, France
Tel & Fax: 011-33-1-4223-5211.

UPDATE BY SETH ACKERMAN: The diplomatic sleight-of-hand at the Rambouillet peace conference in February-March 1999 forces us to ask searching questions about the nature of NATO's Kosovo War. Was it, as NATO says, a desperate recourse to the use of military force, aimed at stopping an imminent genocide from being perpetrated by Yugoslav forces hiding cynically behind claims of national sovereignty? Or was it an American power play—designed to advance Washington's strategic goals in Europe, joined by skeptical European allies brigaded behind a U.S. policy they lacked the military weight to challenge?

Such questions cannot be answered with any certainty until all the diplomatic records are opened—and we will have to wait a long time for that to happen. In the meantime, we can listen to those in some position to know what took place at Rambouillet—as well as before and since. For instance, Eric Rouleau, an influential

French journalist and diplomat, recently published an intriguing account of France's role in Western diplomacy towards Kosovo in the French journal *Le Monde Diplomatique*. In his lengthy analysis, Rouleau, a former French ambassador to Turkey, writes that a senior official in the French foreign ministry admitted to him that the Rambouillet document was unacceptable.

Prominent diplomats, scholars, and Balkan experts have offered their judgments about U.S. diplomacy. Henry Kissinger has said that "the Rambouillet text…was a provocation, an excuse to start bombing" Yugoslavia. Lord David Owen, the European Union's former peace negotiator for Bosnia, has acknowledged that once the U.S. put forward the Rambouillet military annex, with its demand to allow NATO troops throughout Yugoslavia, "there was no question that the Serbs would risk air attacks." He also found it "noteworthy" that this provocative demand failed to materialize in the final June 3 agreement with Yugoslavia.

The famed British foreign correspondent, Robert Fisk, published a report in the November 26 London *Independent* tracing the evidence that Appendix B of the Rambouillet text was designed to provoke a Serbian rejection. Fisk interviewed Serbian officials, including Information Minister Milan Komnenic, a respected figure within and outside Serbia, who is at work on a book about the talks, entitled *The Rambouillet Trap*. Another minister, Goran Matic, who is close to President Milosevic, told Fisk:

"We were ready to accept the political solution of the Kosovo problem and U.N. troops to regulate the implementation— but not NATO troops in occupation." Matic claims that U.N. Security Council Resolution 1244, which set the final peace terms in June, "could have been accepted before the bombing."

To my knowledge, the facts about Appendix B of Rambouillet, Serbia's pre-war concessions, and the American strategic interest in airstrikes, have never been discussed in any depth in the news columns of the major media. In my view, this silence represents the greatest failure of the American press's coverage of Kosovo. Indeed, "failure" is probably too exculpatory. Steven Erlanger of the *New York Times*, one of the best American correspondents in Belgrade, acknowledged in a radio interview last summer that he believes a diplomatic solution to the Kosovo crisis had been possible at Rambouillet. Yet Erlanger, unlike Robert Fisk, has never published an article exploring the question.

Yet the facts are available. One of the best single sources for information about these aspects of the Kosovo War is the Web site of *Z Magazine*, which devotes a special section to Kosovo. That page can be found at www.zmag.org/ZMag/kosovo.htm. Jan Oberg of the Transnational Institute in Stockholm produced some of the earliest and best analyses of the Rambouillet texts and the subsequent diplomacy. His Web site is www.transnational.org.

11 CENSORED

America's Largest Nuclear Test Exposed Thousands

Sources:
COUNTERPUNCH, Summer 1999;
TERRAIN, Fall 1999
Title: "Aftermath of Amchitka"
Authors: Alexander Cockburn &
Jeffrey St. Clair

IN THESE TIMES, August 8, 1999
Title: "30 Years After—The Legacy
of America's Largest Nuclear Test"
Author: Jeffrey St. Clair

Faculty Evaluator:
Eric McGuckin, Ph.D.
Student Researchers:
Tanner May & Fera Byrd

Mainstream coverage: Articles in the *New York Times* on October 30, 1996, and *USA Today* the following day reported the Greenpeace findings, but there have been no follow-up news reports since that time.

Thirty years ago, Amchitka, which sits at the midway point on the great arc of Alaska's Aleutian Islands, was the site of three large underground nuclear tests, including the most powerful nuclear explosion ever detonated by the United States. Despite claims by the Atomic Energy Commission (AEC) and the Pentagon that the test sites would safely contain the radiation released by the blasts

for thousands of years, independent research by Greenpeace and newly released documents from the Department of Energy (DOE) show that the Amchitka tests began to leak almost immediately.

The tests were designed to calibrate the performance of the Spartan anti-ballistic missile that was built to take out the Soviet nuclear arsenal. One of the factors behind the selection of Amchitka as a test site was its proximity to the Soviet Union. Publicly, however, the rationale offered by the AEC and the Defense Department was simply that Amchitka was a remote, and therefore safe, testing ground. Thousands of Amchitka laborers and Aleuts were, however, living on nearby islands. Highly radioactive elements and gasses poured out of the collapsed test shafts, leached into the ground water, and worked their way into ponds, creeks, and the Bering Sea. Dozens of people have died of radiation-linked cancers.

The immediate ecological damage from the blast was staggering. The blast ruptured the crust of the Earth, sucking a creek into a brand new aquifer, a radioactive one. In the months following the explosion, blood and urine samples were taken from Aleuts living in the village of Adak on a nearby island. The samples show abnormally high levels of tritium and cesium-137, both known carcinogens. Despite these alarming findings, the government never returned to Adak to conduct follow-up medical studies. More than 1,500 workers who helped build the test sites, operate the bomb tests and clean up afterward were exposed. The AEC never conducted medical studies on any of these laborers. Still, the DOE claimed that none of the workers had been exposed to radiation, but later was forced to admit that exposure records and dosimeter badges had been lost. The Aleuts in the region, who continue their seafaring lifestyle, are particularly vulnerable to radiation-contaminated fish and marine mammals, and radiation that might spread through the Bering Sea, plants, and ice floes.

In June 1996, two members of Greenpeace, Pam Miller and Norm Buske, returned to Amchitka to collect water and plant samples from various sites on the island. The samples taken revealed the presence of plutonium and americium-241; both are radioactive elements that are extremely toxic and have half-lives of hundreds of years. In 1998, a study by Rosalie Bertell, a former consultant to the Nuclear Regulatory Commission (formerly AEC), found that hundreds of Amchitka workers were exposed to ionizing radiation at five times the level recognized as hazardous. The research is incomplete, however, because many of the records from the Amchitka blast remain classified and others were simply tossed away. In April 1999, the Clinton Administration finally agreed to begin the first health survey of the Amchitka workers. The study was supposed to begin in the summer of 1999, but is languishing without funding.

12 CENSORED
Evidence Indicates No Pre-war Genocide in Kosovo and Possible U.S./KLA Plot to Create Disinformation

Sources:
COVERTACTION QUARTERLY, Spring/Summer 1999
Title: "William Walker: 'Man With a Mission'"
Author: Mark Cook

THE PROGRESSIVE REVIEW, June 1999
Title: "My Multinational Entity, Right or Wrong"
Author: Progressive Staff

EL PAIS, September 23, 1999
Title: "Spanish Police and Forensic Experts have not Found Proof of Genocide in the North of Kosovo"
Author: Pablo Ordaz

Faculty Evaluators: John Kramer, Ph.D. & Andrew Botterell, Ph.D.

Student Researchers:
Fera Byrd & Jeremiah Price

Mainstream coverage: *Los Angeles Times*, October 29, 1999, Editorial

According to the *New York Times*, the "turning point" to NATO's decision to go to war against Yugoslavia occurred on January 20, 1999 when U.S. diplomat William Walker led a group of news reporters to discover a so-called Serb massacre of some 45 Albanians in Racak, Kosovo. This story made international headlines and was later used to justify the NATO bombings.

The day before the "massacre," Serb police had a firefight with KLA rebels that was covered by an Associated Press (AP) film crew. At the end of day, the village was deserted. Then, the next day the village had been reoccupied by the KLA, and it was the KLA who initially led foreign visitors to the alleged massacre site. William Walker arrived at noon with additional journalists, and expressed his outrage at a "genocidal massacre" to the world press.

Walker's story remains shrouded with doubt. "What is disturbing," remarks war correspondent Renaud Girard, "is that the pictures filmed by the AP journalists radically contradict Walker's accusations." Challenges to Walker's massacre story were published in *Le Monde* and *Le Figaro*: "During the night, could the UCK (KLA) have gathered the bodies, in fact killed by Serb bullets, to set up a scene of cold-blooded massacre?" (*Le Figaro*). Belarussian and Finnish forensic experts were later unable to verify that a massacre had actually occurred at Racak.

Walker's pronounced massacre fueled NATO's justification for the air attacks on Serbia as a means of preventing genocide. However, reports from various foreign offices state that genocide was not occurring in Kosovo.

The *Progressive Review* reported that according to internal documents from Germany's Foreign Office and regional courts on January 6, 1999, "No cases of chronic malnutrition or insufficient medical treatment among the refugees are known and significant homelessness has not been observed." On January 12, other records noted: "Even in Kosovo an explicit political persecution linked to ethnicity is not verifiable." In addition, records from February 4 state: "The various reports presented to the Senate all agree the often-feared humanitarian catastrophe threatening the Albanian civil population has been averted." February 24 records state: "Events since February and March 1998 do not evidence a persecution program based on Albanian ethnicity." Records from March: "Ethnic Albanians in Kosovo have neither been, nor are now, exposed to regional or countrywide group persecution in the Federal Republic of Yugoslavia."

Additionally, *El Pais* reports that Spanish forensic experts have not found proof of genocide in the post-war region of northern Kosovo. NATO told the Spanish forensic teams that they were going into the worst part of Kosovo and to be prepared to perform 2,000 autopsies. Only 187 bodies were found in nine villages. They were buried in individual graves (most of which pointed toward Mecca to comply with the Albanian Kidovar religious custom) and without sign of torture.

UPDATE BY AUTHOR SAM SMITH: At about the time the Balkan War broke out, I was working on a memoir of the '60s and read, with no little embarrassment, some of the things I wrote as a 27-year-old in 1965 about Vietnam. I found there the tracks of a Cold-War-liberal upbringing, recent service in the Coast Guard, the memory of a friend who was among the first 40 killed in Southeast Asia, but most of all of a young journalist unwilling to risk looking foolish to others. It took about a year before I could turn such influences aside and stare straight at the facts.

In the end, it was a struggle that stood me in good stead. It taught me that war was the most seductive drama most of us will ever encounter, and that the media too often chooses the role of playwright rather than of honest observer.

The task has become much harder. Not only has military agitprop become infinitely more sly and manipulative, today's typical journalists are without personal experience of the system they celebrate. For this reason, I sometimes suggest a revival of the draft—but only for reporters. That way they would not be so easily conned by the military "experts" they so gladly interview and quote.

A less painful solution, of course, would be a far more aggressive and skeptical journalism that did not repeatedly serve, in Russell Baker's phrase, as a "megaphone for fraud." For my part, I find myself increasingly covering Washington's most ignored beat: the written word. The culture of deceit is primarily an oral one. The soundbite, the spin, and the political product placement depend on no one spending too much time on the matter under consideration.

Over and over again, however, I find that the real story still lies barely hidden and may be reached by nothing more complicated than turning the page, checking the small type in the appendix, charging into the typographical jungle beyond the executive summary, doing a Web search, and, for the bravest, actually looking at the figures on the charts.

THIS MODERN WORLD
by TOM TOMORROW

My work on the Balkan War represents an effort of this sort. It is the result not of investigative journalism, but of something that I fear is even rarer these days: Simple journalistic curiosity, a chronic dissatisfaction with the loose ends of our culture and experience. The piece was just a compilation of what should have been in my morning paper, but was not.

Although the issue with the article "My Multinational Entity, Right or Wrong" is out of print, photocopies of the article can be obtained by sending $2 to the *Progressive Review*. Other coverage of the Balkan War can be found at the following Web sites: http://prorev.com/balkan.htm and http://prorev.com/balkan2.htm.

Sam Smith
The *Progressive Review*
1312 18th St. NW, #502
Washington, DC 20036
Tel: (202) 845-0770 Fax: (202) 835-0779
Web site: http://prorev.com
E-mail: news@prorev.com news

UPDATE BY AUTHOR MARK COOK: Seldom has the power of mass media censorship been so graphically and frighteningly demonstrated as in the William Walker episode in Yugoslavia.

The Kosovo atrocity story Walker trumpeted in January 1999 was almost immediately discredited, not by a small political weekly somewhere, but by the leading newspapers in France. No matter—the discrediting was so completely suppressed in the United States that virtually no one could have heard of it. It was not as if anyone successfully answered the French journalists' claims; practically nobody even tried. As with Orwell's Ministry of Truth, it was found that the best way to kill the story was not to challenge it.

In contrast, Walker's dubious Racak story was loudly and unquestioningly repeated and became the propaganda justification for the bombing war. "Racak transformed the West's Balkan policy as singular events seldom do," wrote the *Washington Post* on April 18, 1999. The

--IF THE PRESIDENT WERE A *SUPERHERO*--JUST GO WITH IT FOR A MOMENT, OKAY?-- AND IN THE COURSE OF HIS NIGHTLY ROUNDS HE HAPPENED ON A *MUGGING*--

GIMME YOUR PURSE, LADY!

OH, DEAR!

--AND HE RESPONDED BY PULLING OUT AN *ASSAULT RIFLE* AND FIRING SEVERAL DOZEN ROUNDS IN THE GENERAL DIRECTION OF THE CRIME--TAKING OUT THE MUGGER AND HIS VICTIM *BOTH*--

STOP, FIEND!

RATATATATATAT

URK

AK

--WOULD YOU THEN NOD YOUR HEAD IN APPROVAL AS HE LOOKED DOWN AT THE CARNAGE AND BIT HIS UPPER LIP AND DECLARED IN A HOARSE YET DETERMINED VOICE--

--I HAD TO DO *SOMETHING!*

...WE DIDN'T THINK SO.

same day, the *New York Times* called Racak "a turning point."

Ironically, Walker had no credibility with the U.S. press corps. His role in El Salvador was so notorious that CBS's *60 Minutes* ran a segment on him twice. The second time was after the principal figure Walker was protecting, Salvadoran army chief of staff Rene Emilio Ponce, turned out to have been the main culprit in the 1989 Jesuit murders.

Since publication, the press has still not backed off the Racak story in the way that was finally done with the Battleship Maine or the Gulf of Tonkin. The revelations in the article have had an effect, however, in Europe as well as here. Many Europeans doubted Walker's Racak atrocity story, but knew little or nothing about his role in Central America. In the period since the article's publication, several European governments are reported privately to have called for his dismissal, arguing that if nothing else, his Salvador reputation made it difficult to use him to sell a "humanitarian" war.

Washington has not given up, however. Aside from Richard Holbrooke, who has a similarly unsavory record in East Asia and has now been appointed Washington's ambassador to the United Nations, there is Undersecretary of State for Political Affairs Thomas Pickering. As ambassador to El Salvador in 1984, Pickering publicly took much the same position that Walker accused the Serbs of taking at Racak—that it was all right to kill unarmed civilians who sympathize politically with armed rebels, since they are, in Pickering's words, "something

more than innocent civilian bystanders" (see "The Salvador Boys," Fall/Winter 1999 issue of *CovertAction Quarterly*).

Readers interested in following the story further can search the Internet under the word "Racak," where the French stories can be found in English translation. Nexus or Internet searches will produce the U.S. Embassy cables from San Salvador published by the *National Catholic Reporter* on September 23, 1994, as well as the articles cited on the Jesuit murders. The Lawyers Committee for Human Rights publication on the Jesuit murders, "A Chronicle of Death Foretold," may be obtained in libraries or from the Committee, 330 Seventh Avenue, 10th Floor, New York, NY 10001.

The findings of the "United Nations Truth Commission on El Salvador" published in 1992-93, do not appear to be on the Internet but can be found in libraries. Unfortunately, the report, "De la Locura a la Esperanza," (*Naciones Unidas*, San Salvador y Nueva York), is available only in Spanish, reportedly because the U.S. government blocked publication in English.

13 CENSORED

U.S. Agency Seeks to Export Weapons-Grade Plutonium to Russian Organization Linked to Organized Crime

Sources:
IN THESE TIMES, Oct. 17, 1999
Title: "Hot Property Cold Cash:
The Plan to Turn Russia into the
World's Nuclear Waste Dump"
Author: Jeffrey St. Clair

COUNTERPUNCH, Vol. 6, No. 16,
September 16–30, 1999
Title: "The MinAtom Conspiracy"
Authors: Jeffrey St. Clair &
Alexander Cockburn

Faculty Evaluator:
Wingham Liddell, Ph.D.
Student Researchers:
Rebecca Aust & Lisa Desmond

The Washington-based Non-Proliferation Trust (NPT) proposes that the U.S. sell nuclear waste to Russia. NPT's plan would make Russia the world's dumping ground for nuclear waste, including weapons-grade plutonium. NPT's partner in this endeavor is MinAtom, Russia's ministry of atomic energy.

NPT is headed up by Daniel Murphy (former deputy director of the CIA), Bruce Demars (former head of the Navy's nuclear program), and William Webster (former director of the CIA and FBI). Although NPT is set up as a non-profit organization, its principals stand to make huge profits off consulting and subcontracting. On the list of potential subcontractors is Halter Marine in Gulfport, Mississippi, a company to which U.S. Senator Trent Lott has close links. Halter Marine would be in line to build the huge container ships needed to transport the waste to Russia.

Yevgeny Adamov, the head of Min-Atom, estimates that the operation could produce $150 billion in revenue, making it the most lucrative operation in Russia. MinAtom is alleged to have links to corrupt government officials and the Russian Mob.

The NPT/MinAtom proposal, which is to last 40 years, would set dangerous precedents by opening up an international market in radioactive waste and by placing nuclear bomb-making materials into the hands of private groups with little or no government oversight. The radioactive waste would be shipped to Russia from Europe and Asia on large ships mounted with an arsenal of weapons designed to ward off nuclear pirates. According to the NPT, the fuel would be either stored in casks or buried in deep geological formations on Russian soil.

Vladimir Silvyak, organizer with the Social Ecological Union, the largest environmental group in Russia states, "If this goes through, the deal will make

MinAtom, an agency that is already barely answerable to the government, the most powerful entity in Russia. Certainly MinAtom will be one of the few agencies with any money and they sure won't spend it on social programs."

The biggest initial hurdle for the NPT are Russian environmental statutes that outlaw the import of spent fuel for storage in Russia. MinAtom has been attempting to overturn these laws for the past few years, but the NPT proposal will make lobbying a lot easier. The trust has pledged to spend at least $3.5 billion on the pet projects of key leaders of the Duma—including $1.8 billion for an underground cave repository for spent-fuel, and $2 billion to "safeguard" weapons-grade plutonium. Hundreds of millions of dollars would be promised for environmental and charitable causes, such as Russian orphans and pensions and salaries for Russian nuclear and defense workers.

So far the U.S. government has rebuffed MinAtom's offer, but a recent federal court ruling favoring the nuclear power industry is changing the situation. The ruling, made earlier this year, states that the U.S. government is obligated to make good a contractual agreement with the nuclear utilities to assume all liabilities and most of the costs for the disposal of the nation's commercial nuclear waste. This may make the U.S. government more anxious to dispose of waste overseas. The NPT plan is also supported by top officials in the Clinton Administration and this connection indicates how tightly wired the group is to the Washington establishment.

14 CENSORED

U.S. Media Ignores Humanitarian Aspects of Famine in Korea

Sources:
PEACE REVIEW, June 1999
Title: "Famine in North Korea"
Author: Ramsay Liem

PEACE REVIEW, June 1999
Title: "Dangerous Communists, Inscrutable Orientals, Starving Masses"
Author: Yuh Ji-Yeon

Faculty Evaluator: Les Adler, Ph.D.
Student Researchers:
Damian Uriarte & Julie O'Conner

The U.S. media used the Korean famine for political propaganda and has failed to cover the huge disaster from a humanitarian perspective. The U.S. media provided only minor coverage of the devastation even though people are suffering severe malnutrition.

A humanitarian food crisis of staggering proportions has been developing in North Korea, yet nowhere has there been an outcry like the one fueled by media worldwide for Ethiopia. Instead, the media chooses to focus on the implication of the threat posed by North Korea as they continue their nuclear testing.

The German Red Cross estimates two million deaths in 1997 due to starvation, the South Korean Buddhists Sharing Movement reported an estimated three million deaths, and the New York Council of Foreign Affairs reported an estimate of one million North Korean deaths due to famine. In May of 1996, the Canadian Food Grains report predicted that the North Korean grain supply had been damaged four times more severely than Ethiopian agriculture during the height of that country's famine in the mid-1980s. As the critical threshold is reached, and some believe it already has been, mortality from famine and famine-related diseases will be unprecedented.

North Korea's entire population shares the deprivation because North Korea's Public Distribution System tries to insure a relatively equal distribution of food. Twenty-three million lives are threatened at once, yet no headlines report these figures. Instead, U.S. media talk about the danger of food relief being given to the North Korean Military instead of the people and the general failure of the Communist political system.

Author Yuk Ji-Yeon writes that North Korea (with whom the U.S. is still technically at war) is still seen as the enemy. While millions of people are starving, the media blames the Communist leaders and ignores the human suffering that is taking place. The media also promote the notion that a proud North Korea refuses aid, rather than focusing on the fact that the U.S. isn't offering much.

UNICEF is actively working in North Korea, surveying 171 of 210 counties, and monitoring food aid distribution from the World Food Program (WFP), an arm of the United Nations. The WFP program's food aid to North Korea is, however, meeting only 50 percent of the need. Meanwhile, the U.S., the food basket of the world, contributes little.

UPDATE BY AUTHOR RAMSEY LIEM: Tragically, hunger in North Korea continues to be an important, if untold, story. Over the half-decade of acute food shortage, hundreds of thousands, if not millions, of Koreans have perished and countless others have been ravished by illness and malnutrition. Accurate statistics on the human costs of this crisis are not available.

Predictably, donor fatigue has been an increasing problem and the U.N. World Food Program has warned repeatedly that failure to respond by the international community threatens long-term suffering in North Korea even if domestic food supplies increase. For example, children who are severely malnourished can experience permanent retardation of their physical and psychological development threatening the loss of an entire generation of young adults.

Fortunately, improved weather conditions during the past year have contributed to improved prospects for food production, and current estimates are that 4.8 of the 6.5 million metric tons of grain needed to feed the population will be produced this year. Although the long-term recovery of North Korean agricultural output is beginning to look more favorable, international aid continues to be vital. Now more than ever, humanitarian aid offers the promise of longer term food security coupled with support for agricultural rehabilitation and the introduction of new varieties of crops and farming methods.

To achieve these objectives, however, the persistent marginalizing and demonizing of North Korea by the United States and her Western allies must end. The most immediate, concrete expression of such a change in policy toward the Democratic People's Republic of Korea (DPRK) would be to end all economic sanctions against North Korea and develop full diplomatic relations based on mutual respect and recognition of one another's sovereignty. While the Clinton Administration has at times shown an inclination to follow this path, Republican hard-liners in the House and Senate have repeatedly attacked the White House for "appeasing" North Korea and sought to undermine the negotiation process. Americans who wish to end the Cold War with North Korea and adopt a truly humanitarian stance toward the food crisis in that country must oppose this mean spirited and self-serving saber rattling.

Coverage of the food crisis in North Korea by the mainstream press was nonexistent during the first two years of shortages (1995–96), and ranged from curiosity to Korea-bashing in 1997 and 1998. Yet coverage has returned once again to virtually total neglect during the past year. The reality of hunger in that country has been replaced by speculation about North Korea's nuclear weapons and long-range missile capabilities in the very limited coverage of North Korea in the U.S. press.

INFORMATION SOURCES FOR THE FOOD CRISIS IN NORTH KOREA: United Nations, NYC—World Food Program (principal coordinator of international food relief in North Korea); United Nations Development Program (UNDP): the UNDP has developed a join proposal with the full partnership of the DPRK for mid-term agricultural rehabilitation.

American Friends Service Committee (AFSC), Philadelphia, PA—Asia Desk: the AFSC has the longest relationship with Korea, north and south, of all NGOs in the United States; they were the first group in the U.S. to initiate food relief programs for North Korea when news of potential famine became public in early 1996.

Institute for Strategic Planning: This Washington, D.C.–based organization of Korean Americans has been supporting food relief programs in North Korea for three years and holding policy briefings in the D.C. area with government officials directly engaged in negotiations with the DPRK.

15 CENSORED

Early Puberty Onset for Girls May be Linked to Chemicals in the Environment and Increases in Breast Cancer

Source:
ENVIRONMENTAL HEALTH
MONTHLY; Pediatrics,
December 1998, Vol. 11, No. 3
Title: "Secondary Sexual
Characteristics and Menses in
Young Girls Seen in Office Practice:
A Study from the Pediatric Research
in Office Settings Network"
Editor: Stephen Lester
Authors: Marcia E. Herman-Giddens,
P.A.; Eric J. Slora, Ph.D.; Richard C.
Wasserman, M.D., M.P.H.; Carlos J.
Bourdony, M.D.; Manju V. Bhapkar,
M.S.; Gary G. Koch, Ph.D.; and
Cynthia M. Hasermeier, B.S.

Faculty Evaluator:
Derek Girman, Ph.D.
Student Researcher: Melissa Bonham

Endocrine disrupters may be responsible for young girls maturing faster, creating an increased risk of breast cancer. A University of North Carolina cross-sectional study, conducted on girls between the ages of 3 and 12 years, found that girls are developing pubertal characteristics at younger ages than suggested by standard pediatric textbooks. The study found that on average, African-American girls begin puberty between 8 and 9 years of age and White girls by 10 years of age, which is six months to a year sooner than previous data suggests. Although it is unclear what is causing this early onset of puberty, environmental exposures have been implicated.

The study, which ran from July 1992 through September 1993, included 17,077 girls from across the United States who were undergoing physical examinations by certified pediatricians. The study data was collected using a one-page, two-sided standardized form for each subject that elicited information on the girl's age, height, weight, race, ethnicity, chronic illness and medication history, presence or absence of menses, and stages of development of breast, pubic hair, and auxiliary hair. The main area of interest were the proportions of girls at a given age with secondary sexual characteristics and menses and the mean ages of onset for each characteristic.

Of the girls studied, 9.6 percent were African American and the remaining 90.4 percent of girls were White. The study found that by three years of age, 3 percent of the African-American girls and 1.2 percent of the White girls showed signs of breast and/or pubic hair development. By the age of seven, these proportions increased to 27.2 percent of African-American girls and 6.7 percent of White girls showing these signs of development. By eight years old, 48.3 percent of African-American girls and 14.7 percent of White girls had begun development.

The mean age of the onset of breast development for African-American girls was 8.87 years old and for White girls was 9.96 years old. Further, the mean age of the onset of pubic hair was 8.78 years for African-American girls and 10.51 years for White girls. The study found that African-American girls entered puberty approximately 1 to 1.5 years earlier than White girls and were beginning menses approximately 8.5 months earlier. No explanation could be given for the statistical differences in the onset of puberty or subsequent menses in the two ethnic groups. The authors concluded that these girls are "....developing pubertal characteristics at younger ages than commonly used norms..." and that "the study strongly suggests that earlier puberty is a real phenomenon, and [that] this has important clinical, educational, and social implications."

The authors specifically raised the issue of how their findings might impact the development of breast cancer. Breast cancer risks include the early onset of puberty that is brought on by the release of natural estrogens in the body. Women who go through puberty early have longer exposure to these estrogens and therefore may be at greater risk of developing breast cancer. In addition, puberty is marked by the rapid growth of breast tissue that may be especially sensitive to the effects of cancer-causing agents. This study raises some troubling questions about whether exposure to endocrine-disrupting chemicals, which mimic the female hormone estrogen, brings on early puberty.

UPDATE BY EDITOR STEVE LESTER: This story is important because it raises questions about the impact of widespread exposure of the American people to low levels of chemicals that interfere with the normal functions of hormones. These endocrine-disrupting chemicals include substances such as dioxin, PCBs, DDT, and many pesticides. Many of these chemicals are known to cause reproductive and developmental abnormalities in wildlife, and now, we are beginning to see increases in some of the same problems in people, including

THIS MODERN WORLD
by TOM TOMORROW

birth defects, breast cancer, prostate cancer, and infertility.

The onset of early puberty in girls is just one such piece of evidence. Research furthers indicates that women who report having had their first menstrual cycle at younger ages have greater lifelong risks of getting breast cancer.

As a direct result of research into the adverse effects of endocrine-disrupting chemicals in people and wildlife, the Environmental Protection Agency (EPA) proposed guidelines in December 1998 for testing more than 15,000 chemicals to determine if they interfere with endocrine function. These chemicals include many common-use substances from cosmetics to plastics to pesticides. The agency plans to use screening tests to identify around 1,000 chemicals for more in-depth testing that will be paid for by the manufacturers. In November 1998, the European Parliament voted for "gradual withdrawal" of hormone-disrupting chemicals from the European market, calling for strict labeling of products containing synthetic chemicals. "The burden should be on the manufac-turers to prove that their products are safe," said Kristen Jensen, who proposed the motion.

(Note: As a direct result of this research, the Pediatric Endocrine Society undertook a comprehensive review of this topic. The primary conclusions of this review have just been published in the *Journal of Pediatrics*.)

There was some coverage in the mainstream press. The Associated Press also ran the story that was picked up by a few local newspapers. Yet overall, there was not much attention given to the story beyond an initial reporting on the day of the release. I don't recall any TV coverage. The TV news programs did not cover it; PBS did do a one-hour special on the general topic of endocrine disrupters, but they did not focus on the issue of premature puberty. Radio gave it very little attention, as did the print newsweeklies. Given that the general population is exposed to so many of these chemicals, that children are the primary target, and that the effects are so severe, though subtle, the story certainly should have gotten much wider coverage.

FOR MORE INFORMATION:

Generations at Risk, Ted Schettler, Gina Solomon, Maria Valenti, and Annette Huddle (Cambridge, MA: MIT Press, June 1999);

Our Stolen Future, Theo Colborn, Dianne Dumanoski, and John Peterson Myers (New York: Dutton/Penguin, March 1996);

Commonweal, P.O. Box 316, Bolinas, CA 94924, Tel: (415) 868-0970, E-mail: dbaltz@igc.apc.org;

Center for Health, Environment and Justice, P.O. Box 6806, Falls Church, VA 22040, Tel: (703) 237-2249, E-mail: cchw@essential.org;

Web site: Endocrine Disruptors Resource Center, International Agriculture and Trade Project: www.iatp.org/edrc.

16 CENSORED

Media Distorts Debate on Affirmative Action

Sources:
NEWS WATCH, Summer 1999
Title: "The Color Game: How Media Plays the Race Card"
Author: Robert Entman

NEWS WATCH, Summer 1999
Title: "It is the Nuances, Stupid"
Author: Linda Jue

Faculty Evaluator:
Elizabeth Martinez, Ph.D.
Student Evaluator: Marni Goodman

The U.S. media oversimplified the debate on affirmative action and deliberately misled the American public. Media coverage at the national level presented the controversy as a conflict primarily between Blacks and Whites. Minimizing the place of Latinos and Asian Americans in the affirmative action debate misrepresents the true complexities involved in evaluating progress toward equality.

In 1995, headlines, visuals, highlighted quotes, and story-line emphasis demonstrated unavoidable conflict of interest between Whites and Blacks. The media portrayed African Americans purportedly gaining at the direct expense of Whites. A *Newsweek* cover shows a Black fist and a White fist, knuckle to knuckle, under the headline "Race and Rage." A *CBS Evening News* story calls affirmative action "deeply divisive" and also distinguishes two camps on the issue: "Jesse Jackson and African Americans" on the one hand, and "the rest of the country" on the other.

In 11 substantive stories about affirmative action that appeared on *CBS Evening News* during 1997 and 1998, six framed the story heavily or exclusively in Black-White terms. Three stories linked Blacks and Latinos against Whites, though Black examples and sources predominated. Just one story emphasized Latinos versus Whites and in one the framing was ambiguous.

Surveys in the mid-1990s indicated widespread support for the principle of affirmative action especially when quotas were excluded. A *Los Angeles Times* poll resulted in a 71 percent favorable rating for affirmative action in 1995, and polls by ABC, NBC, and CNN all found similar results.

Even after these polls, there remained a presumption in media that affirmative action was taking away jobs and opportunities from the dominant group to benefit a particular minority group. The continued use of the misleading negative buzzword "preferences" in conjunction with affirmative action intensified the emotional context of the issue. The news reinforced racial antagonism, while perpetuating the idea that the White majority are fed up with affirmative action. This false perception may have discouraged White politicians who might otherwise have defended the policy.

Since the media has made affirmative action an issue concerning only Blacks and Whites, Latinos and Asians have been left in peripheral positions while women and Native Americans barely register on the radar screen. Journalists say that this depiction of affirmative action distorts the real picture of the program's policies and goals, one where White women have benefited the most. Racial nuances often put Latinos on opposing sides of the affirmative action debate. If you're a dark Hispanic, you'll fall on the Black side. If you're a light Hispanic, you're allowed to choose the other side. Latinos tend to be over-identified with Blacks, and Asian Americans have become honorary Whites.

Media coverage portrayed Asian Americans as monolithically opposed to affirmative action. "We're used as political shills," says Helen Zia. "The claims about us that are made by the partisans in the debate are never challenged by reporters, even when they are presented with opposing evidence."

UPDATE BY AUTHOR ROBERT ENTMAN: The most important recent development in the affirmative action story is probably the emergence of geography-based alternatives to racially-targeted affirmative action in college admissions in California, Texas, and Florida. Most recently, Florida Governor Jeb Bush has pushed a program guaranteeing college admission to all high school graduates who finish in the top 20 percent of their high school classes. The effect is to impose a quota on students from the most affluent, competitive, largely suburban school districts.

These ideas have generated a very positive editorial reaction from such influential newspapers as the *Washington Post* and the *New York Times*. Coverage in those outlets and elsewhere continues largely to assume that public opinion has rejected race-conscious affirmative action, and to use preferences interchangeably with affirmative action still without mentioning the many racially skewed preferences that disproportionately benefit White Americans. The media generally sympathize with the goal of maintaining minority enrollment in colleges. This tendency helps explain the largely favorable response to the Bush plan. And data from Texas do suggest that percentages of minority enrollment has reached about the same level under its geographic plan as under its former affirmative action policy.

Yet whatever individual injustices there were under racially conscious affirmative action still occur under a geographic plan, only they are distributed differently. A hard working, poor minority student who happens to go to a more academically competitive high school and finishes in the 78th percentile of his or her class may be denied admission in favor of a wealthy, lazy White student who coasted to an 81st percentile finish at an undemanding school. Thus, many who decry race-based affirmative action programs for using quotas and preferences are now lauding geographically-based programs that use those very mechanisms. And the new policies impose quotas far more rigidly than even the most "preferential" race-based affirmative action programs, but with far less moral justification (since society has never discriminated against people purely on the basis of their high school of origin).

Beyond ignoring this puzzle, most stories continue implicitly assuming not only that policies explicitly designed to redress racial discrimination are unpopular, but that nothing in current day America, no contemporary pattern of discrimination against minorities or privileges for Whites, might justify racial affirmative action. Consider in this light another recent controversy about race: The one over taxicab drivers' refusal to pick up Black men.

This problem illustrates the blind spot in media coverage, and in the dominant culture more generally. The continued potency of race as a signal of threat, and thus a basis of discrimination, is precisely what should allow us at least to discuss the legitimacy of racially-conscious affirmative action. But the most influential media rarely participate in that discussion.

All this said, if taking geography into account helps to remedy centuries of discrimination, advocates of race-based affirmative action should maintain an open mind. At the same time, journalists and Americans of good will should not forget that discrimination persists, from the taxicabs on the street to the boardrooms on the top floors, that a meritocracy based purely on objective indicators has never been practiced, and that public opinion is not universally hostile to this message.

FOR MORE INFORMATION:

William G. Bowen and Derek Curtis Bok, *The Shape of the River: Long-Term Consequences of Considering Race in College and University Admissions* (Princeton University Press, 1999)

Christopher Edley, *Not All Black and White: Affirmative Action and American Values* (Farrar, Straus, and Giroux, 1998)

Robert M. Entman and Andrew Rojecki, *The Black Image in the White Mind: Media and Race in America* (University of Chicago Press, 2000)

Oscar Gandy, *Communication and Race: A Structural Perspective* (Edward Arnold, 1998)

Lani Guinier, *Lift Every Voice: Turning a Civil Rights Setback into a New*

Vision of Social Justice (Simon and Schuster, 1998)

Nicolas Lemann, *The Big Test: The Secret History of the American Meritocracy* (Farrar, Straus and Giroux, 1999)

Web sites:

The Black Image in the White Mind and related material: www.raceandmedia.com; President Clinton's Initiative on Race: www.whitehouse.gov/Initiatives/OneAmerica/america.html; Fairness and Accuracy in Media report on affirmative action coverage: www.fair.org/extra/9901/affirmative-action.html; Civil Rights Forum: www.civilrightsforum.org/; University of Iowa Site on Gender, Race, and Media: www.uiowa.edu/~commstud/resources/ GenderMedia/; *ColorLines Magazine: Race, Culture, Action* www.arc.org/C_Lines/ArcColorLines.html

17 CENSORED

World Bank's Resettlement Program Displaces Millions

Source:
WORLD RIVERS REVIEW,
December 1998
Title: "World Bank's Record on Resettlement Remains Troublesome"
Author: Lori Pottinger

Faculty Evaluator: Bryan Baker, Ph.D.
Student Researchers: Jennifer Mathis, Melissa Bonham, & Lisa Desmond

The World Bank funds large dam projects, but does little to help the displaced millions who are forced to relocate. A recent report by the World Bank's Operations Evaluation Department (OED), which reviews the Bank's record on complying with its own directives, paints a gloomy picture of the Bank's resettlement record for the people displaced by these large dam projects in the name of development. The most recent data available indicate that 1.9 million people are being displaced by projects in the Bank's current portfolio and that these numbers continue to grow.

The report, "Recent Experience with Involuntary Resettlement," published in June 1998, provides a detailed analysis of the resettlement record of eight dam projects approved between 1984-91 in six countries. To date, the World Bank has helped finance more than 600 large dams.

The OED report acknowledges major problems with the Bank's resettlement record. Their biggest concern is over the Bank's ability to restore the incomes of those resettled. The authors of the report state that the Bank showed only "intermittent interest" in providing follow-through to support its resettlement programs once a loan was disbursed. Another problem stems from the Bank's typical practice of gearing compensation disbursements to a project's construction schedule. This practice results in the

Bank exiting the project before staff can reach the Bank's primary responsibility —restoring or improving incomes and standards of living for the displaced populations.

The report recommends that the Bank move away from its policy of offering replacement land for lands lost to a project. Big dam sites usually eliminate the only productive farming systems in the region, leaving resettlers with barren land. People indigenous to these valleys have few skills that are transferable to activities other than farming. They become displaced and unemployable in a foreign environment. Alternatives to land-for-land compensation such as cash compensations or so-called income generating schemes have been tried for years. Several investigations by the World Bank Inspection Panel demonstrate that, at least in rural settings, such options have universally failed. Even the OED report confirms that the Bank's special income strategies have been uniformly ineffective. Still, they are recommending that the Bank weaken its compensation policy by de-emphasizing the current practice of offering replacement land to displaced farmers. One of the OED report authors has said, "In reality, resettlers lose the best land in the area, river valley land, and it's replaced with the most awful land around, because that is what is left."

AUTHOR UPDATE BY LORI POTTINGER: An estimated 40 to 60 million people have been displaced by large dams in this century, most of them rural poor. The great majority of those displaced have been further impoverished and abandoned by the dam builders and governments responsible for their plight. The World Bank has been a major force behind the world's rush to dam its rivers, and Bank projects as a whole continue to displace nearly 500,000 people a year. The Bank's resettlement policies have long been considered the "gold standard" that forcibly moves people for development schemes. Yet the Bank has failed at resettling people effectively, and instead has increased poverty the world over.

Since the original story was published, the World Bank began to rewrite its resettlement policies, but many non-governmental organizations (NGOs) have criticized the document thus far as far weaker than previous ones, especially on issues of restoring incomes and "land-for-and" compensation. Many NGOs question the entire idea of a policy on forced resettlement. Says Patrick McCully of International Rivers Network (IRN), "[The draft policy] insures that the only people certain to be better off due to Bank-funded involuntary resettlement will be resettlement consultants." IRN and other NGOs propose that the Bank no longer engage in forcible resettlement, which the U.N. Commission on Human Rights calls "a gross violation of human rights," but instead approve projects only after potentially affected people have freely given their consent. "Bank-financed resettlement should be voluntary and based on negotiated settlements with affected people to which project developers can be held accountable. If forced resettlement continues to be normal practice for the Bank, project-affected people and their allies will continue to mobilize against Bank projects," McCully writes in a letter to the Bank.

Even if the Bank were to adopt a stronger resettlement policy, it would still have to rectify problems from past projects. Dam-affected people have increasingly demanded reparations for their losses. One recent example is ongoing protest over Thailand's Pak Mun Dam, one of the few projects described as a success in the World Bank's OED report (the topic of the original story). At press time, 3,000 villagers had occupied the dam site for nearly a year, demanding the dam be removed if the World Bank can't make good on its promises to restore livelihoods. "The OED report did not tell the truth," said a Pak Mun villager, in a new report on the project by International Rivers Network. Villagers are asking Bank staff to come see for themselves how their lives and livelihoods have deteriorated.

Neither the original story about the OED's evaluation of the Bank's resettlement practices nor the ongoing revision of the Bank's resettlement policies have received significant media coverage.

FOR MORE INFORMATION
About dams worldwide:
Lori Pottinger, Director,
Southern Africa Program and Editor,
World Rivers Review
International Rivers Network
1847 Berkeley Way
Berkeley, California 94703
USA

Tel: (510) 848 1155
Fax: (510) 848 1008
Web site: www.irn.org

About the World Bank's role in forcible resettlement worldwide:
Bank Information Center
733 15th Street NW, Suite 1126
Washington, DC 20005
Tel: (202) 624-0623
Web site: www.bicusa.org

Center for International
Environmental Law
1367 Connecticut Avenue NW,
Suite #300
Washington, DC 20036
Tel: (202) 785-8700
E-mail: info@ciel.org
Web site: www.ciel.org

18 CENSORED

California Convicts and Punishes Teenagers as Adults

Source:
THE SAN FRANCISCO BAY GUARDIAN,
January 27, 1999
Title: "The Lost Boys: California is Trying Kids as Adults—and Locking Them Up for Life. No One Knows How Many"
Author: A. Clay Thompson

Faculty Evaluator: Peter Duffy
Student Researchers:
Jeremiah Price & Michael Spigel

In California, minors as young as 14 are being pushed into the adult criminal justice system. As a result children face adult punishments sometimes as severe as life in prison.

Los Angeles County juvenile district attorney Tom Higgins ships more than 600 children into the adult system every year. Higgins states, "The highest violence potential is for people between the ages of 16 and 31. If we have incarcerated a large part of the population for that part of their lives, we have probably made a significant impact on crimes." Justifying these numbers, Higgins claims that "There is a lack of judgment, maturity, reflection in a youth. There is a failure to appreciate consequence, an aura of invincibility."

A fitness hearing trial is used in California to determine whether a minor should be tried as an adult. Paul S. D. Berg, Ph.D., a forensic pathologist who has testified in dozens of fitness hearings states: "The only cases that end up in these hearings are serious cases, so the criterion is met by definition." Though the state does not keep track of how many of their youths go from fitness hearings to adult court, research into prosecution patterns in seven counties reveal that between 80 and 90 percent of juvenile suspects given a fitness hearing do, in fact, end up in adult court. Once these kids end up in adult court, there is little to no tracking process to follow up on

results. The state of California has no idea how many teenagers are being sentenced to life in prison.

Section 707 of the penal code was revamped in 1994 by the then-state assembly members Steve Peace (D-El Cajon) and Chuck Quackenbush (R-San Jose) who were using 707 to attract tough-on-crime votes. Section 707 makes it easier to try teens accused of serious offenses in the adult system. While the lock-kids-up-for-life policy may have sounded like a good idea to many voters sick of violent crime, criminologists say it has no crime-fighting value, and punishes kids who really didn't understand the consequences of their actions.

In 1996, Eric Lotke of the National Center on Institutions and Alternatives and Vincent Schiraldi of the Justice Policy Institute studied the effect of transferring juveniles to adult court. "The data shows that states with higher transfer rates do not have lower homicide rates," their report stated. "Connecticut has the highest transfer rate in the nation, and it has the same youth homicide rate as Colorado, whose transfer rate is nearly zero. Michigan and Massachusetts have nearly the same transfer rates, but their youth homicide rates are among the highest and lowest, respectively."

Professor Thomas Grisso, a leading researcher in developmental psychology and director of forensic training and research at the University of Massachusetts Medical School, says you don't have to be a developmental psychologist to recognize the difference between a 14-year-old and a 24-year-old. "As a parent, imagine your 14-year-old approaching you and saying, 'Dad, I want to get married.' The parent will probably reply with something like, 'They just aren't ready to take responsibility,' or 'They just aren't able yet to see all the consequences of the choices they might make.' That parent is right. Developmental psychologists will tell you that while 14-year-olds on average are capable of considering future consequences, they simply aren't accustomed yet to doing it."

UPDATE FROM AUTHOR A. CLAY THOMPSON: Fueled by a youth-phobic media, politicians at all levels are busy dismembering America's century-old juvenile justice system. With little discussion, more than 40 states in the past decade have passed laws making it easier to cast kids into adult courts and prisons.

"The Lost Boys" is a look at California's juvenile justice rollback—a process that began in earnest in 1994 and is blazing on as I write. Working on the story I was startled by how little information is collected on the kids who are being treated as adults by the courts. Nobody knows how many kids are being shipped to the criminal big leagues, what kind of sentences they're getting, or what happens to them when they get to state penitentiaries. Top-level state officials acknowledged they have almost no data on the trend. Nationwide statistics are skimpy at best. Despite the lack of data—and a half decade of plummeting teen crime rates—politicians across the country are rushing to gut the juvenile justice system entirely.

As our society's ultimate Other, incarcerated kids are voiceless in the mainstream media. For "The Lost Boys," I went to court so one boy might tell his story. Charged with a drive-by slaying, 16-year-old Sou Liem Saechao of Alameda County, California, was awaiting trial as an adult and looking at life in prison. Sou wanted to talk; his lawyer granted me permission to interview him, as did his parents. Yet the county that deemed Sou mature enough to spend perpetuity in the pen said he was too young to speak to the press—even though the daily papers had named him as an indicted murder suspect. I won—or rather, my paper's attorney won—the legal battle to interview the teen, but not until after deadline. To tell Sou's story I was forced to rely on his jailhouse writings and conversations with his family.

The Center on Juvenile and Criminal Justice is tracking the juvenile justice rollback. To learn more, call the center at (415) 621-5661 or check its Web site at www.cjcj.org.

19 CENSORED
Bacterium in Cow's Milk May Cause Crohn's Disease

Source:
CLEVELAND FREE TIMES,
June 16–22, 1999
Title: "The Crohn's Connection?"

Author: Lisa Chamberlain

Faculty Evaluator: Derek Girman, Ph.D.
Student Researchers:
Lisa Desmond & Julia O'Connor

Mounting research shows that a bacterium in cow's milk may cause Crohn's disease, a debilitating chronic inflammatory disease of the gastrointestinal tract. Although four studies indicate that the bacterium, mycobacterium paratuberculosis (Mp), is capable of surviving the pasteurization process, two studies say it is not. Consequently, a strong scientific debate has ensued, primarily behind closed doors, while the American public remains unaware of the hidden dangers. Yet despite scientific concern, little funding has been provided to address this issue.

Estimates are that between 500,000 and 1,000,000 people in the U.S. have Crohn's disease, and that it is spreading rapidly. Approximately 55 Americans, mostly between the ages of 15 and 25, will be diagnosed with this incurable disease every day, and at least half of the Crohn's patients will require surgery for the removal of inflamed intestine. Crohn's disease causes severe diarrhea, excessive weight loss, debilitating abdominal pain, rectal bleeding, bowel obstruction, fistulas, and abscesses.

More than a century ago, Heinrich Johne discovered Johne's disease, a debilitating intestinal disorder in cattle characterized by diarrhea, excessive weight loss, reduced milk production, and ultimately death. The possible connection between infected cow's milk and Crohn's disease in humans was suggested as early as 1913. For more than 70 years the bacterium (Mp) that caused Johne's disease could not be located in human Crohn's patients, but the similarity between the two diseases and recent research implicating that Mp can resist the pasteurization process is too compelling to ignore. Experts agree that Mp "is excreted directly into the milk of infected cows... and it happens before the animal shows signs of Johne's disease."

In a 1981 study, Dr. Rodrick Chiodini, a microbiologist, successfully isolated the same Mp bacterium in six patients with Crohn's disease. This important discovery has led to significant debates among medical and veterinary researchers and the discovery has not led to well-funded research by the government or the dairy industry.

Without well-funded research, however, there are no definitive answers to these vexing questions, such as: Does Mp cause or contribute to Crohn's disease in humans? Does Mp survive the pasteurization process? Is it currently in the retail milk supply? Are our children at risk? And if the answer to any of these questions is even possibly "yes," why isn't the American public aware that this is indeed a concern?

Dr. John Hermon-Taylor, chairman of the department of surgery at St. George's Hospital Medical School in London, is conducting research that will test the retail milk supply in Britain. His initial studies revealed that 7 percent of the retail milk contained the DNA thumbprint of Mp. After growing the cultures for up to three and a half years, he determined that "16 percent of the retail milk samples that originally tested negative came up with long-term cultures which tested strongly positive." The same pasteurization process is used in the United States.

In addition to the strong correlation between the genetic thumbprint for Mp and people with Crohn's disease, Hermon-Taylor says that when he treats patients with antibiotics known to be effective against mycrobacterial infections, between two-thirds and three-quarters of his patients report improvements. Due to Hermon-Taylor's work, the British government announced that they will spend 18 months testing 1,000 samples of all types of milk for Mp. This news made headlines in Britain but not a word was mentioned in the American press.

Crohn's disease is only seen in milk-drinking areas such as the U.S., Australia, South Africa, Europe, Canada, and New Zealand. It is not seen in India where they boil their milk first. Just as Crohn's disease is on the rise, so is Johne's disease in cattle. A 1996 study by the United States Department of Agriculture estimated that 22 percent of U.S. dairies are infected with Johne's organism and that larger herds are more likely to be infected. The same study also shows that 45 percent of dairy producers are either unaware of Johne's disease or know little about it despite the fact that the dairy industry is losing $1.5 billion a year due to infected animals.

UPDATE BY AUTHOR LISA CHAMBERLAIN: I first learned about a possible connection between a bacteria in milk and Crohn's disease while working for a member of Congress, but not from having access to inside information. One of our constituents, whose wife has suffered with the disease for 30 years, had done research on the issue and was asking for our help. Having previously worked in journalism, I understood immediately the implications of this story, and was taking copious notes before he was through.

Using his research as a guide, what I found was that scientists had done serious investigations into the possibility that millions of people worldwide are contracting a debilitating gastrointestinal disease from infected cow's milk. Despite shoestring budgets, credible research shows the theory is not just viable, but likely. The foremost experts on the microbe and the disease are the people who have shown there is, at a minimum, a possible correlation between a bacterium in milk and Crohn's disease. Considering that the suspected organism is known to cause a similar disease in cows and is also known to be shed live in their milk, indicates the relationship is causal.

I first worked on the issue in Congress, which consisted of trying to get a Congressional hearing, among other things, all to little avail. Then I tried to convince a producer I know at 60 Minutes to do the story. His response was something to the effect of, "Unless you can prove it, the story will not happen. After the tobacco stuff, they are not taking any chances."

So upon returning to journalism, I worked on the story myself. It took six more months to conduct the interviews and research, and get over the worst case of writer's block I have ever had. Once the piece was finished, I joked to a friend, "It is my Pulitzer story, but it will probably end up on the Top Ten Most Censored List."

Since the story was reported, not a single other American media outlet has touched it, including other papers owned by the same company as mine. (*Only Now*, Toronto's weekly paper, published the piece.) *Mother Jones* passed on a rewrite of the story, too.

And the most disturbing news has only recently been discovered. The bacteria suspected of causing Crohn's disease has been cultured from the breast milk of two Crohn's patients. Still, not a word about one of the most far-reaching public health/food safety issues has appeared anywhere else in the media.

For more information, visit Paratuberculosis Awareness and Research Association at www.crohns.org.

20 CENSORED

IMF and World Bank Contributed to Economic Tensions in the Balkans

Source:
THIS, July/August 1999
Title: "Banking On the Balkans"
Author: Michael Chossudovsky

Faculty Evaluator: Peter Phillips, Ph.D.
Student Researchers:
Jeremiah Price & Lisa Desmond

The World Bank and International Monetary Fund (IMF) were leading contributors to economic tensions in the Balkans that stimulated the breakup of Yugoslavia. The divisiveness in Bosnia-Herzegovina and Kosovo was reported by media to be caused by "aggressive nationalism" and the ongoing ethnic and religious conflicts. However, other causes involving the IMF and the World Bank contributed to the rise in ethnic tensions.

Declassified documents from 1984 reveal that a U.S. national security decision directive, entitled "United States Policy Towards Yugoslavia," set a policy for destabilizing the Yugoslavian government. U.S. policy was to expand efforts to promote a "quiet revolution" to overthrow Communist governments and parties, while reintegrating the countries of Eastern Europe into a market-oriented economy.

In the early 1980s, the World Bank and IMF provided loans to the former Yugoslavia to supposedly "fix" the economic hardship of the region. The loans from these two organizations included mandated macroeconomic restructuring that, rather than helping, in fact destroyed the industrial sector and dismantled the welfare state. In 1980, when the first phase of macroeconomics reform started, industrial growth began its seven-year decline from 7.1 percent per annum during the years of 1966–79, to 2.8 percent from 1980–87.

Within a climate of severe inflation and wage freezes, restructuring moved on to include new laws, which ushered in import liberalization and a freeze on credit. This caused investment and industrial growth to plummet to zero. Consumer price indexes increased 2,700 percent. Hundreds of firms filed bankruptcy or liquidation, and tens of thousands of industrial workers were laid off. In Kosovo, one of Yugoslavia's poorest provinces, economic depression sparked ethnic conflict between the Albanian majority and Serb minority. Albanian pressure to secede increased and Slobodan Milosevic began moves to suppress Albanian nationalism. In the process, hundreds of Albanians were thrown out of state jobs.

In 1990, the IMF and the World Bank delivered a new "financial aid package" that required new extensive expenditure cuts by the federal government. Belgrade suspended transfer payments to republics and provinces, and real wages collapsed by 41 percent causing half a million workers to have their wages suspended. Inflation began to rise and industrial growth plummeted to 10.6 percent. The entire Yugoslavian banking system began to be dismantled under the supervision of the World Bank. A year later, in 1991, Croatia, Slovenia, and Macedonia declared independence from Yugoslavia and civil war broke out in Croatia.

The IMF and World Bank involvement led to the impoverishment of the population, which in turn led to hatred, confusion, and divisiveness. The United States and NATO wanted to see Yugoslavia become a market-oriented economy, but due to structural adjustment programs the country has experienced out of control inflation and enormous drops in real wages. Now that the economy is in shambles, the U.S. and the European Union have installed a "full-fledged colonial administration" to replace the sovereign economic control of the country. Unfortunately, most of the Western world doesn't realize the root of the problems in the Balkans and sees NATO and the U.S. as the saviors of an "ethnic war."

UPDATE BY AUTHOR MICHEL CHOSSUDOVSKY: The military invasion and occupation of Kosovo is but a stage in the broader process of conquest and political destabilization of Yugoslavia. After the separation of Kosovo from Yugoslavia, the Alliance is intent on promoting the secession of Montenegro, Yugoslavia's only remaining access to the Adriatic. Washington has backed the puppet government of President Milo Djukanovic, politically as well as financially since 1997. Conditional upon the adoption of "free market" reforms, U.S. assistance has included support to the 12,000 strong police force loyal to President Djukanovic, not to mention the financing of the Montenegrin civilian militia. (See U.S. State Department, Press Conference, Washington, DC, June 9, 1999; see also The Statements of Secretary M. Albright and President M. Djukanovic, State Department Press Conference, April 22, 1999).

Advised by Western economists and consultants, the preconditions for Montenegro's "economic separation" from Yugoslavia had been firmly established. The Deutschmark was adopted as the "official" currency in November 1999 leading to Montenegro's *de facto* withdrawal from the Yugoslav monetary system alongside the paralysis of federal transfers to the Podgorica government. A Currency Board was installed on the model of Bosnia-Herzegovina under the Dayton Agreement. Meanwhile, Montenegro's Central Bank had severed its ties with the Yugoslav Central Bank in Belgrade with a view to eventually establishing its own currency pegged to the Deutschmark. The new currency would be established under the currency board arrangement, with the support and financial assistance of the IMF.

By November 1999, the political and economic secession of Montenegro was already *de facto* with the exception of the cutting off of Serbia from its access to the Adriatic. In this regard, the U.S. is intent with the support of the Djukanovic government of mounting an effective blockade of Bar, which is the port of entry for imported oil into Yugoslavia. Meanwhile, the Pentagon had already set out operations plans (OPLANs) "for the invasion and forcible expulsion of Serb forces in Montenegro" (*Truth in Media*, September 29, 1999). The same source indicates "that the unit designated as the spearhead for the invasion of Montenegro, II Marine Expeditionary Force (II MEF), stationed at Camp Lejeune, NC, has an Operational Planning Team (OPT)

in Macedonia calculating how best to secure bridgeheads to militarily support the Montenegrin government should it decide to declare its independence from the Federal Republic of Yugoslavia (FRY)" (*Truth in Media*, September 29, 1999).

Destabilizing Vojvodina: Vojvodina is a "bread basket" and a source of raw materials for Yugoslavia. NATO's ultimate objective is the total collapse of Yugoslavia as a viable national economy. Vojvodina has within Serbia the same status as Kosovo. It is an autonomous province with Novi Sad as its capital. NATO's hidden agenda is to destabilize Vojvodina, calling for the establishment of a "special status." The Budapest government (now a member of NATO) has called for the return of the northern territories ceded from the Austro-Hungarian empire as a result of the Treaty of Versailles after World War I. Barely a month after the end of the bombings, Hungarian Prime Minister Viktor Orban met behind closed doors with U.S. Defense Secretary William Cohen. On the agenda: autonomy to ethnic Hungarians in the north of Vojvodina.

Economic Reconstruction: The so-called "reconstruction" by foreign capital of the Balkans under the "stabilization program" will signify multi-billion dollar contracts to multinational firms to rebuild roads, airports, and bridges that will eventually be required (once the embargo is lifted) to facilitate the "free movement" of capital and commodities. The proposed "Marshall Plan" financed by the World Bank and the European Development

Bank (EBRD), as well as private creditors, will largely benefit Western mining, petroleum, and construction companies, while fueling the region's external debt well into the third millennium.

Free market reforms have been envisaged for Kosovo under the supervision of the Bretton Woods institutions largely replicating the structures of the Rambouillet Agreement. Article I (Chapter 4a) of the Rambouillet Agreement stipulated that: "The economy of Kosovo shall function in accordance with free market principles." The KLA government will largely be responsible for implementing these reforms and ensuring that loan conditionalities are met. In close liaison with NATO, the Bretton Woods institutions had already analysed the consequences of an eventual military intervention leading to the military occupation of Kosovo. Almost a year prior to the beginning of the War, the World Bank conducted "simulations" that anticipated the possibility of an emergency scenario arising out of the tensions in Kosovo (*World Bank Development News*, April 27, 1999).

The "reconstruction" of Kosovo financed by international debt largely purports to transfer Kosovo's extensive wealth in mineral resources and coal to multinational capital. In this regard, the KLA has already occupied (pending their privatization) the largest coal mine at Belacevac in Dobro Selo, northwest of Pristina. In turn, foreign capital has its eyes riveted on the massive Trepca mining complex that constitutes "the most valuable piece of real estate in the Balkans, worth at least $5 billion" (Chris Hedges, *New York Times*, July 8, 1998). The Trepca complex not only includes copper and large reserves of zinc but also cadmium, gold, and silver. Also, it has several smelting plants, 17 metal treatment sites, a power plant, and Yugoslavia's largest battery plant. Northern Kosovo also has estimated reserves of 17 billion tons of coal and lignite.

The most profitable state assets are being transferred into the hands of foreign capital under the World Bank–sponsored privatisation program. Strong economic medicine imposed by external creditors will contribute to further boosting a criminal economy (already firmly implanted in Albania) that feeds on poverty and economic dislocation.

Also, Kosovo is slated to reimburse this debt through the laundering of dirty money. Yugoslav banks in Kosovo will be closed down and the banking system will be deregulated under the supervision of Western financial institutions. Narco-dollars from the multi-billion dollar Balkans drug trade will be recycled towards servicing the external debt, as well as financing the costs of reconstruction. The lucrative flow of narco-dollars thus insures that foreign investors involved in the "reconstruction" program will be able to reap substantial returns. In turn, the existence of a Kosovar "narco-state" insures the orderly reimbursement of international donors and creditors. The latter are prepared to turn a blind eye. They have a tacit vested interest in installing a government that facilitates the laundering of drug money.

21 CENSORED

The Vatican's U.N. Status Challenged

Source:
MS., October/November 1999
Title: "Giving the Vatican the Boot"
Author: Laura Flanders

Faculty Evaluator: Laurel Holmstrom
Student Researchers:
Corey Hale & Katie Anderson

Mainstream coverage: Although some aspects of this story did receive coverage in the *New York Times* and other papers, the extent and reasons behind the Vatican's power in the U.N. were not explored.

A special delegation to the Vatican, the Holy See, holds a position in the United Nations that is more powerful than any other non-governmental organization (NGO). As a "nonmember state permanent observer," the Vatican enjoys the same status as politically neutral Switzerland. When confronted about its problematic "nation" status, the thousand-member male population of the Vatican City legitimizes its position by claiming to be the representative of "the entire people of God." In its position as a nonmember state permanent observer, the Holy See does not have a vote in the General Assembly, but it can speak, lobby, and negotiate on virtually equal footing with any nation.

During more heated proceedings, the priests circulate through the hall, shaking hands and distributing literature to the delegates. This action is a privilege not available to any other NGO. For example, the Vatican wields this power to promote its agendas by threatening to "pull out" of any of the 300,000 health care facilities it owns worldwide if the U.N. should attempt to force any of those facilities to provide abortion services or contraception services. This threat creates a hostage situation for poorer countries who are reliant on the church for poverty relief and basic health care. As governments around the world—such as the U.S.—farm out more health care services to private operators, including the Catholic Church, these countries become more vulnerable to having the Catholic Church's doctrine imposed upon them.

Last spring, the See Change Campaign was launched by over 100 international women's, religious, and reproductive rights groups, to challenge the Vatican's power in the U.N., and to downgrade its status from a nonmember state to a traditional NGO. This campaign was spearheaded by Frances Kissling, president of Catholics for a Free Choice (CFFC). According to Kissling, "the Vatican occupies 100 square acres of office space and tourist attractions in the middle of Rome, with a citizenry that excludes women and children...and should not have a place at the table where governments set policies affecting the very survival of women and children...."

When U.N. committees try to create consensus on issues involving reproducductive rights or contraception, the Holy See is the one consistently dissenting organization. In the case of using condoms for the prevention of sexually transmitted diseases including HIV and AIDS, the Holy See's representatives declare, "We cannot approve." This scene was played out in 1999, at the Cairo+5 conference, which recognized women's empowerment and reproductive health as keys to stemming global population growth. During the conference, the Holy See stalled proceedings for days over language in the final document. In this capacity, the papacy sets its political perimeter not only around a country but around the world.

UPDATE BY AUTHOR LAURA FLANDERS: The United Nations spends lots of time pondering the world's approach to the environment, development, and people's social and political rights. Drop in on one of the organizations' massive conferences, and you will see 185 member nations trying to reach agreement on complex documents that aim to set policy for the globe. From abortion to children's education, the U.N. has a policy document addressing it. That policy is drawn up by the 185 member-nations and one nonmember state—the Holy See, the governing body of the Catholic Church.

The Vatican, the only non-governmental organization, is permitted to debate in the General Assembly, vote on policy at conferences and lobby nation representatives from the floor of the hall, while NGOs are restricted to watching from afar. This consideration has irked women's rights advocates for decades—as they have found themselves at odds with the Church on reproductive rights and health education time and again.

Back in 1995, at the U.N. conference on Women in Beijing, close to 10,000 people signed on to a letter asking the Secretary-General to review the Holy See's status. Still, it has only been in the last year, at the five-year anniversary of the U.N. conference on Population in Cairo, that the campaign has gathered steam. If the Vatican is a state, then EuroDisney deserves a place on the Security Council, says Kissling. At last count, more than 250 groups from around the world had joined with CFEC in the effort to change the Vatican's diplomatic rank.

The See Change story received some coverage this summer and fall, as the General Assembly met. Described as "quixotic" by *Legal Times* (August 16, 1999), the effort has typically been portrayed as a dispute between Kissling and the Vatican (ignoring the powerful groups from South and Central America that are leading participants), and solely about abortion—though the See's interventions go way beyond that. For instance, this spring, the Church's opposition prevented U.N. peacekeepers from distributing RU-486 to rape victims in Kosovo. The larger question raised by the See Change campaign remains woefully under-reported: the Vatican's growing power.

With 300,000 health facilities worldwide, the Roman Catholic Church is a major global health provider. When challenged to provide abortion services, or offer contraception services, the church repeatedly responds that if forced, it will stop health services. As governments privatize social services worldwide, and more and more public hospitals fall under Catholic Church control, the Vatican's power grows. As an adamantly anonymous source in the Secretary General's office put it—the Secretary General's no match for the Pope.

For more information on the See Change Campaign, you can contact Catholics for a Free Choice (CFFC) 1436 U St., NW, Washington DC 20009. Tel: (202) 986 6093; Fax: (202) 332-7995; E-mail: CFFC@igc.apc.org; Web site: www.seechange.org.

22 CENSORED

U.S. and Germany Trained and Developed the KLA

Sources:
THE PROGRESSIVE, August 1999
Title: "Mercenaries in Kosovo: The U.S. Connection to the KLA"
Author: Wayne Madsen

COVERTACTION QUARTERLY, Spring-Summer 1999
Title: "Kosovo 'Freedom Fighters' Financed by Organized Crime"
Author: Michel Chossudovsky

Faculty Evaluators: Rick Luttman, Ph.D. & Phil Beard, Ph.D.
Student Researchers: Michael Spigel & Jeremiah Price

Germany and the U.S. collaborated in supporting the development and training of the Kosovo Liberation Army (KLA) to deliberately destablize a centralized socialist government in Yugoslavia.

Since the early 1990s, Bonn and Washington have joined hands in establishing their respective spheres of influence in the Balkans. Undercover support to the Kosovo rebel army was established as a joint endeavor between the CIA and Germany's Bundesnachrichtendienst (BND). The task to create and finance the KLA was initially given to Germany:

"They used German uniforms, East German weapons, and were financed in part by drug money," according to intelligence analyst John Whitley. As the KLA matured, the U.S. and Germany recruited Mujahedin mercenaries, financed by Saudi Arabia and Kuwait, to train the KLA in guerrilla and diversion tactics.

Since the mid-1990s, there has been a small handful of Pentagon contractors or private military companies providing support to the KLA. One of these contractors is the Military Professional Resources, Inc. (MPRI). In a recent interview retired Army Colonel David Hackworth gave to Catherine Crier of Fox Television, he states that the MPRI used former U.S. military personnel to train KLA forces at secret bases inside Albania.

The MPRI has a starting lineup comprised of retired Pentagon top brass. Its roster includes one retired admiral, two retired major generals, and 10 retired generals. The MPRI employs more than 400 personnel and can access the résumés of thousands of former U.S. military specialists from cooks and clerks to helicopter pilots and Green Berets.

The MPRI has been in the Balkans for years. MPRI military advisers helped plan Storm and Strike, the Croatian offensive that was responsible for driving out 350,000 Croatian Serbs from the Krajina province. In 1996, just one year later, the MPRI received a $400 million State Department contract to train and equip the Bosnian Croat-Muslim Federation Army.

Some of the KLA's military leadership includes veterans of the MPRI-planned operation Storm and Strike. Agim Ceku is the military commander of the KLA and was a former brigadier general in the Croatian army. According to the London *Independent*'s Robert Fisk, Ceku is an ethnic cleanser in his own right. Ceku, along with MPRI military advisers, helped plan the Croatian military offensive that resulted in the ethnic cleansing of the Serbs from Krajina.

UPDATE BY AUTHOR WAYNE MADSEN: The story on the U.S. mercenary connection to the Kosovo Liberation Army (KLA) was virtually ignored by the corporate-controlled media during NATO's Balkans War. Playing into the hands of the Pentagon's information warfare and perception management cadres, as well as Clinton Administration spinmeisters, the major media sang the praises of the KLA, refusing to peer inside the covert assistance program rendered by Pentagon "private military contractors" to this shadowy group long connected to criminal enterprises in both Eastern and Western Europe.

The U.S. private military contractors and police advisory teams associated with the Justice Department's and United Nations peace monitoring teams continue their activity in the world's most volatile trouble spots. As private entities, these companies are not subject to congressional oversight or Freedom of Information requests.

MPRI stepped up its military training activities in Bosnia after the suspension of the firm's arms transfers to the Bosnian army was lifted by the State Department. MPRI activities included training a rapid reaction Bosnian special forces unit and providing direct support to the Bosnian Defense Ministry. Pentagon insiders reported that MPRI also provided weaponry to paramilitary forces loyal to Montenegro's pro-Western President Milo Djukanovic and continued covert assistance to the KLA in Kosovo.

Also, MPRI's activities in Africa increased. Not only did the company's personnel increase their profile in Angola, helping that nation in its war against Washington's former UNITA allies, but the firm's representatives showed up in Abuja, Nigeria, after the swearing in of democratically elected president Olusegun Obasanjo. MPRI is a central player in the Pentagon's African Crisis Response Initiative (ACRI) and Nigeria was long sought as a military partner of the United States in that effort. However, neither former dictator Sani Abacha nor former president-elect Chief Moshood Abiola were acceptable to Washington as military partners. Undersecretary of State Thomas Pickering provided much of the high-level liaison between Obasanjo's government and MPRI. Ironically, Pickering was present during a July 1998 meeting with Chief Abiola when the imprisoned president-elect suffered a heart attack and died minutes later. MPRI is also active in counter-narcotics military operations in Colombia.

There has also been a blurring of law enforcement and military activities of companies like Dyncorp and Science Application International Corporation (SAIC). One of Dyncorp's U.N. police monitors was wounded by pro-Indonesian East Timorese militiamen in the post-referendum violence that swept the ravaged territory. Others, providing police services in NATO-occupied Kosovo, were attacked by both Serb and Albanian militia groups.

SAIC became more active, through the CIA-connected ICITAP, in paramilitary counter-narcotics and counter-insurgency operations in Belize, Bolivia,

THIS MODERN WORLD by TOM TOMORROW

Colombia, Costa Rica, Guatemala, Haiti, and Panama—all long-time favorite haunts of CIA operatives. ICITAP also stepped up training of Bosnian federal and cantonal police units and various South African police services. Former ICITAP director Janice Stromsem was joined by another ICITAP employee, Mick Andersen, who charged that agencies other than the Justice Department were engaging in "illegal activities" in Haiti. Stromsem and Andersen were both forced from their jobs with ICITAP and have been effectively ostracized within the government after blowing the whistle.

During 1999, Dyncorp faced charges that it was raiding police departments around the country luring away experienced officers with six-figure salaries. In September 1999, the mayor of Surf City, New Jersey filed suit against one of his police officers for abandoning his job to join Dyncorp's force in Kosovo. A retired Bloomington, Indiana police officer returned home from Kosovo after becoming disenchanted with his duties. Still others cited difficulties in dealing with the Albanian Mafia in Kosovo. Moreover,

some 10 percent of the U.N. police candidates dropped out of Dyncorp's Fort Worth-based training program after they initially signed up. Aside from radio interviews with progressive radio stations in New York, there was no other media reaction to the story.

For more information peruse the following Web sites:

www.mpri.com
www.dyncorp.com/areas/intlpm.htm
www.saic.com
(key site's search engine for ICITAP)
www.ciponline.org/facts/icitap.htm
www.us.net/cip/icitap3.htm
www.ndu.edu/inss/strforum/
forum84.html
www.whistleblower.org/www/
antigag.htm
www.eucom.mil/programs/acri/

UPDATE FROM AUTHOR: MICHEL CHOSSUDOVSKY: As Western leaders trumpet their support for democracy, state terrorism in Kosovo has become an integral part of NATO's post-war design. The KLA's political role for the "post-conflict"

period had been mapped out well in advance. NATO had already slated the KLA "provisional government" (PGK) to run civilian state institutions. In the weeks following NATO's military occupation of Kosovo, the KLA took over municipal governments and public services including schools and hospitals. The KLA has a controlling voice on the U.N.–sponsored Kosovo Transitional Council, UNMIK. In the weeks following the military invasion, the KLA "Provisonal Government" established links with a number of Western governments.

Under NATO occupation, the rule of law has visibly been turned upside down. Criminals and terrorists are to become law-enforcement officers. With the withdrawal of Yugoslav troops and police, the KLA without delay took control of Kosovo's police stations. Under the formal authority of the United Nations, the Organization for Security and Cooperation in Europe (OSCE) was entrusted with the task of training and installing a 4,000-strong police force with a mandate to "protect civilians" under the jurisdiction of the KLA–controlled "Ministry of Public Order." The evidence suggests that the KLA–controlled police force was also responsible for the massacres of civilians organized in the immediate wake of NATO's military occupation of Kosovo.

Moreover, despite NATO's commitment to disarming the KLA, the Kosovar paramilitary organization is slated to be transformed into a modern military force. So-called "security assistance" has already been granted to the KLA by the U.S. Congress under the Kosovar Independence and Justice Act of 1999.

While the KLA's links to the Balkans narcotics trade (served to finance many of its terrorist activities) had been highly publicized, the paramilitary organization was granted an official U.S. seal of approval as well as being deemed a "legitimate" source of funding. In turn, Washington's military aid package to the KLA was entrusted to Military Professional Resources, Inc. (MPRI) of Alexandria, Virginia, a private mercenary outfit run by high ranking former U.S. military officers.

In September 1999, the KLA was officially dissolved and transformed into the newly formed Kosovo Protection Force that was funded by U.S. military aid. Shift in military labels: KLA Commander Agim Ceku was appointed Chief of Staff of Kosovo's newly created armed forces.

Barely a few weeks after Commander Ceku's NATO sponsored appointment, the International Criminal Tribunal for the former Yugoslavia (ICTY) announced that it was "investigating Ceku for alleged war crimes committed against ethnic Serbs in Croatia between 1993 and 1995" (AFP, October 13, 1999). This information had been withheld by the ICTY during the mandate of Chief Prosecutor Louise Arbour. In other words, the U.N. and NATO knew that Agim Ceku was an alleged war criminal prior to the onslaught of NATO's bombing of Yugoslavia in March 1999. Moreover, KFOR Commander Mike Jackson and UNMIK head Dr. Bernard Kouchner (and 1999 Nobel Peace Laureate as co-founder of Doctors Without Borders) were fully aware of the fact that an alleged war criminal had been appointed as Commander in Chief of the KPF: "If we lose him it will be a disaster," said a diplomat close to Bernard Vouchner, the U.N.'s special representative. "When you get to the second level of the TMK [Kosovo Protection Force], you're down to a bunch of local thugs." American diplomats have suggested any indictment of Ceku would most likely be "sealed" and thereby kept out of the public domain [meaning that public opinion will not be informed of the Court's decision]. Another diplomat said he believed KFOR, the NATO-led peace-keeping force, could not contemplate a public relations disaster with the Albanians by arresting Ceku (Tom Walker, "Kosovo Defense Chief Accused of War Crimes, *Sunday Times*, October 10, 1999).

The ICTY also cautioned that the inquiry did not necessarily imply that Ceku was responsible for wrongdoings in Kosovo: "The court's inquiries relate to atrocities committed in Krajina between 1993 and 1995." Ceku's record in Kosovo itself is not thought to be in question, although the office of Carla del Ponte, the new chief prosecutor, said an investigation into his activities with the KLA could not be ruled out. The possibility that Ceku, a respected figure in Kosovo, could be accused of war crimes, has sent "shivers through the international community in Kosovo..." (*Ibid.*).

In other words, the so-called "international community" has firmly relied on an "alleged war criminal" to replicate in Kosovo the massacres and ethnic cleansing conducted in Croatia against Krajina Serbs. Visibly what was shaping up in the wake of the bombings in Kosovo was the continuity of NATO's operation in the Balkans. Military personnel and U.N. bureaucrats previously stationed in Croatia and Bosnia had also been routinely reassigned to Kosovo. In this context, the assignment of Mike Jackson to Kosovo as KFOR Commander was remarkably consistent with the appointment a few months earlier of Brigadier General Agim Ceku as Commander of the KLA.

KFOR Commander Mike Jackson had also been routinely reassigned to Kosovo following his earlier stint in Bosnia-Herzegovina and Croatia. His experience in "ethnic warfare," however, predates the Balkans. From his earlier posting, while in Northern Ireland as a young captain, Jackson was second in command in the "Bloody Sunday" massacre of civilians in Derry in 1972. Under the orders of Lieutenant Derek Wilford, Captain Jackson and 13 other soldiers of the parachute regiment opened fire "on a peaceful protest by the Northern Ireland civil rights association opposing discrimination against Catholics. In just 30 minutes, 13 people were shot dead and 13 injured. Those who died were killed by a single bullet to the head or body, indicating that they had been deliberately targeted. No weapons were found on any of the deceased" (Julie Hyland, "Head of NATO Force in Kosovo, Second-in-Command at 'Bloody Sunday' Massacre in Ireland," World Socialist Web site, June 19, 1999).

Jackson's role in "Bloody Sunday" "did not hinder his Military career" (*Ibid.*). From his early stint in Northern Ireland, he was reassigned to the theatre of ethnic warfare in the Balkans. In the immediate wake of Operation Storm and the ethnic massacres in Krajina, Jackson was put in charge as KFOR commander, for organizing the return of Serbs "to lands taken by Croatian HVO forces in the 1995 Krajina offensive." And in this capacity General Mike Jackson had "urged that the resettlement of Krajina Serbs not be rushed to avoid tension with the Croatians while also warning returning Serbs of the extent of the land mine threat (*Jane's Defense Weekly*, Vol. 25, No. 7, February 14, 1996). In retrospect, recalling the events of early 1996, very few Krajina Serbs were allowed to return to their homes under the protection of the United Nations. According to Veritas, a Belgrade based organization of Serbian refugees from Croatia, some 10,000–15,000 Serbs were able to resettle in Croatia.

A similar process took place in Kosovo where the conduct of senior military officers conformed to a consistent pattern because the same key individuals were reassigned to a "peace-keeping" role in Kosovo. While token efforts were displayed to protect Serb and Roma civilians, those who fled Kosovo were not encouraged to return under U.N. protection. In post-war Kosovo, ethnic cleansing was carried out by the KLA while under the auspices of NATO and the U.N. It has been accepted by the "international community" as a *fait accompli*.

Moreover, while calling for democracy and "good governance" in the Balkans, the U.S. and its allies have installed in Kosovo a "civilian paramilitary government" with links to organized crime. The outcome is the outright "criminalization" of civilian state institutions in Kosovo and the establishment of what is best described as a "Mafia State." The complicity of NATO and the Alliance governments (namely their relentless support of the KLA) points to the de facto "criminalisation" of KFOR and of the U.N. peace-keeping apparatus in Kosovo. The donor agencies and governments (e.g., the funds approved by the U.S. Congress in violation of several U.N. Security Council resolutions) providing financial support to the KLA are, in this regard, also "accessories" to this criminalization of state institutions. Through the intermediation of a paramilitary group (created and financed by Washington and Bonn), NATO ultimately bears the burden of responsibility for the massacres and ethnic cleansing of civilians in Kosovo.

23 CENSORED

International Conference Sets World Agenda for Peace

Source:
TOWARD FREEDOM, July 1999
Title: "United for Peace"
Author: Robin Lloyd

Faculty Evaluator: Phil Beard, Ph.D.
Student Researcher: Jeremiah Price

The Hague Appeal for Peace (HAP) Conference, which took place in the Hague, Netherlands, in May 1999, has set a "Global Agenda" for world peace in the next century. Over 1,000 groups, from 100 different countries, intended to voice their suggestions on how to make international peace possible. The four-day event yielded a turnout of over 8,000 people and resulted in ground-breaking initiatives and resolutions.

One of the many new campaigns launched at the conference was the International Action Network on Small Arms (IANSA). The IANSA goal is to encourage tracking, protesting, and publicizing the sales and shipments of weapons. Referring to the fact that the U.S. sold $119 billion in arms, some 45 percent of the world's total, from 1989 to 1996, Pierre Sané of Amnesty International stated at the conference that the U.S. is "becoming the arsenal of the world."

The Hague Global Agenda calls for recognition and enforcement of World Court rulings that over 150 countries have endorsed. The United States has been unwilling to submit to the international jurisdiction of the World Court.

A long-term project put in motion at the conference is the Global Action to Prevent War. Its purpose is to establish a coalition of organizations that will build a permanent body of NGOs, individuals, and eventually governments to support world peace.

Heads of some governments avoided the event, although representatives from various governments attended. Several of the attending representatives were ambassadors and ministers, most of whom acknowledge that the majority of governments will only recognize universal values until they interfere with national or economic interests, and that governments often co-opt the language of peace to justify and protect corporate interests.

The following is the agenda that was set forth at The Hague Appeal for Peace Conference. The Global Agenda outlines 10 fundamental principles for a just world order:

1. Every government should adopt a resolution prohibiting war.

2. All states should accept the jurisdiction of the International Court of Justice.

3. Every government should ratify the ICC and implement the Land Mines Treaty.

4. All states should integrate the New Diplomacy—the partnership of governments, international organizations, and civil societies.

5. The world can't ignore humanitarian crises, but every creative diplomatic means possible must be exhausted before resorting to force under U.N. authority.

6. Negotiations for a Convention Eliminating Nuclear Weapons should begin immediately.

7. The trade in small arms should be severely restricted.

8. Economic rights must be taken as seriously as civil rights.

9. Peace education should be compulsory in every school.

10. The plan for the Global Action to Prevent War should become the basis for a peaceful world order.

U.N. Secretary-General Kofi Annan praised the NGOs and civil society organizations for creating the conference. While the conference was covered by Associated Press and released worldwide, the United States media ignored it, with coverage in the back pages of only a handful of small regional papers.

UPDATE BY AUTHOR ROBIN LLOYD: Ten thousand peace activists, Nobel peace prize winners, and celebrities met for four days in May of 1999 at a conference center at the Hague, the Netherlands, to virtually no U.S. (and skimpy international) coverage. A few blocks away, the boys with the big cameras clustered outside the gates of the International Court of Justice, where Yugoslavia was charging NATO with grievous violations of international law.

After all, there was a war going on.

Every day, young people from the conference trooped down with banners, urging the media to provide some coverage. No luck. As a Hague Appeal staffer later explained, "Unless the story has action and can be explained in two seconds, they don't want to cover it."

The conference was spurred by a revolutionary idea: abolishing war in the 21st century. Hopelessly idealistic? As Cora Weiss, president of the Hague Appeal, put it, this end-of-the-century conference was convened "because we want peace to have the last word in this most war-filled, most violent century." That concern also spurred my own participation. I was tired of hearing the millennium being boiled down to an acronym—Y2K. The conference provided a context to talk about renewal and a recommitment to democratic values as we entered a new century.

And it wasn't a bad story, complete with history (the conference occured 100 years after the first Hague conference of 1899), hope for the future, revolutionary fervor, youth, and even some celebrities (Kofi Annan, Bishop Tutu, and Queen Noor, among others). Yet, maybe the best story was: how could this "peace conference"—dedicated to abolishing war, and taking place in the midst of one—avoid taking a stand on Kosovo? Virtually every participant had to answer that question upon returning home.

What was the conference's stand on Kosovo? Officially, it didn't have one. And that may well have been a factor in the press's indifference to both the process and the 21st century agenda that emerged.

But now, after the mobilization against globalization in Seattle, the Hague conference reveals a larger story: the potential role of "civil society" in the new millennium. It's been growing for a while; politely at the Hague, not so politely in Seattle. The people are at the gates, asserting that their interests as human beings are being ignored or manipulated by governments, international financial institutions, and corporations.

"What are these NGOs 'swarming' about?" *The Economist* asked in a December 1999 article. "Are citizens' groups, as many of their supporters claim, the first steps towards an 'international civil society' (whatever that may be)? Or do they represent a dangerous shift of power to unelected and unaccountable special-interest groups?" The way the magazine framed the question suggests that they believe something pretty ominous is happening.

In fact, the number of international non-governmental organizations has increased fourfold, from 6,000 in 1990 to 26,000 today. But the key question is whether civil society can move from knocking on the door of international institutions to taking over the hall and creating a people's parliament. It's not as utopian as it sounds. Remember when the U.S. shifted from electing its senators through state legislatures to letting the people decide?

A Millennium NGO Forum will be held at the U.N. from May 22–26, 2000. Its agenda—to build grassroots and public support for a more effective U.N.—is moderate, but it will also provide an opening for international civil society to push the envelope on global governance. As *Toward Freedom* editor Greg Guma wrote recently in an editorial, "We need to move beyond fear of government and work for democracy at the world level."

The Hague Appeal for Peace can be reached on the Internet at www.hague-peace.org, or e-mail: hapy@ipb.org. The Millennium People's Assembly Network

is at www.ourvoices.org. *Toward Freedom* will continue to track developments on its Web site, www.towardfreedom.com.

24 CENSORED
U.S. Nuclear Weapons Controlled by Unstable Personnel

Source:
MOTHER JONES, November 1998
Title: "Positive Attitude Toward Nuclear Weapons Duty"
Author: Ken Silverstein

Faculty Evaluator: Lynn Cominsky, Ph.D.
Student Evaluator: Jake Medway

Mentally unstable individuals may be in control of U.S. nuclear devices. A screening process called the Personnel Reliability Program (PRP), set in place after a near-disaster in 1959, is supposed to guarantee that only competent, stable, and dependable individuals have access to America's nuclear arsenal. In fact, the PRP looks mainly for self-announced kooks and fails to identify less sensational cases. As a result, numerous unstable individuals are in control of, and have access to, our nuclear weapons.

PRP is a two-step process consisting of an initial screening and post-approval monitoring. Investigators look for traits such as good social adjustment, emotional stability, and a positive attitude toward nuclear weapons duty. Screening includes a cursory medical evaluation, a review of the candidate's personnel file, and a background check of professional, educational, and personal histories. However, no routine psychological testing is done. Between 1990 and 1996, 7,000 people were decertified after passing the PRP screening. These thousands were either temporarily or permanently barred from nuclear weapons duties due to various, sometimes emotional, problems on the job.

Candidates can easily lie about their records with little chance of getting caught. FBI background checks only pick up 5 to 8 percent of people who have had trouble with the law, allowing numerous "bad apples" to receive high security clearance positions. According to the Pentagon's 1996 annual status report on PRP, 758 people were kicked out of the program that year. Out of those, 169 were expelled due to conviction by a military or a civilian court of a serious offense or a pattern of behavior showing contemptuous attitude towards the law.

In several cases, PRP-certified people have gone on to commit murder or suicide, assault, rape, and other serious crimes, exposing unstable mental conditions in their past and present. In one case, where a naval technician committed a murder of two elderly people, investigators were tipped off to his potential violence through interviews with the officer's acquaintances from before his recruitment. These interviews revealed a history including such warning signs as suspected murder, wife beating, lying, stealing, and "continuous fantasizing."

A sonar technician who was expelled from PRP for failing a drug test stated that abuses that should be grounds for expulsion are frequently ignored. An expelled PRP Marine claimed that heavy drinking and depression are overlooked. There have even been cases of people drinking while on PRP duty. In certain cases, individuals still had their PRP clearance while in prison for a felony conviction. One Marine explained that manpower demand at special weapons stations far exceeds the number of qualified personnel.

Herbert L. Abrams, PRP expert at Stanford University's Center for International Security and Cooperation, recommends that the Pentagon strengthen PRP by requiring a physician to examine all candidates, have standardized psychological testing, and improve its post-approval monitoring procedures. Others insist that the entire program be subjected to tough independent scrutiny.

UPDATE BY AUTHOR KEN SILVERSTEIN: This story is important because even if the risks of a problem are relatively small, the consequences of any problem could be enormous. What are the risks? It is hard to say for certain, especially given the Pentagon's refusal to open up its records on the PRP. Still, the fact that a few people involved with the program were willing to talk to me (off the record) about their fears, shows that some key insiders believe the screening system is dangerously inadequate.

No significant new developments have occurred since the story was published, at least that I know of. However, since the Pentagon is generally not eager to disclose problems with the program, it is impossible to know for certain.

There has been no fallout in the mainstream press. I think this is for two reasons. First, it is not exactly the type of story that you can follow up on as, for example, with a campaign finance scandal, where there are always sure to be plenty of emerging developments.

Also, this is the type of story that is unlikely to get a sharp examination until a problem comes to light (in other words, when it is too late). There is no organization that rigorously tracks the PRP. For anyone wanting to do follow-up research, I recommend contacting the sources named in the story. (Or contact me to see about the unnamed sources.)

25 CENSORED
U.S. Military Trains Soldiers to Kill and Eat Tame Animals

Source:
THE ANIMALS AGENDA,
July/August 1999
Title: "Irrational Rations: Animals Used in Military Training"
Author: D'Arcy Kemnitz

Faculty Evaluator: Laurel Holmstrom

Student Researchers:
Rebecca Aust & Aimee Regan

Mainstream coverage:
Seattle Times, July 2, 1999, page B1
Willington-Star News, July 12, 1999, page 3B
News & Observer, Raleigh NC, July 6, 1999, page A1
Spokane Review, Spokane WA, July 2, 1999, page A1
Denver Post, June 30, 1999, page B4

People for the Ethical Treatment of Animals (PETA) have charged that animals are being killed unnecessarily in military training classes. A course titled "Survival Skills" taught at the U.S. Army's Dugway Proving Ground in Utah teaches soldiers to hunt, kill, cook, and eat tame rabbits and chickens.

According to the author, the animals are transported from a local farm to the training grounds by truck. The soldiers then stage an ambush of the vehicle and release, chase, capture, and kill the animals. The officers in charge demand that the soldiers kill the animals with their bare hands.

While PETA was successful in having the class at Dugway discontinued, they also received reports of animal killing at Loring Air Force Base in Maine where soldiers were told to feed and care for rabbits and later to kill and eat them. At Fairchild Air Force Base in Washington, eyewitness accounts describe soldiers who are "required to stroke the rabbit to calm it, then bash it on the head—and the rabbits don't always die with the first blow."

Survival skills training classes began in 1947, in Alaska, to expose Air Force members to the harsh Arctic, and later a training camp was opened near terrain that resembles the former Soviet Union. By 1966, several of these classes were developed to train for the action in Vietnam. Marine Sergeant Joe Bangert told *Life* magazine in 1971, "The day before I went to 'Nam this staff sergeant came out in front of us with a rabbit. Petting it he pulled out a knife and started skinning it, then disemboweled it."

Government documents obtained via the Freedom of Information Act show that two Air Force bases alone used more than 1,500 rabbits each year at a cost of more than $10,000. According to a 1997 Department of Defense (DOD) report, the Air Force kills more rabbits in survival skills courses than does the DOD in all its intramural research facilities combined. PETA estimates that more than 10,000 animals, including chickens, rabbits, and goats are used each year in dozens of classes at military installations around the country.

These exercises seem to serve no practical purpose and teach no relevant skills to soldiers who may one day experience life-threatening, adverse conditions. Soldiers stranded in wartime are not likely to find tame bunnies and hens sitting on a battlefield. These live animal programs are controversial even within the military. Major General Leo J. Baxter of the U.S. Army base in Fort Sill, Oklahoma, stated, "We [at Fort Sill] are in complete agreement that there is no need to utilize live animals for realistic survival skills training."

In the past, there have been instances where such exercises were canceled after receiving national exposure, yet thousands of animals continue to suffer each year on military bases that pursue this training.

UPDATE BY AUTHOR D'ARCY A. KEMNITZ: The story "Irrational Rations: Animals Used in Military Training" outlined a campaign begun when soldiers at U.S. military bases learned they were expected to kill rabbits with their bare hands in "survival skills" training classes. Whistleblowers called animal rights groups to try to get this practice stopped, and their reports marked the lurid beginnings of a national effort to stop one of the most outdated, barbaric, and unjustifiable practices in the military. These exercises result in the deaths of more than 10,000 animals annually—including goats and chickens—usually by soldiers using their bare hands or primitive tools such as rocks and sticks.

The practice dates back to World War II and was designed to teach soldiers how to procure food when separated from their divisions for long periods of time. However, in the modern exercises, soldiers are given tame rabbits before heading out to the training field. Nothing about the exercises simulates combat conditions with regard to "hunting" for food, making the classes as pointless as they are cruel.

Following the story's publication in *The Animals Agenda*, articles appeared in newspapers in areas near large military installations, and *Time* magazine covered the story as well. The Pentagon's public affairs division has frustrated activists by obstructing any communication with decision-makers on the issue.

The mainstream press responded with an emphasis on the gory aspects of small animals being killed by soldiers. Other individuals who were more familiar with such practices took action to stop animals from being killed. For instance, one Seattle-based former survival skills training instructor, who taught rabbit-killing exercises to soldiers going to Vietnam, wrote to members of Congress to help initiate legislation to stop the practice. He stated: "As a former Air Force Sergeant survival instructor at Fairchild Air Force Base from 1968 to 1971... I taught survival in both classroom and field settings. Part of that training was the practice of killing a live rabbit with my own hands and then butchering the rab-bit as one would a larger animal such as a deer. Since the rabbit was caged and hand-fed for a few days before being dispatched, my students often became attached to this animal and were reluctant to see or conduct the killing themselves....The killing and butchering of these live rabbits is wholly unnecessary and does not enhance the survival of military personnel."

What remains now is for military authorities and/or members of Congress to use the information revealed in this campaign and take appropriate action to end this cruel and unproductive practice.

For more information regarding the campaign to stop the use of live animals in military survival skills training courses, contact: *The Animals Agenda*, P.O. Box 25881, Baltimore, MD 21224; Tel: (410) 675-4566; E-mail: office@animalsagenda.org; Web site: www.animalsagenda.org.

COMMENTS BY PROJECT CENSORED NATIONAL JUDGES

MICHAEL PARENTI, author of *America Besieged* and *History as Mystery*: It has been a year in which foreign policy issues have loomed large—as is often the case—and the stories nominated correctly reflect that. The mainstream media seems to be most uncritical of that realm of public policy having to do with the national security state, and the extent to which it serves corporate global domination. The occasional muckraking piece about unsafe products or dangerous medical procedures or the malfeasance of tobacco companies can win attention now and then in the mainstream media, but not the lies and major crimes of the national security state in its tireless campaign to make the world safe for the Fortune 500.

The interests of global finance capital that are served by the kind of military interventionism pursued by Bill Clinton and his predecessors in the White House remain largely unmentioned. So Project Censored is performing an especially valuable service by exposing how the corporate media look the other way, not only in regard to specific corporate abuses but also the larger scope of corporate globalism.

In keeping with this, however, one issue that is lacking in this year's lineup is how the news media suppressed the whole story about GATT, MAI, and the WTO (including the WTO's first 100 decisions, all of which favored corporate capitalism), for several years until that issue exploded in Seattle in November/December of 1999.

ROBIN ANDERSEN, associate professor of Communication & Media Studies, Fordham University: Reading through the *Censored* stories for this year was exhilarating and frightening. Exhilarating because of the skill and dedication demonstrated by the journalists and writers who continue to work and struggle to get their stories out. Frightening because these stories illustrate the connections between corporate power, government, the military, the press, and even non-profit organizations such as the American Cancer Society. Taken together, these stories draw a picture of a world dominated by corporate economic power, and held in place with the help of a media system that does not reveal the human cost of such economic priorities.

Instead of exposing the stories of people poisoned by chemical manufacturers, nuclear testing, and cancer causing pollutants, the media offer narratives of racial exclusion and criminality, claimed as the causes of social and economic problems.

I am sure the "Toxic Gumbo" exposé and the connections between milk consumption, infected cows, and Crohn's disease would be ratings-grabbers. I know the conditions imposed by the army on workers making uniforms would sell newspapers, and I believe the public would have felt differently about the war in Kosovo had they known about the economic incentives. I am left wondering what kind of world we might live in if the information contained in this volume were readily available to the American public. If these stories were repeated as frequently as the lifestyle consumer stories designed to sell us products, demonstrations against the World Trade Organization in Seattle would be only the beginning of a struggle towards a society characterized by peace and justice instead of war and inequality.

JACK NELSON, professor emeritus, Rutgers University: This year, I was struck by the remarkable series of underreported stories about the purposes for and causes of NATO intervention in Kosovo. These stories describe a much more unsavory side of our participation, and deserved a major focus in the mass media for balance and public knowledge. Media attention to Kosovo was certainly and appropriately extensive, but that reportage followed the

U.S. and NATO line that Milosevic and long-lived ethnic hostility and violence accounted for our warring actions; the presumption is that we took the high road by protecting human rights and dealing with a scoundrel. Not well covered were the more nefarious purposes and suspicious events that surrounded our strength of determination in negotiating and supporting NATO intervention.

Media coverage was extensive (some would say excessive) reporting of important world-wide news, but the orientation was unbalanced and misleading—reportage strikingly like that of our early involvement in Vietnam. There remains a lack of coverage of disturbing elements in the Kosovo struggle. As a result, the American public is largely unaware, and highly significant debates over that engagement are missing in public discourse.

I had some difficulty selecting which of the several Kosovo stories, with accounts of economic, massacre deception, gangsterism, or World Bank interest, should be in the top 10, and would like to have had them grouped together to make a larger impact. As it is, I selected two for the list this year, one as number one to illustrate the importance of the lack of reportage. Other stories in my selections represent a variety of appalling and horrendous stories of corporate greed, American racism, corruption of philanthropic purpose, class-based health care, gender and religion issues in the U.N., nuclear control and questionable mental stability, failures of the World Bank in resettling the dispossessed, and toxic environmental issues.

It is always very difficult to separate out the 10 most significant and underreported, since nearly all of the candidates deserved more coverage than they received. There are some recurrent themes each year—environmental disorder, imperialism, and corporate excess—this year is no different, though the examples have changed. It would be easy to become pessimistic over time, but I remain optimistic because of such efforts as Project Censored. Informed criticism is key to social progress. I am proud to have been associated with Project Censored since its inception; it is one of the few means for addressing the public's right to know.

SHEILA RABB WEIDENFELD, President, D.C. Productions: As we begin the third millennium, the "most censored" news stories continue to be about the harm toxic chemicals and hazardous waste do to the world population. The top stories of 1999 include, for example, the possibility of endocrine disrupters increasing the risk of breast cancer. Another story deals with an epidemic of cancer in southeast Louisiana, which appears to be the result of the numerous chemical refineries located there. In the same vein, a story deals with three large underground nuclear test sites in Amchitka and dozens of radiation-linked cancers.

Project Censored is now in its 24th year and every year these same kinds of problems are raised. What will it take for the media to give these stories the attention they deserve?

BILL LUTZ, professor of English, Rutgers University: It may be a cliché, but it's more true than ever: information is power. The paradox today is that as the means of transmitting information has grown in sophistication and availability, the quality of information has significantly decreased. The media has lots of space for the latest manufactured celebrity and non-event, but no space to cover the issues that really matter to people and their lives.

Project Censored brings to public attention those stories that should have been covered but weren't. Every person concerned with the welfare of this country and the world should read these stories.

JULIANNE MALVEAUX, economist and author: The competition for headlines has not trickled down to a competition for content, as was most recently exhibited by coverage of protests at the WTO. We know that people were arrested, but we don't know, generally, what the underpinnings of the protests were about. Nor are we aware, generally, of why foreign news has disappeared from our papers, why economic justice issues are covered only superficially, or why it's more profitable to sustain a little old man's erection than to cure a child's disease.

Capitalism and the profit motive combine, collude, and conspire to produce the lowest common denominator of news. The papers provide us with stories that are easy to digest and do not rock the boat. Still, sometimes papers do provide stories that are contrary to cultural norms.

The news as we know it excludes people's race, gender, nationality, and sexual orientation. It excludes subject matter by complexity, scientific basis, and international focus. There is a journalistic beat that produces carefully reprinted "people style," or "living" stories. Imagine how exponentially better our knowledge base would be if we could get the same kind of coverage of the economy, with every nuance explored, every beneficiary traced. The cliché is that we should "follow the money," but we rarely do. Otherwise, we'd know who pays for the spin.

Information is power, but the people will not gain power from mainstream newspaper headlines. The alternative press and the specialized press are those whose information will deliver all power to the people.

Censored Honorable Mentions for 1999

The following stories were runners-up for 1999's most censored stories list. In the final voting each was supported by a significant minority of the 175 faculty and students at Sonoma State University. In some cases the difference between runner-ups and the top 25 was only a few points. These 30 stories are unranked.

RADIATION INDUSTRY SPREADING DISEASE

Source: NUKE WATCH PATHFINDER
Author: John LaForge

Years after the shutdown of nuclear reactors and the burial of waste, radioactive contamination continues to spread and make people sick. Mysterious cancers and other diseases are afflicting people living near 13 former nuclear weapons reactor sites in the United States.

Since 1991, the government has paid private attorneys more than $54 million to fight thousands of people who believe that the radiation from the Hanford nuclear weapons site made them ill. On October 7, the DOE announced that 35 tons of radioactive trash must be removed from the Richland, Washington city dump and returned to the Hanford nuclear weapons site on the Columbia River. Two weeks later they upped the estimate to 210 tons.

In Sellafield, England, spinach grown near the waste reprocessing machinery is reportedly poisoned with radioactivity seven times higher than normal with Technetium-99, a beta radiation emitter with a half-life of 213 million years. In Apollo, Penn, the former owners of nuclear fuel production systems had to pay $36.5 million to cancer victims or their survivors whose illnesses were caused by gross negligence of the company. One in five people living near the plant were diagnosed with cancer from 1990 to 1994. Tests in both Britain and the U.S. have confirmed that buried waste can rise to the surface by climbing the roots of plants and result in direct exposure from underground storage.

POWER BLOCK; TURKEY AND ISRAEL LOCK ARMS

Source: THE PROGRESSIVE, December 1998
Author: Jennifer Washburn

Arms control and human rights groups protest armsales and contracts between Turkey and other countries due to Turkey's continued persecution of the Kurds. Since 1984, the Turkish military has bombed and depopulated more than 3,000 Kurdish villages in its campaign to eradicate the Kurdish Workers Party, a militant Kurdish opposition group. Turkey's main military supplier is the United States. Over the next 25 years, Turkey plans to spend an astonishing $150 billion to modernize its military. Already, Turkey and Israel have signed a number of arms deals, with many more in the works. Such sales raise questions about whether Israel will become a back door conduit for Turkey to obtain American technology.

Turkey has a burgeoning military partnership with Israel and in 1996, signed a historical military training agreement. Last December, Europe rejected Turkey's application for membership in the European Union, in part because of Turkey's failure to improve human rights. Israeli weapons offer Turkey a way around such sanctions. Israel's eagerness to assist Turkey in a massive buildup of military strength raises many concerns regarding the plight of the Kurds, and Palestinians, Middle Eastern stability, the prospect of Arab-Israeli peace, and regional arms-control efforts.

THE STRUGGLE TO SAVE THE LAST OF AMERICA'S MISFITS

Source: THE ANIMALS AGENDA,
November/December 1998
Author: Laura A. Moretti

The Bureau of Land Management (BLM) is behind yet another scheme to take the land from those who were here first for those who now want it. This time the Bureau of Land Management is removing wild horses and clearing the land for cattle ranchers.

The population of the wild horse was once two million. By 1971, only about 18,000 remained. Many of those horses remaining were run off cliffs, shot in corralled bloodbaths, and buried in mass graves, taking them to the point of extinction.

The wild horses remain caught in a numbers game. Under the Department of Interior's "multiple-use regulations, many cattle, wildlife, and horses roam on federal lands. Wildlife is paid for by taxes, and the revenue obtained from hunting licenses, while cattle are paid for by the meat industry at $135 per head per month. Wild horses take up one "Animal Unit Month" (AUM) but no one is paying their way. Each horse removed from the West frees up another AUM for cattle, sheep, game, and antelope.

The systematic elimination of wild horses from BLM continues unabated. The BLM claims that there are 24,000 wild horses in Nevada alone. According to Jim Clapp, this is an exaggerated number because he documented 300 skulls, and only 8,300 free-roaming horses, over a 250-hour period while flying over Nevada. The removal of more than 9,600 animals—1,300 more than Clapp could even find—has been recommended for removal by the BLM in accordance with their 24,000 figure.

SCHOLARLY PUBLISHERS HOLD UNIVERSITIES HOSTAGE

Source: EXTRA!,
January/February 1999
Author: Nancy Kranich

A few multinational media conglomerates currently have a monopoly on the publication of scholarly journals and monographs. Over the past 10 years, the cost of journals has increased 148 percent and monographs have increased 62 percent. However, the Consumer Price Index has only gone up 44 percent.

Presently, university libraries pay up to $15,000 for one year's subscription to certain journals. Increasingly the money is not in the budgets and libraries must cancel journals. The average research library maintains 15,000 subscriptions at a cost of $3.6 million annually. Journals published by professional associations and societies cost one-third to one-fourth the price of commercial journals with equivalent content. Recent studies show that prices for commercial journals related positively to the firm's portfolio size, and that mergers create significant price increases. Consolidation by large media conglomerates has created a monopoly that's largely responsible for limiting students' access to research and scholarship.

HUMAN RIGHTS TREATIES NOW WORK IN U.S.
Source: CONNECTIONS, February 1999
Author: Ann Fagan Ginger

Recent international treaties give civil rights lawyers new legal tools. On December 10, 1998, President Clinton took the historical step of issuing an executive order on Implementation of Human Rights Treaties in the United States. The three treaties include the Convention on the Elimination of All Forms of Racial Discrimination; the Convention Against Torture and Other Cruel, Inhuman or Degrading Treatment or Punishment—both ratified by the U.S. Senate in 1994—and the International Covenant on Civil and Political Rights, ratified in 1992. Clinton also ordered all federal agencies to notify the States about the rights in these treaties and the need to enforce them in States, on Indian reservations, and in Puerto Rico.

Under the Constitution, treaties are honored as laws. Thus this executive order gives us new legal tools to make complaints on inhuman treatment and discrimination. The treaties require "positive steps" to end racial discrimination. They commit the federal government to train all of its law enforcement officers and military personnel not to mistreat detainees and prisoners.

REFORMING THE IRS... FOR WHOM?
Source: LABOR PARTY PRESS, May 1999
Author: LP Staff

Last year Congress passed a bill to reform the IRS. Yet, the bill was virtually unreported in mainstream media. The reform bill created an oversight board dominated by private sector executives. The board will consist of a Treasury Secretary, the IRS commissioner, a full time government employee representative, and six private sector "experts." The board's duty, according to the IRS, is to oversee the agency's administration, management, conduct, direction, supervision, execution and application of tax. Bob McIntyre of Citizens for Tax Justice states in New York *Newsday* that under the new law the oversight board "will have significant authority over the IRS budget." Private sector representatives will dominate the board and increase the possibility of a pro-business bias.

Republicans on the Senate committee that considered the overhaul plan took exception to the one worker representative on the board, even though corporate executives vastly outnumbered the representative. Still, Senate Majority Leader Trent Lott argued that the presence of both the IRS commissioner and the worker representative on the board would "compromise the board's independence."

LAKOTA OCCUPY ISLAND
Source: ON THE LINE, June 14, 1999
Author: Jerry Wilson

The Lakota Sioux Tribe set up a protest camp on LaFramboise Island to demand that the state of South Dakota fulfill the 1868 Treaty of Fort Laramie. The Lakota Sioux once again face the United States government, while hoping to reclaim land that is rightfully theirs.

The Treaty of Fort Laramie in 1868 recognized Lakota ownership of the Missouri River and millions of acres to the West. Less than a decade later, the U.S. government violated the treaty and took most of that land, forcing the Lakota onto reservations. Five of these reservations were along the Missouri river. In the 1950s, the Army Corps of Engineers took the best of this riverside reservation land to build five massive dams, which in turn

flooded the Indian towns and burial grounds.

Since then, negotiations have taken place between the respective leaders of the region to return some of the land to the Lakota people. Five out of seven Lakota Sioux tribes feel that these attempts are not satisfactory and demand that all of their land be returned. Republican Governor William Janklow proclaimed that he will not honor the 1868 treaty since he did not sign it.

SENTIMENTALITY AND RESPONSIBILITY: PLUTONIUM INJECTIONS EXPERIMENTS
Source: COVERTACTION QUARTERLY, Spring/Summer 1999
Author: Ali S. Zaidi

The hidden history of the University of Rochester (UR) includes plutonium and uranium injection experiments conducted on people during the 1940s, CIA-sponsored mind-control experiments during the 1950s, and lead injection experiments during the 1960s. Human medical experimentation at UR has continued into the 1990s. The uranium experiments that occurred at UR in the '40s and '50s were specifically designed to harm the subjects. According to one subject's son, the subjects were never asked for consent.

One example of UR placing its subjects at risk during human experimentation happened in 1996. The subject involved, a woman, was paid $150 dollars to participate in an experiment that involved having cells extracted from her lungs in order to study the effects of smoking and pollution. The woman left the bronchoscope unit trembling from an overdose of lidocaine, entered a hospital due to seizures, and died a few days later.

HIGHER JUSTICE, OR HIRED JUSTICE
Source: COVERTACTION QUARTERLY, Fall 1999
Author: Diana Johnstone

FORMER AG: CLINTON'S A CRIMINAL: CLARK WANTS JUSTICE
Source: SPOTLIGHT, August 2, 1999
Author: Margo Turner

The International Action Center (IAC) headed by former U.S. attorney general Ramsey Clark has charged President Clinton and other NATO leaders with war crimes. This indictment is one of two indictments charging Clinton and other NATO leaders with war crimes in former Yugoslavia.

The IAC hopes to bring recognition to the general public that the U.S. and NATO deliberately targeted Yugoslavian civilians and civilian infrastructure. Thus, NATO destroyed Yugoslavia's economical foundation, especially any State-owned sector of the economy; used cluster bombs and other prohibited weapons; willfully ruined the environment; used radioactive depleted uranium weapons; and committed numerous other warcrimes. After several months of hearings, the commission plans to convene a final war crimes' tribunal and issue a public verdict.

Fifteen lawyers and law professors from around the globe have recently filed a lawsuit charging President Clinton and 60 other heads of state, foreign ministers, defense ministers, and NATO officials with violations from the following organizations: The U.N. Charter; the NATO treaty; the Geneva Convention; and the Principles of International Law recognized by the Nuremberg Tribunal.

ABORIGINES AND URANIUM
Source: IF MAGAZINE, July/August 1999
Author: Sam Perry

For the past two decades, the Aboriginal people of Australia (the Mirrar) have struggled to survive the threats to their land. Currently, the Mirrar find themselves in battle with the Australian government who want to extract valuable uranium from land that the Mirrar claims as theirs.

For over 50,000 years, the Mirrar Aboriginal clan has traced their ancestral land claim to what is currently the Kakadu National Park. Still, for over twenty years the Australian government has allowed ERA to mine uranium on land within Kakuda. Now the government is pushing to open a second uranium mine in an area called Jabiluka. Even though various studies have shown uranium mining to be dangerous to the ecology of the region, the Australian government has denied or ignored the Mirrar's opposition. Due to political maneuvering and exemptions, the Jabiluka project is scheduled to proceed without Mirrar consent. Despite UNESCO and international pressure, the Australian government appears committed to the continued historic exploitation of the Aboriginal people and their land.

CONGRESS PUTS CONTRA-COKE SECRETS BEHIND CLOSED DOORS
Source: IF MAGAZINE,
July/August 1999
Author: Robert Parry

The House Intelligence Committee conducted a secret hearing on the Contra-cocaine issue. On May 25, the panel announced that they had no plans for a public session. When questioned why Congress was acting more secretively than the CIA, an official, who spoke on condition of anonymity, responded that a closed hearing gave the members a chance to "step back and look at what they would be interested in without having to worry about classification."

The report indicates that every major cocaine smuggling network used the Contra operation in some way, and that the Contras were connected—directly or indirectly—with possibly the bulk of cocaine that flooded the United States in the 1980s. A government official said the committee supported the work done by the CIA inspector general. "We believe the unclassified version was a good piece of work," the official said.

Both the CIA and the Justice Department issued reports last year, denying that the federal government willfully colluded with the Contra operatives to smuggle cocaine into the United States.

Parry reports that the CIA knew about the Contra-cocaine smuggling, obstructed criminal investigations, and systematically covered up evidence that might have been politically harmful to President Reagan's pro-Contra policies. Most big newspapers downplayed the disclosures or wrote nothing at all. This neglect stems from the refusal of the major news organizations to acknowledge that they had missed—or misreported — one of the worst scandals of the 1980s.

THE UNASKED QUESTION: U.S. NUKE WEAPONS IN EUROPE
Source: THE BULLETIN OF ATOMIC SCIENTISTS, July/August 1999
Author: Paolo Cotta-Ramusino

Nearly 10 years after the fall of the Berlin Wall, the U.S. still believes it necessary to have tactical nuclear weapons in Europe. At the NATO summit in April, the U.S. squashed German and Canadian initiatives that proposed a reduction in nuclear weapons and the adoption of a "no first use" policy, calling the debate over nuclear doctrine "nonproductive and damaging." Presently, about 180 American-made and -controlled variable-yield B61 bombs are located in seven different NATO countries. Construction of new Weapons Storage and Security Systems, vaults that shelter the tactical weapons, have recently been completed at nine air bases. The new Strategic Concept maintains that although NATO's nuclear forces no longer target any country, NATO will maintain adequate sub-strategic forces based in Europe.

Eliminating U.S. nuclear bombs from NATO territories would alleviate hostility between NATO and Russia. Public opinion in Europe shows very little concern for the risks or the political consequences related to having American nuclear weapons on European soil. As a result, the governments of NATO countries face little opposition to the residual nuclear force, and most news operations and opinion makers simply ignore the fact that nuclear bases still exist in Europe.

AN UNLIKELY THREAT HYPES DANGER OF TERRORIST ATTACKS

Source: THE BULLETIN OF
THE ATOMIC SCIENTISTS,
July/August 1999
Authors: Jonathan Tucker & Amy Sands

In January, President Clinton warned that "the enemies of peace realize they cannot defeat us with traditional military means" and therefore the military is working on "new forms of assault," including the development of chemical and biological weapons (CBW).

The Clinton Administration's federal budget for fiscal year 2000 calls for nearly $1.4 billion to protect U.S. citizens against terrorist chemical or biological attacks, more than double the fiscal 1999 spending. Justification for this spending seems mostly about convincing the public of hypothetical dangers and thus a need for stronger powers for law enforce-

ment. Still, a mass-casualty attack with chemical weapons has never occurred in the United States. The largest related incident occurred in 1984, when members of the Oregon based Rajneeshee cult deliberately contaminated restaurant salad bars in the town of Dallas with salmonella bacteria that temporarily affected 751 with a diarrhea illness. Other than this incident, only one person has died from a chemical terrorist attack in the United Sated since 1900. That attack happened when the Symbionese Liberation Army used cyanide-tipped bullets to assassinate a California school superintendent in 1973.

Eighty percent of the CWB terrorist threats investigated by the FBI in 1998 turned out to be hoaxes and the remainder threats were very small-scale attacks that failed. The tendency of U.S. government officials to exaggerate the threat of chemical and biological terrorism has been reinforced by sensational reporting in the press and an obsessive fascination with catastrophic terrorism in Hollywood films. This combination leaves Americans with the misguided perception that massive terrorist threats are on the increase.

SAME-SEX SPOUSES IN CANADA

Source: THE NATION,
July 12, 1999
Author: E. J. Graff

On May 20, 1999, Canada's Supreme Court declared 8 to 1 that for the purposes of family law, same-sex partners must be considered "spouses." This decision confers "common law" marriage status on cohabiting same-sex couples. Same-sex couples in Canada still cannot marry, but by living together for several years, common-law status is obtained. Common-law Canadian gay and lesbian couples now come under laws for alimony, child support, shared taxes, separation oversight, rights to pensions, wrongful-death benefits, immigration rights, hospital visitations, and much more.

U.S. mainstream media completely failed to cover this important Canadian Supreme Court decision. Our country has passed laws—both at the federal level and in 29 states—forbidding recognition of same-sex marriage. These laws are being used to threaten even the most basic domestic-partnership same-sex statutes. U.S. states have spent this century dismantling—instead of creating—common-law marriage forms, so we have little recent legal history of recognizing families that do not start with wedding bells.

THE SELLING OF SMALL TOWN AMERICA NEWSPAPERS
Source: THE WASHINGTON SPECTATOR, June 15, 1999
Author: Mary Walton

Half of all the "hometown newspapers"—dailies with a circulation of less than 13,000—remain caught in a "selling spree" in which 70 percent have changed owners since 1994, some more than once.

The *American Journalism Review* (AJR) reports that "there are 1,489 daily

newspapers nationwide and they are changing hands at a dizzying clip." In addition, the AJR reports that from 1994 to 1998 there were 545 transactions, and in 183 of those transactions the same paper was turned over to a new owner a second, a third or even a fourth time.

Often the new owners retain publishers. Papers like the Community Newspaper Holdings, Inc., of Birmingham, AL, also keep their names off the masthead. As a result, small-town leaders may be only dimly aware that the rampant "chain-store" phenomenon has claimed yet another local enterprise—their newspaper.

WHAT THE COX REPORT DOES & DOES NOT SAY ABOUT ISRAELI TECHNOLOGY TRANSFER TO CHINA
Source: THE WASHINGTON REPORT ON MIDDLE EAST AFFAIRS, July/August 1999
Author: Shawn L. Twing

On May 25, 1999, the U.S. House of Representatives released a declassified version of its investigation into China's illegal acquisition of U.S. nuclear and military technology. The Cox Report details China's attempts to obtain U.S. military technology and hardware by buying it from Third World countries. What the report does not say is that Israel is giving China U.S. arms technology in direct violation of U.S. arms export laws that forbid the retransfer of that technology to other countries without U.S. permission.

Israel has given China a cruise missile that incorporates sensitive U.S. technology, air-to-air missiles, a re-engineered version of the U.S. made AID-9 "Sidewinder," anti-tactical ballistic missile technology related to the U.S. Patriot missile, and laser weapon technology.

The impact of China's illegal acquisition of an airborne early warning system will "significantly erode the military technological edge held by U.S. and Taiwan that is necessary for deterring China."

INEQUALITY IN LATIN AMERICA

Source: DISSENT, Summer 1999
Author: Forrest D. Colburn

THE NEO-LIBERAL WORLD ORDER: THE VIEW FROM THE HIGHLANDS OF GUATEMALA

Source: NACLA REPORT ON THE AMERICAS, July/August 1999
Author: John D. Abell

The first generation of reforms suggested by the IMF, the World Bank, the IDB, and AID (known as the Washington Consensus), in response to the recession of the 1980s, curbed inflation but did not help the poor. Income inequality, widespread poverty, and low education affect those Latin Americans who suffer from extreme poverty.

A comprehensive 1998–1999 Inter-American Development Bank (IDB) report entitled "Economic and Social Progress in Latin America" documents huge inequalities. The most inequitable countries are Brazil, Chile, Guatemala, Ecuador, Mexico, Panama, and Paraguay. Taken as a whole, the wealthiest 5 percent of the population receive 25 percent of national income; the wealthiest 10 percent receive 40 percent. By contrast, the poorest 30 percent of the population receive only 7.5 percent of total income. More than 150 million Latin Americans, roughly one-third of the population, have income levels of under $2 a day. Most of the poor still live in the countryside and the poorest 30 percent have an average of 6.3 members in their household. The majority of Latin Americans are in favor of reforms that would address pressing social needs such as the need for education, health care, and income generation for the poor.

TOMAHAWK MISSILES, RAYTHEON, CAMPAIGN MONEY

Source: COVERTACTION QUARTERLY, Winter 1999
Author: Lee Siu Hin

The August 20, 1998, missile attacks in Sudan and Afghanistan, as well as the December missile attacks on Iraq, involved huge amounts of money, manpower, and resources. The assaults were, however, only part of a larger web involving campaign donations, international military sales, U.S. military contracts, and the U.S. military buildup in the Middle East.

The Raytheon Company, one of the biggest military contractors, based in Lexington, Massachusetts, manufactures

Tomahawk and Patriot missiles worth billions of dollars in annual sales. The Tomahawk cruise missiles cost $750,000 each, more than a conventional bomb delivered by manned aircraft. *Aviation Week & Space Technology* reported that the U.S. fired 79 cruise missiles at up to seven targets in the August 20 attack. That attack amounted to over $100 million spent in one night.

While Raytheon receives new military contracts worth billions of dollars, they are also one of the largest political donation providers. Since 1995, Raytheon and its subsidiaries have donated over one million dollars in campaign contributions. For example, House Majority Leader Dick Armey received $48,201 from Raytheon. The series of U.S. military threats and air strikes around the globe, against "terrorists" and "military dictators," creates excuses for policy makers to spend increasing amounts of money on weapons for years to come.

SOCIOLOGIST DEPICTS THE NEW SLAVERY

Source: THE CHRONICLE OF
HIGHER EDUCATION, May 7, 1999
Author: D. W. Miller

After pioneering research involving many case studies, sociologist Kevin Bales exposed a phenomenon called "New Slavery," a product of demography and global capitalism, in his book *Disposable People: New Slavery in the Global Economy*. Bales claims that as many as 27 million people around the globe endure forced servitude and are "in a relationship in which one person is completely controlled by another person through violence or the threat of violence for the purpose of economic exploitation," from which the rest of us benefit.

Bales states, "the population explosion plus the globalization of the economy have pushed a lot of people into economic vulnerability." When capital flows where labor remains cheap, then bribery undermines labor laws. As a result of such corruption, workers become easily replaced or "disposable." Currently, slaves across the world work and sweat and build and suffer for products that we all use. Slaves in Pakistan may have made the shoes that you are wearing and the carpet that you stand on. Slaves in the Caribbean may have put sugar in your kitchen and toys in the hands of your children.

Debt bondage forces many men into near starvation and often they die from starvation conditions. As many as 45,000 children in India make fireworks and matches in factories while the gunpowder they handle often corrodes and blisters their already scarred fingers. Bales estimates that about 35,000, or one in 20, of the women in the huge commercial sex industry in Thailand are slaves. In some case, families sell their own children into prostitution.

STRANGE BUT TRUE: ARE U.S. PLANES SOWING THE SKY WITH POISON?

Source: SUNDAY TELEGRAPH
(London), January 31, 1999
Author: Paul Sieveking

SKY SAMPLES ANALYZED—CONTRAILS MYSTIFY

Source: LYCOS:ens.lycos.com/ens.
apr99/1999L-04-22-01
Authors: William Thomas
& Eriminia Cassani

People across the U.S. are reporting crisscross patterns of jet contrails. Many believe that these sightings are evidence of the U.S. government doing biological testings on civilian population areas. Described as unmarked taker-type aircraft, the aircraft have been reported in 11 states and several foreign countries. The U.S. military says that they are simply created by heavy air traffic, or by planes dumping fuel before landing.

Samples of the chemical substance have now been identified as a JP-8 fuel additive, a brownish substance used by the Air Force for bioremediation. This biological additive creates a brownish gel that was found on houses, barns and dwellings, nearby any fly-by-fuel dumping place. The jet-fuel additive is also a known carcinogen capable of causing severe upper respiratory problems and blood inflections in humans. Numerous people have reported becoming sick with flu-like symptoms after exposure. Two samples of the substance tested from different regions were found to be contaminated with Strepomyces and various other bacteria and molds.

THE CVX DECISION: A RARE OPPORTUNITY

Source: RACHEL'S ENVIRONMENT
& HEALTH WEEKLY, August 12, 1999
Author: Peter Montague

Although people may think nuclear power is dead because of its danger and expense, the United States Navy remains the one sector of the U.S. economy where new nuclear reactors are being built. Recently, the Navy began planning for the new CVX class of aircraft carriers that run on nuclear reactors instead of cheaper diesel fuel.

The military defends its position stating that nuclear power is more modern than diesel powered engines because it allows for unlimited and quicker travel without refueling. What the military does not explain is that the cost of maintaining such a carrier is so expensive that the military will have to retire the carrier before the end of its service life. In addition, the U.S. General Accounting Office (GOA) said that a 50-year-lifetime cost of a nuclear-powered carrier exceeds the lifetime cost of a conventional carrier by $8.1 billion. The GOA finds that nuclear-powered carriers provide no significant military advantage.

HIGH-CALIBER: U.S. PROMOTES WEAPONS BAZAARS

Source: MOTHER JONES,
July/August 1999
Author: Ken Silverstein

The U.S. government supports two dozen International Arms Carnivals or Arms Shows around the world. Latin America Defentech, or LAD '99, brought 200 firms from around the world to Rio de Janeiro in April 1999, in hopes of drumming up business with Brazil, the region's biggest arms importer.

Defentech is one of about two dozen stops on the international arms circuit, which includes exhibition sites on every continent outside Antarctica. Arms shows are largely a mixture of hype and machismo. For example, at the International Defense Exhibition in Abu Dhabi, live-fire range attendees sipped umbrella drinks while observing surgical strikes on dummy targets. This display gives industry personnel a chance to make the hard sell to potential clients.

Presently, critics of the exhibitions, like Representative Pete Stark (D-CA) want support for a bill that bans Pentagon participation in weapons exhibitions. The work on the bill began when the Pentagon started leasing military equipment to companies for display at such shows and paid for military escorts to ensure the weapon's safety. As the weapons industry prepares to face the new millennium, its strategy for keeping production lines open includes selling arms to Third World countries that do not necessarily have the money or need for them. For example, Brazilian president Fernando Henrique Cardoso recently spent $59.7 million on high-speed torpedoes in a country that is severely poverty stricken.

PRESCRIPTION: PROTEST
Source: THE NATION,
August 6, 1999
Author: Neil Shulman, MD

Protests erupted in Atlanta when the 1,035-bed Grady Memorial Hospital, the only public hospital in the Atlanta metropolitan area, raised the price of prescriptions by a substantial rate. An internal Grady document projected that without access to discounted medications, 6,500 people would suffer or die within 30 to 60 days. This decision also affects more than 26,000 patients, many of whom need life-sustaining medicines. The chairman of the hospital explained that the facility had a $26.4 million deficit and that the price increase was essential to maintain its fiscal viability. Grady's pharmaceuticals policy is America's health care crisis in a microcosm.

Throughout the country, hundreds of people are suffering or dying every year because they cannot pay for medications. Of late, the matter of prescription costs has surfaced as Congress considers changes in the Medicare program, with politicians sensing a galvanizing issue for the 2000 elections. The confrontation with Grady's trustees, which took place on March 4, 1999, was only the opening shot in a battle that, at least temporarily, reinstated the minimal prescription fees and, by June 8, secured $4.6 million in public money. Still, the fundamental problem remains. Access to medication is the ultimate bottleneck in the health-care system. The United States is the only industrialized country that places no ceiling on the price of drugs, and prescription prices are becoming too costly for millions of Americans.

WHAT WAS ABOARD FLIGHT 1862?
Source: EARTH ISLAND JOURNAL,
Winter 2000
Author: Gar Smith

Seven years after El Al Flight 1862 crashed just outside Amsterdam, authorities have just recently discovered what was aboard the plane. Originally, Israeli officials claimed that Flight 1862 was carrying only "a regular commercial load," consisting of perfume and gift articles. Since the crash, 850 survivors, police and rescue workers have sought medical treatment for a host of maladies.

The denials collapsed on October 4, 1998, when the Dutch daily *NRC Handelsblad* printed a leaked copy of a page from the plane's cargo manifest. According to the previously secret freight documents, Flight 1862 was hauling 10 tons of chemicals, including hydrofluoric acid, isopropanol, and dimethyl methylphosphonate (DMMP). These chemicals make up three of the four chemicals used in the production of sarin nerve gas. The DMMP had been supplied by Solkatronic Chemicals of Morrisville, Pennsylvania. The shipment was destined for the Israeli Institute for Biological Research (IIBR) in New Ziona, outside of Tel Aviv. While the export of DMMP is strictly controlled by the U.S. government, the U.S. Department of Commerce had no problem granting Solkatronic's license to ship DMMP. Still, Israel maintains that the chemicals were to be used to test gas masks but this explanation is puzzling since it only takes a few grams to conduct such tests. These findings have raised serious questions about the transportation of undeclared hazardous materials.

WASHINGTON'S 10% SOLUTION

Source: PROGRESSIVE POPULIST, May 11, 1999
Author: Wayne O'Leary

Nine-tenths of all stocks remain in the hands of the richest 10 percent of Americans. The wealthiest 5 percent of Americans own three-quarters of the market and a full half of the market is owned by the top 1 percent, whose annual family income exceeds $250,000 or have an average net worth of $650,000.

Most of the millions of Americans who are technically participating in the stock market are not active investors. Most current stockholders have a little 401(k) money in mutual funds (typically less than $5,000). Instead they have a traditional pension where the employer invests into a particular mutual fund and sometimes without consulting the employee.

Significant advantage in the formation of government policy goes to the leading stockholders in the U.S. The non-investing public at large, the bottom 60 percent (or more accurately, 90 percent), currently has little effective representation in national politics or government. Government policies directly or indirectly reward Americans who own stock; the opposite side of the coin, of course is that they often simultaneously harm those who are stockless.

SCHOOL TIES

Source: IN THESE TIMES, October 31, 1999
Author: Terry J. Allen

Vermont's Norwich University, a private military college, is training Indonesian students who will serve in an Indonesian military unit known for its gross violations of human rights. In 1997, 11 students listed their billing address as the headquarters of Kopassus, an elite unit that has for years been accused of torture and conducting covert psychological warfare.

A 1998 law prohibits federal assistance or military training of any unit of security forces when there is credible evidence that any member of the unit has committed human rights violations. Since Norwich receives federal funds in the form of grants and other assistance, the U.S. government has been subsidizing the training of Indonesian soldiers. On September 10, 1999, President Clinton froze all relations with the Indonesian military. Yet Norwich argues that restrictions on training are irrelevant to their school.

COLOMBIA ON THE BRINK

Source: IN THESE TIMES,
October 31, 1999
Author: Ana Carrigan

Trying to avoid an outright civil war, the Colombian Government and the Revolutionary Armed Forces (FARC), a 40 year leftist insurgency in the southern part of Colombia, were trying to restart peace negotiations this past summer. To repress this peace process, the U.S. announced further military and anti-drug aid of some $500 million per year for the next three years to fight drugs specifically focusing in the FARC–held areas. FARC officials pledged to stop growing drugs if a peace process could be developed. Yet under the guise of drug suppression, the U.S. continues to arm the Colombia military in an effort to defeat the FARC.

The Drug Enforcement Agency (DEA) says that there are actually more drugs being grown, processed and shipped in right-wing paramilitary regions in the north of Colombia than in the south. It is widely accepted that the paramilitaries are closely linked to the Colombia military and that human rights abuses and death squads are more likely associated with the right-wing narcoterriorist than the left-wing revolutionaries. Both the left

and right wings grow and sell drugs to support their political movements.

BLOOD MONEY

Source: SALON, December 1998
Author: Suzi Parker

While President Clinton was governor of Arkansas, HIV- and hepatitis C–tainted blood plasma from Arkansas' Cummins Prison was sold to and infected thousands of Canadians.

Despite repeated warnings from the Food and Drug Administration, Arkansas kept its prison plasma program running until 1994. Administrators of Cummins Prison sold the blood plasma to brokers who in turn sold it to other states, plus to Japan, Italy, Spain, and Canada. Arkansas was the last state to cease selling the plasma of its prisoners. More than 7,000 Canadians may die as a result of this blood scandal.

Many former Arkansas inmates, who claim they contracted hepatitis C and AIDS as a result of improper procedures during the donation of blood plasma, plan to bring a lawsuit against the following: Arkansas Department of Corrections, Health Management Associates Inc. (HMA) and Pine Bluff Biologicals (the two companies that held the prison's plasma contracts), the state of Arkansas, and Clinton and his administration.

CITY SLICKERS

Source: SALON, July 1999
Author: Jake Tapper

U.S. cities and counties are suing gun manufacturers and dealers for distributing dangerous products. Since October 1998, more than 20 U.S. cities and counties have filed lawsuits against gun dealers and manufacturers for negligence and irresponsibility. However, some of these same cities and counties—including New Orleans, Boston, Detroit, and Alameda County, California—have been more than willing to engage in quiet deals with these same manufacturers to trade in their old police weapons, and have sometimes even confiscated criminal weapons, for new guns for their officers.

CHAPTER 2

Censored Déjà Vu: What Happened to Last Year's Most Censored Stories

BY CORRIE ROBB, MELISSA BONHAM, BONNIE FAULKNER, COREY HALE, WILLOW LYONS, PAUL STUTRUD, KATIE SIMS, VICTORIA CALKINS, & PROJECT CENSORED

Chapter 2 is designed to give readers an update on the top stories from previous years that have been covered in the news in 1999. This year's reviews focus on coverage of stories from 1998. For follow-ups on previously undercovered news stories in the United States, an excellent reference is *20 Years of Censored News* by Carl Jensen & Project Censored (Seven Stories Press, 1997). *20 Years* provides updates on the most Censored stories for the years 1976 to 1995 and is available direct from the publisher (Tel: (800) 596-7437), from the Quality Paperback Book Club, and in bookstores nationwide.

SECRET INTERNATIONAL TRADE AGREEMENT UNDERMINES THE SOVEREIGNTY OF NATIONS

The proffered intent of the Multilateral Agreement on Investment (MAI) was to safeguard the investments of multinational corporations. However, the corporate protections that the international trade treaty was meant to put into place challenged the sovereignty of member nations by granting corporations rights that equalled or superseded the regulatory authority of nation-states and local governments. Additionally, MAI would have overreached the North American Free Trade Agreement (NAFTA) and The General Agreement on Tariffs and Trade (GATT) by allowing corporations to directly sue any level of government—state, municipal, or federal—for perceived financial losses (including future profits) due to legislative action, strikes, or boycotts.

The MAI would have thrust the world economy much closer to a transnational laissez-faire system where international corporate capital would hold free rein over the democratic wishes and socio-economic needs of its people.

The investments to be protected by the MAI were broadly defined as any assets such as factories, products, services, currency, and stocks that may be located in one country, but owned by a company, corporation, or individual in another country. Pushed by the International Chamber of Commerce and U.S. Council on International Business, the MAI agreement would have required "national treatment" for all foreign investors. Consequently, local governments would no longer have been able to treat domestic firms more favorably than foreign firms, and it would have become illegal to implement restrictions on what foreign firms could own. Subsidy programs which focused on assisting and developing domestic industries would have been eliminated as host nations became legally liable for lost competitiveness and profits. Lawsuits would have been heard before secret tribunals consisting of unelected trade officials of the Organization for Economic Cooperation and Development (OECD). The agreement made no provisions for local citizens and communities to have legal recourse.

The MAI would also have had devastating effects on a nation's legal, environmental, and cultural sovereignty, forcing countries to relax or nullify human, environmental, and labor protection in order to attract investment and trade. Necessary measures such as food subsidies, control of land speculation, agrarian reform, and the implementation of health and environmental standards could have been challenged as "illegal" under the MAI. Compromise of national sovereignty would have been extended to community control of forests, local bans on the use of pesticides and hormone-induced foods, clean air standards, limits on mineral, gas, and oil extraction, and bans on toxic dumping. The MAI would have exacerbated the pressure on undeveloped nations to deplete their own agricultural, mining, fishing, and forestry assets, seriously undermining the capacity of local communities and municipalities to govern sustainably and democratically.

SOURCES: Joel Bleifuss, "Building the Global Economy," *In These Times*, January 11, 1998; Bill Dixon, "MAI Ties," *Democratic Left*, Spring 1998; Miloon Kothari & Tara Krause, "Human Rights or Corporate Rights?" *Tribune Des Droits Humains*, April 1998.

COVERAGE 1999: In April 1998, unable to resolve several issues including exemptions for cultural industries and a proposal to allow European Union members to give each other preferential treatment, negotiators for the MAI took a six-month break. Reconvening in October, France announced it was withdrawing from the talks as they were unwilling to relinquish the amount of control over its own economy that the MAI would require. In November, Australia and Canada followed suit. On December 4, 1998, the 29-member OECD, which hosted the negotiations in Paris, announced the formal suspension of talks.

During the three-year negotiations, which started in 1995 after the passage of GATT, the proceedings received virtually no mainstream press coverage in the United States. The foreign press, on the other hand, dedicated significant attention to MAI proposals and reported on anti-MAI demonstrations which took place throughout Europe.

Critics of the agreement both here and abroad included labor unions, environ-

mentalists, political activists, and non-governmental organizations such as the Public Citizen's Global Trade Watch. These were pivotal influences in the treaty's demise.

When the OECD decision to indefinitely suspend talks was announced, officials from the member countries agreed that it was imperative to continue discussing the need to protect overseas investment. "There is a general recognition of the importance of some agreement. I don't think you are going to see something emerge called MAI. I do think it's in everyone's interest, including France's, that there be some investment framework," said Donald Johnston, OECD Secretary-General. France and Canada asserted that the World Trade Organization (WTO), not the OECD, was the proper venue for such talks. The United States and OECD officials disagreed, pointing out that if a treaty agreement could not be reached with the 29-member OECD, it would not be reached with the 135-member WTO.

Anticipating the revival of MAI international trade rules within the framework of the WTO, critics and protestors from around the world converged on Seattle, Washington, from November 30–December 3, 1999, for the third ministerial WTO talks. What scanty press coverage the MAI received in the domestic press in 1999 came late in the year and in articles about the WTO ministerial meeting amidst critics' fears that MAI investment principles would be included in the negotiations.

SOURCES: *Washington Times*, December 5, 1998; www.citizen.org; www.preamble.org

1998 #2 CENSORED STORY

CHEMICAL CORPORATIONS PROFIT OFF BREAST CANCER

The leaders in cancer treatment and information are the same chemical companies that also produce carcinogenic products.

Breast Cancer Awareness Month (BCAM), initiated in 1985 by the chemical conglomerate Imperial Chemical Industries and now known as Zeneca Pharmaceuticals, reveals an uncomfortably close connection between the chemical industry and the cancer research establishment. As the controlling sponsor of BCAM, Zeneca is able to approve—or veto—any promotional or informational materials, posters, advertisements, etc. that BCAM uses. The focus is strictly limited to information regarding early detection and treatment, avoiding the topic of prevention. Critics have begun to question why.

While 49 percent of Zeneca Group's 1997 profits came from pesticides and other industrial chemicals, another 49 percent were from pharmaceutical sales, one-third of which were cancer treatment drugs (about $1.4 billion). The remaining 2 percent of Zeneca's profits derived from health care services, which include the 11 cancer treatment centers Zeneca operates across the United States. The herbicide acetochlor, considered a probable human carcinogen by the Environmental Protection Agency (EPA), accounted for close to $300 million of Zeneca's 1997 sales; tamoxifen citrate (Nolvadex), the most prevalent breast cancer treatment drug, accounted for $500 million. Zeneca strongly promotes the tamoxifen option for breast cancer as part of their "risk reduction" plan, implementing its use in each of its treatment centers. Actual cancer prevention would clearly conflict with Zeneca's business plan.

Hormones have been at the center of breast cancer research for the past two decades. Five years ago, however, researchers began to consider the possibility that chlorinated chemicals might be a contributing factor in the rising occurrences of breast cancer. In response to what it perceived as a threat, the Chemical Manufacturers Association and the Chlorine Chemistry Council banded together to develop a strategy to discount the research, which included hiring a public relations firm to discredit the scientific investigation and its resulting data.

SOURCES: Peter Montague, "The Truth About Breast Cancer," *Rachel's Environment & Health Weekly*, December 4, 1997; Allison Sloan & Tracy Baxter, "Profiting Off Breast Cancer," *Green Guide*, October 1998.

COVERAGE 1999: The merging of massive chemical corporations with large pharmaceutical companies has led to a conflict of interest in the cancer treatment and chemical production sectors. Zeneca pharmaceuticals merged with Astra chemical corporation on April 6, 1998, effectively forming the world's third largest pharmaceutical and third largest agrochemical company.

In regard to the use of drugs to treat breast cancer, most of the 1999 mainstream press coverage appears to be corporate press releases thinly veiled as news stories. Riding this wave of positive press coverage, AstraZeneca kicked off an ad campaign encouraging healthy women to assess their breast cancer risk, and urging them to then contact the company for further information.

Formerly available only for breast cancer treatment, tamoxifen was approved by the FDA in October 1998 to reduce the incidence of breast cancer in healthy women at high risk. This decision was reached after a four-year trial by the National Cancer Institute of 13,388 "high risk" women, which found that tamoxifen decreased breast cancer incidence by almost one-half. Unfortunately, women in the tamoxifen group also had twice the incidence of uterine cancer, three times the rate of blood clots in the lungs, and 50 percent more cases of blood clots in major veins. Five women in each group died: in the placebo group all five died from breast cancer, while in the tamoxifen group three died from breast cancer and two from drug side effects. Ironically, tamoxifen itself is considered a probable human carcinogen by the World Health Organization.

Tamoxifen has been aggressively marketed to women with no mention of these potentially life-threatening side effects. Television ads for tamoxifen in 1999 first discredited ideas women may have had about why they would not get breast cancer, then urged them to call Zeneca to find out what they could do to reduce their risk. The blatant promotion of this carcinogenic drug is not exclusive to its manufacturer, but is supported by the American Cancer Society of Clinical Oncology which recommends "offering" the drug to healthy women who have an increased risk of breast cancer. Rowan Chelbowski of UCLA said "[they] are not recommending that women take tamoxifen, but rather [they] are recommending it be offered."

A Zeneca spokeswoman told the *New York Times* that 29 million women are at increased risk for breast cancer. If only 10 percent take tamoxifen at its average annual cost of $1,000 for the recommended five years, tamoxifen sales would come to $14.5 billion.

This attitude prompted Ann Pappert of *Ms.* to suggest "this may be just another chapter in the sad history of 'medical miracles' for women, like DES and the Dalkon Shield, that turned into nightmares." Her opinion is supported by a letter sent from the Food and Drug Administration (FDA) to Zeneca, which warns the company that their advertising brochure for physicians was inaccurate. The original brochures stated that endometrial cancer associated with tamoxifen was "uncommon" and had inadequate information on the side effects of tamoxifen for all women over 60 even if their risk factor is less than 1.67 percent.

In 1999, the Justice Department launched an antitrust investigation into

Zeneca and the company's deal with the generic-drug maker Barr Laboratories, which competitors say may have cost consumers millions of dollars. Government officials are concerned that Zeneca's settlement, which gave Barr Laboratories $21 million dollars and a nonexclusive deal to distribute a generic form of tamoxifen manufactured by Zeneca, is more than just competitive, and has in effect prevented other generic-drug makers from entering the market and kept the drug's price high. Barr now realizes approximately $30 million a year from the deal.

AstraZeneca and Swiss drug giant Novartis have unveiled plans for a merger and spinoff of their agricultural-chemical businesses. The new company will spin off into a new company called Syngenta, becoming the biggest agrochemical business in the world, with sales of $7.9 billion.

Other corporate-cancer profiteers include: Rhone Poulenc Rorer's pharmaceutical division, which churns out the breast cancer treatment drug docetaxel (Taxotere). Similar in nature to Zeneca's situation, this company also manufactures 56 crop protection products that contain ingredients that are probable or suspected carcinogens." Also, Novartis, which at $4.15 billion is the 1998 world leader in agrochemical sales, makes the pamidronate compounds used to treat bone metastases in breast cancer patients. On one web page, this multinational company states that "Novartis intends to lead the fight against cancer by introducing therapies that battle the disease and alleviate the patients' suffering." On another page it declares that "Novartis Crop Protection is the leader in fungicides."

Eli Lilly and Co. sells millions of dollars of raloxifene (Evista) to treat breast cancer. But a huge cash cow for Elanco, Lilly's animal health division, is the cattle hormone Rumentin. It has been suggested that eating hormone-treated meat alters estrogen levels, which in turn may contribute to increased cancer risk.

Other breast cancer profiteers include General Electric and DuPont, who manufacture mammography machines and x-ray film. The two companies are tied for managing the highest number of SuperFund toxic waste sites in the country.

SOURCES: *Sierra*, September/October 1999; *Denver Post*, June 6, 1999; *San Diego Tribune*, July 30, 1999; *Ms.*, October/November 1999; *In These Times*, August 8, 1999; *New York Times*, July 30, 1999 & August 3, 1999; *SFGate*, May 19, 1999; *Pacific Sun*, October 27, 1999; *Extra!*, January/February 1999; *Green Guide*, January 1999.

COVERAGE OF ANTITRUST: Ellence, and STAR Trial: *USA Today*, June 28, 1999 & September 30, 1999; *New York Times*, March 28, 1999; The Associated Press, May 26, 1999 & September 16, 1999.

For more information on health risks, or to find out more about the toxic link, contact: The National Women's Health Network, Tel: (202) 347-1140; Breast Cancer Action, Tel: (877) 2STOPBC,

Web site: www.bcaction.org; The Toxic Links Coalition, Tel: (415) 243-8373, Web site: www.igc.org/justice/tlc; The National Women's Health Network, Tel: (202) 347-1140; Mothers & Others, Web site: www.mothers.org, E-mail: greenguide@mothers.org.

1998 #3 CENSORED STORY
MONSANTO'S GENETICALLY MODIFIED SEEDS THREATEN WORLD PRODUCTION

Monsanto Corporation has been working to consolidate the world seed market and is now poised to introduce new genetically engineered seeds that will produce only infertile seeds at the end of the farming cycle. Farmers will no longer be able to save seeds from year to year and will be forced to purchase new seeds from Monsanto each year.

On March 3, 1998, Delta and Pine Land Company, a large American cotton seed company, and the U.S. Department of Agriculture (USDA) announced that they had been awarded a patent on a technique that genetically disables a seed's ability to germinate when planted a second season. This patent covers not only the cotton and tobacco varieties, but, potentially, all cultivated crops. Scarcely two months after the patent was awarded, Monsanto, the world's largest seed corporation and second largest agrochemical corporation, began the process of acquiring Delta and Pine Land with its rights to this new technology.

If commercialized, the USDA stands to earn 5 percent of the royalties from the net sales of this technology. Historically, the USDA has received government money for research aimed at benefiting farmers, but recently the USDA has been turning more and more often to private companies for funding. As a result, for the first time in history, research is being done for the benefit of corporations, sometimes in direct opposition to farmers' interests.

Dubbed "Terminator Technology" by Hope Shand of the Rural Advancement Foundation International (RAFI), Monsanto's new seeds have diverse implications including the disruption of traditional farming practices around the world, the altering of the Earth's biodiversity, and possible impacts on human health.

Monsanto has euphemistically called the process by which seeds are disabled the "technology protection system." A primary objective of Terminator Technology is to grant and protect corporate rights to charge fees for patents and products that are genetically modified. Terminator Technology offers no advantage by itself, but when coupled with the production of the strongest, highest yielding seeds, farmers may be compelled to buy single-season plants.

SOURCES: Leora Broydo, "A Seedy Business," *Mojo Wire*, http://www.motherjones.com/news_wire/broydo.html, and http://www.motherjones.com/news_wire/usda-inc.html, April 27, 1998; Chakravarthi Raghavan, "New Patent Aims to Prevent Farmers From Saving Seed," *Third World Resurgence* No. 92;

Hope Shand & Pat Mooney, "Terminator Seeds Threaten an End to Farming," *Global Pesticide Campaigner* and *Earth Island Journal*, June 1998 & Fall 1998; Brian Tokar, "Monsanto: A Checkered History" and "Revolving Doors: Monsanto and the Regulators," *The Ecologist*, September/October 1998, Vol. 28, No. 5.

COVERAGE 1999: The debate about the ethics of genetically modified foods finally arrived in America during 1999 after having been a major issue globally for the last several years. Like the coverage of the Comprehensive Test Ban Treaty (1999 #6 *Censored* story), the debate about Terminator Technology and genetically modified organisms (GMO) in food was widely featured throughout the year. The centerstage visibility in mainstream U.S. media accomplished Project Censored's goal—exposure of the pros and cons of genetic engineering and its implications for the world food supply.

In early October 1999, hundreds of media sources reported on Monsanto's formal announcement that it would not "market seeds that produce crop plants that are themselves infertile." Although Monsanto is the world leader in seed sterility technology, another company which Monsanto hoped to purchase developed the specific Terminator Technology. Final approval of this purchase was blocked by antitrust investigators.

While the media coverage about the ethics of genetic modification remained strong, the concern over the domination of transgenic crop and livestock development by a handful of multinational corporations was largely absent. In countless polls, editorials, and letters to the editor in publications worldwide, the public overwhelmingly stated that there was not enough information available about how genetic engineering might affect the food they ate and the world in which they lived. Equally troubling was the notion that the science behind the technology has been largely profit-driven, and funded by a handful of some of the largest global corporations. Mergers and consolidations continue at the highest levels in the biotech and pharmaceutical industries, putting more independent genetic technology into the hands of those whose ulterior goals may not represent the best interests of the consumer.

On December 20, 1999, there was wide press coverage about Monsanto's merger with Pharmacia and Upjohn Inc., which formed one of the largest pharmaceutical companies in the world worth an estimated $52 billion. Monsanto is the producer of the chemical herbicides Roundup, Harness, and Lasso, the artificial sweetener NutraSweet, the arthritis drug Celebrex, the numerous variety of Ortho lawn and garden products, and POSILAC, the brand of rBGH milk-producing hormone given to cows. Citing intense criticism and pressure, the merging companies announced plans to "spin off" the agricultural division of Monsanto, which would conduct its own stock offering separate from the rest of the company.

The action and protest by opponents of GMOs culminated with the December 15, 1999 announcement of a major class-action lawsuit filed by several prominent antitrust lawyers on behalf of six farmers. The farmers accused Monsanto of rushing genetically engineered seeds to the agricultural marketplace before properly testing them for safety, and of forming an international cartel which conspired to control the world's production of corn and soybean seeds. In addition to discussing how U.S. exports had been severely impacted, especially to Europe and Japan, the farmers noted that Monsanto had spent over $8 billion in acquiring seed companies over the last decade. The actions of the farmers are widely supported and assisted by environmental groups from around the world.

Despite the fact that the U.S. Food and Drug Administration (FDA) opposes the labeling of any genetically engineered food, and has since 1995, FDA officials are having to rethink their position in the face of foreign market demands. Europeans are forcing American food exporters to segregate and label all genetically engineered food. This firm statement by the Europeans is seriously undermining the FDA's argument that labeling would be an unnecessary and wasteful proposition. Many farmers have benefited from the increased yields of genetically engineered seeds from Monsanto and other biotech firms, but they have been unable to sell their yields abroad since the international community put its foot down in the summer of 1999. In response the U.S. food and biotech industries have shifted into full crisis mode, mounting a massive public relations blitz in an attempt to prevent the backlash from washing up on American shores.

The *Nation* reported several attempts at such publicity including the Alliance for Better Foods run by the public relations firm BSMG. This same firm also represents Philip Morris and Monsanto. In December 1999, Monsanto's main public relations company, Burson-Marsteller, bused 100 members of a Washington, D.C., Baptist church to conduct a pro-GMO rally outside an FDA hearing. Some protesters reported being paid.

The FDA held three public forums in cities around the nation during 1999 to allow private industry, government, and the public to discuss genetic engineering and food. These gatherings drew considerable regional and national coverage. South Korea, Australia, New Zealand, some European nations, and Japan have all passed laws requiring the labeling of genetically modified foods. The two leading manufacturers of baby food in the United States, Gerber and Heinz, announced in July that they will not allow any genetically modified corn or soybeans into their products. The American Corn Growers Association told its members to strongly consider only planting traditional corn for fear that growers may not be able to export GMO corn.

In February 1999, representatives from 170 countries met at the United Nations Convention on Biological Diversity in Cartagena, Colombia. At this meeting, the U.S. interests led an attack that destroyed the world's first international biosafety protocol on genetically engineered organisms and products. *Third World Resurgence* and the *New York Times* were just two sources that reported on these negotiations leading up to the World Trade Organization (WTO) meetings in Seattle. As a means of protecting themselves from developed nations dumping unlabeled GMOs, developing nations wanted the protocol to extend to all genetically modified products. The United States was adamant about excluding agricultural products and worked closely to defeat the agreement with other nations where American multinational corporations have significant vested interests—Canada, Australia, Argentina, Chile, and Uruguay.

SOURCES: *Time*, February 1, 1999; *New York Times*, August 29, November 4, December 8, 14, & 20, 1999; the *Nation*, March 8 and December 27, 1999; *Wall Street Journal*, July 21, 1999; *Guardian* (London) August 25, 1999; *Financial Times* (London) December 6, 1999; *New Scientist*, November 27, 1999; *Business Week*, December 20, 1999; *Global Pesticide Campaigner*, December 1998; *Third World Resurgence*, August 1999.

1998 #4 CENSORED STORY
RECYCLED RADIOACTIVE METALS MAY BE IN YOUR HOME

Special government permits currently allow some U.S. companies to sell "decontaminated" radioactive metal for the manufacture of everything from knives, forks, and belt buckles to zippers, eyeglasses, dental fillings, and IUDs. The Department of Energy (DOE), the Nuclear Regulatory Commission (NRC), and the radioactive metal processing industry want to eliminate the need for these special permits and are advocating for new, more relaxed radiation standards. Present standards oblige metal companies to scrub contaminated metal until the radiation level is nearly unmeasurable. The new standards will allow a level of radiation whose concentration could result in nearly 100,000 additional cancer fatalities in the United States alone.

The current standards still allow some radiation to remain on recycled metal, exposing consumers to low-dose radiation from some common consumer products. Certain scientists argue that continual exposure to low-level radiation is potentially more harmful than a one-time high-level dose. The greatest threat to consumers may be from seemingly harmless everyday household products such as pots, pans, bed frames, and metal desks. In 1980, a survey of the domestic jewelry market revealed that out of more than 160,000 pieces of jewelry studied, over 170 pieces were found to be radioactive. Although these represented a very small percent of the total jewelry studied, at least 14 people developed finger cancer and several others were forced to endure the amputation of fingers and/or parts of their hands.

While the DOE, NRC, and radioactive metal processing industry endorse lowering the recycled metal standards for U.S. production, they engage in selling high-level contaminated metal to foreign markets. In fact, three major U.S. oil companies shipped 5.5 million pounds of radioactive scrap metal to China in 1993. In June 1996, Chinese officials stopped a U.S. shipment of 78 tons of radioactive scrap which exceeded China's safety limit as much as 30-fold. As of January 1998, 178 Taiwan buildings containing 1,573 residential apartments had been identified as radioactive due to the use of recycled radioactive building materials. Residents suffered from congenital disorders, various cancers, and unusual chromosomal and cytogenetic damage. Tom Gilman, U.S. Ecology accounts manager, centers the issue as an economic debate and dismisses public health concerns by stating that recycling radioactive metal is "turning wastes into assets" and that "there is always going to be some level of radioactivity."

SOURCE: Anne-Marie Cusac, *The Progressive*, "Nuclear Spoons," October 1998.

COVERAGE 1999: In mid-1999, the issue of radioactive metal recycling received some mainstream news coverage when two lawsuits were filed, one against the DOE and the other against a high-profile contract between the DOE and British Nuclear Fuel Limited (BNFL). Prior to the lawsuits, coverage of the potential dangers of recycled scrap metal was virtually nonexistent. In fact, in early 1999 the only issues about scrap metal recycling being explored by the mainstream press were those regarding the acquisition of metal recycling plants by large corporations and the potential financial gains being made in the 'waste-to-energy' industry.

A ruling by U.S. District Court Judge Gladys Kessler on June 29, 1999, concerning a 1997 quarter-billion-dollar contract awarded by the DOE to BNFL received substantial news coverage in select papers. The contract in question permitted a subsidiary of the BNFL to decommission and decontaminate three uranium enrichment plants at the DOE's Oak Ridge, Tennessee, nuclear reservation. The Oak Ridge facilities contain an estimated 100,000 tons of radioactive metal, which the BNFL can cleanse and then sell to the scrap metal market for the manufacture of such intimate everyday items as forks, frying pans, teeth braces, and baby carriages.

Judge Kessler ruled in favor of the DOE because of a loophole in federal law which prevented her from halting the project. However, she stated that it was "quite troubling" that the DOE and BNFL provided no explanation why an amendment in the EPA's Environmental Agreement was finessed to evade "public notice and comment opportunities." Kessler stated that the absence of opportunity for "public scrutiny or input on a matter of such grave importance" was both "startling and worrisome," and that the "potential for environmental harm is great, especially given the unprecedented amount of hazardous materials which the defendants seek to recycle."

In August 1999, Congressional leaders, steel industry officials, and scores of environmental groups called on the Clinton Administration to reconsider the Oak Ridge program. Public Citizen, a watchdog group, was one of more than 185 organizations that signed a letter to Vice President Gore on August 11, demanding a halt to the controversial program. A 1996 plan promoted by the Vice President had endorsed restricting the use of recycled metal for use in batteries only. However, the final contract does not provide for this restriction, leaving the public with no way of knowing if the metal objects in their homes or offices are made from recycled radioactive metal. As of November, 1999, Gore has still declined to comment on the matter.

In October, the *Tennessean* reported that despite the June ruling, federal lawmakers appeared "close to putting the brakes" on the controversial plan to "clean and recycle atomic bomb-making machinery from the Oak Ridge" site. U.S. Representative Bart Gordon is reviewing the plan, but feels confident that "Congress will reach a compromise agreement that would have the U.S. Nuclear Regulatory Commission, not individual states, rule on the matter." Legislators fear that the Tennessee state ruling may "become the de-facto national standard." Currently, U.S. Energy Secretary Bill Richardson is reviewing the case and a "hush-hush" attitude about the issue remains.

The second high-profile lawsuit was filed against the DOE by three former operators of the U.S.-owned Paducah Gaseous Diffusion Plant in western Kentucky. It was first reported by the *Washington Post* on August 8, 1999, and picked up by the *Los Angeles Times* on August 14. The ex-employees contend that the plant failed for years to properly screen gold and other metals for radioactive content. They state that some metals bound for private markets may have been highly radioactive when they left Paducah. This unscreened metal could have been recycled into a number of consumer products.

The Paducah case is extremely disturbing because it charges that thousands of "unsuspecting workers inhaled plutonium-laced dust brought into the plant for 23 years as part of the flawed government experiment." The *Washington Post* stated that "the government and its contractors did not inform workers about the hazards for decades, even as employees in the 1980s began to notice a string of cancers." Paducah plant workers further allege that radioactive waste was deliberately dumped into nearby fields, abandoned buildings, and a landfill not licensed for hazardous waste. The implications of such charges are far-reaching, considering the fact that this activity may have gone unmonitored for several decades.

To date, mainstream coverage about the recycling of radioactive metals has been seen in the *Washington Post, San Francisco Examiner,* and *Los Angeles Times* as well as on television stations ABC, MSNBC, Fox, UPN, and KQED. Multiple alternative sources have been diligent in covering the issue. The recycling of radioactive metal into the domestic market has been occurring for decades, posing a serious threat to public health. Only now, after lawsuits have been filed, has the mainstream press turned its attention to the problem.

SOURCES: *Washington Post*, August 8 & 14, 1999; *The Tennessean*, August 11 & 15, & October 1, 1999; The Associated Press State & Local News Wire, February 4, June 30, July 19, & August 12, 1999; *San Francisco Examiner*, September 19, 1999.

1998 #5 CENSORED STORY
U.S. WEAPONS OF MASS DESTRUCTION LINKED TO THE DEATH OF A HALF-MILLION CHILDREN

U.N. sanctions advanced by the United States against Iraq have taken the lives of more Iraqi citizens than did the military actions of the Gulf War itself. The Iraqi people are being punished for their leader's refusal to comply fully with the U.S.-supported U.N. demands "to search every structure in Iraq for weapons of mass destruction."

The sanctions imposed on Iraq are causing shortages of food, medical supplies, and medicine. In May 1996, then-U.N. ambassador Madeleine Albright acknowledged on *60 Minutes* that more than half a million children under the age of five had died since the war ended. UNICEF reported in 1998 that child mortality continued at 150 per day. The United States holds the position that sanctions against Iraq must continue until it can be proven that the country is unable to build biological and chemical weapons. Of these deaths, many are attributed to depleted uranium (DU) weapons or have been linked to birth defects known to be caused by radiation exposure. The rate of cancer in Iraqi children has increased dramatically.

Few Americans are aware of the enormous human toll caused by the continuing war with Iraq. In updates to the original Project Censored stories, the authors explain that the mainstream press has characterized the deaths, disease, and hardships of Iraq as "claims" while misunderstanding and grossly understating the damage and potential health hazards caused by the sanctions and the use of depleted uranium.

In another surprising insight into the Iraqi "situation," a 1994 Senate panel reports that between 1985 and 1989, U.S. firms supplied microorganisms needed for the production of Iraq's chemical and biological warfare. U.N. inspectors found and removed chemical and biological components identical to those previously furnished by the United States to Iraq. The Simon Wiesenthal Center in Los Angeles reported in 1990 that more than 207 companies from 21 western countries, including at least 18 from the United States, were contributing to the buildup of Saddam Hussein's biological and chemical arsenal.

SOURCES: Dennis Bernstein, "Made in America," *San Francisco Bay Guardian*, February 25, 1998; Bill Blum, "Punishing Saddam or the Iraqis," *IF Magazine*, March/April 1998; Most Rev. Dr. Robert M. Bowman, Lt. Col., USAF (Ret.), "Our

Continuing War Against Iraq," *Space & Security News*, May 1999.

COVERAGE 1999: There has been little U.S. mainstream news coverage about the almost one million Iraqi children who have either starved to death from U.N.-imposed sanctions, or become the victims of cancer and other maladies from chemical and biological weapons exposure. News about Iraq is more typically about the ongoing debate to pressure the country's leadership into complying with U.N. demands (the policy of "containment plus" to keep Saddam Hussein within the confines of the two "no-fly" zones). Some publications, though, have made a point of covering the more controversial elements in Iraq's current history. The poignant page-two feature article in the November 1999 *National Geographic*, and a series of investigative articles in the *Christian Science Monitor* are the most noteworthy examples.

A UNICEF report released in August caused a small flurry of coverage, especially in the foreign press. According to London's *The Independent*, "[UNICEF] argues that about 500,000 Iraqi children who have died in that time would have lived but for the sanctions." They report infant and child death rates doubling since 1989, and one in five children having stunted growth from malnourishment. According to a *Chicago Sun-Times* report on UNICEF's findings, the toll is especially heavy in central and southern Iraq, home to 85 percent of the country's population. Although officials insist that this proves Iraq's government is responsible for the woes of the country, a UNICEF representative argues that "the differences could be explained partly by the heavy presence since 1991 of humanitarian agencies helping the [northern] Kurdish population."

In the *San Francisco Chronicle*, UNICEF was reported to have claimed that 4,500 Iraqi children under the age of five die each month, and the number of Iraqi children with cancer has increased sevenfold. When asked about the effects of the sanctions on the plight of Iraq's children, U.S. Secretary of State

THIS MODERN WORLD

by TOM TOMORROW

SO IT TURNS OUT THAT THE U.N. WEAPONS INSPECTION TEAM WAS PROBABLY SPYING ON IRAQ FOR U.S. INTELLIGENCE AGENCIES! DO YOU *UNDERSTAND* THE IMPLICATIONS OF THIS?

SADDAM *CLAIMED* THE INSPECTORS WERE SPYING ON HIM, AND REFUSED TO COOPERATE WITH THEM--

--WHICH WAS USED TO JUSTIFY THE U.S. DECISION TO *BOMB* IRAQ... BUT IF THE U.N. TEAM REALLY *WAS* SOMEHOW INVOLVED IN SPYING--

Madeleine Albright said, "It's a hard decision, but we think the price… is worth it." The *Houston Chronicle* expounded on Albright's position, stating that Washington refuses to take responsibility for the human toll from economic sanctions.

A January 1999 *New York Times* story quotes one White House official as saying, "Containment doesn't bring about a decisive resolution quickly. It's unsatisfying and ungratifying by its nature. But 40 years of containing the Soviets in the Cold War paid off. You've got to be patient." Denis Halliday, a former U.N. assistant secretary general and coordinator of its Humanitarian Program in Iraq, resigned his post in protest as did American U.N. weapons inspector Scott Ritter, both disgusted with the failure of the sanctions. Ritter lost patience with Saddam Hussein's cat-and-mouse game, but Halliday stated he no longer wanted to be a part of the devastating effects of the sanctions on the children: "Sanctions are starving to death 6,000 Iraqi infants every month, ignoring the human rights of ordinary Iraqis and turning a whole generation against the West."

Halliday has gone on to write in various newspapers about the U.S. violation of the goals of U.N. Resolution 687 (the cease-fire-sanctions resolution), and the almost-daily air strikes in the "no-fly zones" created without U.N. approval by the United States, Great Britain, and France (France has since withdrawn from the triumvirate). According to a *Houston Chronicle* article on U.N. Resolution 687, Iraq's disarmament must be in the context of regional disarmament: there must be a nuclear weapons–free zone as well as a "weapons of mass destruction–free zone" created throughout the Middle East including Saudi Arabia, Iran, and Turkey.

Although the question of radiation fallout from the Gulf War use of depleted uranium has been ongoing in foreign news reports, the discussion was finally picked up in the U.S. press with a series of investigative articles in the *Christian Science Monitor. Monitor* reporter Scott Peterson not only personally investigated the presence of radiation in the war fields of Iraq, but explored Pentagon, Nuclear Regulatory Commission, and other gov-

--IT MEANS THAT CLINTON'S RATIONALE FOR THE BOMBING WAS AN UTTER *FABRICATION* AND HE *KNEW* IT! IN THE NAME OF INTERNATIONAL LAW, THE U.S. *VIOLATED* INTERNATIONAL LAW-- AND DELIBERATELY *MANUFACTURED* AN EXCUSE TO BOMB IRAQ!

I CAN SEE YOUR BEAK MOVING, BUT I CAN'T UNDERSTAND A WORD YOU'RE SAYING.

YOU'RE PROBABLY NOT THE ONLY ONE, MY FRIEND.

ernment and military reports to trace the history and controversy about the use of depleted uranium. Seventeen countries have arsenals of DU bullets, many procured from the United States, England, France, and Russia. A 1990 U.S. Army study "links DU with cancer and states that 'no dose is so low that the probability of effect is zero.'" The Pentagon has now backpedaled on that position. Still, U.S. handlers of DU are ordered to treat the substance as "low-level radioactive waste." Peterson states, "If there is a connection between human suffering and DU, then its use in the future will mean that lands of conflict will remain contaminated for the 4.5 billion years—a figure comparable to the age of the solar system—that DU remains radioactive."

Reports further implicating DU in the incidence of Gulf War Syndrome surfaced in the back pages of several newspapers after a September convention in Las Vegas of Persian Gulf War veterans. Physicians and researchers revealed their suspicions that exposure to a "toxic soup" of various chemicals and biological entities as well as DU radiation is responsible for the rearrangement of RNA (which helps decode genetic instructions) found in chronically ill Gulf War veterans. The Pentagon continues to dispute the contribution of depleted uranium to Gulf War Syndrome which affects an estimated 110,000 veterans.

DU continues to plague troops and victims alike in other war-torn countries. In December, *60 Minutes* reported on a military coverup of the use of DU in not only the Gulf War but also in Kosovo. As

in the Gulf War, troops in the Kosovo conflict were not informed of the hazards of DU. The military reports it "lost track" of the number of DU shells used in the 78-day NATO campaign in the Balkans, and continues to insist that there is no evidence that depleted uranium shells cause cancer.

Project Censored was unable to uncover any further reports regarding the United States' role in supplying materials for Iraq's production of biological and chemical weapons.

SOURCES: *New York Times*, January 3 & August 24, 1999; *Post-Standard, Houston Chronicle*, March 4, 1999; *Christian Science Monitor*, April 29 & October 5, 1999; *Chicago Sun-Times*, August 13, 1999; *San Francisco Chronicle*, September 19, 1999; *National Geographic*, November 11, 1999; *The Independent*, London, December 18, 1999; *60 Minutes*, December 26, 1999.

1998 #6 CENSORED STORY

U.S. NUCLEAR PROGRAM SUBVERTS U.N.'S COMPREHENSIVE TEST BAN TREATY (CTBT)

When scientists in India conducted a deep underground test on May 11, 1998, the world saw it as a violation of the United Nations' Comprehensive Test Ban Treaty (CTBT). However, two months before, the United States carried out a similar test that went largely unnoticed by the American media. Code-named "Stagecoach," the U.S. experiment called for the detonation of a 227-pound nuclear bomb at the Department of Energy's (DOE) Nevada Test Site, co-managed by Bechtel Corporation, Lockheed Martin, and Johnson Controls. While perceived as a hostile act by many nations of the world, U.S. officials claim that since it was a "subcritical" test, meaning no nuclear chain reaction was maintained, it was "fully consistent with the spirit and letter of the CTBT." Furthermore, they claimed that the test was necessary to insure the "safety and reliability" of America's aging nuclear arsenal.

Disputing this "safety and reliability" promise, foreign leaders believe that "Stagecoach" was, in fact, designed to test the effectiveness of America's weapons if, and when, they are ever used again. Though India refused to sign the treaty because it wasn't comprehensive enough, the countries that did sign felt that the CTBT would halt new weapons development and promote the move toward disarmament. The European Parliament officially warned the United States that further experiments might open the door for other nations to progress to full-scale testing. Leaders from China and Japan also harshly criticized the United States, calling for America to stop "skirting its responsibility for arms reduction."

According to the original *Nation* article, underground experiments aren't the U.S. government's only method of subverting the treaty. In July 1993, Clinton introduced the Stockpile Stewardship Program (SSP) which allots $45 billion over the next 10 years to finance new research facilities. Even when adjusted for inflation, this amount is larger than the per-year budget during the Cold War when much of the cost went to actually producing the nuclear arsenal. One of the most controversial elements of the SSP is the Accelerated Strategic Computing Initiative (ASCI) which is intended to develop a virtual nuclear testing program. The supercomputers comprising ASCI will allow scientists to continue testing and developing new weapons while bypassing actual experimentation. These supercomputers will conduct and monitor virtual explosions creating a new frontier of nuclear technology and the potential for massive weapons defense spending.

SOURCE: Bill Mesler, "Virtual Nukes—When is a Test Not a Test?" *The Nation*, June 15, 1998.

COVERAGE 1999: The debate about the U.S.'s failure to ratify the Comprehensive Test Ban Treaty (CTBT) was a major 1999 media event. Thousands of articles graced the front pages of every major publication in the world. When all was said and done, the U.S. Senate rejected a major international treaty for the first time in 80 years. Hopes rose that the United States could take a strong role in nonproliferation leadership by ratifying the treaty, especially in the context of the India-Pakistan arms race. When polled, 82 percent of Americans supported ratifying the CTBT.

The U.S. scientific community protest was one of the loudest ever voiced. In an unprecedented incident of collaboration, all 32 living Nobel Laureates in

Physics signed a statement that it was imperative that the Senate approve the treaty "to halt the spread of nuclear weapons." This signed note of protest did receive news coverage, but on page A16 of the *New York Times*. Meanwhile, the partisan politics that the statement left in its wake took center stage on page A1 during the second week of October 1999. The American Geophysical Union and the Seismological Society of America also released yet another unprecedented joint statement expressing "confidence in the treaty's verification scheme."

The U.S. media failed to make the connection between the fact that the U.S. government continues to pressure and strongly criticize foreign governments for their development and testing of nuclear technology while continuing to conduct nuclear tests and expand its nuclear technology through the Stockpile Stewardship Program. Since 1994, the U.S. government has conducted seven underground tests. These subcritical tests (tests that do not maintain a chain reaction) and the accompanying protests were reported in papers all around the globe outside the United States.

The subcritical underground tests have continued. One was carried out on February 9, 1999, and three more in the fall of 1999. All four tests—bringing the total since 1997 to 10—were conducted with less than 170 grams of plutonium and were carried out in the name of "continuing to understand the aging state of our nuclear arsenal." U.S. officials argue that these tests do not violate the CTBT because they do not sustain the chain reaction necessary for a true nuclear explosion. Russia is the only other country to have carried out such tests in the last decade.

Looking beyond the nationalistic rhetoric, these tests have sent a significant message to the global community: the United States can do what it wants while other nations exploring nuclear technology are a "threat to world peace and security." The media has yet to focus on how the rest of the world perceives U.S. actions and our apparent hypocrisy. There was little coverage of the massive outcry and protest going on outside the United States. European leaders Tony Blair and Gerhardt Shroeder along with many other heads of state voiced their collective support for the Senate's ratification of the agreement. These leaders poignantly raised the issue that the rest of the world was watching to see what the "leader of the free world" would do. A December 3, 1999, *Washington Post* article noted, "with the Senate rejection, the United States has bounced the check it wrote when it signed the test ban treaty in 1996." The CTBT has for decades been viewed as the ultimate test by non-nuclear states of the nuclear powers' commitment to nonproliferation. Little media mention was paid to the threat that non-ratification may have upon the over-arching Nuclear Proliferation Treaty (NPT) and Ballistic Missile Treaty (BMT).

The work that continues on ASCI has exceeded the initially allotted $45 billion (over a 10-year period), and has resulted in the United States alone possessing a battery of the world's fastest super computers for conducting simulated nuclear explosions.

In the summer of 1999 the General Accounting Office strongly criticized the Department of Energy's ASCI program, citing weak management, inconsistent progress and an absence of performance measures. The budget overrun has risen into the billions of dollars for the period 1996 to 2004.

SOURCES: *The Statesman* (India), October 22, 1999; *Malaysian National News*, February 8, 1999; *Japan Economic Newswire*, October 1, 1999; *Washington Post*, October 1 & December 3, 1999; *Inside Energy with Federal Lands*, February 2, 1999; *Los Angeles Times*, October 5, 1999; *Energy Daily*, April 29, July 31, & July 7, 1999.

1998 #7 CENSORED STORY
GENE TRANSFERS LINKED TO DANGEROUS NEW DISEASES

A major public health crisis is brewing as both emergent and recurring diseases reach new heights of antibiotic resistance. At least 30 new diseases have emerged over the past 20 years, and familiar infectious diseases like tuberculosis, cholera, and malaria are returning in new more vigorous forms. By 1990, nearly every common bacterial species had developed some degree of antibiotic resistance, many to multiple antibiotics. A major contributing factor, in addition to antibiotic overuse, just might be the transfer of genes between unrelated species of animals and plants, which takes place during genetic engineering. There is currently no independent investigation of the relationship between genetic engineering and the etiology (cause, or origin) of infectious diseases.

The technology of genetic engineering, or biotechnology, uses manipulation, replication, and transference techniques to insert genes "horizontally" to connect species which otherwise cannot interbreed. Normal genetic barriers and defense mechanisms are in this way broken down. Genetic engineering can also result in antibiotic-resistant genes, which can inadvertently spread and recombine to generate new drug and antibiotic resistant pathogens. This, say the authors, has occurred. Horizontal gene transfer and subsequent genetic recombination may have been responsible for bacterial strains that caused a 1992 cholera outbreak in India, and for a streptococcus epidemic in Tayside, Scotland, in 1993.

Biotechnology is presented to the public as a highly precise science. Genes never work in isolation, but rather in extremely complicated networks with other genes which can cause genes to replicate, reorganize, or even travel outside the organism. DNA released from cells may not be readily broken down in the environment, so it can retain the ability to transform other organisms.

Biotechnology firms have billions of dollars invested in these new technologies, and are concerned that their speculation bubble may burst before they can recoup their investments. In Europe, where the public support for such programs is dismal at best, EuropaBio, the non-government organization representing the interests of the biotech industry, hired public relations firm Burson-Marsteller to initiate a campaign to promote the benefits of biotechnology.

There is an urgent need to reassess the safety regulations pertaining to genetic engineering, and it is vital that this research be conducted by independent groups. Opposition to gene biotechnology has "skyrocketed " in Europe.

SOURCES: Mae-Wan Ho & Terje Traavik, "Sowing Diseases, New and Old," *Third World Resurgence*, No. 92; Mae-Wan Ho, Hartmut Meyer, & Joe Cummins, "The Biotechnology Bubble," *The Ecologist*, May/June 1998, Vol. 28, No. 3.

COVERAGE 1999: Although an upsurge in the number of cases of drug-resistant diseases often grabbed the headlines of U.S. newspapers and television news programs in 1999, popular consensus has been to attribute the cause to the overuse of antibiotics. The possibility of the transgenic mutation of disease bacteria has been overlooked by all but the most specialized publications. And although there was the beginning of a dialogue in 1998 about the possible dangers of generating new strains of viruses and bacteria through biotechnological blunders, most of the attention has been diverted to that of genetically modified foods (see 1998 *Censored* story #3).

Meanwhile, the domestic biotechnology industry scored a standoff at a U.N.-sponsored summit in February 1999 on the dangers of genetic engineering. The U.S.-led coalition of six countries (a.k.a., the Miami group) blocked approval of a Biosafety Protocol on transgenic crops. Still, the summit represented the first unified attempt to assess and regulate the risks of biotechnological engineering. Ironically, the United States could not vote on the issue since the Senate had failed to ratify the 1992 biodiversity agreement in Rio de Janiero. The biosafety debate went almost unnoticed in the United States, although questions surrounding "Frankenstein foods" and the regulation of the biotech industries were heavily scrutinized outside our media borders. When the U.N. biosafety negotiations resume in Montreal in January 2000, countries will once again try to write "a treaty-like protocol among nations to govern the movement of genetically modified foods."

Some medical professionals did take the threat of transgenic disease bacteria seriously, though. In May, the British Medical Association (BMA) "called for a moratorium on growing transgenic crops and importing unlabeled transgenic foods." The BMA questioned whether antibiotic-resistant genes engineered into crops might increase the spread of drug-resistant pathogens. In a *Richmond Times-Dispatch* article, a Virginia Commonwealth University professor and infectious disease expert, Dr. Richard P. Wenzel, urged colleagues to consider what impact the possibility of biological warfare might have on the medical field. According to the *Dispatch*, Wenzel believes that "[t]errorists using biological weapons now have the frightening ability to alter the genetic makeup of producing organisms—pathogens—to make them resistant to antibiotics and vaccines."

SOURCES: Joseph B. Verrengia, "Summit Under Way On the Dangers of Genetic Engineering," Associated Press, February 19, 1999; Peter Bacque, "Biological Terrorism Professor Urges Hospitals to Train Teams, Be Ready," *Richmond Times-Dispatch*, April 1, 1999; "Transgenic Food Fight," *Chemical Week*, May 26, 1999; Bill Lambrecht, "Tumultuous Talks on Trade Set Tone for Debate on Gene-Altered Food"; *St. Louis Post-Dispatch*, December 5, 1999.

1998 #8 CENSORED STORY
CATHOLIC HOSPITAL MERGERS THREATEN REPRODUCTIVE RIGHTS OF WOMEN

Hospital mergers with Roman Catholic Church medical facilities nationwide are threatening women's access to abortions, sterilization, birth control, and in vitro fertilization. In 1996, over 600 hospitals merged with Catholic institutions in 19 states. These mergers and partnerships with hospitals and health maintenance organizations (HMOs) are impacting and impairing reproductive health care rights across the nation.

These collaborations have made the Roman Catholic Church the largest private health care provider in the nation. Why would they want to join forces with secular hospitals?

"The big money in the hospital comes when you have a closed system of doctors, HMOs, and hospitals all feeding each other in a closed loop," writes author Christine Dinsmore.

In response to community pressure for access to reproductive medical care, some Catholic health care agreements have resulted in the formation of independently run women's health clinics. Some activists, however, say it is a poor solution because separate women's health clinics are often easier targets for anti-abortion extremists. In addition, Catholic hospitals often claim they will set up a separate women's health clinic as part of a partnership agreement, and then simply don't follow through.

These mergers also affect men's reproductive medical rights. When a hospital moves to free-standing clinics for women only, men seeking vasectomies are forced to go elsewhere. Health care workers, clergy, women's groups, and HIV/AIDS advocates are creating coalitions to inform the public about possible future mergers. Currently there are few laws requiring community notification of impending non-profit partnerships, but activists are pressuring state lawmakers to pass protective legislation. California and New York are two states which introduced bills for legislative review. In response, a lobby called the New York Catholic Conference has made defeating these bills "a priority." Such lobbies see these bills as forcing "Catholic entities to abandon their moral and ethical principles." Stopping these bills has become "second only to banning late-term abortions," says *Ms.* magazine.

SOURCES: Christine Dinsmore, "Women's Health: A Casualty of Hospital Merger Mania," *Ms.*, July/August 1998.

COVERAGE 1999: While there has been a clear increase in mergers between Catholic and secular hospitals in 1999, there has been no proportionate reaction from the media. In fact, there has been no coverage or follow-up on the mergers' impact on affected community services nor on how these changes have significantly impacted people's lives. These mergers often result in the public's inability to receive desired and often necessary reproductive health care.

Catholic mergers have accelerated. In 1994 there were six Catholic acquisitions of non-Catholic hospitals. In 1999, the Catholic church acquired 38 new hospitals, of which 25 were secular. The Catholic Health Association claims that only about 1 percent of hospital mergers result in a discontinuation of reproductive services. However, as reported by *USA Today*, Catholics for a Free Choice, a group that opposes the mergers because of the loss of reproductive services says that "of 127 Catholic/non-Catholic hospital mergers this decade, reproductive services were eliminated or greatly restricted in 48 cases."

The *Los Angeles Times* reported, "Catholic Health Care West (CHCW), the largest owner of hospitals and the biggest merger participant in California, owns 46 hospitals. Tenet Health Care (a secular provider), by comparison, owns 42." In a telephone study of 589 Catholic hospitals conducted by Catholics for a Free Choice concerning rape victims and their right to abortion, the group found that though Catholic health directives permit post-rape contraception in many circumstances, 82 percent of Catholic hospitals did not offer this service. "Of those hospitals that denied the service, nearly one-third, or 31 percent, provided no further referral useful in getting the so-called morning-after pills that could prevent pregnancy," wrote the *Boston Globe*.

In addition to the abortion issue, other problems remain, including those of birth control counseling, family planning, and emergency procedures categorized as "reproductive." There is concern over the underreported and therefore silent absorption of women's and men's reproductive health care rights into large conglomerates overseen by Catholic directives. Unbeknownst to the general public, persons and families in need of these services have become casualties of what author Christine Dinsmore refers to as "Merger Mania." In particular, there is a growing concern among the opposition to these mergers that in cases of rural and low-income Medicaid recipients, mergers may mean the complete loss of birth control and other reproductive services.

Not only has the mainstream U.S. press neglected to inform the public of mergers between secular hospitals and the Roman Catholic church, it has neglected to address those groups fighting for and against such mergers. Paul Yde, an antitrust lawyer with Vinson &

Elkins who represents Christus Health, says, "The Catholic systems have no interest in monopolizing the family planning services prohibited by its religious directives. Their goal is to have no connection with those activities." According to *USA Today*, Michael Pruitt, an attorney, and the vice president of mergers and acquisitions for Christus goes on to say, "It's a religious issue.... Our health care directives control how we express our faith through the provision of health care."

Opponents to the mergers—the National Organization for Women, the National Family Planning and Reproductive Health Association, and others—redirect the argument, maintaining it is a health rather than a religious issue. They have employed "antitrust guidelines" in fighting the mergers, and are using the National Women's Law Center's antitrust handbook. It has been handed out in communities that are being affected by Catholic hospital mergers and at family planning conferences. Experts say the activists can be strong deterrents to Catholic hospitals' expansion plans.

California Assembly Bill 525, introduced by Democratic Assemblywoman Sheila James Kuehl, also went almost completely unnoticed. As briefly reported by the *Los Angeles Times*, Kuehl's bill, the Health Care Access Bill would have required "all health plans, including commercial HMOs, to guarantee the full range of services within their provider network, require[d] all HMOs to inform patients about how to access the full range of services and any limitations on services purchased through their plan, and require[d] that any health facility that receives tax dollars through public bond or loan programs make all reproductive services available by contracting with others, where necessary, to provide them." The bill would also have required "any merger where non-profit assets are being transferred or acquired be approved by the attorney general, and that one aspect of approval involve the impact on the provision of reproductive health service."

Regardless of one's stance on reproductive healthcare issues, without mainstream U.S. coverage on this topic and the availability of knowledge that would follow, neither the topic nor the issues can be addressed by the public. As Assemblywoman Sheila Kuehl reminds us, "If you are among the majority of Americans who believe that the ability to make choices concerning reproduction is secured in the Constitution, think again. The struggle, primarily by women, to secure reproductive health services... has shifted from the halls of justice to the halls of medical centers and hospitals. Women, who spend 68 percent more on health care per year than men yet earn significantly less per capita, deserve at least to be certain that hard-won rights do not disappear, one hospital at a time."

SOURCES: *Wall Street Journal*, February 1999; *Boston Globe*, March 21, 1999; *USA Today*, April 8, 1999; *Los Angeles Times*, April 18, 1999; *San Diego Union-Tribune*, June 5, 1999; *New York Times*, October 9, 1999.

U.S. TAX DOLLARS SUPPORT DEATH SQUADS IN CHIAPAS

The passage of the North American Free Trade Agreement (NAFTA) ushered in an era of unprecedented military and corporate domination over the already beleaguered indigenous citizens of Mexico. On the day NAFTA went into effect, the Zapatistas of Chiapas in southern Mexico rose up in rebellion against the exploitation that they feared they would incur. Though the initial violence did not last long, the Zapatistas have continued to resist intrusions into their communally held lands, or *ejidos*. Owned and inhabited by the indigenous people of Mexico, the *ejidos* have been farmed collectively since the Mexican Revolution after the turn of this past century. With the passage of NAFTA, the Mexican government is pushing for the elimination of these communally held lands. By privatizing the land, the government hopes to make lucrative deals with multinational corporations.

Many Zapatista-controlled lands in Chiapas sit on major petroleum reserves that are second in size in the Western hemisphere only to Venezuela. Major deals have already been brokered between the Mexican government and multinational corporations for the development of forest and petroleum resources in the country. The absence or lack of enforcement of environmental and labor regulations in Mexico makes the nation particularly attractive to corporations from more regulated industrial nations.

One company, Pulsar, has presented a project to plant (non-indigenous) eucalyptus trees over 300,000 hectares throughout Chiapas and surrounding territories, and has contracted to sell the wood to International Paper (IP).

In December 1997, 45 unarmed indigenous Mayan Indian men, women, and children were massacred, their bodies dumped into a ravine near the town of Acteal. Accounts of torture continue to surface as the local Indians mount a campaign of primarily peaceful resistance. The group allegedly responsible for these and other atrocities are members of the Mexican Army Airborne Special Forces Group (GAFE)—a paramilitary unit trained by the U.S. Army Special Forces. Mexican soldiers are being trained with U.S. tax dollars to fill the GAFE ranks and fight an alleged War on Drugs. The 1998 Clinton Administration budget allocated $21 million for the Mexican Drug War. Anti-drug efforts continue to focus on Chiapas when, in fact, it is the least active of all Mexican states in drug production and trafficking. The level of autonomy desired by the Zapatistas both politically and economically stands to significantly affect multinational business ventures and Mexican government control of future oil and plantation agriculture development.

SOURCES: Viviana, "U.S. Paper Companies Conspire to Squash Zapatistas," *Earth First!*, Summer 1997; Slingshot Collective, "Mexico's Military: Made in the USA," *Slingshot*, Summer 1998; Darrin Wood, "Bury My Heart at Acteal," *Dark Night Field Notes*, Winter 1998.

COVERAGE 1999: As the Zapatista movement enters its sixth year, the Chiapas dispute continues to receive significant U.S. and international coverage. December 22, 1999, marked the second anniversary of the Acteal massacre. Relations between the Zapatistas and the PRI government remain tense and peace talks have been stalled. Throughout 1999, the Zedillo-led central government made several unsuccessful "attempts" to restart the peace process. The Zapatista National Liberation Army (EZLN) has not engaged the government, protesting that an agreement was already brokered in the form of the 1996 San Andres Accords for Indigenous Rights which would have granted limited autonomy to indigenous villages. The Mexican government rejected this agreement and refused to abide by it until significant "Zapatista changes" were made, leaving the situation in its present stalemate. The EZLN responded by implementing the accord itself, establishing civil courts, village commissions, and decision-making assemblies according to indigenous law, and taking over government functionaries within its territory.

The Mexican military has continued its campaign of large-scale militarization in the region, bringing in over 50,000 troops. This equals one soldier for every nine inhabitants in an area which has only one doctor for every 18,000 residents according to the Mexican government's own statistics.

Small conflicts continue to occur as the Mexican military works to move further into the Zapatista-controlled jungles. An August *New York Times* article describes several Zapatista acts of civil disobedience against the Mexican government's road building and surveying crews. The *Times*, among others, explained the importance of such roads to the Mexican government, which plans to use the new transportation infrastructure to harass the rebels and continue paper-tree plantation development. When the Mexican military was brought in to protect construction crews, students from Mexico City arrived *en masse* in response to a Zapatista call for support. The Mexican government quickly agreed to halt construction on August 26, 1999.

Conservative estimates put the number of displaced indigenous people at tens of thousands. The Mexican military persecutes locals arbitrarily perceived to be "cooperating" with the Zapatista rebel forces. President Zedillo and Chiapas Governor Roberto Albores Guillen continue to work closely in coordinating the military activities and presence.

The majority of media outlets do not explain precisely why the Indians of Chiapas are revolting against the government, nor the level of military support the U.S. provides. Because of the inattention to overarching conditions and specific details, the media coverage tends to add to the confusion of an already complex issue. First, the Mexican government continues to work with multinational export corporations and paper manufacturing companies to privatize the collective landholdings of the local people. An article from *Dark Night Field Notes* dated December 1998 states that the policy of the Mexican government continues to be that of taking valuable agricultural or undisturbed lands and turning them into plantation agriculture or eucalyptus mass monocrops for the international paper and pulp industries.

All the while Mexico cannot feed its own people. Chiapas is home to 3.2 million people. Approximately 40 percent of its population suffers from some level of malnutrition, and 50 percent is illiterate. Hundreds of millions of Mexican federal dollars have been poured into the conflict zone as the government attempts to selectively wean entire rebel villages away from the Zapatista movement. Chiapas now receives more assistance from the Mexican government for education, health care, and housing assistance than any other state.

Chiapas has been exposed to foreign business activities since the 1960s when the World Bank moved in and converted large tracts of indigenous land into privately held cattle ranches. The 1970s oil boom that followed resulted in a massive degradation of the local environment and the loss of already-scarce farmland.

The Mexican government and military came under condemnation from myriad sources in 1999 for their human rights abuse. An official delegation of Spanish observers who visited Chiapas concluded that the Acteal massacre could not have taken place without the complicity of the Mexican army. The report was submitted to the European Union and the United Nations. The U.S. State Department released other reports with similar findings as did the non-profit monitoring groups Human Rights Watch and the Inter-American Human Rights Watch Commission.

The French news-gathering organization, Agence France Presse, was one of a few media outlets to cover the introduction of a resolution in Congress calling on U.S. Secretary of State Albright to broker a peace deal in Chiapas. A coalition of U.S. Senators headed by Vermont Democrat Patrick Leahy drafted the proposal, which stated that the U.S. military should have no part in the ongoing human rights violations in Chiapas. The news that the head of the pro-government paramilitary squad responsible for the Acteal massacre was sentenced in a Mexican court to 35 years in prison while 23 other men were sentenced to lesser terms also went widely unreported.

In November 1999, the Mexican government indicated it would cease accepting all future counternarcotics funding from the U.S. government. This bold move stems from mounting dissatisfaction on the part of the Mexican military with the "my game, my rules" U.S. funding. It has expressed discontent with the quality of military hardware received, especially outdated helicopters. In addition, the U.S. government began implementing stricter rules and monitoring practices for funds and equipment given to Mexico to insure they were used only for the drug war. Prior to the refusal of aid, the Mexican government was the largest recipient of International Military Education and Training (IMET) funds in Latin America. Without the power inherent in a financial relationship as powerful as "the drug war," the United States has lost any influence it may have had to prevent human rights abuses throughout indigenous conflict zones like Chiapas. The *Dallas Morning News* was one of only a handful of papers to cover the significant event.

Mexico may be trying to hide rampant corruption in the upper ranks of its military from the U.S. Drug Enforcement Agency (DEA). Still, the training of elite Mexican paramilitary forces at the School of the Americas (SOA) in Fort Benning, Georgia is scheduled to continue. In fact, the number of Mexican graduates from the SOA has increased from approximately 15 per year in 1994, to well over 300 in more recent years, an increase of 2,000 percent.

The U.S. government continues to assert that it has no direct involvement with the Chiapas operations. Yet independent observer reports have documented the temporary detention of two U.S. military personnel by Zapatista forces in their region. The U.S. military is responsible for providing the Mexican paramilitary forces with state-of-the art telecommunications technology that enables them to move between indigenous villages with destructive efficiency. The difference between counterinsurgency and counternarcotics with the Mexican forces can be described as fuzzy at best.

The U.N. High Commissioner for Refugees, Mary Robinson, went on a fact-finding mission in Chiapas in early December 1999. She found herself "overwhelmed" by the documentation of refugee atrocities, and called for a significant reduction in the number of Mexican national forces present in the region. The list of noted abuses included arbitrary detentions, torture, disappearances, violence again women and harassment. The *Los Angeles Times* quoted Robinson as saying that the troop deployments are "very oppressive in certain areas, especially indigenous communities. I feel compelled to speak out about the level of violations, of cases of officials acting with impunity. I hope my visit has drawn attention to the problems."

Finally, the regional debut of the recently released film *Chiapas* by Canadian filmmaker Nettie Wild drew moderate coverage in community papers around the country. Wild documented the repercussions of NAFTA on the poorest of Mexico's poor: the Mayan Indians. The international attention the Chiapas issue is receiving has embarrassed President Zedillo and the PRI, the ruling political party that has been in power for over 70 years. The events in Chiapas may have domestic political implications as well when the Mexican population goes to the polls for national elections in the summer of 2000.

SOURCES: *Louisville Courier-Journal*, January 2, 1999; *Chicago Sun-Times*, June 4, 1999; *Los Angeles Times*, September 8 & November 18, 1999; *New*

York Times, August 31 & September 12, 1999; *Dark Night Field Notes*, December 1998; *El Universal*, May 1999; *Irish Times*, December 4, 1999; Agence France Presse, October 13, 1999; *Milwaukee Journal Sentinel*, September 14, 1999; *Atlanta Journal Constitution*, October 27, 1999; *San Diego Union-Tribune*, August 7, 1999; *Houston Chronicle*, August 8, 1999; *SourceMex*, January 20, 1999; Inter Press Service, March 1, 1999; *Baltimore Sun*, February 2, 1999; *Courier-Journal* (Louisville, KY), February 1, 1999. Internet links: Global Exchange—Mexico Campaign: www.globalexchange.org/campaigns/mexico; Human Rights Watch—Mexico Campaign: www.hrw.org; Amnesty International: www.amnesty.org

1998 #10 CENSORED STORY

ENVIRONMENTAL STUDENT ACTIVISTS GUNNED DOWN ON CHEVRON OIL FACILITY IN NIGERIA

On May 28, 1998, Nigerian soldiers in helicopters owned and operated by Chevron were flown to an oil facility, also owned by Chevron, off the coast of Nigeria in order to attack student demonstrators who had peacefully occupied the oil barge. After multiple assaults, two students lay dead, and several others were wounded. One hundred and twenty-one youths from 42 different communities had gathered to oppose the environmental destruction brought on by Chevron's oil extraction practices.

For decades, the people of the Niger Delta have been protesting the destruction of their wetlands. Discharges into the creeks and waterways have left the region a dead land, resulting in the Niger Delta becoming one of the most heavily polluted regions in the world. The students voiced their concerns many times but received no response. They organized the protests around the Chevron barge in order to draw the corporation's attention to the environmental injustice. According to student leader Bola Oyinbo, approximately 20 of the 121 students surrounding the barge in small boats went on board to meet with a Nigerian Naval officer who was working for Chevron. Oyinbo stated that the students wanted to speak to a Mr. Kirkland, Chevron's managing director. Although the director never came, other Chevron officials did arrive the next day and promised to set up a meeting with the students at the end of May.

The students agreed to leave the platform and attend the proposed meeting. As they were preparing to disembark, Nigerian soldiers in three helicopters piloted by Chevron employees opened fire on the students. Two young protesters were killed. Eleven students were detained by the Chevron-backed "security force" and taken to the city of Akure for prosecution. Despite their previous agreement to meet with the nonviolent protesters, Chevron filed a complaint against the group, saying they were pirates and should be interrogated.

During his imprisonment, one activist said he was handcuffed and hung from a ceiling fan hook for hours for refusing to sign a statement written by Nigerian federal authorities.

SOURCES: *Environmental Rights Action/Friends of the Earth Nigeria*, "Chevron in Nigeria—ERA Environmental Testimonies," AINFO News Service, July 10, 1998; Amy Goodman & Jeremy Scahill, "Drilling and Killing: Chevron and Nigeria's Oil Dictatorship," Pacifica Radio—*Democracy Now*, Summer 1998.

COVERAGE 1999: The actions and positions of Chevron and other oil companies in Nigeria, as well as the disastrous relationship between Chevron and Nigeria's indigenous people, remain a mystery to most of the American public as U.S. media sources continue to fail to report on the events unfolding along the Niger Delta.

After *Democracy Now!* broke the story in 1998, and a host of alternative publications including Project Censored drew attention to the issue in 1999, Chevron released a series of statements that eventually admitted involvement in the incident. One account by a Chevron employee stated that the company had no control over the actions of the military forces that arrived. Chevron simply called them and they came. However, only the Chevron helicopter pilots possessed the skill and expertise needed to land on the oil platform. Another Chevron statement acknowledged that the company brought the soldiers in with Chevron helicopters flown by Chevron pilots.

In 1999, Chevron Corporation contradicted its previously released statements when it claimed that the military forces called in were merely defending themselves against the armed protesters. They later admitted, however, that the protesters were unarmed. According to a first-hand account by protest leader Bola Oyinbo on *Democracy Now!* the military forces fired from the helicopters both before and during landing.

Political and environmental upheaval continues to grip the southern Chevron-controlled delta region of Nigeria. In late November 1999, Nigerian soldiers murdered at least a dozen residents of the town of Odi in Bayelsa State. The campaign of violence, allegedly provoked by the kidnapping and killing of 12 policemen in Odi by anti-oil activists, went on for several days. Approximately 300 Nigerian soldiers were moved in to occupy Odi. Locals reported that almost all major buildings and most homes were razed as a retaliatory move on the part of the government-controlled forces. At the same time a letter written by Nigerian president Obasanjo threatening the governor of Bayelsa State that action "must be taken" was leaked to the local press. Obasanjo spoke of reassuring the oil executives that the government was "very much aware of the concerns of the oil-producing companies for law and order."

The town of Odi has at least three capped oil wells owned by Chevron. Other communities that are under attack are also sites of Chevron wells. Five hundred soldiers were deployed on these assaults. "We will not allow the federal government of Nigeria to massacre us with military weaponry acquired with our God-given resources," the Federated Niger Delta Ijaw Communities group said in a statement. But the violence continues to escalate as frustrated activists, continuously beaten, killed, and harassed during peaceful protests, begin to target oil facilities and workers.

The *Houston Chronicle* reported in November 1999 that according to the Sierra Club the environmental damage along the Niger Delta is "so extensive that the U.N. Conference on the Environment and Development has listed it as one of the most endangered river deltas in the world." The gas flares in the region, which have occurred 24 hours a day for the last 40 years, is a "major contributor to global warming."

After decades of military authoritarianism in Nigeria, a new civilian government is taking measures to hold the multinational oil companies accountable for environmental degradation and the death of Wiwa. In one of literally hundreds of foreign articles highlighting the situation in Nigeria during 1999, the British press (including the *Times* of London, the *Guardian*, and the *Independent*) covered the Nigerian government announcement and its implications. The newly elected president called upon the oil multinationals to take responsibility for the destruction in the delta and for creating a restoration plan.

The plight of the inhabitants of southern Nigeria is but one example of the exploitation and host of injustices thrust upon indigenous peoples in the name of corporate and government mineral

extraction. Multinational oil companies repeatedly state that they do not want to work behind military shields, yet hundreds of Nigerians died in oil-related violence in 1999. Nigeria is Africa's most populous nation and its hopes for a future economic, political, and social rebirth rest with the country's rich oil reserves, while the severe poisoning of its people and land continue.

SOURCES: *San Francisco Chronicle*, November 19, 1998; *CNN WorldView*, November 21, 1998; Inter Press Service, February 16, 1999; Pacifica News Urgent Action—*"Democracy Now,"* February 15, 1999; *Project Underground, Drillbits & Tailings*, Vol. 4, No. 18/November 9 & No. 20/ December 11, 1999; *Houston Chronicle*, November 6, 1999; *The Independent* (London), October 26, 1999; *Financial Times* (London), October 26, 1999. Internet Resources: Project Underground: www.moles.org; Pacifica Radio's *Democracy Now!*: www.pacifica.org/programs/democracy_now/

1998 #11 CENSORED STORY
PRIVATE PRISON EXPANSION BECOMES BIG BUSINESS

Private prisons are one of the fastest growing industries in the United States. Under contract by the government to run jails and prisons, and paid a fixed sum per prisoner, firms operate as cheaply and efficiently as possible to insure a profit. This means lower wages for staff, no union, and fewer services for prisoners. Substandard diets, extreme over-crowding, and abuses by poorly trained personnel have all been documented as practices of this private business approach to incarceration.

The "need" for more prisons was created in the 1980s, say the authors, when many businesses in the United States decided to take their factories out of the country, seeking higher profits and lower wages. Most seriously hurt by these plant closures and layoffs were African Americans and semi-skilled workers in urban centers. Both a drug economy and the international prison industrial complex have filled the gaping economic hole left by the exodus of jobs from U.S. cities. Currently, 1.8 million people are behind bars in the United States. Many, who once made a living wage, are now making only 22 cents per hour behind prison walls.

For those who have invested in private prisons, prison labor is like a pot of gold. There are no strikes, no unions, no unemployment insurance, or workers' compensation. Prisoners can now be found doing data entry for Chevron, telephone reservations for TWA, raising hogs, shoveling manure, and sometimes making lingerie for Victoria's Secret.

Investment houses, construction companies, architects, and support services such as those that provide food, medical supplies, transportation, and furniture, all profit by prison expansion. The investment firm, Smith & Barney, is partial owner of a prison in Florida. American Express and General Electric have invested in private prison construction in Oklahoma and Tennessee. Communication giants such as AT&T, Sprint, and MCI are getting into the act as well, gouging prisoners with exorbitant rates for phone calls which are often six times the normal long distance charge.

With the transformations in the global economy that have occurred over the past two decades, wage decreases and standards for workers have suffered. Privatization of prisons contributes to this cycle as the prison industrial complex rapidly becomes a primary component of the U.S. economy.

SOURCES: Eve Goldberg & Linda Evans, "The Prison Industry and the Global Complex," *Turning the Tide*, Summer 1998.

COVERAGE 1999: The expansion of private prisons has become an increasing part of the American criminal justice system, yet the major U.S. media outlets have found the subject to be of little concern. There was only minor mention of private prisons if a new facility opened, or when a legal grievance was scheduled for trial.

The alternative press further expanded its investigation into private prisons by focusing in four major areas: the growth of the industry and the players involved, the privatization of juvenile detention centers and foster programs, the decline of human rights and conditions in private facilities, and the rise of the "new slavery" behind bars.

According to the *Progressive Populist*, billions of dollars are being spent each year on the construction of new private prisons while funds for crime prevention and rehabilitation continue to decrease. Four major corporations, says *North Coast Xpress*, have emerged as the big winners of private prison construction contracts including Corrections Corporation of America (CCA), Wackenhut Corporation, Correctional Services Corporation (CSC), and Cornell Corrections. The boards of directors of these companies include the chairman of major health care corporations, the executive director of The Rainbow Coalition, a board member of Knight-Ridder news service and the *Miami Herald*, and an administrator for the Washington, DC school system.

The *Progressive Populist* maintains that there is a "relatively new fad that has hit state governments—turning juvenile jails and foster programs over to private industry." This has led to "corruption and abuse, and lax oversight by the state governments that have entered into contracts with the for-profit companies." According to *Prison Legal News*, children have endured sexual and physical abuse, neglect, and even death while detained at private juvenile facilities.

Conditions continue to decline behind bars throughout the prison industry, and this is especially true of private prisons, according to Eric Bates in his *Nation* article concerning the growth of CCA. Minimal training and low guard wages increase the possibility of abuse while an emphasis on profits has caused the quality of health care and food provisions to reach an abysmal low. "[One] former guard explained how CCA got workers to take food from inmates to boost profits,"

says Bates. According to *In These Times*, the situation is no better in women's prisons. "The problem of rape and sexual assault is exacerbated in America's booming private for-profit prisons, where guards have minimal accountability to prisoners or the public." At the same time allegations of wrongful death and denial of healthcare are at an all time high.

Perhaps the most frightening aspect is the expanding use of prisons by corporations as sources of cheap or free labor. The storage and transportation of prisoners is itself profitable through the acquisition of lucrative government contracts at taxpayers' expense. Yet the use of prisoners as a slave workforce makes them doubly valuable. The private prison corporation can charge rent for the use of prison labor (or for providing the space) while corporations such as IBM, Nike, AT&T, and United Airlines get their work done for as little as 17¢ an hour. "Next to robots, corporate America can't imagine a better workforce... sub-minimum wages, no health benefits, no unions, no vacation," says the *American Prospect*. Daniel Harr in *Social Policy* maintains that at the same time for-profit prisons are "heavily invested in lobbying efforts to sponsor 'get tough on crime' legislation designed to place ever-increasing numbers of men and women behind bars for longer periods of time."

SOURCES: The *American Prospect*, September/October 1999; *In These Times*, December 27, 1999; The *Nation*, June 7, 1999; *North Coast Xpress*, Winter 1998/1999; *Prison Legal News*, January 1999;

Progressive Populist, November 1, 1999; *Social Policy*, Summer 1999; *Washington Free Press*, September/October 1999.

1998 #14 CENSORED STORY
POLITICAL CONTRIBUTIONS COMPROMISE AMERICA'S JUDICIAL SYSTEMS

America's justice system is being compromised by campaign contributions to judges from special interest groups and corporate Political Action Committees (PACs). Although campaign fundraising scandals have drawn new attention to the way moneyed interests buy political favors in Washington, many of these same donors operate unchecked in a different venue: the state courts. The cost of judicial races is rising at least as fast as that of either Congressional races or presidential campaigns, as candidates for the bench pay for sophisticated ads, polls, and consultants. A recent study by the California Commission on the Courts found that the cost of the average superior court race in the Los Angeles area has more than doubled every year, increasing 22-fold from 1976 to 1995.

Fueling these campaigns is an influx of money from the tobacco industry, casinos, insurance companies, doctors, and businesses. Other contributors include defense lawyers and trial lawyers, unions and, recently, the religious right. It adds up to a system of justice in which judges are compromised by the time they take the bench, and those who are perceived as unsympathetic to well-funded interest groups often end up simply kicked out of office.

The pleas from the legal community to regulate these contributions are being ignored. The American Bar Association, the American Judicature Society, and the Fund for Modern Courts have all recommended setting spending caps for candidates, putting limits on donations and providing free advertising. But effecting real changes is up to the states.

In 1996, the National Voting Rights Institute filed suit in Los Angeles on behalf of a coalition of civil rights groups, challenging private financing of judicial elections there. The group says that under the current system, money determines the outcome of judicial races, effectively shutting out those without sufficient means. *The Nation*'s coverage of this case illustrates the threat posed to our nation's judicial system by a campaign process gone amuck.

SOURCE: Sheila Kaplan, "The Buying of the Bench," *The Nation*, January 26, 1998.

COVERAGE 1999: During the past year, the U.S. media wrote extensively about campaign funding reform. States and special interest groups on both sides of the issue argued for and against campaign fund restrictions for local and national offices. However, little was mentioned about the effects of the election process and campaign funding on judges and the ultimate influence on their bench decisions.

The *Atlanta Journal-Constitution* exposed how cigarette companies use campaign contributions and court challenges to insure that their products do not come under the scrutiny of the Food and Drug Administration (FDA). The issue came to the Supreme Court after split decisions in the lower courts. A North Carolina U.S. District Court judge agreed with the FDA that cigarettes are essentially drug-delivery systems. However, a Virginia appeals court reversed that ruling stating that by ruling in favor of the FDA, tobacco could be banned, something Congress never intended. The U.S. Supreme Court has agreed to decide whether the FDA can regulate cigarettes. A ruling favoring the FDA could dramatically alter the way our government and society treat tobacco.

The American Bar Association, which sponsors the Model Code of Judicial Conduct adopted in most states, amended the code to call for limiting campaign contributions and disqualifying judges from any case involving contributors who gave large contributions. This is the first nation-wide step to address the problems inherent in judicial elections.

The *Washington Post* ran a story about how some federal appellate judges have ruled on cases involving companies in which they own stock. (It overlooked the fact, however, that state and local judges receive substantial campaign contributions from trial lawyers.) In Denver, one story exposed how campaign funding for judges created a mini-crisis in Cincinnati, Ohio, over a case involving Chiquita Banana. Three judges had to recuse themselves because of having received campaign funds from Chiquita. A fourth judge took the case, even

though she, too, had the same conflict of interest. Her explanation, "Such a removal encourages judge shopping and delays in getting cases resolved."

SOURCES: *Journal of Law and Economics*, University of Chicago Law School, April 1999; *Atlanta Journal-Constitution*, April 29, 1999; *Washington Post*, September 22, 1999.

1997 #4 CENSORED STORY
EXPOSING THE GLOBAL SURVEILLANCE SYSTEM

The ECHELON system, designed and coordinated by the U.S. National Security Agency (NSA), is one of the world's biggest, most closely held intelligence projects. Unlike many of the Cold War electronic spy systems, ECHELON is designed primarily to gather electronic transmissions from nonmilitary targets: governments, organizations, businesses, and individuals in virtually every country. The system works by indiscriminately intercepting very large quantities of communications and using computers to identify and extract messages of interest from the mass of unwanted ones. Computers at each secret station in the ECHELON network automatically search millions of messages for pre-programmed key words. For each message containing one of those key words, the computer automatically notes time and place of origin and interception. It also gives the message a four-digit code for future reference.

Computers that can automatically search through traffic for key words have existed since at least the 1970s, but the ECHELON system was designed by NSA to interconnect all these computers and allow the stations to function as components of an integrated whole. Using the ECHELON system, an agency in one country may automatically pick up information gathered elsewhere in the system.

ECHELON allows spy agencies to monitor public and private telephones, e-mail, and telex communication networks. It potentially affects every person communicating between (and sometimes within) countries anywhere in the world. The exposure of ECHELON occurred after New Zealand journalist Nicky Hager interviewed more than 50 people who work or have worked in intelligence and related fields. Materials leaked to Hager include precise information on where the spying is conducted, how the system works, the system's capabilities and shortcomings, and other details such as code names.

The potential abuses of and few restraints around the use of ECHELON have prompted other intelligence workers to come forward. In one example, a group of "highly placed intelligence operatives" from the British Government Communications Headquarters (GCHQ) came forward protesting what they regarded as "gross malpractice and negligence" within the establishments in which they operate, citing cases of GCHQ surveillance of charitable organizations such as Amnesty International and Christian Aid.

SOURCE: Nicky Hager, "Secret Power: Exposing the Global Surveillance System," *CovertAction Quarterly (CAQ)*, Winter 1996/1997.

COVERAGE 1999: Since Project Censored's 1998 yearbook, media exposure on the vast ECHELON system has grown, and public awareness of secret global surveillance has increased. Although mainstream media coverage on the issue has been moderate at best, interest in this secret spy network has been quite evident in alternative and foreign media since early 1998. Despite an overall low level of public awareness, ECHELON has been an object of concern for U.S. Representative Bob Barr who has endorsed ECHELON-focused Congressional hearings and has helped to pass an amendment protecting American rights to privacy.

Nicky Hager, New Zealand journalist and Project Censored source, was immensely successful in gaining ECHELON exposure through his 1996 publication, *Secret Power: New Zealand's Role in the International Spy Network*. Several current news sources quoted Hager's extensive investigation into the closely held NSA project. In early 1998, the disclosure of an official European Parliament report entitled "In Appraisal of Technologies of Political Control" sparked a widespread panic throughout Europe concerning ECHELON. "While the report did draw needed attention to ECHELON, it and subsequent European press coverage built ECHELON up into some super-elaborate system that can listen in on anyone at any time, which goes beyond what Nicky Hager wrote," stated a 1999 *Village Voice* article. Knowledge on the precise capabilities of ECHELON has yet to be made public.

Duncan Campbell, a British investigative journalist, prepared a report on ECHELON entitled, "Interception Capabilities 2000." The European Parliament's Science and Technology Options Assessment Panel (STOA) commissioned Campbell to uncover vital information about the ECHELON system because, stated STOA member Glyn Ford, "what is missing here is accountability, clear guidelines as to who they can listen to and under what circumstances these laws apply." According to Citizens for Overt Action, "The report details how intelligence agencies intercept Internet traffic and digital communications and includes screen shots of traffic analysis from NSA computer systems."

Campbell contends in his report that the ECHELON system targets the communications systems of known diplomats, criminals, and industrialists of interest to the intelligence community. The report charges that popular software programs, such as Lotus Notes and Web browsers, include a "back door" through which the NSA can gain entrance to an individual's personal information.

"Interception Capabilities 2000" also provides an account of a previously unknown secret international organization led by the FBI called International Law Enforcement Telecommunications Seminar (ILETS). ILETS is working on building back door wiretap capabilities into all forms of modern communication including satellite communications systems. The United States has never officially recognized ECHELON's existence, but dozens of reports over the past decade similar to "Interception Capabilities 2000" have revealed a maze-like system with ECHELON's capabilities.

Hager is quoted as saying, "ECHELON has a huge potential for violating privacy and for abuses of democracy.... Because it's so powerful and its operations are so secret there are no real constraints on agencies using it against any target the government chooses...[t]he use of intelligence services in these cases had nothing to do with national security, but everything to do with keeping tabs on critics."

Indeed, cases have been cited in a *St. Petersburg Times* article in which NSA is accused of using the ECHELON network to eavesdrop on Princess Diana and other high profile individuals and on institutions in order to steal proprietary secrets from European corporations to aid U.S.–based companies. According to the April 1999 article, a "former NSA employee appeared on German television last year and disclosed that the American government has spied on [a] German energy company" and then used the information to obtain a patent on the stolen idea. The former employee stated that the sale of the same company's products in the United States was later banned.

A *Washington Post* article contends that Congressional interest in the ECHELON system was heightened when Representative Porter J. Goss, chairman of the House Permanent Select Committee on Intelligence, asked the NSA for internal documents about its compliance with the 1978 Foreign Intelligence Surveillance Act (FISA). Goss felt that the NSA might have been too cautious in approving new surveillance programs. However, NSA claimed attorney-client privilege and declined his request. This caused significant congressional unrest and prompted Goss to withhold NSA's budget. According to the Post article, "Barr immediately joined the dispute from the opposite flank, suggesting that the NSA had refused Goss's request because it was violating Americans' privacy by indiscriminately vacuuming up communications."

An article in the *Los Angeles Times*, acknowledging Barr's strong conservative views (he was a supporter of the Clinton impeachment hearings), stated, "Barr is apparently such a foe of the federal government that he is taking on the federal intelligence agencies, organizations not accustomed to being challenged by Republicans." Regardless of his politics, which has kept some strong civil liberties groups from supporting his ECHELON endeavors, the congressman played an important role in informing the American public about the potential dangers of the unregulated spy system.

On May 17, 1999, Barr was successful in amending the Intelligence Reauthorization Act, requiring U.S. intelligence agencies to report to Congress on the legal standards justifying surveillance activities directed at U.S. citizens. In August, Congress released a press release stating that Barr and colleague Burton agreed to hold hearings on government surveillance programs.

October 21, 1999, was the first annual "Jam ECHELON Day" in which e-mail activists banded together in an effort to overload ECHELON databases. Organizers urged users to send as many messages as possible containing words such as "bomb" and "assassinate" in an attempt to overload NSA's supercomputers. These "hactivists" were responsible for the first mass protest using electronic mail as the primary weapon.

The sheer magnitude of such a spy network has been of deep concern to many and was actually used by the producers of the major motion picture *Enemy of the State*. The film portrayed the NSA as an out-of-control agency listening in on unwitting citizens. Concerned with real-life implications, the *Washington Post* stated, "As the nation begins a new century, congressional hearings to redefine the agency's boundaries are the best way to prevent life from imitating art." A civil liberties group filed a lawsuit against the NSA on December 3, 1999, seeking information about ECHELON's network.

SOURCES: "ECHELON Listens Around the World," *St. Petersburg Times*, April 18, 1999; Niall McKay, "Spying on the Skies," Citizens for Overt Action, May 10, 1999; "The Cutting Edge," *Los Angeles Times*, August 16, 1999; "Spy in the Sky," *San Diego Tribune*, October 17, 1999; "Loud and Clear," The *Washington Post*, November 14, 1999; "ACLU Plans to Observe ECHELON Global Spy Network Online," *Newsbytes*, November 16, 1999. Internet Resources: www.ECHELON-watch.org; www.villagevoice.com

THIS MODERN WORLD

by TOM TOMORROW

IT'S TIME FOR YET ANOTHER CABLE TV *CELEBRITY BIOGRAPHY!* FIRST, WE GLIMPSE THE DIFFICULT EARLY YEARS...

> SPARKY NEVER DID REALLY FIT IN AROUND HERE.

> HE WAS AN ODD ONE, THAT PENGUIN. ALWAYS COMPLAINING.

> AND WHAT WAS THE DEAL WITH THOSE *SHADES,* ANYWAY?

...THEN, THE METEORIC RISE TO STARDOM...

> --AND WHEN *THE WRATH OF SPARKY* WAS PUBLISHED, WE MUST HAVE BEEN SELLING TWO OR THREE COPIES A *WEEK!* I'D NEVER SEEN ANYTHING *LIKE* IT!

> AT LEAST, UM, IN TERMS OF OBSCURE ALTERNATIVE WEEKLY CARTOON COMPILATIONS.

> SO AM I GONNA BE ON TV?

Welcome to Your Friendly Neighborhood **CORPORATE BOOKSTORE**™

SERVING YOUR NEEDS WITH CENTRALIZED EFFICIENCY SINCE 1997

STAR WARS DIET PLAN

STAR WARS GUIDE TO BETTER SEX

STAR WARS EXERCISE PLAN

$00.00

HELLO MAY I HELP YOU?

...FOLLOWED, OF COURSE, BY THE INEVITABLE *DOWNWARD SPIRAL.*

> HEY! ONE OF YOU HO'S GET ME SOME MORE FRESH HERRING--AND I MEAN *NOW!*

> I'M SPARKY THE *WONDER PENGUIN,* DAMMIT!

(A RE-ENACTMENT)

FINALLY, WE LEARN OF EITHER THE STAR'S UNTIMELY *DEMISE*--OR THEIR UPLIFTING ROAD TO *REDEMPTION...*

> --BUT I SURE DIDN'T FEEL WONDERFUL *INSIDE*--UNTIL I FOUND *JESUS,* THAT IS.

> I'VE BEEN DOING SOME CARTOONS FOR THE *CHURCH BULLETIN,* YOU KNOW! THEY'RE VERY POPULAR WITH THE *CONGREGATION!*

> I'M MUCH HAPPIER NOW. REALLY.

GOD BLESS THIS MESS

TOM TOMORROW© 9-1-99 ... tomorrow@well.com ... www.thismodernworld.com

CHAPTER 3

News Abuse of 1999

BY COREY HALE. Research and editing assistance from Amy Danziger; administrative assistance from Katie Anderson and Jennifer Mathis. Special thanks to Elizabeth Holmes for help in the creation of the new chapter title.

Previously titled "Junk Food News," this chapter switches focus to those overreported news stories that fill our media (and minds) with fluff or "fat" and take attention away from the more substantial stories that comprise the rest of the book. This process is "news abuse."

Thanks to the members of the Organization of News Ombudsmen who were asked to rate their choices for the most obsessively overreported stories of the year.

1. Tinky Winky and Jerry Falwell's Theory on this Purple Teletubby
2. Pokémon
3. Y2K
4. Millennium
5. Pamela Lee Anderson's Breasts
6. *Star Wars*
7. Clinton—The Clinton's Search for a House; Monica Searches for an Apartment; the Release of Monica's Book; Hillary's Side of the Story Interview.
8. Columbine/Teen Shootings; Killer Classmates; Marilyn Manson Delays Video Release
9. John F. Kennedy, Jr.
10. George W. Bush and Cocaine

When the brainstorming began for this year's News Abuse chapter, no one needed to have actually owned a TV, subscribed to a mainstream newspaper, or listened to a mainstream radio station in order to have known about the stories that won the dubious honor of becoming a part of this year's edition of News Abuse (NA).

These awards do not negate the overabundance of coverage these stories received in the last year in mainstream media. What the News Abuse awards succinctly illustrate is how stories that are often irrelevant, inflammatory, or simply self-serving information conduits can insinuate themselves into the fabric of our daily existence. Once stories reach the heights that the top 10 choices for this year have, how plugged-in you are has become all but irrelevant.

One example of a self-serving new story is the story about Jerry Falwell's fixation with the purple star of Teletubby fame, Tinky Winky. Tinky was pinpointed by Falwell as a menace to our social fabric, and he viewed the gender neutral character as the deliverer of subversive messages to children, influencing them to accept homosexuality. According to Falwell, Tinky's purpleness, his purse, and of course, the triangle headpiece, are clear signs of homosexuality. Indeed, malice on the part of a national figure toward a children's television character is news, but should not reach the sensationalized frenzy of a major mainstream news story.

When a story reaches the sensationalism boiling point, and however newsworthy an issue's roots may have been, the story can deteriorate from genuine to pulp to infotainment. These stories create the macabre manifestation of voyeurism impersonating national dialogue. As News Abuse stories reach mythical proportions they insinuate themselves into the social conversation, to the exclusion of thousands of stories carrying the weight of real news.

This phenomenon is poignantly illustrated by the Columbine killings story. When we return to the tragic scene in Littleton for the cleanup and the first day back, and the funerals, and the first football game, and the last football game, it becomes News Abuse. Readers, viewers, and other news consumers become addicted to the endless stories of terror and grief. Television news ran the same footage, over and over again, for weeks, milking every bit of sensationalism out of the tragic shooting spree and ensuing deaths of the young teens. Other stories of teen shootings were dredged up to further drag out the story. The abuse of the media sent every news outlet to Littleton while failing to report other news of daily importance.

Not willing to stop the exploitation of the Littleton teens and their parents, media also gave free air time to celebrities, however remotely connected with the case they might be. One high-profile press release came from Marilyn Manson, who used it as a PR opportunity to promote his new violent music video, announcing he would delay it out of respect for the Columbine victims. Not willing to be outdone, *Buffy the Vampire Slayer* star Seth Green, bothered that the Columbine shootings focused criticism on violence in entertainment, said, "I think that's the wrong way to go. You can have 10,000 kids watch *Natural Born Killers*, and only one or two are going to go shoot people...." Nice spin, Seth.

It seems our list is never complete without the requisite blockbuster movie release. This year's production, *Star Wars*, made a valiant effort at becoming the movie release promotion of all time. Not only did we get to hear about the new *Star Wars* movie, but we got to hear about its producer, his entire list of works, the early editions of *Star Wars*, the stars of *Star Wars*, where they are now, the making of *Star Wars*, and the expansion of Lucas Film Industries, and Industrial Lights and Magic. Perhaps the most uproarious speculation of all was the discussion of a possible economic collapse, as predictions warned of a high worker absenteeism on the film's opening day. Of course, this story would not have been complete without the in-depth coverage of the waiting lines, who was in them, how long they had been there, and how many times they had gone to see the movie. The only question we are left with is, What were you doing the day *Star Wars* was released?

More somber, but no less fetishized, was the coverage given to the plane crash of John F. Kennedy, Jr. Since a generation of people remember where they were the day President John F. Kennedy was assassinated, many viewers took it to heart when the son they had watched grow up disappeared in a mysterious plane crash. Mainstream media clutched this story to its metaphorical bosom, capitalizing on the death of this beloved celebrity, just as they had with the death of Lady Di. Media unscrupulously gorged on historical footage, falling over themselves in their frenzy to get JFK, Jr.'s picture on their magazine covers, inflicting endless map drawings of the Vineyard upon audiences.

This obsessive coverage was not limited to the United States. In war-torn Iraq, where the high death toll from the bombing and sanctions has affected everyone's families, a woman approached a U.S. journalist. "When you get back to America, please send a letter to the Kennedy family saying a woman in Iraq is very sorry to hear of their loss." How many Americans are sending sympathy cards to the millions of grieving Iraqi families? Then again, they were not all over the news.

The eventual discovery of the wreckage of JFK, Jr.'s plane did little to alleviate the crush of Kennedy information. Instead, the press used each new release of information as a further opportunity for exploitation and a reason to discuss Kennedy's personal finances, his prenuptial agreement, and the debate over whether the recipients of his money were worthy.

At Project Censored headquarters, we are well aware of the paradox created with the News Abuse chapter, as we select overcovered stories for the dubious honor of a place in our NA Top Ten, ambivalently giving them just a bit more coverage. As if to exemplify this quandary, in the number seven spot, down from its number one spot in last year's *Censored 1999* Junk Food News List, we again find President Clinton and his entourage of faithful followers. Embraced by the press, Clinton's sex life continued to be the topic of conversation with the release of Monica Lewinsky's book, and prominent interviews of both her and Hillary Clinton, for their respective sides of the story.

The endless prattling about Clinton's sex life was supplemented this year by an enthralling account of the Clinton's hunt for a house, and Monica's hunt for an apartment. A story that did not make it into the Top Ten is Hillary's run for Senate, which, of course, was primarily a sidebar of the story of the Clinton's search for real estate.

Coverage of the private lives of politicians did not stop with the Kennedys and the Clintons. Presidential candidate George W. Bush and his alleged use of cocaine was an irrepressible NA story throughout 1999. The debate raged over whether he used seven, or fifteen, years ago, and whether he was a better man than Clinton for being honest about his use, or non-use. The mainstream press deemed this an appropriate measure of his ability to be president, rather than discuss his historical ties to the Savings & Loan scandals, the media, or discuss the fact that the same man, as Texas governor, has been

THIS MODERN WORLD  by TOM TOMORROW

especially ruthless and unforgiving to drug convicts in Texas. That shining example of hypocrisy also unfortunately escaped much of the media. This hashing-over of politicians' private lives is out of control.

We may just have to finally acknowledge that politicians are human and get on with it. It hardly matters what they stand for; we all know the real issues here are promiscuity, drug use, and personality.

Then there was Pokémon. This newest craze in a long line of crazes has succeeded in capturing more airtime than two other airtime monopolizers, the Furbies and the Beanie Babies. We are sure that this had some deep, meaningful impact on the manufacturers of these fad toys, but we are unclear as to its national importance, especially in relation to the many undiscovered or ignored stories about *real* news events around the nation and the world.

Coming in at our number five NA spot are Pamela Lee Anderson's breasts. Over the span of only a few years we have been subjected to the intimate details of her marriage to Tommy Lee, his incarceration for domestic violence, their eventual breakup, and their much touted reconciliation. What the nation's media took most to heart, however, was the news of her breast reduction. What a relief it was to hear that she and Tommy would be renewing their vows after the surgery, this time in the nude.

Ending on a somewhat ambiguous note, our last two stories are similar in content, but have their own idiosyncratic natures. By the time this book is released, the consequences (if any) of Y2K, and the impending millennium, will already have been revealed. For now the media satisfies its gluttonous appetite for calamity by maintaining a voracious stranglehold on news that is not news, exploring the possibilities of a catastrophic outcome, based on an arguably arbitrary date set 2,000 years ago. The predictions for the mil-

lennium range from those of apocalyptic proportions, volcanic eruptions, earthquakes, and tidal waves, to the prophesy of the second coming of Jesus Christ. The millennium has become one giant cash cow, as companies see dollar signs and fan the flames of fear inspired by mainstream media's extemporaneous predetermination.

The current barrage of coverage regarding Y2K is dramatically underscored by its utter lack of coverage in the previous decade, during which time scientists vainly attempted to draw attention to this potential problem. When Y2K became a trend and a selling point, then the discussion was reared its head regarding an impending crisis.

Other stories under consideration for News Abuse included the World Wrestling Federation (WWF) and Jesse "The Body" Ventura; the proliferation of stories of multiple births; Bill Gates and Microsoft; the Dow Jones hitting 10,000; and the weather, including cyclones, hurricanes, earthquakes, El Niño, and El Niña. This year we also had a list of previous Junk Food title holders, including O. J., the ever present Viagra, JonBenet Ramsey, the Jenny Jones murder trial, and Jerry Springer. Stories that were nominated by our ombudsman judges but did not receive enough votes to get into the Top Ten were the Egypt Air and Swiss Air crashes; *The Blair Witch Project*; and Warren Beatty for President.

Finally, the following comments were submitted from individual ombudsmen in response to our questionnaire.

CARL JENSEN, founder of Project Censored: It is a wonder the United States survived 1999. Employees shirked work to sit out on sidewalks to purchase over-priced tickets to see Star Wars; Bill Gates, a.k.a. the anti-Christ, monopolized the computer industry and threatened to take over all electronic communications; Jesse "The Body" Ventura inspired wrestlers, boxers, and other extreme sports figures to take over the political process; Viagra aroused thousands of over-sexed males to attack women; and Y2K threatened to end life as we know it.

Fortunately we survived all the News Abuse. But we did not learn much about the real problems that plagued America—including the 25 critical issues raised in this book.

However, we will not have to worry about the typical junk food news in the year 2000. The news media in 2000 will be dominated by the most apocalyptic of all News Abuse—the quadrennial explosion of political News Abuse. The media will loudly decry the trivialization of the presidential election and the influence of money but then go on to portray it as an expensive horse race, characterized by endless polls, political scandals, and unending 20-second television sound bites.

EMERSON STONE, columnist at *News Practices* and *The Communicator Magazine*: On JonBenet Ramsey: Ye Gads! Can't we ever shuck this tawdry unexceptional schlock? And on air crashes: Unending coverage. Twenty years ago such crashes got a day or two in news and were gone. Now, we must learn about every grief counselor, every caregiver, every non-denominational service, every flower wreath floated out to sea, every... But why do I go on?

THIS MODERN WORLD

by TOM TOMORROW

WELCOME TO "*WHO WANTS TO BE A BILLIONAIRE!*" OUR FIRST CONTESTANT IS ONE OF THE THREE FACELESS BUREAUCRATS WHO SIT ON THE WORLD TRADE ORGANIZATION'S *RULING TRIBUNAL*--WEARING A DISGUISE TO PRESERVE HIS *ANONYMITY*, OF COURSE!

LET'S GET STARTED, ANONYMOUS BUREAUCRAT! FOR $100, WERE THE PROTESTERS IN SEATTLE--

--(A) A BUNCH OF KNOW-NOTHING, ANTI-CAPITALIST SUBVERSIVES WHO PROVE THE NEED FOR A NEW SEDITION ACT--

--OR (B) AMERICAN CITIZENS CONCERNED ABOUT THE ANTI-DEMOCRATIC EFFECTS OF A SECRETIVE GLOBAL BODY EMPOWERED TO OVERRULE ANY NATION'S LAWS IN THE NAME OF FREE TRADE?

WELL, BILL--THE ANSWER IS CLEARLY (A)!

FINAL ANSWER?

YES, FINAL ANSWER. BUT BEFORE WE GO ANY FURTHER, I'M GOING TO HAVE TO ASK YOU TO DECLARE ME THE *WINNER* AND GIVE ME THE BILLION DOLLARS.

UM--THAT'S NOT REALLY HOW THE RULES OF THE GAME ARE SET UP--

THE W.T.O. DOESN'T CARE ABOUT YOUR LITTLE RULES! THE W.T.O. MAKES ITS *OWN* RULES--AND THEY'RE *NOT* SUBJECT TO APPEAL! YOU KNOW THAT, YOU SCHMUCK-- YOU SIGNED THE TREATY!

NOW HAND OVER THE DAMN CHECK-- OR FACE HARSH SANCTIONS FOR EXPROPRIATING MY POTENTIAL *PROFITS!*

WELL, FOLKS--IT LOOKS LIKE WE'VE GOT A *WINNER!* TUNE IN NEXT TIME--WHEN OUR CONTESTANT WILL BE *RALPH NADER!*

I'VE GOT A FEELING *HE'LL* FIND OUR GAME A LITTLE MORE ... CHALLENGING...

PAY TO THE ORDER OF: ANONYMOUS BUREAUCRAT ONE BILLION DOLLARS

TOM TOMORROW ©12-8-99 ... tomorrow@well.com ... www.thismodernworld.com

CHAPTER 4

Is the Press Really Free?

We asked a panel of four media activists and academics to answer the question, "Is the press really free in the United States?" Carl Jensen, founder of Project Censored, Janine Jackson with Fairness and Accuracy in Reporting (FAIR), Justin Lewis from University of Massachusetts, and Robin Andersen from Fordham University each approached this issue from a different perspective.

Who is Killing the Press?
BY ROBIN ANDERSEN

If court were about to convene and if this were the trial of the century to find the culprit, who would be charged with the crime of killing the press? There are many suspects. In fact, the evidence suggests it is not a single crime. Narrowing down the charges would be difficult, but murder is certainly at the top of the list. There are those who have killed individual stories, stories that never got a chance to lead a full life in the public sphere. Investigative reporters have also been struck down, robbed of their pro-fessional dignity, and sometimes even their livelihoods. They were never allowed to expose details, criticize corporate malfeasance, or affect public policy debates. Clearly a number of charges will have to be made, but a clever prosecutor will quickly understand that some suspects have to be tried jointly; separate convictions would fail. While much evidence has been amassed, in many cases a smoking gun has not been recovered. Part of the prosecution's team will point to a conspiracy. Others will argue that these misdeeds would not have occurred outside a sinister subculture of greed, profit margins, and the willingness to deceive.

Finding witnesses will sometimes pose a problem for the people's case. Some are willing to testify; others are not. Any astute prosecutor would call the most credible and willing witnesses first. Jane Akre and Steve Wilson would tell their story under oath, the one they were not able to tell on the Fox TV station in Florida about Monsanto and bovine growth hormone. The story was killed, even after over 80 attempts to revive it with rewrites. They will argue on the stand that public safety is still under threat in Florida and that the people's right to know has suffered a serious blow. A hostile witness for the prosecution would be called; the new manager hired to make sure the story would never see the light of day. Would he admit under oath what he said to the journalists?: "We paid $3 billion for these television stations. We'll decide what the news is. The news is what we say it is" (Peter Phillips & Project Censored, 1999). And if he did go on the stand, would he be featured in live coverage of the trial, or in a ratings-grabbing tabloid story with the footage slowed into a grainy-gray, unsavory criminalized depiction? Would the same production gimmicks used to grab ratings and distract the public from the real censored news be used to criminalize this witness like all those scary suspects we see on nightly broadcasts?

In showing a "pattern and practice" to the court, the fearless prosecutor would call as her next witness, the tough investigative reporter, Brian Ross from ABC News. Known for his dramatic, pulsating reports, he would be asked to go on record with his story about cases of child sexual assault at Disney World, a story killed by ABC News president David Westin. Westin would be questioned about his real motives for killing the story. Was he afraid of Disney, ABC's parent company? After all, if he told Ross to go ahead with the story, why did he kill it later? Ross's longtime producer Rhonda Schwartz might also be called to counter claims that the story was flawed, inaccurate, or unimportant. She had become upset by the amount of evidence they had found at Disney's theme park, and Disney's refusal to cooperate with law enforcement and other child protection agencies. After all, she has a child of her own. But Westin, underscoring his claim that the story was flawed, would defend his decision confirming that he does not succumb to corporate pressures: "There's a large moat built around any news organization. If anybody starts messing with it, op-ed pieces start being written, columns, and work [is] leaked" (Stevens, 1998). "But isn't that exactly what has happened here?" the prosecutor might ask on cross-examination.

It will be up to the jury to decide the credibility of witnesses for the defense. Would they believe David Westin and blame the journalists for constructing a bad, sensationalized story? After all, there is no smoking memo. There rarely is.

But in a dramatic turn of events, the prosecution might decide that the newsroom is not really the scene of the crime. Instead, she would submit into evidence images of revolving doors showing members of the board of directors of Fortune 1000 companies going in and out of the newly decorated corporate conference rooms of the global media mega-corporations. She would submit corporate financial statements, consolidation and synergy profit projections, and merger agreements. She would call new witnesses in the ABC case, this time Michael Eisner, CEO of Disney, ABC's parent company. She would ask him what he meant when he said on September 29, 1998, on National Public Radio's *Fresh Air*, "I would prefer ABC not cover Disney...I think it's inappropriate for Disney to be covered by Disney. By and large, the way you avoid conflict of interest is to, as best you can, not cover yourself...." The prosecutor's follow-up would be tense and pointed, "But what about the ABC special on the 25th anniversary of Disney World? Isn't that covering Disney?" She might also call ABC News's senior VP for editorial quality, Richard Wald, and ask him about the statements he made in October of 1997, at a panel discussion at Columbia University titled,"News for Sale? Profits vs. the Press." When asked about the potential for a network to censor itself when it comes to producing tough stories on its parent company, his response was described by *Brill's Content* as vehement: "We do not do that. There is no instance in which we have done that. There will be no instance in which we will do that.... We do not play around with the integrity of the central question of our lives, which is to report fully and fairly what we know" (Stevens, 1998). But, the prosecutor

might quip, "you seem to have done it now!" Eisner would be recalled. This time the prosecutor would take off the kid gloves and demand, "Isn't it true then, that you are willing to censor the press, ignore the people's right to know and flaunt your First Amendment guarantees, all in order to increase your precious corporate bottom line!" At this point, reporters will dash out of the courtroom, rushing to be the first with the biggest headline, "Prosecution Accuses Corporate Chieftains of Killing Real News for Profits."

Or would they?

Would this dramatic revelation in the trial of the century finally result in hard-hitting news coverage, the type of coverage that would point out what's at stake for the public interest when yet another megamerger and media business deal is struck? Could the press be revived? Maybe it's not a case of homicide yet.

If Tom Brokaw were called to the stand and asked to report on the latest, biggest merger, the Viacom/CBS deal, a deal that creates the world's second largest media corporation, worth $80 billion, and a vertically integrated company that controls two TV networks and reaches more than 35 percent of the national audience with their stations, he would probably repeat what he said on NBC TV (September 7, 1999): "What does that mean for the average viewer? Well, probably not very much." Maybe if the people sent out their most ingenious, dogged investigator to find expert witnesses and credible researchers, they would call next Jim Naureckas, editor of

Extra! and *Extra!Update*. He would, no doubt, testify that Tom Brokaw's comments were consistent with evidence he discovered, that overall, the news coverage of the Viacom/CBS deal "skirted issues that might cast the merger in a bad light" (*Extra!Update*, October 1999). Such testimony might convince the jury that the victim is terminal; the press is dying.

How would the people's case be made when such vertical integration is not in the public's interest and poses a lethal threat to the press? Would the Viacom/CBS deal mean the same thing for CBS News that Disney ownership means for ABC News—that the corporate interests of the parent company will not be criticized? Michael Eisner would be recalled and asked about the Disney requirement that anyone under contract with them get clearance from corporate public relations before talking to the press about any Disney projects. Eisner would probably return, "no comment," and a death knell for the free press would be heard in the courtroom.

Detectives would deliver a subpoena to Viacom chairman Sumner Redstone, and the prosecutor would demand that he explain his statement that news organizations should not be unnecessarily offensive to foreign governments. He would probably explain how such coverage would be bad for business: "There are 3 billion people in Asia and 2 billion of them are in the MTV generation. That's who we're after" (Hentoff, 1999). A good prosecutor would ask, "Is that why you went to China with Jack Welch, chairman of General Electric (which owns NBC) and Gerald Levin, chairman of Time Warner, who invited you to a global forum celebrating the 50th anniversary of China's Communist party, to open markets in China, too? Did you know Mr. Levin refused to meet with human rights representatives before the conference, and that Amnesty International documented 34 prisoner executions before the celebration?"

Xiao Qiang, executive director of New York–based Human Rights in China, would testify that every time "constructive engagement" occurred, increasing trade with China, repression in China increased as a result (Hentoff, 1999). But there is little coverage of China, and even less critical coverage of the consequences for Chinese and U.S. workers if China enters the World Trade Organization. With corporate media CEOs joining over 300 of the world's foremost corporate leaders to increase trade and expand global corporate holdings, how can corporate news organizations be critical of global business practices?

To make the people's case, the jury would be shown *The Insider*, a film illustrating how difficult it is to get a story on TV about the effects and extent of corporate power. In fact, the prosecutor might ask the jury to wonder why the point has to be made by a fictionalized feature film?

The prosecutor would recall Sumner Redstone and ask him, "Even though Viacom is willing to overlook abuses and do business with China, will you allow CBS to cover China without fear or favor?

Could CBS News expose the exploitation of Chinese workers and the environmental destruction taking place?" Redstone may take the Fifth, or offer "no comment." He might even testify under oath that he would not tell editors and news managers what to say or not say.

Redstone's comments might cause the people's case to suffer a setback, but a clever assistant DA would identify another assailant attacking the press. He'd call new witnesses. A number of journalists, former journalists, and even researchers would be asked about the dreaded, rapidly growing virus infiltrating the very heart of the press—self-censorship. The virus is hard to detect, but antibodies can be traced to those who were exposed and are willing to tell their stories. The people would call former top CBS producer Richard Cohen to ask how the virus can be detected. He would testify that the boundaries of acceptable reporting are implicitly defined: "If you know that they really don't want certain kinds of stories at the top, you're not going to do those kinds of stories" (Baker and Sanders, *Fear and Favor in the Newsroom*, 1997).

But there is another guilty party responsible for media concentration, that 2,000-pound gorilla sitting on top of the press. If President Clinton were asked to testify as to his whereabouts on February 8, 1996, he would have to admit he was signing the Telecommunications Act. He is certainly not the only government official responsible for the megacorporate media that this act created. In fact, it was the Republican Congress that invited the industry into the backrooms to forge the bill, and the assistant prosecutor wants to subpoena the subcommittee, but it's considered too politically risky. Instead, they play a segment from *Nightline* that introduced the bill to the public: "It's possibly the most important communications bill in history, and here's what the networks had to say about it. NBC said, 'No comment.' ABC suggested that we talk to CBS, who told us 'No comment.' And Fox? They said, 'No comment.'" The bill allows a single company to own TV stations that reach as many as 35 percent of the nation's households—the previous limit was 25 percent. For the first time, TV networks can also own cable systems; and existing networks can begin new affiliate networks.

The People will make the case that radio became the biggest victim when national limits on station ownership were lifted. They will submit into evidence the ledgers on the 4000 stations that have changed owners since the 1996 law. They will call the CEO of Clear Channel Communication and ask about the buyout of AMFM, the largest radio acquisition in history: "And how many stations do you own now, 830? Is there room for community programming in this world of radio centralization? To answer the question she will call Joe Marshall, volunteer host of the community call-in program *Street Soldiers*, and founder of the Omega Boys Club. On the air at KMEL-FM in San Francisco since 1992, the program reaches out to young people living in violence-prone, under-served communities, offering a forum on everything from drugs and gangs to teen pregnancy. The prosecution will ask, "And were you taken off the air at the flagship station KMEL, even though you reach half a million youth nationwide?" He will answer, "Yes, we remain in 40 small and medium markets, but we are blocked from the larger urban FM stations that form the bulk of our listenership." But he will add, "We are petitioning the FCC." Maybe there is hope for revival of the press.

In another surprise move to counter defense strategies, the prosecution would add another charge to this list: reckless endangerment. They would call Mark H. Willes, former publisher of the *Los Angeles Times*, as an unfriendly witness for the People. The prosecutor would ask, "Is it true that when you started at the *Times* you had been a vice chairman at General Mills? And is it true that you quickly acquired the nickname Captain Crunch and the Cereal Killers for all the cuts you made to the news budget? And do you admit to saying that you were going to take a bazooka to the sacred wall that separates editorial judgment and practices from advertising and marketing departments?" Feeling uneasy, he might admit, "Yes, it's all true. But we increased advertising revenue and profit margins, by practicing 'entrepreneurial creativity!'"

The next witness would be Willes's hand-picked successor Kathryn M. Downing, the current publisher of the *Times*, a person with no newspaper background. Offered into evidence will be the 164-page single-issue edition of the *Times' Sunday Magazine* (October 10, 1999), all about the opening of the Staples Center sports arena. The alternative paper *New Times* revealed that the issue was a profit sharing venture with the Staples Center itself. The *Times* is one of the "founding partners," and the paper shared the magazine's advertising profit with the center. The prosecution will enter into the record the testimony of a subscriber to the *Los Angeles Times* who tells the court that it was very hard to distinguish between what was editorial copy written by journalists and what was advertising content. Asked if she will resign over the controversy, even admitting that she has a "fundamental misunderstanding" of editorial principles, Downing will answer adamantly, "No" (Barringer, 1999a).

Speaking on tape behind a screen with voices digitized so as not to be recognized, two high-ranking *Times* editors will testify that business executives continue to come to the news side with possible projects, and a daily editorial feature titled, "Stories that Shaped the Century," had its genesis in the advertising department (Barringer, 1999b).

At this point, the court would be filled with 300 editorial staff members from the *Los Angeles Times* carrying a petition that states the financial deal with the Staples Center compromises the paper's integrity and editorial heritage. Portions of the petition would be entered into the court record, "As journalists at the *Los Angeles Times*, we are appalled by the paper entering into hidden financial partnerships on editorial products with the subject we're writing about." They would demand that the wall separating editorial judgment from advertising concerns be rebuilt and the dying press would start to breath again.

The tenacious prosecutor would stay up all night to work on her summation. Like her courageous fictional counterparts on the hour-long crime dramas who prove to the viewing public every night that justice is done and that truth is revealed in America, she would make the People's case. Having become an expert on the absolute necessity of a thriving free press in a healthy democracy, she would rest the People's case with these words: "And so ladies and gentlemen of the jury, it's time to decide if the defendants are guilty of killing the press, or guilty of the lesser charges of attempted murder and reckless endangerment. It's up to you to decide. And if they are guilty, it's up to all of us to do something about it."

REFERENCES

Felicity Barringer, "Day of Contrition at the *Los Angeles Times*," *New York Times* (October 29, 1999a: C2.

Felicity Barringer, "After a News-Ad Clash, a 'Wall' May Go Up Again At the *Los Angeles Times*," *New York Times*, November 1, 1999b: C19.

Randy Baker and Beth Sanders, *Fear and Favor in the Newsroom*, 1997.

Nat Hentoff, "Blood on the CEOs Profits," *Village Voice*, November 23, 1999: 43.

Peter Phillips & Project Censored, *Censored 1999: The News that Didn't Make the News* (New York: Seven Stories Press, 1999): 154.

Elizabeth Lesly Stevens, "mouse-ke-fear," *Brill's Content*, December 1998: 94–103.

Objectivity and the Limits of Press Freedom
BY JUSTIN LEWIS

What does it mean to talk about a free press? In spite of the importance of the concept in the history of journalism, this question is rarely asked. Once we pose such a question, two things become clear. First, freedom is a contingent rather than an absolute term.[1] The meaning of freedom is dependent upon specific forms of limitation, restriction and containment from which one is free. A poor person living in a pure market economy might be free from government, but this same liberty will make him less free from the restrictions of poverty and disease than his counterpart in, say, a Scandinavian-style economy where the government provides a range of services for citizens regardless of ability to pay.

Second, despite well-meaning utopian sentiments to the contrary (such as "no one is free when others are repressed"), there are many ways in which freedom for some will rely upon restrictions for others. The freedom of the Disney corporation or Time Warner to maximize profits is, in this sense, in direct conflict with the freedom of their employees to protect and improve their standards of living. Similarly, the freedom to report on the lives of the rich and famous will mean a certain decrease in the freedoms enjoyed by the rich and famous.

These are hardly obscure, philosophical points, and yet we live in a culture where words like freedom or liberty are routinely banded about without qualification—as if we all agreed what it is that we want to be free of and all stood to gain from having more of it (whatever "it" might be). In the United States, the word "freedom" has enormous power but very little innocence. Its dominant meaning tends to reflect a corporate set of interests: thus the freedom of the press is generally signified as freedom from government restriction or regulation, while the constraints of a corporate, advertising-based system tend to be ignored. Nonetheless, as Project Censored has demonstrated over many years, a commercial, ad-based system of news production is likely to suppress a whole range of news stories, notably those that do not suit specific or general business interests.[2]

Just as there is no pure or absolute freedom, there is no absolute freedom of the press. The best we can do, in this instance, is to prioritize a range of freedoms and to say which freedoms we regard as important.[3] Thus we might say that the freedom to report truthful information is more important than the freedom to report irrelevancies and lies. Or that the press should be free to report those stories that do not reflect the interests of the wealthy and powerful. Such freedoms, if we pursue them, may fly in the face of other freedoms, such as the freedom of media corporations to enjoy

unrestricted growth.[4] Either way, discussions of freedom of the press have little meaning in any vague abstract sense. It is more useful, I would argue, to consider the question in relation to specific freedoms and the more significant structures of constraint in the contemporary media system.

The restrictions of a corporate media system have been well documented by scholars like Edward Herman and Robert McChesney, and I will not elaborate upon them here. Suffice to say that many of these restrictions often have very little to do with the kind of mass market populism often bemoaned as causing the decline of "serious" journalism. Most of the neglected stories that Project Censored has sought to bring to wider attention are not ignored because they would be seen as unpopular or dull—they are ignored because the various elites who define news frameworks would rather tell a different set of stories. So, for example, PBS's *NewsHour*—which could hardly be accused of appealing to popular taste—is generally as likely to ignore Project Censored stories as ABC or CBS. Conversely, the "horse race" coverage that dominates U.S. politics persists, even though it is regarded by most people as neither informative nor interesting. In short, we cannot blame the omission of important stories on the predilections of viewers and readers.

Simply put, the ownership and control of news media by an increasingly small and select group of business owners is bound to restrict the kinds of stories that get widely reported. But journalists are also constrained by customs and practices that have little to do with their views (which tend, like other members of a professional class, to be liberal on civil liberties issue and conservative on fiscal or spending issues) or the more pervasive conservative ideology of someone like Rupert Murdoch. Indeed, one of the most important structural factors that limits the news information system—and that makes Project Censored so necessary—is the notion of objectivity itself.

Since objectivity is a fairly uncontested term like freedom, most people are likely to claim some form of allegiance to it. Still, this may seem an odd statement to make. After all, isn't Project Censored on the side of objectivity? And yet if we look at the way objectivity operates, the way it is generally interpreted within informal journalistic codes of conduct, we can see that being objective often means excluding those stories that Project Censored brings to our attention.

In common journalistic practice, the notion of objectivity masks a fundamental contradiction. It is, on the one hand, linked to the notion of independently verifiable truth, or more specifically, the idea that there are objective facts and subjective opinions. In its quest for this objective truth, serious news journalism thereby insists on distinguishing facts from opinions (facts on the front page, opinions in the op-eds or editorials).

And yet, while journalists profess their faith in this objective world, they have little confidence in their ability to recognize it. The norms of "objective reporting" thus involve presenting "both sides" of an issue with very little in the way of independent forms of verification. So, for example, a Republican will present one set of facts and a Democrat will present another set of facts. The objective journalist reports both, regardless of their veracity. We thus have the poignant irony that a journalist who systematically attempts to verify facts—to say which set of facts is more accurate—runs the risk of being accused of abandoning their objectivity by favoring one side over another. On those occasions when journalists do attempt to evaluate competing claims, they invariably cloud the issue by referring to instances of truth and veracity on both sides.

In this muddled world, objective reporting requires that an environmental advocate who makes a truthful claim about corporate pollution be given weight equal to that of a corporate voice attempting to obfuscate this truth. The objective reporter will thereby play a part in this obfuscation. In other words, journalists who try to be faithful to an objective model of reporting are simultaneously distancing themselves from the notion of independently verifiable truth.

A common defense of this practice is to suggest that it gives the viewer or reader the freedom to decide for themselves. And yet one might reasonably ask how the reader or viewer is supposed to be able to make such a judgment? When the Reagan Administration denied the existence of the state-sponsored massacre in El Mazote in El Salvador, how were we to know that their accounts were completely false? The Reagan Administration's renowned PR acumen would certainly have meant that they would have looked and sounded credible at worst, speakers of a partial truth in the "two sides" paradigm.

The "two sides" model of journalistic objectivity makes news reporting a great deal easier since it requires no recourse to a factual realm. There are no facts to check, no archives of unspoken information to sort through. It relies entirely on the credibility of the sources chosen to make up the privileged duopolies who give us "both sides" of an issue, and it is at this point that the notion of objective reporting becomes bound to limited views of the world and, ultimately, to constraining the freedom of the press. If Tweedledum fails to challenge a point made by Tweedledee, the point remains unchallenged. If Tweedledum and Tweedledee are both talking nonsense, then objectivity dictates that nonsense prevails.

So, for example, in 1999, both President Clinton and the Republican party favored increasing the massive military budget (as the *Washington Post* stated on May 29: "Consensus builds for increased defense spending"). Since the U.S. already outspends the next five biggest military powers put together (and most of the other big spenders are allies rather than adversaries), this may seem to many to be an absurd use of resources, particularly when so little is done about more immediate threats to life, such as global warming or the lack of health insurance for the working poor. But to challenge the "consensus" in favor of increased military spending—even though most polls show a majority favor other priorities—is to step outside this cozy objectivity and risk being seen as adversarial.

Research by political scientists, sociologists, and media scholars, from a range of perspectives, has repeatedly demonstrated the degree to which journalists rely on political and corporate leaders to define the world. Being in authority, it is erroneously assumed, makes one an authority. For many professional journalists, the objective world is therefore one that is already circumscribed and defined by various elites, a framework that dictates what is relevant and what is not. A journalist's freedom to move beyond this world is thus limited by an ideology of objectivity pinned to the notion that politics is defined by political elites. If Project Censored's annual lists of overlooked stories have one thing in common, it is that they are all irrelevant to the terms of this elite discourse—a discourse described caustically by Robert Parry as informed by the narrow confines of a "conventional wisdom."

Since the body politic is pushed to the right by the presence of corporate money in elections and the crafting of legislation, the range of discourse that this conventional wisdom makes available often ignores ideas that polls suggest are consistently popular.[5] Thus, for example, the single-payer health care option often commands widespread support in polls (a plurality or a majority, depending on how the question is framed), and yet the lack of support for such an option by political elites makes discussion of single-payer irrelevant to mainstream media coverage of health care reform. Stories that informed the single-payer option were thus "censored" from the health care reform debate in Clinton's first term. During the health care reform debate, for example, both the U.S. General Accounting Office and the Congressional Budget Office calculated that public or government run health care systems were considerably more efficient than the private system favored by leaders of both political parties. Yet these reports fell outside the discourse espoused by political elites and they were almost entirely ignored by the news media.

If the "two sides" model of objective reporting limits what can be widely reported, it also tends to promote a specific ideology. Lurking within this model is a specific philosophical assumption about where truth lies. Since the model tends to assume that both sides will always be speaking partial truths (a proposition that, however implausible, allows reporters to remain agnostic), it is easy to infer that the whole truth must lie somewhere in the middle. This idea often translates into the proposition that while one cannot be objective in siding with the political left or right, one is able to speak for the politics of the center with fewer inhibitions. So, for example, on June 14th, 1999, ABC and NPR reporter Cokie Roberts told the audience for *Morning Edition* that campaigning politicians were "moving to the center, where the voters are." It is not simply that this statement is misleading (it may be where the potential vote-switchers are, but this tends to be a minority of the electorate), but that she felt able to make such a statement without feeling that she was threatening her objectivity.[6] Many reporters would—regardless of the evidence—be much more circumspect in declaring most voters to be on the right or left.

The notion that the center is a less ideological space than right or left (particularly in terms of Washington politics, where the center is distinctly more pro-corporate than most citizens tend to be) may be naive, but it is partly sustained by the way in which journalistic objectivity is used and understood. We are thereby swept along with the Washington consensus even when it departs, as for example in the case of NAFTA, from majority opinion.

Once notions of objective reporting become enshrined within a system in which politics is defined by political elites, objectivity effectively becomes the delivery system for forms of censorship. Objectivity, as it is currently practiced, may not be responsible for the narrow field of facts and ideas that make up the conventional wisdom, but it gives this limited framework both solidity and legitimacy, and it constrains journalists from speaking truths for their own sake.

NOTES

1. See, for example, Edward Herman, *The Myth of the Liberal Media* (New York: Peter Lang, 1999); Robert W. McChesney, *Corporate Media and the*

Threat to Democracy (New York: Seven Stories Press, 1997).

2. See, for example, M. Edelman, *Constructing the Political Spectacle* (Chicago: University of Chicago Press, 1988); T. Ferguson & J. Rogers, *Right Turn: The Decline of the Democrats and the Future of American Politics* (New York: Farrar, Strauss and Giroux, 1986); Todd Gitlin, *The Whole World is Watching* (Berkeley: University of California Press, 1980); Ed Herman & Noam Chomsky, *The Manufacture of Consent* (New York: Pantheon, 1988); S. Iyengar, *Is Anyone Responsible?* (Chicago: University of Chicago Press, 1991); B. Page & R. Shapiro, *The Rational Public* (Chicago: University of Chicago Press, 1992); G. Tuchman, *Making News* (New York: Free Press, 1978); J. R. Zaller, *The Nature and Origins of Mass Opinion* (Cambridge: Cambridge University Press, 1992).

3. Robert Parry, *Fooling America* (New York: Morrow, 1992).

4. See, for example, J. Harrigan, *Empty Dreams, Empty Pockets: Class and Bias in Amercian Politics* (New York: Macmillan, 1993); or D. Hellinger & D. Judd, *The Democratic Façade* (Pacific Grove, CA: Brooks Grove Publishing, 1991).

5. See, for example, J. Harrigan, *Empty Dreams, Empty Pockets*. [Full citation in Note #4, above.]

6. The national Election Studies at the University of Michigan show that independent voters do not always fall between Democrats and Republicans—their ideological leanings are both complex and distinct. Similarly, research by Williams and Wollman in 1996 found no evidence to support the conventional journalistic wisdom that the electorate favors moderate candidates. On the contrary, in their study of comparable performance, the more left-wing Democratic candidates actually did better than their more moderate counterparts. ("Pundits Had It Wrong: The Voters Did Not Embrace Moderation," *Roll Call*, December 12, 1996).

JUSTIN LEWIS is a professor at the Department of Communication, University of Massachusetts at Amherst. He has written several books about the politics of media and culture. His most recent book is an analysis of the media and public opinion, to be published by Columbia University Press.

Is the Press Really Free in the 21st Century?

BY JANINE JACKSON

"If candidates for the United States Senate were required to possess $10 million, and for the House $1 million," wrote journalist and press critic A.J. Liebling, "we could still be said to have a freely elected Congress: anybody with $10 million (or one, if he tailored his ambition to fit his means) would be free to try to get himself nominated, and the rest of us would be free to vote for our favorite millionaires or even abstain from voting."

"In the same sense," he went on to say, "we have a free press today." Anyone with at least $10 million "is free to buy or found a paper in a great city like New York or Chicago"; and "as to us, we are free to buy a paper or not, as we wish."

Liebling wrote this in 1947, but, like much of his press criticism, its resonance for us today is downright eerie. The monopolistic tendencies of the media industry, the discouragement of diversity by the sheer amount of capital required to be a major player, and the journalistic and ethical compromises born of regarding information like any other widget to be bought and sold—these problems were noted decades ago by spirit guides of media criticism like I. F. Stone and George Seldes. But they have reached a kind of crisis today. Public distrust and dissatisfaction with media are high; commercialism is omnipresent and omnivorous; potentially democratizing new technologies are harnessed to provide a media palette with many apparent options but little substantive choice.

Today's media would seem to have something like "freedom." They are free to bombard us with images of bloody car crashes, "animal attacks," and abusive police officers chasing and tackling poor people. They're free to make prodigious profits by tailoring their content to the interests and whims of advertisers, and to exert overweening influence over the electoral system, in part by controlling candidates' ability to get their message out.

It's true, media outlets today employ dedicated, talented, creative people who sometimes provide art and information that teaches us and enriches our lives.

But to be free—free to do critical, challenging reporting and creative work—the press must be without compromising ties to government or corporate power. That is, after all, what we rely on journalism to do: to scrutinize the powerful, fearlessly and honestly. Two of the most powerful social forces, in the turn-of-the-millennium United States, are corporations and the state. A press corps that is not independent of these is not independent in a way useful to democracy.

IS THE PRESS INDEPENDENT OF GOVERNMENT POWER?

The First Amendment prevents Congressional interference with the press, and media are nominally free to report critically on government officials and policy. At times they've made efforts to do so, as when the *New York Times* published the Pentagon Papers, revealing the secret policy U.S. in Vietnam.

Unfortunately, those proud moments are part of a history that includes a great deal of acquiescence and self-censorship. The same *New York Times* that ran the Pentagon Papers pulled their correspondent from Guatemala at the CIA's request just before the 1954 coup, and the paper toned down its treatment of the Bay of Pigs and Cuban missile crisis at the behest of President Kennedy. *Washington Post* owner Katharine Graham's outlook is reflected in comments she made to a group of senior CIA employees: "We live in a dirty and dangerous world. There are some things the general public does not need to know and shouldn't."

During the Persian Gulf War, reporters were restricted to press pools under military control. In 1992, a group of human rights organizations (and media watch groups) had to sue the Defense Department for press access to camps in Guantanamo Bay, Cuba, where the U.S. was holding Haitian refugees.

But more distressing than the barriers to press scrutiny the state still sometimes throws up is how rarely the press takes them on. Instead we see, most notably in times of war, a kind of identification of interests between reporters and the state. News anchors use personal pronouns to refer to military actions, like during the Gulf War, when we heard things like, "We hit Saddam again today," or "How badly are we hurting him?" At that war's end, CBS's Dan Rather concluded an interview with a general by pumping the man's hand and gushing, "Congratulations on a job wonderfully done!"

Now the NATO/Kosovo War is being transformed from news to history, and the media are writing a very pro-establishment book. In October 1999 CNN chief international correspondent Christiane Amanpour (also the spouse of the State Department's chief spokesman) delivered a post-war "wrap-up" that relied overwhelmingly on NATO officers for sources and treated military assertions as fact. And there's the "we-we" problem again as Amanpour says, "When the defiant Yugoslav army was finally forced to pull out of Kosovo, we were stunned to see how much of their hardware they managed to take with them—intact." Who was stunned—CNN or NATO? She doesn't say, or give any indication that the distinction is meaningful.

Indeed, press/state closeness during the Kosovo War was such that when a Fox News channel anchor introduced a segment by saying, "Let's bring in our Pentagon spokesman—excuse me, our Pentagon correspondent," it could be seen as an understandable mistake.

Media outlets don't need to be forced to promulgate the official line on many social issues as well, even in the face of widespread public disagreement. At a time when polls showed the idea of universal or "single payer" health care enjoying majority public support, for example, mainstream media dismissed such plans as not "viable," reserving all of their attention for the Clinton Administration's "managed competition" proposal. "The debate over health care reform is over," the *New York Times* announced in October 1992. "Managed competition has won." Coverage of so-called "free trade" pacts pushed by the administration has been similarly lopsided, with critics marginalized in the press no matter how prevalent they are among the public.

Far from a healthy adversarialism, many media see themselves as "partners" with the state. Some reporters described things just that way in justifying practices like the police "ride-along," that involve compromisingly close ties between the press and law enforcement. The Supreme Court challenged deals in which media accompany cops onto private property as potentially violating Fourth Amendment rights; but the deals are defended by outlets like ABC News, which described them as "an arrangement between police and the news media that seems to serve the needs of both groups." The "needs" of media were defined not as truthful reporting on the criminal justice system, but "gritty stories and dramatic pictures."

Some of the cozyness between reporters and government comes from the "top down" approach of traditional journalism, which always privileges the "official" voice (even if those officials are unnamed) over the perspectives of policy critics, activists, or the public. But it also has a great deal to do with the fact that newspapers and radio stations are, first and foremost, major corporate entities with a vested interest in working out favorable relationships with the state. The media industry's staunch opposition to reforming the campaign finance system—of which they are prime beneficiaries—illustrates how a press/state alliance can serve both interests.

Like other major corporate actors, media companies routinely seek to influence legislation in ways favorable to their industry's profitability; the trouble is, their bargaining chip is their powerful influence on public awareness and opinion. In January 1995, then House Speaker Newt Gingrich held a little-noted series of closed door meetings with the chief executives of virtually every leading media and telecommunications firm in the country. Republicans were poised to give media owners a veritable cornucopia in the form of the evisceration of rules limiting concentration and cross-ownership, long-standing barriers to monopolization. Gingrich & Co. were clear about what they expected in return: favorable coverage. Or as Gingrich reportedly put it to Time Warner chair Gerald Levin, "Get your children to behave."

That kind of anti-democratic quid pro quo is no secret in the media industry or the halls of Congress; it's just the public that's out of the loop.

IS THE PRESS INDEPENDENT OF CORPORATE POWER?

Such a question is hardly coherent anymore, since the vast majority of media outlets are themselves corporate "holdings," and media companies rely on corporate advertising to sustain them. Not only that, but the media corporations and the sponsoring corporations are themselves tightly interlocked. The barriers to journalistic independence presented by such a system are myriad; some conflicts are glaring, others are more subtle, and new ones turn up every day.

We can start with the fact that media outlets tend to move toward monopoly, so the profitability of the industry doesn't translate to a proliferation of outlets, or a diverse range of owners. More and more places are becoming "one-paper" towns, and the country's number one newspaper chain, Gannett, has shown that it will stop at nothing to drive out competing dailies and even weeklies in their markets (see Richard McCord, *The Chain Gang: One Newspaper vs. the Gannett Empire*). Minority ownership is tiny and decreasing.

Each time media companies merge or take one another over, maneuvers that "make sense" from a business perspective, the public has fewer choices for sources of information. Since the deregulatory Telecommunications Act of 1996, roughly half of U.S. radio stations have been sold. Radio is now dominated by a few mega-companies, each of which owns hundreds of stations—as many as eight in a single market.

Concentration's poisonous effects on journalism extend beyond the elimination of outlets. As with other mergers, media mergers generally involve downsizing and drastic cost-cutting, both of which hit news departments hard. Overworked reporters have little time (or incentive) to do long-term investigations, or sometimes to do much more than re-work press releases and press conference speeches. There are countless stories reporters are practically unable to write, though theoretically "free" to do so.

And then there are stories that, because of the corporate ownership and control of media, reporters are not free to tell at all. In 1998, Fox sold out two of its own reporters, Jane Akre and Steve Wilson, who had produced a program on bovine growth hormone that ruffled feathers at Monsanto, makers of the synthetic hormone rBGH. Monsanto threatened to sue Fox over the report, though they couldn't prove it was in any way inaccurate. Rather than support their journalists, as an independent outlet would, Fox made a series of corporate decisions—first to sit on the story, then to try to force Akre and Wilson to re-write it in terms the reporters described as "misleading," and finally to fire them when they refused to play along. At one point during the negotiations, a Fox station manager told the veteran reporters, "We paid $3 billion for these television stations. We will decide what the news is."

"No newspaper which is supporting one class of society is independent," George Seldes tells us, but, as wealthy corporate capitalists, today's media owners represent only a narrow and elite sector of society, and their content reflects those values. The evidence is ample. Think of the *Washington Post*, which editorialized against a ban on "replacement" workers, with the stated rationale that the Washington Post Co. itself had employed such strike-breaking devices, to good effect.

Add to this media's need to reach, not the largest audience, but the audience advertisers want to target, and you explain the surfeit of reporting aimed at the upper-income investor class, and the skewing of news generally toward a happy view of the socioeconomic status quo that benefits that class. This slant has a way of affecting the most apparently straightforward coverage. For instance, the Associated Press published a report purporting to illustrate the impact of proposed tax changes on American families. The report used five hypothetical households to represent the U.S. public: one household with an income of $35,000, one with an income of $48,500, one with $72,750, one with $100,000, and one with $1,000,000 in income. In reality, AP's poorest household, with $35,000 in annual income, represents nearly half the U.S. public—

the median household income is about $38,885; 20 percent of families have a net worth of zero or less.

Advertisers have abilities to influence editorial content beyond skewing programming toward their "desired demographics." When CBS signed up Nike to sponsor coverage of the Nagano Olympics, part of the deal was that CBS correspondents—not just sports reporters, but "hard news" folk too—were to wear Nike paraphernalia, hats, jackets, etc. on air. There was some outcry over this obvious and embarrassing overstepping, and CBS backed down.

While the reporters as billboards gaffe got some attention, few heard about a more serious breach brought on by CBS's Nike deal. The network killed a news report by veteran consumer reporter Roberta Baskin, a follow-up to her award-winning exposé of Nike sweatshops in Vietnam. When Baskin complained, she was demoted. Press critics who had upbraided CBS for the more cosmetic offense had little to say about the more grave incident.

Such heavy-handed tactics are not usually necessary, and sponsors generally seem to favor a more preemptive approach to shaping the news. There's no finer illustration than a letter sent by an ad agency representing Coca-Cola to magazines hoping to snag the soft drink company as a sponsor. Coca-Cola has a "very specific" policy about the editorial context in which their ads are placed, the letter explained. "We consider the following topics to be inappropriate, and require that our ads are not placed adjacent to articles discussing the following issues: Hard news; sex-related issues; drugs (prescription or illegal); medicine (chronic illnesses such as cancer, diabetes, and AIDS); health (mental or physical medical conditions); negative diet information (bulimia, anorexia, quick weight loss); food; political issues; environmental issues; articles containing vulgar language; religion." More celebrity fashion coverage, anyone?

Another growing trend is sole sponsorship. *Time* magazine launched a special environmental series, "Heroes for the Planet," with a single sponsor: Ford Motor Company. No, *Time* editor Charles Alexander acknowledged, the magazine's "environmental" series would not likely devote any attention to air pollution.

The *Los Angeles Times* recently published a special issue of their magazine with a single sponsor: the Staples Center arena in downtown L.A. It was subsequently revealed that the paper was sharing profits from the issue with the Staples Center, an ostensible subject of their news coverage. Publisher Kathryn Downing stated publicly that the deal, which outraged *Times* reporters, resulted from her "fundamental misunderstanding" of journalistic principles. Misty recollections of a "golden age" of journalism may be largely apocryphal; yet it seems safe to say that at another time, a publisher might have been ashamed to admit that.

Yes, each individual journalist is free to fight such predations when they occur, at substantial risk to their career prospects. But these conflicts are the result not of individual "lapses" but of the very institutional structure and culture of media corporations, which is powerfully hard to resist. It seems more likely that, increasingly, those reporters who have a problem with the way things are done will be weeded out, or just won't go into mainstream journalism at all.

Unfortunately, the public's need for a press corps with the integrity to really speak truth to power, no matter who is offended, to represent a wide range of voices in debate, not just the powerful, and to make decisions based on journalistic principles, not business rules, is as desperate as ever.

REASONS TO BE CHEERFUL

The conflict between the goals of media as a profit-driven business and the goals of journalism to serve the public interest is vivid and undeniable. To return to Liebling, the press has become "the weak slat under the bed of democracy. It is an anomaly that information, the one thing most necessary to our survival as choosers of our own way, should be a commodity subject to the same merchandising rules as chewing gum, while armament, a secondary instrument of liberty, is a government concern. A man is not free if he cannot see where he is going, even if he has a gun to help him get there."

But if the current media situation is a crisis, it is also an opportunity. As the public has become increasingly dissatisfied with media as it is, many have become active in figuring out ways to change it.

There are organizations dedicated to fighting media concentration at the legislative level and at the grassroots, groups that specifically address media's influence on public understanding of economic, environmental, and political issues. And media watch groups like FAIR, that just a dozen years ago were virtually alone in attempting to call attention to the limitations of commercial establishment media, are now echoed widely.

Most significant, there is a noticeable shift in public consciousness, in the way we look at media. People are abandoning the notion of television and newspaper reporting as a neutral window on the world and are engaging it critically, and talking back. And many are coming to value and support those alternative, noncommercial outlets we do have—outlets that, usually on tiny budgets, provide respite from the dominant worldview, and offer space for the kind of broad-ranging debate and diversity of perspectives that are vital to democracy.

No, as we go into the 21st century, the press is emphatically not free. But we are sowing the seeds of the mass movement that will free it.

JANINE JACKSON is program director of FAIR (Fairness and Accuracy In Reporting), the national media watch group, and producer/host of FAIR's weekly radio show, *CounterSpin*. She co-edited *The FAIR Reader: An EXTRA! Review of Press and Politics in the '90s* (Westview).

What Free Press?

BY CARL JENSEN

Before gazing into a murky crystal ball to contemplate the status of press freedom in the new millennium, we should first pause to examine how free the press really was at the end of the old millennium. On the surface, it would seem that the press was about as free as any of us are, subject as we all are to the constraints of laws, ethics, morals, etc. Following are some of the more obvious constraints that will continue to impact press coverage in the future: The press can't publish military secrets because of national security; it can't print names of victims and witnesses because of law enforcement requirements; it can't print embarrassing information about individuals because of the right to privacy; it can't print trade secrets because of corporate rights; it can't print pornographic materials because of obscenity laws; it can't print false or misleading advertising because of rules regarding commercial speech and so on.

But given these exceptions, we could say the press is free to print whatever it likes. Or, could we? It seems there are other, less well-known influences that determine what should or should not be printed. Many of them are rooted in the "old boys" school of mutual self-interest. Who would be fool enough to rock the boat by exposing a colleague when he's in the same boat?

However, the most important factor determining the content of the daily headline is the quarterly bottom line. Once upon a time, the heralded goal of the press was to keep the people informed. Now the primary objective is to make a profit. If the media should neglect to report a story that would jeopardize some corporation's profits, that is now perfectly understandable and acceptable in a capitalist society driven solely by the bottom line. We can't expect to see an NBC journalist expose the hazards of nuclear power as long as General Electric, a major manufacturer of nuclear power plants, signs the NBC paychecks. We can't expect to see an ABC journalist expose some illicit activity at Disneyland. In fact, Michael Eisner, chairman of Disney, which owns ABC, once said, "I would prefer ABC not cover Disney. I think it's inappropriate." And we can't expect to see a CBS journalist expose human rights violations in important trade partners.

Sumner Redstone, chairman of Viacom, the pending new owner of CBS, once warned that news organizations should take care to report the news without being "unnecessarily offensive" to foreign governments. As the CEO of Westinghouse, a major media player, said in *Advertising Age* in 1997, "We are here to serve advertisers. That is our *raison d'être*." That sounds like something famed madame Sally Stanford might once have said.

Unfortunately, we, as a society, accept these "nuances" when it comes to a free press. In fact, propaganda over the years has led us to believe the press is free. We even have a Constitutional amendment guaranteeing a free press and free speech. You won't find that in any of those authoritarian or socialist societies. The fight for a free press and free speech is not a recent phenomenon or exclusively an American one. It's an honorable battle that dates back at least to Socrates who knocked back a shot of hemlock rather than be gagged by his colleagues.

But as we begin a new millennium, it appears that we are beginning to lose the good fight. First, we know that a free press and a well-informed public are best served by a variety of sources competing to bring information to the people. With the pending sale of CBS, the last major independent television network, to Viacom, an insatiable advertising network, we have seen the media merger madness attain a new unparalleled height. Viacom now provides an inter-generational cradle-to-grave media market monopoly.

When media monopoly monitor Ben Bagdikian first published his landmark *Media Monopoly* in 1983, critics were surprised and alarmed over his warning that some 50 corporations controlled more than half of America's news media outlets. By his fifth edition, in 1997, Bagdikian had to reduce that figure to just 10. And there was no similar surprise or outrage.

Soon there will be just six massive media monopolies that control most of the world's information: Time Warner, Viacom/CBS, Disney, Bertelsmann, General Electric, and the News Corp. Even San Francisco, that once multi-newspaper-proud feisty Baghdad by the Bay, is being reduced to a wimpy one-paper town.

Political cartoonist Don Wright, of the *Palm Beach Post*, succinctly characterized the power of today's mega-media monopoly, "Do not attempt to change the channel. We own all of them. Do not attempt to turn off the set. If you do, we will cut the electricity. We own the power company. And if you try to get a drink or use the toilet, there will be no water. We own that utility, too. Do not try to call for help. We own the phone company. Sit back and enjoy the show. Now! We know where you are."

Next, the press is starting to lose its credibility as a watchdog of society. Public opinion polls continue to reveal a growing dissatisfaction with the media as an institution. A 1999 survey of public attitudes about First Amendment freedoms, sponsored by the First Amendment Center at Vanderbilt University, revealed that more than half of all Americans, 53 percent, believe the press has too much freedom. Equally alarming, the survey found that increasing numbers of respondents believe that newspapers should not be allowed to publish freely without government approval. It appears that the public does not fully understand that its own right to free speech, which it dearly cherishes, is co-mingled with the right to a free press. It is the press that allows the public to express itself through publication and dissemination.

Indeed, the future of the press in the new millennium appears bleak. Given the new monopolization of the old monopolies, we find an increasingly smaller group of white men dictating what all the rest of us see and hear. As the century-old "man bites dog" defensive dirge persists in defining news, we can expect to see continued growth in cheap-to-produce "junk food news."

Project Censored first warned about this inordinate focus on individuals or issues undeserving of press coverage in 1984 with Clara Peller's widely-publicized "Where's the beef?" Since then the Project has monitored the continuing increase in "junk food news" and the corresponding decline in hard news.

What's wrong with that? Well, consider for a moment what a truly aggressive free press—more interested in hard news than in O.J. Simpson or Monica Lewinsky—could do for us. The press has the power to stimulate people to clean up the environment, prevent nuclear proliferation, force crooked politicians out of office, reduce poverty, provide quality health care for all people, and even to save the lives of millions of people as it did in the Ethiopia famine in 1984. But instead we are using it to promote sex, violence, and sensationalism and to line the pockets of the already wealthy media moguls.

If there is any hope of awakening the sleeping watchdog press in the new millennium, we must support those individuals and groups who continue to put up a good fight despite the odds. These quixotic warriors include individuals like Ben Bagdikian, Noam Chomsky, George Gerbner, Hugh Downs, Frances Moore Lappé, Robert McChesney, Ralph Nader, and Michael Parenti; groups like the Association of Alternative Newsweeklies, Center for Investigative Reporting, Center for War, Peace, and the News Media, Fairness and Accuracy in Reporting (FAIR), Freedom Forum, Media Alliance, and the Reporter's Committee for Freedom of the Press; and media like *Brill's Content*, *CovertAction Quarterly*, *In These Times*, *Mother Jones*, *Multinational Monitor*, the *Nation*, *PR Watch*, the *Progressive*, *San Francisco Bay Guardian*, and the *Village Voice*. Project Censored, the nation's longest running news media censorship research project, is proud to be allied with these warriors struggling to force the press to be all that it can be.

Since its inception in 1976, Project Censored has identified thousands of important stories the major news media ignore. Through this process, the Project prompts people to be more critical of what they see and read and it encourages the news media to rethink their antiquated definition of news. The battle for a truly free press in the new millennium may seem quixotic but, given the alternative, it is imperative.

The Reverand Jesse Jackson once warned us that the most dangerous enemy of press freedom in the United States is the press itself because of the accelerating media monopoly. Calling the Big Media just another subdivision of Big Business, he said, "The spirit of the First Amendment will be revived when truth, rather than profit, becomes once again the object of a free and uninhibited press." While one hopes the new millennium might bring this about, it is unlikely we will see that happen until people like Michael Eisner and Sumner Redstone realize that the truth is also profitable.

CARL JENSEN, PH.D., is the founder and director emeritus of Project Censored.

THIS MODERN WORLD

by TOM TOMORROW

THEY SMILE REASSURINGLY AND TELL YOU EVERYTHING'S FINE, THAT THE ECONOMY'S GOING GANGBUSTERS AND A RISING TIDE LIFTS ALL BOATS--BUT YOU KNOW THAT SOMETHING'S WRONG HERE. YOU KNOW THAT 85% OF THE WEALTH IS CONTROLLED BY 20% OF THE POPULATION... THAT THE WAGES OF A MAJORITY OF AMERICANS ARE ACTUALLY LOWER, IN REAL DOLLARS, THAN THEY WERE IN *1973.*

YOU KNOW THAT YOUR LEADERS HAVE BEEN BOUGHT AND PAID FOR, THAT CORPORATE MONEY SETS THE POLITICAL AGENDA. YOU KNOW THAT THE FREE MARKET HAS BECOME THE DOMINANT RELIGION OF OUR AGE... THAT ANYONE FOOLISH ENOUGH TO SUGGEST TEMPERING THE QUEST FOR PROFIT WITH A MODICUM OF CONCERN FOR HUMAN RIGHTS OR THE ENVIRONMENT IS VIEWED AS A HERETIC--IF NOT AN UTTER LUNATIC.

YOU KNOW THAT SOMETHING IS DEEPLY, FUNDAMENTALLY WRONG.

BUT WHAT CAN YOU DO? YOU DON'T MATTER. YOUR VOTE DOESN'T MATTER. YOUR PROTESTS DON'T MATTER. GO AHEAD, MARCH IN THE STREETS AND CHANT YOUR LITTLE SLOGANS. THE POLITICAL SOPHISTICATES AND MEDIA ELITES WILL SMIRK AT YOUR NAIVITÉ, YOUR MISGUIDED NOSTALGIA FOR THE SIXTIES, AND THEN THEY WILL STEER THE CONVERSATION BACK TO THE STOCK MARKET OR THE FABULOUS NEW RESTAURANT THEY'VE RECENTLY DISCOVERED. THEY'RE NOT WORRIED ABOUT YOU.

AND YET... SOMETHING EXTRAORDINARY JUST HAPPENED IN SEATTLE. DEMONSTRATORS TOOK TO THE STREETS AND MADE THEIR VOICES HEARD-- AND IT *MADE A DIFFERENCE.* THE MEDIA WERE FORCED TO ADDRESS ISSUES THEY HAD PREVIOUSLY SWEPT UNDER THE RUG, TO EXPLAIN WHY ANYONE COULD POSSIBLY BE OPPOSED TO UNFETTERED GLOBAL CAPITALISM. IN A FEW SHORT DAYS, THE ENTIRE DEBATE WAS ALTERED, PERHAPS IRREVOCABLY.

YOU KNOW SOMETHING'S WRONG. MAYBE IT'S TIME TO START MAKING SOME NOISE ABOUT IT.

HAPPY NEW MILLENNIUM.

TOM TOMORROW©12-22-99 ... tomorrow@well.com ... www.thismodernworld.com

CHAPTER 5

Oligopoly: The Big Media Game Has Fewer and Fewer Players

BY ROBERT W. McCHESNEY
Reprinted with Permission from *The Progressive*, November 1999.

When Viacom announced its offer to gobble up CBS for $37 billion in September 1999, it capped off a decade of unprecedented deal-making and concentration in the media industries. The new Viacom would be one of only nine massive conglomerates—all of which took their present shape in the last 15 years—that dominate the U.S. media landscape.

These giants—Time Warner, Disney, Rupert Murdoch's News Corp., Viacom, Sony, Seagram, AT&T/Liberty Media, Bertelsmann, and GE—to a large extent furnish your TV programs, movies, videos, radio shows, music, books, and other recreational activities. They do a superb job of maximizing profit for their shareholders but a dreadful job of providing the basis for a healthy democracy. Their entertainment fare is tailored to the needs of Madison Avenue; their journalism to the needs of the wealthy and powerful.

By any known standard of liberal democracy, such a concentration of media power in a few self-interested firms run by some of the wealthiest people in the world poses an immediate and growing threat to our republic. As James Madison put it in 1822, "A popular government without popular information, or the means of acquiring it, is but a prologue to a farce or a tragedy, or perhaps both."

When the Viacom/CBS deal was announced, *Time* and *Newsweek* lavished attention on the personalities of Viacom's Sumner Redstone and CBS's Mel Karmazin. To the extent that there was analysis, it centered on the how the deal would affect Viacom's profits and the strategies of its main competitors. The *Washington Post*'s "Outlook" section featured a lead story entitled, "Clap If You Love Mega-TV! Without the Conglomerates, You Can Wave Goodbye to Free, High-quality Shows." Written by Paul Farhi, a reporter for the *Post*'s "Style" section, the article said: "Now is the time to root for the big guys, the conglomerates, the mega-studios."

Aside from some notable reports in the *Boston Globe*, *Boston Herald*, *Chicago Tribune*, and the *New York Times* that broached the question of whether this deal might not be good for people, the issue was off-limits. And even those papers that waved at it did not follow up, so the story died.

This paucity of press coverage makes it easier for the federal government to shirk its duties. Far from regulating the media giants, the government has served as the handmaiden to these electronic robber barons.

This oligopoly would never have passed legal muster if the regulators at the Federal Communications Commission and in the antitrust division of the Justice Department were doing their jobs, or if the Telecommunications Act of 1996 were not railroaded through Congress.

The regulators have let these mergers slide, under tremendous pressure from the telecommunications and entertainment industry. And it looks as though the Viacom/CBS merger will sail through as well. Virtually no one in government is looking out for the public's interest in the media field.

The main defense provided by the government for its laxity is that the Internet upends the rationale for regulating media mergers—or for regulating media at all. It used to be that the major media companies possessed the only access to millions of Americans. Now, with the Web, the argument goes, anyone can launch a site at marginal expense and compete directly with the existing media giants. So there is no need to worry about conglomerates. Proponents of the Internet act as though it is a massive comet crashing onto the Earth that will drive media giants into extinction.

This is nonsense. The Internet is certainly changing the nature of our media system. But after five years, it has not spawned a competitive media marketplace; the giants have too many advantages to be seriously challenged. They have the programming, the brand names, the advertisers, the promotional prowess, and the capital to rule the Internet.

Media concentration is not a new phenomenon, but it has accelerated dramatically in the last decade, and it is taking a new and dangerous form. Classically, media concentration was in the form of "horizontal integration," where a handful of firms tried to control as much production in their particular field as possible. The U.S. film production industry, for instance, has been a tight-knit club effectively controlled by six or seven studios since the 1930s. That remains the case today; the six largest U.S. firms accounted for more than 90 percent of U.S. theater revenues in 1997. All but 16 of Hollywood's 148 widely distributed films in 1997 were produced by these six firms, and many of those sixteen were produced by companies that had distribution deals with one of the six majors.

The newspaper industry underwent a spectacular consolidation from the 1960s to the 1980s, leaving half a dozen major chains ruling the roost. U.S. book publishing is now dominated by seven firms, the music industry by five, cable TV by six. Nearly all of these are now parts of vast media conglomerates.

That's why looking at specific media sectors fails to convey the extent or the nature of the system today, for no longer are media firms intent on horizontal integration. Today, they seek "vertical integration," not only producing content but also owning distribution. Moreover, they are major players in media sectors not traditionally though to be related. These conglomerates own some combination of television networks, TV show production, TV stations, movie studios, cable channels, cable systems, music companies, magazines, newspapers, and book publishing firms.

This has all come about seemingly overnight. In 1983, Ben Bagdikian published *The Media Monopoly*, which chronicled how some 50 media conglomerates dominated the entirety of U.S. mass media. By today's standards, that era was downright competitive.

The mega-media firms have enjoyed a staggering rate of growth in the last decade. In 1988, Disney was a $2.9-billion-a-year amusement park and cartoon company; in 1998, Disney had $22 billion in sales. In 1988, Time was a $4.2 billion publishing company and Warner Communications was a $3.4 billion media conglomerate; in 1998, Time Warner did $26 billion business. In 1988, Viacom was a measly $600 million syndication and cable outfit; the new Viacom is expected to do $22 billion worth of business in the coming year.

Moreover, each of these firms averages at least one equity joint venture—where they share actual ownership of a company—with six of the eight other media giants. Rupert Murdoch's News Corp. has at least one joint venture with each of them. AT&T/Liberty owns nearly 10 percent of both News Corp. and Time Warner. This looks more like a cartel than it does the fabled competitive marketplace.

For decades, U.S. laws and regulations forbade film studios from owning movie theaters, and television networks from producing their own entertainment programs, because it was understood that this sort of vertical integration would effectively prohibit newcomers from entering these production industries. Likewise, regulations forbade companies from owning more than one radio or TV station in the same market and put a strict cap on the total number of stations that could be owned by a single family. Such restrictions have been relaxed or eliminated in these deregulatory times, and, as the Viacom/CBS merger shows, producers and distribution networks are racing to link up with each other.

What these media conglomerates have learned is that the profit whole is greater than the sum of the profit parts. Viacom/CBS, for instance, will now be able to produce a movie at Paramount or a TV show at Spelling studios, air it on Showtime and CBS, advertise it on MTV, VH1, Nickelodeon, and CBS and its 34 TV stations, as well as on the 163 Infinity Radio stations that CBS owned, and then sell it at Blockbuster Video, all owned by the same merged company.

Vertical integration enables a company to increase market power by cross-promoting or cross-selling a show. If a media conglomerate has a successful motion picture, for instance, it can promote the film on its broadcast properties and then use the film to spin off television programs, CDs, books, merchandise, and much else. "When you can make a movie for an average cost of $10 million and then cross-promote and sell it off of magazines, books, products, television shows out of your own company, the profit potential is enormous," Redstone said, even before he put his money down on CBS.

Take Time Warner. It owns leading film companies (Warner Bros., New Line Cinema, Hanna-Barbera, and Castle Rock), cable TV systems (the second largest in the United States), cable TV channels (CNN, HBO, TBS, TNT), magazines (*Time, People, Sports Illustrated, Fortune*), publishing companies (Little, Brown and Warner Books), and music labels (Warner Bros. Records, Elektra, Atlantic, Sire, and Rhino). In the sports field, it owns the Atlanta Braves, the Atlanta Hawks, and World Championship Wrestling.

For its part, Disney has the ABC network, 10 TV stations, 30 radio stations, cable programming (ESPN, the Disney Channel, A&E, E!, Lifetime), film studios (Miramax, Walt Disney Pictures, Touchstone, Hollywood), Hyperion book company, ESPN magazine, music labels (Walt Disney Records, Mammoth, Lyric Street), and amusement parks. It also owns the Anaheim Angels and the Mighty Ducks.

Murdoch's News Corp. owns the Fox network and 15 TV stations. It produces cable programming (Fox News, Fox Sports, Fox Family Channel). Its studios are 20th Century Fox, Fox Animation, and Searchlight. It owns the *New York Post*, along with hundreds of newspapers worldwide. It also owns the conservative *Weekly Standard* and the book company HarperCollins. Its sports teams are the Los Angeles Dodgers and the National Rugby League in Australia.

These mega-media companies have contributed to the rampant commercialization of U.S. childhood. "More and more companies are realizing," the head of the Fox Family Channel stated, "that if you develop a loyalty with the kids of today, they eventually become the adults of tomorrow." What's more, children age four to twelve are a formidable market in their own right. They spent $2.4 billion in 1997, three times the figure of a decade earlier. And no better medium exists for the delivery of the youth market than television. By age seven, the average American child is watching 1,400 hours and 20,000 TV commercials per year. By age 12, that child's preferences are stored in massive data banks by marketers of consumer goods.

In the 1990s, commercial television for children may well have been the most rapidly growing and lucrative sector of the U.S. industry, with 1998 ad revenues pegged at approximately $1 billion. Each of the four largest U.S. media giants has a full-time children's cable TV channel to capture the 39 million viewers in the two-to-eleven age group. (Viacom was touted as the "perfect match" for CBS in large part because Viacom's Nickelodeon network, with its young demographic, complements CBS's stodgier audience.)

In 1998, broadcasters even began targeting one-year-olds to get a toehold on the youth market. In a moment of candor, one Time Warner children's television executive conceded that "there's something vaguely evil" about programming to kids that young. Nobody knows what the effects of this unprecedented commercial indoctrination of children will be years down the road. The only thing we know for sure is that the people responsible for it don't care.

Perhaps nowhere is the effect of concentrated corporate control on media more insidious than in journalism, democracy's lifeblood. I do not wish to romanticize the nature of U.S. journalism in the old days. It was highly flawed in key respects, and many of the current problems are only exaggerated forms of those that existed yesterday. But in today's corporate media system, journalism—and by that I mean the rigorous accounting of the powers-that-be and the powers-that-want-to-be, as well as wide-ranging coverage of our most urgent social and political issues—has nearly ceased to exist on the air and has been greatly diminished elsewhere. The reason is simple: Good journalism is bad business, and bad journalism can be very, very good for business.

The corporate assault on journalism assumes many forms. It is bad business, for example, to employ editors and reporters when a small staff can generate the same amount of material, albeit at lower quality. Since the mid-1980s, there has been a 50 percent reduction in the number of broadcast network reporters in Washington. This shifts more power to the PR industry and its corporate clients, which are ever eager to provide news fare to the media.

It is bad business, too, to do hard investigative work on corporations and powerful government agencies that primarily serve elite interests, like the Pentagon, the CIA, and the Federal Reserve Board. Such exposés can lead to expensive lawsuits and acrimonious relations with major advertisers, corporate brethren, and political heavyweights.

It is far better business practice to cover trivial stories about celebrities, natural disasters, train wrecks, sensational crimes, the Kennedys, and the royal family, and to limit "political" reporting to mindless speculation about campaign tactics and the regurgitation of mainstream politicians' soundbites. This is relatively inexpensive and rarely antagonizes anyone in power. The corporate and commercial pressure of the 1990s has softened news standards. Welcome to the age of fluff.

For network and cable television, news has gone from being a loss-leader and a mark of network prestige to being a major producer of network profit. At present, NBC enjoys what is regarded as "the most profitable broadcast news division in the history of television," according to *Electronic Media*, with annual advertising revenues topping $100 million. NBC is renowned not so much for the quality of its news as for its extraordinary success in squeezing profit from it. NBC uses QNBC, a high-tech statistical service, to analyze its news reports to see exactly how its desired target audience is reacting to different news stories, and to the ads.

The owners of the networks are increasingly hostile to airing reports that may call into question some of their other activities. And, given the reach of those activities, there may be a lot of uncovered territory in the years to come.

In 1998, Disney-owned ABC News killed a 20/20 segment by Brian Ross, its leading investigative reporter, about Disney World in Florida. Ross was prepared to air charges that Disney was so lax in doing background checks on employees that it had hired pedophiles. Although ABC News claimed the cancellation was due to factors other than pressure from above, the stench of conflict-of-interest could not help but fill the air.

The same censorship mentality spills over into programming. This May, NBC heavily advertised a two-part mini-series called *Atomic Train*, which was originally about a runaway train carrying nuclear waste. But just days before broadcast, NBC started to pull the ads for the program and dubbed out all references to nuclear waste, choosing the more generic "hazardous material." Not incidentally, General Electric, which owns NBC, is a major nuclear energy producer.

In 1996, the news story that NBC gave the most time to was the Summer Olympics in Atlanta, an event that did not even rank among the top 10 stories covered by CBS, ABC, or CNN. What explains NBC's devotion to this story? NBC had the television rights to the Olympics and used its nightly news to pump up the ratings for its prime-time coverage.

NBC is not alone here. "Various shows on ABC, now owned by Disney, have devoted a great deal of time to several movies produced by Disney, although the network has maintained in each instance that there was justified journalistic interest in the films," an article in the *New York Times* noted on July 10, 1998.

Don't expect the new Viacom to be any better. At MTV, it was policy under Redstone to provide editorial coverage—and ample promotional tie-ins—only to those film studios that purchased large amounts of advertising on MTV. The music station even required the studios to pay the production costs for the special shows on MTV about their movies.

The commercial media is increasingly cozy with other wealthy corporations. A News Corp. station in Florida in 1997, for instance, fired, two of its on-air reporters, Jane Akre and Steve Wilson, for refusing to water down their investigative story on Monsanto's bovine growth hormone.

And CBS News last year rebuked Roberta Baskin, one of its 48 Hours correspondents, who was responsible for an acclaimed 1996 exposé of Nike's labor practices in Vietnam. What was her apparent crime? She had protested too loudly when CBS on-camera correspondents wore the Nike logo and Nike gear during the CBS telecasts of the 1998 Winter Olympics, for which Nike was a major sponsor. Baskin said this undermined the network's credibility and detracted from her original story. She also charged that CBS refused to rebroadcast that story for fear of offending Nike, which CBS denied. But the network confirmed that it refused to let Baskin respond to criticisms of her story in the *Wall Street Journal*. And Baskin says CBS would not permit her to do a follow up story, even though she had uncovered an internal Nike report substantiating her original charges.

In sum, concentrated corporate control of the media has produced a broadcast journalism that is great at generating profit, pleasing advertisers, and protecting powerful institutions from scrutiny, but lousy at what it's supposed to do: informing the citizenry and confronting abusers of power. If we are serious about democracy, we need decent journalism. And to get decent journalism, we need to make fundamental reforms in our media system. Even among those who deplore conglomeration, hypercommercialism, and the decline of public interest journalism, there is a fatalistic sense that this is the way it must be. But the U.S. media system is the result of a series of political decisions, not natural law or holy mandate. The U.S. government and the citizens of the United States did not—and do not—have to turn over the broadcast spectrum to nine mega-corporations interested only in maximizing profit.

At any time in the last century, the American people might have chosen to establish a truly non-profit and noncommercial radio and television system; they have always had the constitutional right to do so. The first major law for U.S. broadcasting was the Communications Act of 1934; the second was the Telecommunications Act of 1996. In 1934, there was considerable opposition to corporate domination of radio broadcasting, but those who led the opposition had barely any influence in Washington. In 1996, there was nowhere near the organized opposition that existed in 1934, and the communications lobbies pushed the law through at breakneck speed.

The striking feature of U.S. media policymaking is how singularly undemocratic it has been—and remains. Crucial decisions are made by the few for the few behind closed doors. Public participation has been minuscule.

That has got to change. We, as citizens, need to let our voices be heard. The airwaves belong to the people. We should demand a democratic media, not one that is controlled by Time Warner, Rupert Murdoch, Disney, GE, or Viacom/CBS.

I'd like to offer four general proposals for media reform. They are by no means explicit blueprints; they are meant only to get the discussion going.

1. SHORE UP NON-PROFIT AND NONCOMMERCIAL RADIO

The starting point for media reform is to shore up a viable non-profit, noncommercial media sector. Such a sector currently exists in the United States and produces much of value, but it's woefully small and underfunded. This sector is unbeholden to corporations, and its views are undistorted by the profit motive. It thus has the inclination to air stories that run counter to the interests of the huge corporations; it publishes viewpoints on national issues that get short shrift elsewhere, and it engages in the kind of public-spirited debates that we need more of in our democracy.

Foundations and organized labor could and should contribute far more to non-profit media. And government itself should foster this sector. It could extend lower mailing costs for a wide range of non-profit publications. Or it could permit tax deductions for contributions to non-profit media.

To leave the non-profit, noncommercial sector to starve as the commercial sector gets fatter and fatter makes no sense at all.

2. STRENGTHEN PUBLIC BROADCASTING

Public broadcasting today is really a system of non-profit commercial broadcasting, serving a sliver of the population. What we need is a system of real public broadcasting, with no advertising, one that accepts no grants from corporations or private bodies, one that serves the entire population, not merely those who have high-brow tastes and disposable income to contribute during pledge drives.

A new system should include more national networks, local stations, fully utilized and subsidized public access television, and independent community radio stations. Every community should also have a stratum of low-power television and micropower radio stations.

Where will the funds come from to pay for such a service? At present, the federal government provides $260 million annually. The public system I envision—which would put per capita U.S. spending in a league with Britain's and Japan's—may well cost $5 billion to $10 billion annually. I have no qualms about drawing the funds from general revenues. A system of genuinely non-profit, noncommercial, and public broadcasting is essential if we are to be not just consumers but citizens, too.

3. TOUGHEN REGULATION

Media reformers have long been active in this arena, if only because the public ownership of the airwaves gives the Federal Communications Commission a clear legal right to negotiate terms with the chosen few who get broadcast licenses. Still, broadcast regulation has largely been toothless, with the desires of powerful corporations and advertisers rarely challenged.

In my view, commercial broadcasters should be granted licenses only on the following terms:

First, they will not air any paid political advertising during electoral campaigns unless every candidate on the ballot is given equal time, free of charge, immediately following the paid spot of a rival. This would go a long way toward clearing up the campaign spending mass that is destroying electoral democracy in the United States.

Second, we should follow the lead of Sweden and ban advertising to children under 12. Likewise, we should remove advertising from TV news broadcasts.

Third, broadcasters should donate some percentage of their revenues to subsidize several hours per day of noncommercial children's and news/public affairs programming. Educators and artists should control the children's programming; journalists the news programming.

4. ANTITRUST

If ever there was a need for antitrust laws, that need is painfully clear in the area of media conglomerates. Not only do the media giants make a mockery of free competition; they impede the very functioning of democracy. Antitrust laws were put on the books at the turn of the last century to counteract the power of a few huge companies over both our economic and our political system. We should recall those concerns today as we wrestle with the media behemoths.

What is needed is a new media antitrust statute, similar in tone to the Clayton and Sherman Acts, that lays out the general values to be enforced by the Justice Department and the Federal Trade Commission. It would put an emphasis on valuing the importance of ideological diversity and noncommercial content. The objective should be to break up the media conglomerates and smash their vertical integration so that their book publishing, magazine publishing, TV show production, movie production, TV stations, TV networks, cable TV channels, cable TV systems, retail store chains, amusement parks, and so on all become independent firms. With reduced barriers to entry in these specific markets, new firms could more easily join in, and something resembling fair competition could ensue.

The aim of these combined measures is to produce a media system that is fair and accurate, that scrupulously examines the activities of the powerful, that provides a legitimate accounting of the diverse views and interests of society. It would provide a culture based on artists' interactions with people and ideas, not on the orders from Madison Avenue. The only bias is a fervent commitment to democracy.

There is no reason why we must have a system that gives the wealthy and powerful high-quality information so they may rule the world while the rest of the population is fed a diet of schlock. The only way to gain some popular control over the communications field is to mobilize a popular movement for it. As the agitator Saul Alinksy noted, to beat organized money, you need organized people. The issue of media reform can attract the enthusiastic support of many citizens who have not been previously active. There's a general disgust with the media and entertainment industry, and there's a wellspring of populist resentment toward media giants.

While the fight for a democratic media is a necessary component—even a cornerstone—of any democratic movement, it cannot be won in isolation. Media reformers need to work with those involved in campaign finance reform, organized labor, civil rights, women's rights, gay and lesbian rights, immigrant rights, environmental protection, health care, and education. We need a broad movement to reshape our society, redeem its democratic promise, and put power in the hands of the many.

It won't be easy. On the media front, the giants are unusually canny, and they have the means at their disposal to get their own views across.

Unless we marshal the forces on our side, we will have no choice but to sit back and watch more mergers like Viacom/CBS—and to listen to the pundits tell us how good they are for us.

ROBERT W. McCHESNEY is an associate professor at the Institute of Communications Research and at the Graduate School of Library and Information Science at the University of Illinois, Urbana-Champaign. He is the author, most recently, of *Rich Media, Poor Democracy: Communication Politics in Dubious Times* (University of Illinois).

THIS MODERN WORLD

by TOM TOMORROW

OUR TOP STORY TONIGHT: THE GOVERNOR OF *IOWA* LAUNCHES AN AIR STRIKE AGAINST NEW YORK CITY STRONGMAN *RUDY GIULIANI!*

HIS SECURITY FORCES ARE *TERRORIZING* THE REGION'S ETHNIC POOR!

WE *MUST* DEGRADE HIS CAPABILITIES!

CROP DUSTERS RETROFITTED WITH STATE-OF-THE-ART "STEALTH" TECHNOLOGY UNLEASH IOWA'S VAST ARSENAL OF *FARMING BYPRODUCTS* ON THE CITY!

IS THIS WHAT I *THINK* IT IS..?

I'M AFRAID SO, SIR! NOW, PLEASE--WE'VE GOT TO GET YOU TO YOUR *BUNKER!*

DAMN THOSE CORN-EATING IMPERIALISTS!

SPLAT! SPLAT!

THE ISSUE IS DEBATED ON CABLE ACCESS CHANNELS THROUGHOUT THE STATE!

IF WE IOWANS DON'T SET A MORAL EXAMPLE-- WHO *WILL?*

YES, BUT WHAT'S OUR *END-GAME STRATEGY?* CAN MIDWESTERNERS *REALLY* SOLVE THE PROBLEMS OF A CITY WITH SUCH A LONG HISTORY OF ETHNIC AND RELIGIOUS STRIFE?

GROUND TROOPS MAY EVENTUALLY PROVE NECESSARY-- BUT SO FAR, IOWANS REMAIN ADAMANTLY *OPPOSED* TO THE IDEA...

YOU WOULDN'T GET *ME* NEAR THAT PLACE! NO *WAY!*

IT'S SO DIRTY AND CROWDED! AND PEOPLE DRIVE LIKE *MANIACS!*

MY UNCLE WENT THERE ONCE--AND GOT LOST ON THE SUBWAY FOR *THREE DAYS!*

COMING UP NEXT: WILL HOSTILITIES SPILL OVER INTO NEIGHBORING *NEW JERSEY?* STAY TUNED!

TOM TOMORROW©99

CHAPTER 6

The Media and their Atrocities

BY MICHAEL PARENTI

For the better part of a decade the U.S. public has been bombarded with a media campaign to demonize the Serbian people and their elected leaders. During that time, the U.S. government has pursued a goal of breaking up Yugoslavia into a cluster of small, weak, dependent, free-market principalities. Yugoslavia was the only country in Eastern Europe that would not dismantle its welfare state and public sector economy. It was the only one that did not beg for entry into NATO. It was—and what's left of it, still is—charting an independent course not in keeping with the New World Order.

TARGETING THE SERBS

Of the various Yugoslav peoples, the Serbs were targeted for demonization because they were the largest nationality and the one most opposed to the breakup of Yugoslavia. But what of the atrocities they committed? All sides committed atrocities in the fighting that has been encouraged by the Western powers over the last decade, but the reporting has been consistently one-sided. Grisly incidents of Croat and Muslim atrocities against the Serbs rarely made it into the U.S. press, and when they did they were accorded only passing mention.[1] Meanwhile, Serb atrocities were played up and sometimes even fabricated, as we shall see. Recently, three Croatian generals were indicted by the Hague War Crimes Tribunal for the bombardment and deaths of Serbs in Krajina and elsewhere. Where were the U.S. television crews when these war crimes were being committed? John Ranz, chair of Survivors of the

Buchenwald Concentration Camp, USA, asks: Where were the TV cameras when hundreds of Serbs were slaughtered by Muslims near Srebrenica?[2] The official line, faithfully parroted in the U.S. media, is that Bosnian Serb forces committed all the atrocities at Srebrenica.

Are we to trust U.S. leaders and the corporate-owned news media when they dish out atrocity stories? Recall the 500 premature babies whom Iraqi soldiers laughingly ripped from incubators in Kuwait? A story repeated and believed until exposed as a total fabrication years later. During the Bosnian war in 1993, the Serbs were accused of pursuing an official policy of rape. "Go forth and rape" a Bosnian Serb commander supposedly publicly instructed his troops. The source of that story never could be traced. The commander's name was never produced. As far as we know, no such utterance was ever made. Even the *New York Times* belatedly ran a tiny retraction, coyly allowing that "the existence of 'a systematic rape policy' by the Serbs remains to be proved."[3]

Bosnian Serb forces supposedly raped anywhere from 25,000 to 100,000 Muslim women the stories varied. The Bosnian Serb army numbered not more than 30,000 or so, many of whom were engaged in desperate military engagements. A representative from Helsinki Watch noted that stories of massive Serbian rapes originated with the Bosnian Muslim and Croatian governments and had no credible supporting evidence. Common sense would dictate that these stories be treated with the utmost skepticism—and not be used as an excuse for an aggressive and punitive policy against Yugoslavia.

The "mass rape" propaganda theme was resuscitated in 1999 to justify the continued NATO slaughter of Yugoslavia. A headline in the *San Francisco Examiner* (April 26, 1999) tells us: "Serb Tactic is Organized Rape, Kosovo Refugees Say." No evidence or testimony is given to support the charge of organized rape. Only at the bottom of the story, in the 19th paragraph, do we read that reports gathered by the Kosovo mission of the Organization for Security and Cooperation in Europe (OSCE) found no such organized rape policy. The actual number of rapes were in the dozens "and not many dozens," according to the OSCE spokesperson. This same story did note in passing that the U.N. War Crimes Tribunal sentenced a Bosnian Croat military commander to 10 years in prison for failing to stop his troops from raping Muslim women in 1993—an atrocity we heard little about when it was happening.

A few dozen rapes is a few dozen too many. But can it serve as one of the justifications for a massive war? If Mr. Clinton wanted to stop rapes, he could have begun a little closer to home in Washington, DC, where dozens of rapes occur every month. Indeed, he might be able to alert us to how women are sexually mistreated on Capitol Hill and in the White House itself.

The Serbs were blamed for the infamous Sarajevo market massacre. But according to the report leaked out on French TV, Western intelligence knew that it was Muslim operatives who had bombed Bosnian civilians in the marketplace in order to induce NATO involvement. Even international negotiator David Owen, who worked with Cyrus Vance, admitted in his memoir that the NATO powers knew all along that it was a Muslim bomb.[4]

On one occasion, notes Barry Lituchy, the *New York Times* ran a photo purporting to be of Croats grieving over Serbian atrocities when in fact the murders had been committed by Bosnian Muslims. The *Times* printed an obscure retraction the following week.[5]

The propaganda campaign against Belgrade has been so relentless that even prominent personages on the left—who oppose the NATO policy against Yugoslavia—have felt compelled to genuflect before this demonization orthodoxy, referring to unspecified and unverified Serbian "brutality" and "the monstrous Milosevic."[6] Thus, they reveal themselves as having been influenced by the very media propaganda machine they criticize on so many other issues. To reject the demonized image of Milosevic and of the Serbian people is not to idealize them or claim that Serb forces are faultless or free of crimes. It is merely to challenge the one-sided propaganda that laid the grounds for NATO's aggression against Yugoslavia.

THE ETHNIC CLEANSING HYPE

Up until the NATO bombings began in March 1999, the conflict in Kosovo had taken 2,000 lives altogether from both sides, according to Kosovo Albanian sources. Yugoslavian sources put the figure at 800. Such casualties reveal a civil war, not genocide. Belgrade is condemned for the forced expulsion policy of Albanians from Kosovo. But such expulsions began in substantial numbers only after the NATO bombings, with thousands being uprooted by Serb forces especially from areas where KLA mercenaries were operating.

We should keep in mind that tens of thousands also fled Kosovo because it was being mercilessly bombed by NATO, or because it was the scene of sustained ground fighting between Yugoslav forces and the KLA, or because they were just afraid and hungry. An Albanian woman crossing into Macedonia was eagerly asked by a news crew if she had been forced out by Serb police. She responded: "There were no Serbs. We were frightened of the [NATO] bombs."[7] I had to read this in the *San Francisco Bay Guardian*, an alternative weekly, not in the *New York Times* or *Washington Post*.

During the bombings, an estimated 70,000 to 100,000 Serbian residents of Kosovo took flight (mostly north but some to the south), as did thousands of Roma and others.[8] Were the Serbs ethnically cleansing themselves? Or were these people not fleeing the bombing and the ground war? Yet the refugee tide caused by the bombing was repeatedly used by U.S. warmakers as justification for the bombing, a pressure put on Milosevic to allow "the safe return of ethnic Albanian refugees."[9]

While Kosovo Albanians were leaving in great numbers—usually well-clothed and in good health, some riding their tractors, trucks, or cars, many of them young men of recruitment age—they were described as being "slaughtered." It was repeatedly reported that "Serb atrocities"—not the extensive ground war with the KLA and certainly not the massive NATO bombing— "drove more than one million Albanians from their homes."[10] More recently, there have been hints that Albanian Kosovar refugees numbered nowhere near that.

Serbian attacks on KLA strongholds or the forced expulsion of Albanian villagers were described as "genocide." But experts in surveillance photography and wartime propaganda charged NATO with running a "propaganda campaign" on Kosovo that lacked any supporting evidence. State Department reports of mass graves and of 100,000 to 500,000 missing Albanian men "are just ludicrous," according to these independent critics.[11] Their findings were ignored by the major networks and other national media.

Early in the war, *Newsday* reported that Britain and France were seriously considering "commando assaults into Kosovo to break the pattern of Serbian massacres of ethnic Albanians."[12] What discernible pattern of massacres? Of course, no commando assaults were put into operation, but the story served its purpose of hyping an image of mass killings.

An ABC *Nightline* broadcast made dramatic and repeated references to the "Serbian atrocities in Kosovo" while offering no specifics. Ted Koppel asked a group of angry Albanian refugees what specifically had they witnessed. They pointed to an old man in their group who wore a wool hat. One of them reenacted what the Serbs had done to him, throwing the man's hat to the ground and stepping on it "because the Serbs knew that his hat was the most important thing to him." Koppel was appropriately horrified about this "war crime," the only example offered in an hour-long program.

A widely circulated story in the *New York Times*, headlined "U.S. Report Outlines Serb Attacks in Kosovo," tells us that the State Department issued "the most comprehensive documentary record to date on atrocities." The report concluded that there had been organized rapes and systematic executions.

But as one reads further and more closely into the article, one finds that State Department reports of such crimes depend almost entirely on information from refugee accounts. "There was no suggestion that American intelligence agencies had been able to verify, most, or even many, of the accounts... and the words "reportedly" and "allegedly" appear throughout the document."[13]

British journalist Audrey Gillan interviewed Kosovo refugees about atrocities and found an impressive lack of evidence or credible specifics. One woman caught him glancing at the watch on her wrist, while her husband told him how all the women had been robbed of their jewelry and other possessions. A spokeman for the U.N. High Commissioner for Refugees talked of mass rapes and what sounded like hundreds of killings in three villages, but when Gillan pressed him for more precise information, he reduced it drastically to five or six teenage rape victims. But he had not spoken to any witnesses, and admitted that "we have no way of verifying these reports."[14]

Gillan notes that some refugees had seen killings and other atrocities, but there was little to suggest that they had seen it on the scale that was being reported. One afternoon, officials in charge said there were refugees arriving who talked of 60 or more being killed in one village and 50 in another, but Gillan "could not find one eye-witness who actually saw these things happening." Yet every day Western journalists reported "hundreds" of rapes and murders. Sometimes they noted in passing that the reports had yet to be substantiated, but then why were such unverified stories being so eagerly reported in the first place?

THE DISAPPEARING "MASS GRAVES"

After NATO forces occupied Kosovo, the stories about mass atrocities continued fortissimo. The *Washington Post* reported that 350 ethnic Albanians "might be buried in mass graves" around a mountain village in western Kosovo. They "might be" or they might not be. These estimates were based on sources that NATO officials refused to identify. Getting down to specifics, the article mentions "four decomposing bodies" discovered near a large ash heap.[15]

It was repeatedly announced in the first days of the NATO occupation that 10,000 Albanians had been killed (down from the 100,000 and even 500,000 Albanian men supposedly executed during the war). No evidence was ever offered to support the 10,000 figure, nor even to explain how it was arrived at so swiftly and surely while NATO troops were still moving into place and did not occupy but small portions of the province.

Likewise, repeatedly unsubstantiated references to "mass graves," each purportedly filled with hundreds or even thousands of Albanian victims also failed to materialize. Through the summer of 1999, the media hype about mass graves devolved into an occasional unspecified reference. The few sites actually unearthed offered up as many as a dozen bodies or sometimes twice that number, but with no certain evidence regarding causes of death or even the nationality of victims. In some cases, there was reason to believe the victims were Serbs.[16]

On April 19, 1999, while the NATO bombings of Yugoslavia were going on, the State Department announced that up to 500,000 Kosovo Albanians were missing and feared dead. On May 16, U.S. Secretary of Defense William Cohen, a former Republican Senator from Maine now serving in President Clinton's Democratic Administration, stated that 100,000 military-aged ethnic Albanian men had vanished and might have been killed by the Serbs.[17] Such widely varying but horrendous figures from official sources went unchallenged by the media and by the many liberals who supported NATO's "humanitarian rescue operation." Among these latter were some supposedly progressive members of Congress who seemed to believe they were witnessing another Nazi Holocaust.

On June 17, just before the end of the war, British Foreign Office Minister Geoff Hoon said that "in more than 100 massacres some 10,000 ethnic Albanians had been killed [down from the 500,000 and 100,000 bandied about by U.S. officials]."[18] A day or two after the bombings stopped, the Associated Press and other news agencies, echoing Hoon, reported that 10,000 Albanians had been killed by the Serbs.[19] No explanation was given as to how this figure was arrived at, especially since not a single war site had yet

THIS MODERN WORLD by TOM TOMORROW

been investigated and NATO forces had barely begun to move into Kosovo. On August 2, Bernard Kouchner, the United Nations' chief administrator in Kosovo (and organizer of Doctors Without Borders), asserted that about 11,000 bodies had been found in common graves throughout Kosovo. He cited as his source the International Criminal Tribunal for the Former Republic of Yugoslavia (ICTY). But the ICTY denied providing any such information. To this day, it is not clear how Kouchner came up with his estimate.[20]

As with the Croatian and Bosnian conflicts, the image of mass killings was hyped once again. Repeatedly unsubstantiated references to "mass graves," each purportedly filled with hundreds or even thousands of Albanian victims, were publicized in daily media reports. In September 1999, Jared Israel did an Internet search for newspaper articles appearing over the previous three months including the words "Kosovo" and "mass grave." The report came back: "More than 1,000—too many to list." Limiting his search to articles in the *New York Times*, he came up with 80, nearly one a day. Yet when it came down to hard evidence, the mass graves seemed to disappear.

Thus, in mid-June, the FBI sent a team to investigate two of the sites listed in the war-crimes indictment against Slobodan Milosevic, one purportedly containing six victims and the other 20. The team lugged 107,000 pounds of equipment into Kosovo to handle what was called the "largest crime scene in the FBI's forensic history," but it came up with no reports about mass graves. Not long after, on July 1, the FBI team returned home, oddly with not a word to say about their investigation.[21]

Forensic experts from other NATO countries had similar experiences. A Spanish forensic team, for instance, was told to prepare for at least 2,000 autopsies, but found only 187 bodies, usually buried in individual graves, and showing no signs of massacre or torture. Most seemed to have been killed

by mortar shells and firearms. One Spanish forensic expert, Emilio Perez Puhola, acknowledged that his team did not find one mass grave. He dismissed the widely publicized references about mass graves as being part of the "machinery of war propaganda."[22]

The *Washington Post* reported that 350 ethnic Albanians "might be buried in mass graves" around a mountain village in western Kosovo. Or they might not. Such speculations were based on sources that NATO officials refused to identify. Getting down to specifics, the article mentions "four decomposing bodies" discovered near a large ash heap, with no details as to who they might be or how they died.[23]

In late August 1999, the *Los Angeles Times* tried to salvage the genocide theme with a story about how the wells of Kosovo might be "mass graves in their own right." The *Times* claimed that "many corpses have been dumped into wells in Kosovo... Serbian forces apparently stuffed... many bodies of ethnic Albanians into wells during their campaign of terror."[24] Apparently? Whenever the story got down to specifics, it dwelled on only one village and only one well—in which one body of a 39-year-old male was found, along with three dead cows and a dog. Neither his nationality nor cause of death was given. Nor was it clear who owned the well. "No other human remains were discovered," the *Times* lamely concluded. As far as I know, neither the *Los Angeles Times* nor any other media outlet ran any more stories of wells stuffed with victims.

In one grave site after another, bodies were failing to materialize in any substantial numbers or any numbers at all. In July 1999, a mass grave in Ljubenic, near Pec (an area of concerted fighting), believed to be holding some 350 corpses, produced only seven after the exhumation. In Djacovica, town officials claimed that 100 ethnic Albanians had been murdered, but there were no bodies because the Serbs had returned in the middle of the night, dug them up, and carted them away, the officials seemed to believe. In Pusto Selo, villagers claimed that 106 men were captured and killed by Serbs at the end of March, but again no remains were discovered. Villagers once more suggested that Serb forces must have come back and removed them. How they accomplished this without being detected was not explained. In Izbica, refugees reported that 150 ethnic Albanians were executed in March. But their bodies were nowhere to be found. In Kraljan, 82 men were supposedly killed, but investigators found not a single cadaver.[25]

The worst incident of mass atrocities ascribed to Yugoslavian leader Slobodan Milosevic allegedly occurred at the Trepca mine. As reported by U.S. and NATO officials, the Serbs threw 1,000 or more bodies down the shafts or disposed of them in the mine's vats of hydrochloric acid. In October 1999, the ICTY released the findings of Western forensic teams investigating Trepca. Not one body was found in the mine shafts, nor was there any evidence that the vats had ever been used in an attempt to dissolve human remains.[26]

By late autumn of 1999, the media hype about mass graves had fizzled noticeably. The many sites unearthed, considered to be the most notorious, offered up a few hundred bodies altogether, not the thousands or tens of thousands or hundreds of thousands previously trumpeted, and with no evidence of torture or mass execution. In many cases, there was no certain evidence regarding the nationality of victims.[27] No mass killings means that the Hague War Crimes Tribunal indictment of Milosevic "becomes highly questionable," notes Richard Gwyn. "Even more questionable is the West's continued punishment of the Serbs."[28]

No doubt there were graves in Kosovo that contained two or more persons (which is NATO's definition of a "mass grave"). People were killed by bombs and by the extensive land war that went on between Yugoslav and KLA forces. Some of the dead, as even the *New York Times* allowed, "are fighters of the Kosovo Liberation Army or may have died ordinary deaths"—as would happen in any large population over time.[29] And no doubt there were grudge killings and summary executions as in any war, but not on a scale that would warrant the label of genocide and justify the massive death and destruction and the continuing misery inflicted upon Yugoslavia by the Western powers.

We should remember that the propaganda campaign waged by NATO officials and the major media never claimed merely that atrocities (murders and rapes) occurred. Such crimes occur in every war, and indeed, in many communities during peacetime. What the media propaganda campaign against Yugoslavia charged was that mass atrocities and mass rapes and mass murders had been perpetrated, that is, genocide, as evidenced by mass graves.

In contrast to its public assertions, the German Foreign Office privately denied there was any evidence that genocide or ethnic cleansing was ever a component of Yugoslav policy: "Even in Kosovo, an explicit political persecution linked to Albanian ethnicity is not verifiable...The actions of the [Yugoslav] security forces [were] not directed against the Kosovo-Albanians as an ethnically defined group, but against the military opponent and its actual or alleged supporters."[30]

Still, Milosevic was indicted as a war criminal, charged with the forced expulsion of Kosovar Albanians, and with summary executions of 100 or so individuals, again, alleged crimes that occurred after the NATO bombing had started, yet were used as justification for the bombing. The biggest war criminal of all is NATO and the political leaders who orchestrated the aerial campaign of death and destruction. But here is how the White House and the U.S. media reasoned at the time: Since the aerial attacks do not intend to kill civilians, then presumably there is no liability and no accountability, only an occasional apology for the regrettable mistakes—as if only the intent of an action counted and not its ineluctable effects. In fact, a perpetrator can be judged guilty of willful murder without explicitly intending the death of a particular victim—as when the death results from an unlawful act that the perpetrator knew would likely cause death. George Kenney, a former State Department official under the Bush Administration, put it well: "Dropping cluster bombs on highly populated urban areas doesn't result in accidental fatalities. It is purposeful terror bombing."[31]

In sum, through a process of monopoly control and distribution, repetition and image escalation, the media achieve self-confirmation, that is, they find confirmation for the images they fabricate in the images they have already fabricated. Hyperbolic labeling takes the place of evidence: "genocide," "mass atrocities," "systematic rapes," and even "rape camps"—camps which no one has ever located. Through this process, evidence is not only absent, it becomes irrelevant.

So the U.S. major media (and much of the minor media) are not free and independent, as they claim, they are not the watchdog of democracy but the lapdog of the national security state. They help reverse the roles of victims and victimizers, warmongers and peacekeepers, reactionaries and reformers. The first atrocity, the first war crime committed in any war of aggression by the aggressors, is against the truth.

MICHAEL PARENTI is the author of *Against Empire* and *America Besieged*. His most recent book is *History as Mystery* (City Lights Books).

NOTES

1. For instance, Raymond Bonner, "War Crimes Panel Finds Croat Troops 'Cleansed' the Serbs," *New York Times*, March 21, 1999, a revealing report that has been ignored in the relentless propaganda campaign against the Serbs.

2. John Ranz in his paid advertisement in the *New York Times*, April 29, 1993.

3. "Correction: Report on Rape in Bosnia," *New York Times*, October 23, 1993.

4. David Owen, *Balkan Odyssey*: 262.

5. Barry Lituchy, "Media Deception and the Yugoslav Civil War," in *NATO in the Balkans*: 205; see also *New York Times*, August 7, 1993.

6. Both Noam Chomsky in his comments on Pacifica Radio, April 7, 1999, and

Alexander Cockburn in *The Nation*, May 10, 1999, describe Milosevic as "monstrous" without offering any specifics.

7. Brooke Shelby Biggs, "Failure to Inform," *San Francisco Bay Guardian*, May 5, 1999: 25.

8. *Washington Post*, June 6, 1999.

9. See for instance, Robert Burns, Associated Press report, April 22, 1999.

10. For example, *New York Times*, June 15, 1998.

11. Charles Radin and Louise Palmer, "Experts Voice Doubts on Claims of Genocide: Little Evidence for NATO Assertions," *San Francisco Chronicle*, April 22, 1999.

12. *Newsday*, March 31, 1999.

13. *New York Times*, May 11, 1999.

14. Audrey Gillan, "What's the Story?," *London Review of Books*, May 27, 1999.

15. *Washington Post*, July 10, 1999.

16. See for instance, Carlotta Gall, "Belgrade Sees Grave Site as Proof NATO Fails to Protect Serbs," *New York Times*, August 27, 1999.

17. Both the State Department and Cohen's figures are reported in the *New York Times*, November 11, 1999.

18. *New York Times*, November 11, 1999.

19. Associated Press release, June 18, 1999. Reuters (July 12, 1999) reported that NATO forces had catalogued more than one hundred sites containing the bodies of massacred ethnic Albanians.

20. Stratfor.com, Global Intelligence Update, "Where Are Kosovo's Killing Fields?" Weekly Analysis, October 18, 1999.

21. Reed Irvine and Cliff Kincaid, "Playing the Numbers Game," www.aim.org/mm/1999/08/03.htm.

22. *Sunday Times* (London), October 31, 1999.

23. *Washington Post*, July 10, 1999.

24. *Los Angeles Times*, August 28, 1999.

25. Stratfor.com, Global Intelligence Update, "Where Are Kosovo's Killing Fields?" Weekly Analysis, October 18, 1999.

26. Richard Gwyn in the *Toronto Star*, November 3, 1999.

27. See for instance, Carlotta Gall, "Belgrade Sees Grave Site as Proof NATO Fails to Protect Serbs," *New York Times*, August 27, 1999.

28. Richard Gwyn in the *Toronto Star*, November 3, 1999.

29. *New York Times*, November 11, 1999.

30. Intelligence reports from the German Foreign Office, January 12, 1999 and October 29, 1998 to the German Administrative Courts, translated by Eric Canepa, Brecht Forum, New York, April 20, 1999.

31. Teach-in, Leo Baeck Temple, Los Angeles, May 23, 1999.

THIS MODERN WORLD

by TOM TOMORROW

Panel 1:

IF NOT FOR THE SEATTLE PROTESTS, DISCUSSION OF THE WORLD TRADE ORGANIZATION WOULD HAVE REMAINED AT A NEAR-KINDERGARTEN LEVEL.

FREE TRADE BENEFITS *EVERYONE*, BOYS AND GIRLS! ANYONE WHO DOESN'T UNDERSTAND *THAT* IS A *BIG SILLY-HEAD!*

CAN *YOU* SAY "BIG SILLY-HEAD"?

I KNEW YOU COULD!

Panel 2:

OF COURSE, THERE *IS* A BIT MORE TO THE STORY... I.E., THE PROFOUNDLY ANTI-DEMOCRATIC NATURE OF THE W.T.O., WHOSE SECRETIVE THREE-MEMBER TRIBUNAL IS EMPOWERED TO OVERRULE THE LAWS OF ANY MEMBER NATION IN THE NAME OF *FREE TRADE...*

I DON'T SEE ANY PROBLEM WITH THAT.

I DON'T HEAR ANYONE COMPLAINING.

I HAVE NO COMMENT.

World Trade Organization

Panel 3:

...WHICH BRINGS US TO THE HEART OF THE PROBLEM: THE GROWING DOMINANCE OF AN ECONOMIC SYSTEM IN WHICH GOVERNMENTS PLACE THE NEEDS OF LARGE CORPORATIONS OVER THOSE OF THEIR *OWN CITIZENRY...*

--A SYSTEM THE ITALIANS LONG AGO TERMED "ESTATO CORPORATIVO"--

--OR, MORE POPULARLY, "*FASCISM.*"

YOU'RE MAKING ONE OF YOUR LITTLE POINTS AGAIN, AREN'T YOU?

Panel 4:

IF ONLY THERE WERE SOME WAY TO COUNTER THIS TREND.

YES--IF ONLY WE HAD A SYSTEM IN WHICH EVERY CITIZEN HAD AN *EQUAL* VOICE-- *REGARDLESS* OF THEIR SOCIAL OR ECONOMIC STATUS!

AND SOME METHOD FOR--WELL--*TALLYING* THEIR BELIEFS, SO THAT THE WILL OF THE *MAJORITY* COULD SOMEHOW BE IMPLEMENTED!

WELL-- I SURE CAN'T THINK OF ANYTHING LIKE *THAT!*

CHAPTER 7

The Media Battle of Seattle

BY NORMAN SOLOMON

When thousands of protesters gathered in Seattle at the end of November 1999 to challenge the global summit of the World Trade Organization (WTO), they were on a collision course with a decade of media support for "free trade."

Many of America's mainstream news outlets had been rumbling with apprehension all fall. Four weeks before the pivotal trade talks were set to begin, the *Washington Post* echoed the anxiety with a front-page article under the headline "Trade Body Summit Targeted for Protests." The influential newspaper reported that the WTO had long faced "virulent opposition"—an assessment not quoted or attributed to anyone, presumably just a matter of fact.

"Virulent"? According to my dictionary, the mildest definition of the word is "intensely irritating, obnoxious, or harsh." The other definitions: "extremely poisonous or pathogenic; bitterly hostile or antagonistic; hateful." After this characterization of WTO opponents in the fourth paragraph, the *Washington Post* article prominently quoted several pro-WTO sources: the head of the organization, a top executive at the Goldman Sachs investment firm, the U.S. trade representative, and a member of the British House of Commons. But foes of the WTO got few words in edgewise.

The tone and sourcing of the *Post*'s news article were consistent with long-established journalistic baselines for informing the public about trade issues. Yet the impending demonstrations at the WTO ministerial meeting added a worrisome element to the mix. The November 8 issue of *Business Week* featured a downbeat piece by Jeffrey Garten, a former undersecretary of commerce in the Clinton Administration, who declared: "In late November, Seattle is likely to be the scene of a big test for global capitalism. That's when more than 1,000 non-governmental organizations (NGOs) are planning to disrupt the kickoff of a new round of global trade negotiations."

Similar concerns were voiced by many other media commentators. What were they afraid of? Undue democratic participation in decision-making. NGOs "have skillfully exploited the void between shrinking governments unable to cushion the impact of change on ordinary citizens and multinational companies that are the agents of that change," Garten wrote.

Translation: Huge firms had been shaping government policies, while "ordinary citizens" suffered dire consequences. Rather than passively accept the results, activist groups were resisting—and worse, they were getting somewhere.

"While governments and chief executives bore the public and the media with sterile abstractions about free markets," Garten added, "NGOs are sending more nuanced messages sensitive to the anxieties of local communities around the world. At the same time, they are preparing sophisticated strategies to influence television networks, newspapers, and magazines."

Translation: Activists were threatening to usurp the prerogatives of big money to determine the main media messages.

"If Washington and Corporate America don't move decisively," Garten warned, "NGOs could dominate public opinion on global trade and finance."

Translation: Washington and Corporate America must make sure that they continue to dominate public opinion.

But the fears of some were the hopes of others. Since the launch of the World Trade Organization in 1995, grassroots oppositional movements had emerged to monitor secretive WTO activities and to work together—across boundaries of race, class, language, culture, and nationality. Those movements were insisting that truly democratic procedures—not unelected WTO officials—should determine the rules of the global economy. The implications were profound: for workers, human rights, public health, and the environment.

But during the 1990s, for most of the U.S. media, the virtues of corporate globalization were self-evident, like motherhood and apple pie—and the media "debate" resembled the sound of one side clapping.

Six years before the battle of Seattle, a brief flurry of news coverage marked the end of the "Uruguay Round" of GATT negotiations that set the stage for the founding of the World Trade Organization. Here's how a news story began on page one of the *New York Times*: "Free trade means growth. Free trade means growth. Free trade means growth. Just say it 50 more times and all doubts will melt away." Accompanied by a pedantic headline—"How Free Trade Prompts Growth: A Primer"—the article concentrated on quoting economists who lauded "free trade." When ABC News anchor Peter Jennings introduced a report on what GATT "means for the U.S.," only one person appeared to provide the answer—the head U.S. trade negotiator, Mickey Kantor. He was succinct: "Jobs. Wealth. Increased standard of living. Growing capital. More profits."

Greatly aided by such glowing media treatment, the GATT pact gained congressional approval in late 1994, and the United States joined with more than 100 other countries to establish the World Trade Organization. Soon the WTO took action that gave ample reason for alarm. But the U.S. media paid very little attention.

In mid-January 1996, the World Trade Organization ruled that the U.S. law known as the Clean Air Act was unacceptable because of restrictions it placed on pollutants in imported gasoline. Although the WTO decree would mean higher levels of toxic auto emissions, it was a blip on the U.S. media screen. Five months later the Clinton Administration opted to comply with the WTO's decision, agreeing to change how the U.S. government would apply environmental regulations of gasoline imports.

But activism began to impinge on policy prerogatives. In November 1997, the House of Representatives refused to grant the president fast-track authority over trade agreements. Major media outlets responded with disgust. An angry *Wall Street Journal* editorial charged that AFL-CIO President John Sweeney had "busted up a Democratic president's attempt to maintain American trade leadership in the emerging global economy." A heated *New York Times* editorial concluded that "narrow political interest has carried the day." The *Washington Post* fumed that Congress "caved in to the special pleaders."

The *Post* editorial told a somewhat resentful tale: "Trade liberalization benefits most people, but it also invariably hurts a few.... In the political process, the losers and potential losers naturally lobby vociferously; the winners, a larger but more diffuse group, don't." The *Post* didn't mention that corporate trade "winners" had been able to lobby vociferously in its own pages. During the six months leading up to fast track's demise in the House, the *Post*'s op-ed page ran 12 articles in favor of fast track—and just four against it.

Meanwhile, a lot of news and commentary echoed the sentiments of Commerce Secretary William Daley, who depicted citizens living outside the Beltway as ill-informed dummies: "Even though we all know the benefits of globalization, obviously the people out there don't know it." In general, the big victory over fast-track legislation—won by labor, environmentalists, and human rights activists—was widely reported as a triumph for ignorance and narrow special interests.

Despite the defeat of fast track, most media continued to present corporate globalizing as an irresistible force. Yet resistance kept gaining strength. And when the WTO finally held its long-awaited ministerial meeting in late 1999, the conflicts were much too big to be swept under the media rug.

As thousands of WTO delegates and demonstrators converged on Seattle, no one could accuse the U.S. media of downplaying the WTO summit. Quantity of coverage would not be a problem. But quality was another matter.

The spin, already frenetic, approached warp speed. Key media outlets were inclined to portray anti-WTO activists as simplistic naysayers trying to spoil the corporate party in Seattle. A front-page *New York Times* article reported on November 28 that the WTO talks would "test support for freer trade in both rich and poor countries, especially since delegates will face a giant, 1960s-style protest campaign meant to mobilize worldwide opposition to new trade efforts." Just to make sure readers got the (stereotypical) point, the *Times* explained in the second paragraph of another prominent article the same day that protesters "are planning to turn what initially sounded like the yawner of all international meetings—a gathering of trade ministers from 135 countries to start the 'Millennium Round' of trade liberalization talks—into the Woodstock of the era of globalization."

While polishing such clichés, the press also supplied plenty of policy-wonking. The paper-of-record *Times*—devoting lots of ink to intricate tangles of trade, economics, politics, and nationalism—constructed most of its coverage on the bedrock notion that the WTO helps to enhance the future of humanity. A typical *Times* editorial was emphatic on November 28, just before the summit opened: "Lost among the disputes is the fact that open trade promotes prosperity." Such statements are rarely exhumed for critical examination—least of all in the media outlets propagating them.

For instance, how is the WTO fostering "open trade" when it sets about rigorously imposing rules that are protectionist for multinational corporations? And what is the meaning of "prosperity" when huge numbers of people are poor, income disparities are outrageous, labor rights are trampled, and rampant environmental destruction continues?

"The goal of trade talks," the *Times* editorial summarized, "is to guarantee that countries that want to export can find countries willing to import—a goal that can start to be met if the trade ministers drop proposals that cannot yet be resolved by consensus and focus on the few that can." Like other big media, the *New York Times* was eager to see the WTO staying afloat and steaming ahead.

——

For the World Trade Organization, five years of a free ride in U.S. mass media came to a crashing halt on the last day of November 1999.

Fully accustomed to operating with scant media scrutiny in this country, the WTO was apt to seem distant, aloof, and fully protected from the intervention of mere mortals. But on Tuesday, November 30, thousands of mere mortals threw themselves onto the gears of global trade designed by the rich and powerful. The Oz-like curtain shielding the operators of corporate machinery went up in smoke—symbolized by the tear gas and pepper spray wafting over Seattle. December began with the acrid smell of illusions turning to ash. After a little more than half a century, Bretton Woods was burning down.

The broad base of the anti-WTO protests in Seattle compelled media attention. The unions, religious groups, NGOs, activist coalitions, and other organizations represented in the streets were clearly and deeply rooted in communities across North America and every other continent. The emerging alliances that literally and figuratively disrupted the best-laid plans of the WTO were, for corporate media, somewhat odd—and ominous. For the guardians of systemic inequities on a global scale, the expectations for a ministerial gathering had turned nightmarish.

The default position of U.S. news coverage had always been implicit: When government leaders and top corporate officials reach agreement on economic rules for the planet to live (and die) by, those rules are basically sound. Such assumptions were so automatic that few journalists seemed to think twice about them. But as the smoke cleared in Seattle, there were bound to be some second thoughts.

In downtown Seattle, the scene was perversely logical. Relying on heavily armed police and National Guard troops to salvage its summit, the WTO did what anti-democratic organizations have often done, resorting to militarized solutions. But in the process, the happy-face stickers fell off the World Trade Organization. Under intense pressure, masks were slipping.

Promoters of the WTO's image got a break when a small group of people went on a window-smashing spree and drew massive media attention. It's easy enough for TV cameras to videotape scenes of vandalism in a shopping district. A far more difficult task would be to cover the institutionalized violence that is a quiet part of daily life. When Western banks collect interest on loans to poor countries, the suffering—and the links between wealth and poverty—go largely unreported. That's how 20,000 children worldwide continue to die each day from preventable diseases.

Without visible opposition, reigning power brokers are glad to pose as tolerant leaders. But at the crossroads in Seattle, when the WTO found itself unable to proceed with business as usual, it was time to exchange the velvet glove for the iron fist. Police kept attacking nonviolent protesters with rounds of pepper spray, tear gas, and rubber bullets. Armored personnel carriers moved in. Some policemen arrived on horses. National Guard troops donned gas masks. Day after day, helicopters droned steadily overhead.

In a perverse way, it all seemed to make sense. While boosters of the World Trade Organization talk incessantly about "free trade," the consequences of contempt for democracy include more contempt for democracy. Officials of the WTO, a supremely undemocratic institution, deliberate in secret and issue edicts that deem local or national laws to be unfair "trade barriers" if they impede the pursuit of profits. Laws that protect workers or the environment or human rights are supposed to get out of the way.

Overall, the corporate media of the United States declined to acknowledge that the historic events in Seattle represented the emergence of a global pro-democracy movement. The vibrant social forces that arrived in that Pacific Northwest city—and proceeded to deflate the WTO summit—were complex, diverse, and sometimes contradictory. Yet the threads of their demands formed a distinct weave: insisting on democratic rights for all people.

Fervent about the glories of the WTO, marketeers were determined to preserve the kind of social order described a century ago by writer Anatole France: "The law, in its majestic equality, forbids the rich as well as the poor to sleep under bridges, to beg in the streets, and to steal bread." Genuine pro-democracy movements are always profoundly threatening to those with their polished boots on the necks of the poor. In the United States, corporate-owned media—like corporate-leased politicians—don't tend to see any fundamental problem.

America's punditocracy is adept at changing the subject, away from the basics. What is out in the open—like the purloined letter in Edgar Allan Poe's classic tale—is often so omnipresent that it goes unnoticed. Every daily newspaper in the U.S. has a business section; none has a labor section. Even though "Public" is NPR's middle name, there's not even a weekly labor update on that radio network—which airs an hourly "NPR business update."

The Capital Gang on CNN is just one of many TV programs providing an incessant national chorus of corporate-friendly political pundits. It's an apt metaphor: We're supposed to assume that the name of the show is a reference to Washington, DC, but actually the "Capital" in *Capital Gang* could be much better understood as financial capital.

The common media pretense that wealth creates all labor is simply another inversion of reality. What passes for journalism routinely stands on its head in order to serve corporate interests.

———

When the World Trade Organization summit collapsed in Seattle, major American news outlets seemed to go into shock. The failure to launch a new round of global trade talks stunned many journalists who were accustomed to covering the WTO with great reverence. In the wake of the crucial meeting, the mainstream media plunged into the four stages of grief:

SHOCK

Misled by its own reporting and punditry, the media establishment was unprepared for the breakdown of the summit. According to conventional media wisdom, the United States can prevail over Third World countries by brandishing various carrots and sticks at trade negotiations. That mindset did not prepare the press corps for what happened in Seattle, where delegates from poor nations refused to knuckle under.

The usual haunts of reporters covering politics and economics—Pennsylvania Avenue and Wall Street—insulated them from the growing anger against corporate globalization at the grassroots. For years, largely ignored and discounted by mainstream media, community-based activists had been making headway in organizing against the WTO. Not coincidentally, the protests in the streets of Seattle resonated across the nation—especially among people on the lower rungs of the economic ladder. A Pew Research Center survey in spring 1999 found that "among Americans in families earning $75,000 or more, 63 percent see globalization as positive." In sharp contrast, "among the half of American adults in families earning less than $50,000, the positive view of globalism is held by just 37 percent."

If prestigious journalists and their bosses weren't in high income brackets, they'd probably be more in touch with how the other half lives. And thinks.

DENIAL

Despite the enormous volume of coverage in the closing weeks of 1999, few news accounts illuminated the anti-democratic core of the World Trade Organization. Instead, much of the reporting and commentary remained stuck in deep denial.

Near the top of its December 13 cover story, *Newsweek* flatly described the WTO as "the small, Geneva-based bureaucracy that the United States and 134 other nations set up five years ago to referee global commerce." Days earlier, *New York Times* syndicated columnist Thomas Friedman wrote: "The more countries trade with one another, the more they need an institution to set the basic rules of trade, and that is all the WTO does." Reporters and pundits continued to lose credibility when they insisted on denying what had become apparent to so many people: The WTO is a global institution that serves the interests of multinational corporations, placing profits above all else.

ANGER

Unwilling to allow WTO foes to have much time or space in mass media to directly state their case, the biggest news outlets were preoccupied with caricaturing—and often vilifying—the demonstrators.

While the summit was coming unraveled, Friedman devoted a column to lashing out at anti-WTO protesters—"a Noah's ark of flat-Earth advocates, protectionist trade unions, and yuppies looking for their 1960s fix." A week later, in a postmortem piece, Friedman could hardly hold back his tears of rage. "The biggest negative fallout from Seattle," he sputtered, "is the way it smeared free trade."

SADNESS

Countless news stories and commentaries grieved because events in Seattle interfered with the WTO's next leap forward. The diverse protests had raised key issues about democracy and corporate power. But it was still tough for strong critics of the WTO to find much of a platform in big media outlets.

Working within the limits of corporate-owned media, some journalists sounded wistful as they described unconstrained media efforts during the summit. On *World News Tonight*, ABC correspondent Brian Rooney reported: "The meeting of the World Trade Organization was a turning point for the so-called independent media—small, partisan news organizations and individual reporters with political opinions they could never express in the mainstream media."

But why are there widely held "political opinions" that American reporters "could never express in the mainstream media"? The ABC News report didn't explain. But it did provide a clue, mentioning that independent journalists "got out a worldwide message about the working poor, endangered species, and the power of the World Trade Organization."

The nation's largest newsweekly, *Time* magazine, responded to the events in Seattle with seven pages that articulated key policy concerns of corporate America. The main story's penultimate paragraph closed with a quote from a U.S. Chamber of Commerce official, who emphasized that "those who want to promote trade are going to have to make their case much more vigorously to all the American people." Then *Time* concluded: "It is a pretty compelling case. And if they can make it with anywhere near the vigor that was demonstrated by the antis last week in Seattle, free trade may yet win the day."

Both of the commentaries in *Time*'s post-Seattle package stressed the foolishness of the "antis" and the wisdom of corporate globalizing known as "free trade." In a piece headed "Return of the Luddites," Charles Krauthammer mocked what he called the "kooky crowd" protesting in Seattle—"one-world paranoids"; "apolitical Luddites, who refuse to accept that growth, prosperity, and upward living standards always entail some dislocation"; and "the leftover left." Krauthammer's essay was typeset around a photo of union activists protesting the WTO. The picture had a pithy caption: "Kooky Crowd. Motley Remnants of the Old Left Found their Voice in Seattle."

To accentuate the positive, *Time* gave Michael Kinsley a page to explain the errors of anti-WTO thinking. For years, Kinsley appeared as co-host of CNN's *Crossfire* while purportedly representing "the Left." Now he is editor of Microsoft's online publication *Slate* and writes for the flagship magazine of Time Warner, the world's largest media conglomerate. (A liberal fellow, fitting in nicely.) In response to the WTO summit, Kinsley wrote an ode to corporate "free trade" that ended with these reassuring words: "But really, the WTO is O.K. Do the math. Or take it on faith."

Also on magazine racks was *Newsweek*'s cover story—an 11-page spread, heavy on photos and breathless descriptions of the street upheaval in Seattle. The only commentary piece ran under the name of Fareed Zakaria, managing editor of *Foreign Affairs*, with a long headline: "After the Storm Passes. The Protesters Didn't have their Facts Right, and may Hurt the Very Causes They Claim to Care About. Why Good Drama can make Bad History." Chosen by *Newsweek* to illuminate it all, the pundit came through. "What happened in Seattle was an unmitigated disaster," Zakaria asserted, going on to decry "a disparate and motley crew of protesters" and bemoan "the carnival tactics of a small but effective minority." He explained: "The expansion of free trade has been one of Washington's most remarkable acts of global leadership this century—benefiting hundreds of millions of Americans and billions of people across the world."

Among "history's striking regularities," Noam Chomsky has observed, is that "those in a position to impose their projects not only hail them with enthusiasm but also typically benefit from them, whether the values professed involve free trade or other grand principles, which turn out in practice to be finely tuned to the needs of those running the game and cheering the outcome."

NORMAN SOLOMON is a nationally syndicated columnist on media and politics. His most recent book is *The Habits of Highly Deceptive Media: Decoding Spin and Lies in Mainstream News*.

CHAPTER 8

Information Equity for the 21st Century

BY NANCY KRANICH

Free people read freely. That was the theme of this year's Banned Books Week, a week that celebrates our most basic freedom in a democratic society—the freedom of speech. Yet we cannot take this freedom for granted. Books and information access continue to be banned throughout the United States and elsewhere in the world. Part of living in a democracy means respecting each other's differences and the right of all people to choose for themselves what they will read and think.

Most publicized challenges to content involve materials dealing with sexuality, evolution, or witchcraft. But far more subtle are the attempts to limit access to unpopular ideas and the public's right to know. Censorship by any means—government, the marketplace, religious zealots—results in the erosion of our basic freedoms. We must be ever-vigilant of challenges to these rights and stand firm against attempts to limit free expression.

Access to information is fragile. All sorts of barriers can restrict the public's access to ideas. Best known are blatant book banning attempts. But every link in the information chain can either strengthen or weaken public access. The chain begins with the information creators. Without doubt, the elite are far more likely to assume this role than those who are less advantaged. The marketplace for ideas is another key link in determining which voices will be heard—and which will be heard the loudest. But after the sale of an idea, information and knowledge are not used up or consumed like other commodities. They still have many chances to influence thought when they are collected, archived, and preserved for future generations. Among the various barriers to sustained public access are classification, copyright or other licensing restrictions, funding, filtering, and other censoring actions. Any of these actions can limit the public's access to constitutionally protected speech.

As the information revolution has changed the way we work, learn, and live, we cannot simply assume that we have equitable access to all the resources and points of view that we desire. Access to abundance does not insure access to diversity. Instead, we now have access to more and more of the same ideas, with alternatives marginalized more by such forces as corporate profiteering, political expediency, and the whimsy of the marketplace. The promise of new technologies is imperiled by powerful political and economic forces. Attempts to restrict the public's right to know have accelerated over the past year. The battles to protect our First Amendment freedoms, fair use, information equity, and the free flow ideas have increased and public interest stakeholders must now recognize the serious threats facing their basic freedoms.

In 1999, struggles to protect and promote intellectual freedom were waged on many fronts. In schools and libraries around the country, censors tried to deny children the right to read their treasured Harry Potter books. The study of evolution was banned in Kansas. *Snow Falling on Cedars* was removed from a Texas high school curriculum. Religious right groups waged well-organized campaigns to restrict access to the Internet in public libraries

and schools. The Mayor of New York denied funds to the Brooklyn Museum after deriding the exhibit "Sensation" as "sick stuff," claiming that, "you don't have a right to government subsidy for desecrating somebody else's religion." The digital divide between rich and poor grew ever wider. And several well-healed database companies tried to restrict the public's right to facts. Indeed, the last year of the 20th century has proven to be a highly contentious year for the public's First Amendment rights, with little relief in sight for the new millennium.

GOVERNMENT INFORMATION

Over the last decade, access to government information has improved after the repressive Reagan years. Nevertheless, government censorship took several turns for the worse during 1999. The inconclusive investigation over security leaks at Los Alamos led Congress to reverse the promising trend toward declassification of many scientific research reports. Commerce Secretary William Daley called for the shutdown of the National Technical Information Service without a plan for providing access to the nation's scientific research reports and translation of foreign research documents. A proposal forwarded by the library community to insure permanent public access to ethereal electronic government documents was ignored while Internet links to important documents disappeared in droves. A Court of Appeals reversed a lower court ruling which will now allow federal agencies to destroy electronic documents resident in word processing or electronic mail systems once a copy is made for recordkeeping. Clearly, public access to government information produced at taxpayer expense failed to advance in 1999.

COPYRIGHT AND FAIR USE

Over the past year, Congress proposed and even passed a number of bills to further protect the rights of copyright owners at the expense of public access. The delicate balance between creators' and users' rights, carefully negotiated over the past century for print materials, is now tilting toward intellectual property owners. The Digital Millennium Copyright Act, a new law which criminalizes for the first time illegal use of digital materials, places additional limits on the rights of electronic information users. Fair use, only negotiated into the bill after the library and public interest community threatened defeat, was barely preserved under new restrictions regarding unauthorized access to technologically restricted work. The act prohibits the "circumvention" of any effective "technological protection measure" used by a copyright holder to restrict access to its material unless adverse affects on the fair use of any class of work can be demonstrated. Industry representatives have pressed hard to create these and other new protections for their intellectual property while eroding users' rights in order to achieve a competitive advantage in the digital age.

Another copyright-related bill, the Collections of Information Antipiracy Act, would protect investment rather than creativity for database companies and overturn over 200 years of information policy, which has consistently supported unfettered access to factual information. This bill, supported by a small but powerful group of database publishers including: Lexis-Nexis (owned by Reed Elsevier), the New York Stock Exchange, and the National Association of Realtors, would allow a producer or publisher unprecedented control over the uses of information including facts and government works. Even though the Supreme Court held that constitutional copyright principles prohibit ownership of facts or works of the federal government and current copyright law already sufficiently protects database companies, certain corporate interests continue to press hard for this overly broad legislation. This represents a radical departure from the current intellectual property framework that protects expression—not investment—and endangers the doctrine of fair use. If these narrow interests prevail, we will transform into a pay-per-view digital economy where the free flow of ideas is limited to the quaint world of print and photocopy machines.[1]

UNIVERSAL SERVICE AND FILTERING

Under the universal service provisions of the Telecommunications Act of 1996, the Federal Communications Commission has authorized landmark rules to insure that schools and libraries enjoy the lowest possible telecommunications rates that were once only offered to the largest corporate customers. Known as the E-rate, over $2 billion in discounts and grants was earmarked for distribution from fees collected by long distance phone carriers this year. The E-rate helps bridge the ever-widening digital divide by expanding access and connectivity to needy communities.[2] Telecommunications companies agreed to this amendment to the 1996 Telecommunications Act in return for deregulation of their markets. But several of the major carriers who benefited most from deregulation, including MCI and AT&T, have tried to sabotage this nominal fee by highlighting the universal service charge on consumer bills without explanation, thereby maddening their enormous customer base. Other telecommunications companies tried to sue in federal court, but were unsuccessful in stopping the program. Often referred to as the "Gore Tax," this program remains in great jeopardy, even as funds are finally flowing to local communities and the significant benefits are becoming tangible.

Congress has picked up where corporate attempts to stop the flow of subsidies to schools and libraries ended. A number of bills are pending that require local communities to install filters to protect children from obscenity and child pornography as a condition for receiving E-rate funds. One of them, the Children's Internet Protection Act, which is part of the House-passed version of the Juvenile Justice bill, seeks to protect children from violence by focusing on Internet censorship—while doing nothing to control guns in schools. Attempts to tie federal funding to content restrictions raises serious Constitutional questions similar to those brought forward in the *ACLU v. Reno* case (which challenged the Communications Decency Act) and the *Giuliani v. the Brooklyn Museum* case. These bills seek to impose federal regulation over local, community control of information access.[3]

Many states are trying to pass similar laws to restrict Internet access in schools and libraries through mandating a filtering requirement in order for these institutions to receive state and local funding. Unfortunately, filters do not work; they sweep too broadly, blocking only some sites with indecent materials while restricting access to legal and useful resources. In the small portion of libraries that employ filters, users complain that they block such home pages as the Mars Exploration site (MARSEXPL), a site on swan migration in Alma, Wisconson (swANALma), *Mother Jones* magazine, the National Rifle Association, and thousands of other legitimate sites of interest. Filtering systems have trouble distinguishing between a 6-year-old and a 16-year-old, which essentially makes all information received through them appropriate for the youngest users at the expense of all others. Furthermore, filters are not effective in blocking much material that some consider undesirable for children; they give parents a false sense their children are protected from harm; and they do not take the place of preferred routes that include the development of community-based Internet Access Policies, user education programs, links to great sites, and safety guidelines. The extraordinary benefits of Internet access are too often overshadowed by controversies fueled by local family groups. These groups revive old fears about the power of images and words and raise questions about the ownership and control of information. According to a recent study by the National Coalition Against Censorship, "the evidence of harm from Internet access at public institutions is at best equivocal, and the blunt-edged approach advocated by pro-censorship advocates ignores the individualized need of children and their parents. Fortunately, most libraries have found ways of balancing the interests of all parties effectively, without censorship."[4]

MARKETPLACE CENSORSHIP

Project Censored and others have successfully documented how multinational media conglomerates have made undemocratic decisions that affect people's lives. Less well-known, however, is the impact on scholars' access to information and new ideas. Over the last 10 years, as mergers have squeezed out smaller publishers and media producers, the cost of scholarly materials has skyrocketed. These high costs have caused severe stress for the nation's libraries as they try to keep up with the enormous increase in the volume and price of journals—particularly in science, business, technology, and medicine. Canceled subscriptions and decreases in the purchase of monographs have eroded access to the world's increasing output of research and scholarship, and have undermined the market for specialized monographic literature.

Journal costs in particular have risen at an astounding 150 percent over the last decade. Lucrative journal publishing has stretched budgets beyond the breaking point by an industry now dominated by a handful of multinational conglomerates who also control much of the market for electronic products: Reed Elsevier, Walters Kluwer, and Wiley. For years, Reed's electronic database subsidiary Lexis-Nexis, has led efforts to privatize government information and is a principle proponent for the database bill that will further erode users' rights. Reed Elsevier's 1,200 scientific and technical journal titles account for close to 25 percent of the payments for journals made by many research libraries. Prices for these titles have increased 151 percent over the past 6 years and they are among the most costly items purchased (several exceed $15,000 per year for a subscription.) While libraries have canceled millions of dollars worth of serials, they have spent even less on monographs which now constitute one-third rather than two-thirds of their annual expenditures for materials. As a result, the scholarly monograph is endangered with university and small presses suffering the most. The reduced purchasing power of university libraries which once accounted for the purchase of 80 percent of university press sales is now closer to 40 percent. Press runs formerly of 2,000–3,000 copies have dropped down to 1,250–1,500, sending the price of monographs soaring.

Increasingly, librarians and others in the academic community have concluded that they can no longer sustain a system where their own faculty sign away the rights to their scholarship to commercial publishers who in turn sell this content back at astronomical prices to a nearly captive market—university libraries. Alternative models that are emerging for disseminating scholarly resources are unlikely to relieve budgetary pressure on libraries anytime soon. Already, most commercial publishers have abandoned the scholarly monograph market and few university presses remain willing to take risks with more esoteric titles. As a result, less popular voices are less likely to be published and distributed.[5]

INSURING INFORMATION EQUITY

Censorship in America is likely to flourish into the next century. The culprits, whether public officials, private interests, or decency groups, employ a variety of techniques that have evolved over time. Whatever their form, attempts to control free expression deny the cherished democratic rights of citizens. The promises of the 21st-century information society must not be placed in peril by those content on restricting public access to information and the free flow of ideas. A high-tech society must not become a highly-controlled society. The vigilance and activism of those concerned with protecting free expression is more important than ever, if the American ideals embedded in the First Amendment of the Constitution are to remain the beacon of our way of life in the new millennium.

The stakes are high. Corporate profit alone should not determine how the public will receive and distribute information. We must counter the heavy influence of commercial corporations by harnessing our strength as voters, educators, and activists who know how to act up if our rights and liberties are at risk. Too often, the information marketplace is considered the sole domain of the industries building the information infrastructure. We simply cannot afford to sit back and let the information infrastructure debate be framed by special interests whose profits depend on the proliferation of info-tainment and home shopping. We must make public access happen for all the public, not only for corporate interests, not only for those who can afford high prices, not only for those concerned with family values, not only for those who can utilize highly sophisticated computer software and hardware, and not only for those who peddle legislative influence. We must speak up and fight for information equity for all. Otherwise, we will endanger our most pre-cious right in a democratic society—the right of free speech and inquiry.

NANCY KRANICH is president, 2000–2001, of the American Library Associ-ation; and associate dean, New York University Libraries.

NOTES

1. For up-to-date information about copyright issues, see the American Library Association Washington Office Web site, www.ala.org/washoff, with links to numer-ous other sites concerned with protecting fair use in the digital age.

2. For more information about the E-Rate, see the American Library Association Washington Office web site: www.ala.org/washoff. The National Telecommunications and Information Administration (NTIA) recently issued: *Falling Through The Net: Defining the Digital Divide* (Washington, DC: U.S. Department of Commerce, 1999) which provides data on the extent of technology inequality in America.

3. See the National Coalition Against Censorship, *The Cyber-Library: Legal and Policy Issues Facing Public Libraries in the High-Tech Era* (New York: NCAC, 1999): 8; the American Library Association, Office of Intellectual Freedom Web site: www.ala.org/oif.html; and the Freedom to Read Foundation web site. Up-to-date infor-mation about Congressional bills that require filtering is available on the ALA Wash-ington Office Web site on E-rate issues: http://www.ala.org/washoff/e-rate.html.

4. See Nancy Kranich, "Scholarly Publishers Hold Universities Hostage: Monop-oly On Journals Causes Prices To Soar," *Extra*, publication of FAIR (January 1999): 24–25, and the Association of Research Libraries Office of Scholarly Communica-tion Web site: http://www.arl.org/scomm/index.html.

5. For a review of current public perception about the First Amendment, see First Amendment Center, *State of the First Amendment* (Nashville, TN: First Amendment Center, 1999).

CHAPTER 9

Media Accountability: News Councils and Ombudsmen

BY CHARLES L. KLOTZER

The freedom to communicate is buttressed in the United States by tradition, culture, and most important, by a religious faith in the legal system. Its god is the U.S. Constitution. This strengthens the system of government with the fervor of faith. Even miniscule extremist groups advance their cause by invoking the U.S. Constitution and claiming that America has abandoned its principles.

No aspect of the Constitution is cited as often as the First Amendment, which is the only section that upholds the free exercise of a profession, the press.

All publications, including those that are subversive to the established order, find a safe haven under the umbrella of the First Amendment. That political consensus legitimizes the judiciary to sustain the exercise of free expression. Attempts to circumscribe that freedom by various branches of government have been attempted in the past and, no doubt, will be in the future. The system, as a whole, is self-correcting.

Yet the commercialization of the media is so all pervasive, so limiting to the free expression of alternative ideas and social solutions, that to talk of a free press one must first define what we are talking about. A reporter's freedom to investigate private or official corruption? The corporate media's freedom to gobble up other media and further concentrate control and wealth?

Media mergers, as reported by the Associated Press, have accelerated since Capital Cities Communications Inc. bought American Broadcasting Company (ABC) for $3.5 billion early in 1986. Since then, 22 mergers, involving more than $633 billion, have consolidated 34 of these media conglomerates into 13. Is that an exercise of press freedom?

Robert W. McChesney, among others, has documented how corporate media has cemented a system "whereby the wealthy and powerful few make the most important decisions with virtually no informed public participation." He suggests an array of media reforms, which involve massive organizational drives by labor, progressives, and other groups; support of noncommercial media, and ways to affect regulations, the legal system, and campaign reform efforts. All excellent, but long range, ideas.

Meanwhile, the consumer of news has an additional option: press criticism. In view of the power of the media, and irrespective of how it is interpreted by our judicial system, press freedom will remain a noble but abstract concept unless this freedom can be applied locally and daily, not only by the media but also by the consumer.

The media define influence and often join forces with particular interests that may or may not serve the public. While politicians must always keep the electorate in mind, business leaders their stockholders, and labor leaders their members, who calls the media to account for their treatment of news?

Accountability of the media to the public and applicability of review by the public are the two ingredients that make press freedom come alive.

Press freedom is a two-way street. Most often it refers to the right to pre-

THIS MODERN WORLD   by TOM TOMORROW

YOU CAN READ THE DAILY PAPER AND WATCH THE CABLE NEWS CHANNELS AND TRUST THE RESPONSIBLE VOICES OF AUTHORITY TO TELL YOU WHAT YOU NEED TO KNOW -- ABOUT IRAQ, SAY...

IF SADDAM WAS GOING TO KEEP TREATING THE U.N. INSPECTORS LIKE SPIES--

--WE HAD NO CHOICE BUT TO BOMB HIM!

THAT MADMAN HAS NO RESPECT FOR THE INTERNATIONAL RULE OF LAW!

...AND WHEN IT TURNS OUT THAT THERE WAS MORE TO THE STORY THAN YOU WERE TOLD, YOU CAN TREAT IT AS SOME SORT OF FREAKISH ABERRATION...

WHADDYA KNOW! THE UNSCOM TEAM REALLY WAS SPYING FOR THE U.S.!

SO OUR GOVERNMENT SUBVERTED U.N. AUTONOMY AND ESSENTIALLY MANUFACTURED AN EXCUSE TO BOMB IRAQ?

OH WELL! I'M SURE IT WILL NEVER HAPPEN AGAIN!

sent news without governmental interference. Yet it also applies to the right of the consumer of news to observe, critique, and correct the news product. Since most of the media will not provide self-criticism accessible to the public, the consumer of news must draw on other sources of review: news councils, journalism reviews, and media critiques in alternative publications and by professional organizations.

These avenues, briefly reviewed below, are few in number except for letters-to-the-editor sections that are featured in most print publications. Some U.S. dailies—only 38 out of 1,540—also feature internal editorial guardians, most often called ombudsmen, who handle complaints by readers or who may initiate inquiries on their own. Depending upon the degree of independence these critics enjoy, they represent a respected and mature approach to ferret out editorial shortcomings.

News councils operate on a national, regional, or local basis. While these councils may publish ethical guidelines, send out speakers, or organize media activities, their principal reason for existence is to adjudicate complaints against the media, conduct hearings, and issue reports.

Press councils were suggested as early as 1930 and again by the Hutchins Commission in 1947. A National News Council was formed in 1973 and financed for three years by two foundations. The lack of support by the major media, such as the *New York Times*, the *Washington Post*, and CBS doomed it from the start. The Council folded in 1984.

This collapse suggests that a truly independent council on a national level will most likely never be supported, i.e. financed, by the media. Walter Cronkite has been quoted as being ambivalent, Al Neuharth has become a supporter, and Mike Wallace is campaigning for a National News Council. But little came from a national session with various media personalities that

was held recently to consider resurrecting such a council. The chances seem very slim that such a council will ever come back to life.

Many foreign countries, on the other hand, have news or press councils which apparently function effectively. A study of how they operate may be beneficial for those favoring a National News Council.

The story of state and local news councils is more promising. While few in number, a couple of councils have survived for many years and have made a lasting contribution to their communities.

The first statewide council ever formed was set up in 1971 in Minnesota by the state's newspaper association. It considers complaints against the local media. The Council has 12 journalists and 12 members of the public presided over by an associate justice of the Minnesota Supreme Court. Only recently, in 1998, was a second state news council formed in Washington. Efforts are currently being made in Oregon to form a state news council there.

Both the Minnesota and the Washington Councils have managed to involve representatives of the mass media, labor, business, academia, the judiciary, and other professions. They have an impressive and prestigious list of financial supporters. Both have a full-time staff member and are assisted by volunteers. They have established a procedure which asks complainants to sign a waiver of the right to sue.

While a number of local news councils were tried as early as the 1950s and 1960s, today only one local council is functioning: the Honolulu Community-Media Council.

The Honolulu Council grew out of a dispute between the city's mayor and local newspapers in 1970. It is composed entirely of volunteers and is primarily active on the island of Oahu but also responds to requests from other islands. The Council has come to cover all aspects of communication, not just the media themselves, including, for example, news access to public information. It is active in education, freedom-of-information and First Amendment issues, and hears about four to five complaints per year.

Whether on a wider geographic base or just locally, to establish a news council requires a group of representative organizers, the voluntary participation of all local media, sufficient funding, and volunteers to administer such a council (Bob Shaw, founding member of the Minnesota News Council offers some excellent advice in "How to Start a News Council" on www.mtn.org/newscouncil/General/Shaw.html).

The smallest rural weekly or the *New York Times* can only publish some of the news, some of the time. This limitation also applies to all broadcasting outlets, including CNN. It is in this shadowy area of partial truth and selective presentation of news that media reviews find their principal vocation. The primary job for reviews is uncovering the inevitable incomplete, and occasionally slanted presentation of news in the day-to-day routine operation of the media.

While there are many media publications, some national journalism reviews, and other local media critics, the local journalism reviews—except for St. Louis—are practically extinct. The nearly 30 local reviews, which flowered in the late 1960s and early 1970s, most of them established by volunteers, expired within a few years.

Local print reviews, established with the cooperation of journalists, academics, and other professionals, can gain a following and be recognized even in the face of neglect or outright opposition by the mass media. This is their major advantage over news councils. They are independent and deal not only with sins of commission, but also of omission. Local journalism reviews exercise peer pressure and involvement by the public.

Peer review is a powerful tool. From time to time, it has been suggested that if journalism reviews would publish just a few hundred copies and circulate them exclusively to media personnel, the effect would be the same. But having a general circulation base offers more than just inviting pressure on the media. It invites the public to share their reaction and their concerns with the media community transforming a journalism review from being merely a critic to becoming a bridge between diverse views which otherwise may never come to the attention of the media or the public.

Journalism today is not just the work of a reporter on the beat, but rather a regimented structure with allocated inches for every discipline or for every minute on the air, orchestrated to produce the highest circulation or the highest ratings. Opportunities for critics abound who are not limited by the pressure of profits and editorial restraints.

How can a review sustain itself without a subsidy or without a separate source of income? While it is unlikely that an independent, private journalism review can become profitable, a periodical combining media criticism with more general fare may succeed. The advent of the plush, colorful *Content* magazine may be successful where others have failed. But *Content* is a national journal which does not offer the effectiveness of a local review.

One of the best resources of "Media Accountability Systems" (MASs) is Claude-Jean Bertrand, professor emeritus at the University of Paris. He has done pioneering work on U.S. journalism reviews and other MASs that have in common a concern to find non-governmental means of insuring that the media respect ethical rules. Many of his ideas are presented in his book, *Media*

Ethics and Accountability Systems (Piscataway, N.J. & London: Transaction, 1999).

The Internet, of course, is an ever-growing source of media information and criticism, but the accuracy of these reports is questionable and, equally important, not local.

Many alternative publications review local media, usually found in a dedicated column. They should expand their coverage by inviting local media organizations to contribute and edit a page or two by discussing the local media.

Professional organizations in the field of communications, such as the Society of Professional Journalists or Press Clubs, should expand their programs beyond social activities and featured speakers. They should evaluate local media by either publishing regular reviews or, at least, schedule discussions at which local media issues are considered. Some of these organizations which have difficulties enrolling or retaining members, might be invigorated by such activities.

Instead of merely endorsing a free press in the abstract, which journalists are apt to do even without provocation, such programs would translate their beliefs into actual practices. Moreover, the local media confronted by such reviews would have to decide how open and receptive they are to criticism and whether others are entitled to the same rights they claim for themselves and practice daily.

Today, there are only spotty and intermittent opportunities to hold the U.S. media accountable. Rare are the occasions where the public can apply criticisms. This diminishes not only the media's ability to address public mistrust and doubts, but also the public's ability to voice their frustrations.

In many autocratic countries, the powers that run the press are closely allied with governments. In those countries, press criticism challenges not only the press but also the government.

However, even in more democratic countries, without criticism of the press, press freedom becomes meaningless.

CHARLES L. KLOTZER is the founder and editor/publisher emeritus of the *St. Louis Journalism Review*.

CHAPTER 10

The Battle for Free Speech Radio

BY DENNIS BERNSTEIN

In July of 1999, thousands of activists, writers, school teachers, students, street people, workers, politicians, and artists of every ilk rose up in defense of freedom of speech. The dispute had been simmering for several years; a dangerous spark was struck on March 31, 1999; and the explosion finally came on July 13, when my bosses at Pacifica Radio arrested me and dozens of my co-workers and supporters for "trespassing" in our own offices and studios. What finally pushed Pacifica into dropping all pretense of reason and showing its true, brutal nature, was my report on a Pacifica proposal to dumb-down, reprogram, and possibly sell KPFA out from under the community that invented it and had nourished it for 50 years. KPFA in Berkeley was the first listener-sponsored radio station in the world, founded in 1949 by Quakers and militant anti-war activists who deplored violence as much as they treasured free speech.

THE PALMER E-MAIL

The report that led to our arrest by Pacifica included a 15-minute clip of a public press conference called by the San Francisco–based watchdog group Media Alliance. Media Alliance had obtained a copy of a highly damaging e-mail from Houston-based Pacifica board member Michael Palmer to board chair Mary Frances Berry, discussing the possibility of selling KPFA and WBAI, its sister station in New York City.

The Palmer e-mail discussed the shutting down and reprogramming of KPFA. "I was under the impression," Palmer wrote, "that there was support in the proper quarters, and a definite majority, for shutting down that unit and reprogramming immediately. Has that changed? Is there consensus among the national staff that anything other than that is acceptable/bearable?"

After discussing the planned shutdown and reprograming of KPFA, Palmer went on in his e-mail to talk about the potential sale of KPFA. "As an update for you and Lynn [Executive Director Lynn Chadwick], I spoke with the only radio broker I know last week and his research shows the primary signal would lend itself to a quiet marketing scenario of discreet presentation to logical and qualified buyers. This is the best radio market in history. Private media companies would be the most aggressive in terms of price, which [the broker] thinks could be in the $65-75M range depending on various aspects of a deal."

Palmer also stated in his e-mail to Berry that it might be less dicey and more profitable to sell WBAI in New York because "there is a smaller subscriber base without the long emotional history as [in] the Bay Area, far more associated value, a similarly dysfunctional staff, though far less effective, and an overall better opportunity to redefine Pacifica going forward. It is simply the more strategic asset."

I never expected to be censored by armed thugs and arrested for reporting the truth at a Pacifica station—even if that truth was about Pacifica. Indeed, I came to Pacifica 20 years ago because of the network's reputation for having taken on Joe McCarthy, and for having been at the center of the Free Speech Movement. KPFA was the first station to broadcast Allen Ginsberg's revolutionary poem, "Howl," and it was the first to give a real voice to the Black Panthers.

Now, to my shock and profound disappointment, Pacifica, guided by extraordinary amounts of ignorance and arrogance, had been transformed from a network created to "speak truth to power" to one apparently committed to using all power necessary to suppress the truth.

ARMED GOONS SEIZE FREE SPEECH RADIO

On June 26, 1999, a sleepy Berkeley Saturday, Pacifica had sent in a squad of armed agents from a private police organization called IPSA International to end free speech at KPFA. Several days earlier, and without warning, Pacifica had cancelled the door codes of all staff members. Station personnel saw these actions as a preemptive strike, intended to silence the rising voices of dissent and on-air protests triggered by the unexpected termination on March 31st of KPFA's station manager, Nicole Sawaya.

When KPFA staff queried Executive Director Chadwick about Sawaya's sacking, Chadwick refused to comment. Chadwick then made KPFA history by ordering the News Department not to report on the Sawaya termination. Chadwick later hand-delivered a written directive ordering co-news director Aileen Alfindary not to report on the firing. Alfindary resisted Chadwick's censorship and informed KPFA listeners that the coup had begun in earnest. She reported on both Sawaya's firing and on Chadwick's attempt to censor the station's news broadcast, the first such in KPFA history: "In a move that sent shock waves through KPFA, the executive director of Pacifica today fired general manager Nicole Sawaya. Sawaya said she was shocked and dismayed and believes her firing was part of a larger strategy. She did not elaborate. Sawaya says Chadwick told her the reason for her termination was that Sawaya 'was not a good fit.'"

The following day, the paid and unpaid staff responded to the Sawaya firing with an on-air statement which was read hourly, calling for Sawaya's immediate rehiring and demanding an explanation. Six producers (including myself) were warned to stop reading the statement or be fired. All six refused to stop on-air protests.

In the weeks that followed, KPFA broadcasters continued to comment on the situation. Larry Bensky, a virtual fixture at KPFA and host of a daily show carried by three Pacifica stations and syndicated to some of the 65 affiliates, was fired for violating the gag order by commenting on Sawaya's ouster. Shortly thereafter, a popular music producer, Robbie Osman, was fired for commenting on Bensky's ouster. On-air protests continued, as other broadcasters violated Pacifica's gag order as a matter of principle. By June, protest had moved beyond the KPFA staff. Sit-ins and demonstrations in support of the station, its broadcasters, and its insistence on speaking out, had led to a number of citizen's arrests by Chadwick. Rather than quelling the uproar, these arrests only exacerbated the situation. Apparently fearing that matters were getting out of hand, Pacifica installed a pair of uniformed but unarmed (and generally peaceful) guards from a local security service. These guards were replaced on June 26 by the menacing crew of armed plainclothes "security consultants" from IPSA. These "consultants" were a squad of tough, bulky white males. Internet research indicates that their backgounds include high-level experience as agents of various federal security agencies. IPSA president Russ Owens, for example, was at one point a consultant for the Federal Bureau of Investigation and later director of security for IBM. "During hostile terminations," IPSA's Web site boasts, "our protection specialists provide a virtual safety net. They can help diffuse an emotionally charged environment and bring about a sense of calm. No national security company can match our success." The IPSA group also provides military trained sharpshooters and other non-traditional services for the new corporate executive.

KPFA staff members were horrified. They considered the hiring of armed former intelligence agents and police to roam the corridors and offices of a small radio station, with unfettered access to sensitive files and Rolodexes, and to hover outside on-air studios during broadcasts, an obvious attempt to intimidate and silence them. Meanwhile, staff members felt their bosses were working to disembowel the station's powerful, politically-progressive message.

As many as a dozen poker-faced IPSA guards, who refused to identify themselves by name, informed the on-air engineer that they had come to seize the station and secure the premises, and that they were armed. They stood guard at KPFA's front and side entrances and flashed an extraordinary memorandum from Executive Director Chadwick. The memo stated that extreme measures were being imposed because "The Pacifica Board of Directors and management are deeply concerned with the ongoing protest activities in which some members of the community, staff, and volunteers are engaged..." Astonishingly, the station that had taken on Joe McCarthy and had later become the electric voice of the Free Speech Movement and the Black Panthers, was being locked down.

The memo stated that "Security personnel will be stationed... around the clock.... Authorized personnel will identify themselves with picture ID.... One guest will be admitted and escorted per authorized station staff member." The memo concluded with the warning that "All staff and volunteers are expected

THIS MODERN WORLD — by TOM TOMORROW

to follow these procedures or face disciplinary action, including possible suspension or termination."

KPFA workers who tried to enter the building on June 26 and thereafter were treated as strangers, told to produce IDs, and ordered to sign in by agents who consistently refused to identify themselves. Some staff members were threatened when they failed to comply. I was personally pursued by one agent, pushed, and told to "get the fuck out of the station" that I had risked my life to report for. At one point, the agent appeared to be going for his weapon but then pulled out a cell phone. I was terrified. The guard and his five bulky colleagues had a good laugh.

The new extreme security measures made it next to impossible for producers to do their work. On Sunday morning June 27, the day after IPSA seized the station, music producer Mary Berg was prevented from bringing guests on her program. Two members of the noted Bay-Area vocal ensemble, SoVoSu, had been scheduled for an eight o'clock joint interview on Berg's show. Because of Chadwick's new draconian one-guest limit, SoVoSo's Joey Blake was refused entrance and prevented from appearing on air. Blake, a long-time collaborator with Bobby McFerrin, was outraged by the experience. "I've never been to a station where I couldn't even get access to a reception area," he said. "Since when do you need armed guards" at a community radio station, he asked.

On another occasion, a late night producer found herself staring into a flashlight in a darkened building. The rather petite, African-American woman was followed into her studio by the armed agents and ordered to open the studio curtain so they could keep an eye on her. They explained their order, "That's the way we like it."

It is of particular note that IPSA's armed seizure of KPFA came on the same day that a large delegation from KPFA had traveled to Washington to meet with Berry during a Pacifica national board meeting, in the hopes of achieving reconciliation.

Pacifica insisted that the new security measures were for the staff's own safety, and in response to a rumored radical takeover of the station. Staff members suspected that Pacifica's real motive was to prevent the reporting of the planned shutdown and reprogramming outlined in the Palmer memo. For weeks Pacifica Archives had been shipping cartons of old tapes to Berkeley, tapes that could be used to fill KPFA's airwaves when the station was taken over. Pacifica had also purchased special transmitter equipment that would permit KPFA's airwaves to be programmed and streamed in from Houston.

The Houston Pacifica station, KPFT, had once been a bastion of multicultural and multilingual broadcasting. But by now it had been neutered into a popular music station with a playlist under the management of a junior member of the Berry-Chadwick-Palmer axis, one Garland Ganter.

On July 12, national board chair Mary Frances Berry arrived in Oakland and with Lynn Chadwick by her side and Ganter in the room, held a bizarre press conference. Attendance was by invitation only; the purpose was to talk about the very same Pacifica issues that Bensky and Osman had been fired for bringing up on the air. Pacifica's then communications director, Elan Fabbri, using hotel security, tried to prevent certain KPFA reporters from entering the room. She attempted to grab a tape recorder out of my hands and blocked a television camera in an attempt to prevent interviews of journalists who had been forbidden entrance. Afterwards, the television cameraman said Fabbri was acting "more like [Nazi propaganda chief] Goebbels" than a spokesperson for a community radio network.

The next day Lynn Chadwick called a staff meeting at KPFA along with Gene Edwards, Pacifica's ironically titled human resources consultant. It was Edwards who had selected IPSA to seize the station just weeks after Edwards had assumed his duties. At this meeting, standing side by side with Marc Torres of the Pacifica Archives, I was told by Garland Ganter that despite Pacifica's "non-disclosure" policy (i.e., the gag rule), KPFA news reporters would be allowed to cover whatever was being widely reported in the mainstream media. This pledge turned out to be a setup, as Pacifica was by now prepared to seize the station and were obviously looking for an excuse.

A few hours later, after I had played the clip from the Media Alliance press conference with Ganter's approval, Ganter pursued me into the newsroom, where he and two armed IPSA agents attacked me and tried to grab me and drag me from the room. In the process, they backed me into a broadcasting tape player, inadvertently sending the scene live on the air.

The entire KPFA listenership heard the rest, and in the next few days a tape of the incident was broadcast and rebroadcast. I can be heard shouting, "I belong here!" In the best tradition of Gandhi, Martin Luther King, and KPFA founder Lewis Hill, I went limp. As the story spread, the tape was heard all over the country and all over the world. My picture appeared in newspapers and magazines. Without intending to, I had achieved my "15 minutes of fame," and the leaders of Pacifica had created a martyr and given themselves a huge black eye in the process.

SILENT TOO LONG

For a dozen years, I had produced a daily magazine at Pacifica stations, and I never once mentioned internal Pacifica matters on the air, though I knew there were serious questions being raised about the motives and direction of national leadership, its handling of our very valuable archives, and other key issues of concern to the future of this noncommercial network. But until March 31, I bought into the idea that public silence was best and that working within channels was the way to resolve problems.

When our highly effective station manager, Nicole Sawaya, was fired, two weeks before a major celebration of KPFA's 50th anniversary, with barely a word of explanation, I realized that my silence had been a huge mistake. The termination of Sawaya, a proud Lebanese American with a vision for radio and an abiding respect for her co-workers, was regarded by the entire KPFA staff as outrageous, unwarranted, and highly provocative.

It is my own belief that she was fired because she had dared to take on the coup makers. She told the truth to her staff about the implications of recent board by-law changes that cut out local input by disenfranchising community boards. She further refused to become a hatchet woman and a censor for Pacifica and she paid for it with her job.

In testimony before the Joint Legislative Audit Committee of the California Legislature, investigating Pacifica's extreme actions and potential misuse of listener contributions, Sawaya summed up the implications of changes in Pacifica's by-laws made by the board under Berry's leadership. "With the recent by-law changes of the Pacifica Foundation, the board is now self-appointing, governing and overseeing all the financial aspects with no accountability to the stations, the financial stakeholders, the subscribers, or donors.

In effect the Pacifica leadership has privatized a public institution and they didn't have to pay a dime."

Pacifica executive director Lynn Chadwick refused to tesitify at the Audit Committee. After using shockingly brutal tactics to silence the KPFA staff and community, Chadwick stated that such testimony would be a violation of "the principle of independent noncommercial broadcasting," which she asserted was to be "free from unnecessary intrusion by governmental and political bodies." She said in a letter to the committee, that "this tradition has been cherished by Pacifica and KPFA for 50 years. Because I value the principle of independence to public broadcasting, I will not appear as a witness in today's hearing."

It is noteworthy, however, that this "principle of independence" didn't stop Berry, who also holds the post of Chair of the U.S. Civil Rights Commission, from intervening. She contacted high level Justice Department officials and persuaded at least one such official to telephone the Berkeley police department and complain that they weren't cracking down hard enough on KPFA protesors.

Chadwick did assure the committee that "all of the extraordinary actions and expenses that Pacifica has taken has been a measured and reasonable response to the extraordinary actions taken against the station." According to Pacifica documents obtained by the Joint Audit Committee, Pacifica spent at least $390,000 on armed security, $58,000 to a San Francisco public relations firm, and $7,000 to board up the windows and padlock the station. Independent estimates go a lot higher. A measured and reasonable response? Out of which account does half a million dollars come, at a network that could barely afford to send one reporter to cover the entire war in Yugoslavia?

CORPORATE RAID ON COMMUNITY RADIO

Pacifica cobbled together a SWAT team to crush KPFA as we know it, and spent well over a half million dollars to carry out their plan. Included in the mix were a high-powered private national security downsizing armed police force, a corporate PR firm, a union busting attorney, a downsizing employment specialist, and a board member who works for one of the most powerful corporate real estate firms in the world.

A five-line press release from Pacifica stated that [the new "human resources consultant"] Edwards was hired to review and update personnel files. According to a report in the *East Bay Express* (a highly-regarded weekly serving Berkeley, Oakland, and environs), "Edwards has a long history of advising companies in the process of terminating employees en masse; for several years in the mid-'90s Edwards developed 'employee transition' programs for the consulting firm Lee Hecht Harrison, a subsidiary of the giant temporary employment agency Adecom. Lee Hecht Harrison are downsizing specialists with an expertise in imposing mass layoffs at companies."

The termination of free speech radio had been on the minds of this new Pacifica crew for years. They brought in a notorious union busting firm, Mitchell, Silberberg, and Knupp (MSK), to break the union first and later represent Chadwick in meetings with the staff after Sawaya's firing. MSK's Web site advertises a firm proud of its union busting activities. Its list of anti-union activities include many victories against organized labor, including "extensive union avoidance work in communications, apparel, publishing, financial services, and health care industry," and an incident in which they "guided a company with approximately 400 employees through an economic strike by the Teamsters Union, and ultimately obtained decertification of the union."

When things got really hot, Pacifica terminated Elan Fabbri, who had misled the press so often she was no longer taken seriously. In her stead, the new corporate team at Pacifica hired the San Francisco–based firm of Fineman and Associates, whose clients included the corporate beneficiaries of sweatshop labor at Walt Disney. But after a brief relationship (and at a fee of $60,000) Fineman declined to continue to represent Pacifica.

Berry had repeatedly denied that any serious plans to sell KPFA were being discussed. She even denied it after the Palmer e-mail story broke and KPFA had been locked down and reprogrammed from Houston. But a public statement by Berkeley-based national board member Pete Bramson put the lie to Berry's repeated claims. "I take no pleasure being here today," stated Bramson at a well attended press conference in front of the Berkeley Municipal Court House. "But I cannot remain silent while Pacifica's national board holds serious discussions in secret about selling KPFA. KPFA is a national treasure," said Bramson, "my commitment is to the KPFA staff and listening community. I hope that by making this public, we can help convince the rest of the board not to go through with this tragic plan. Pacifica Board Chair Mary Francis Berry has repeatedly said during this past several weeks that she has no intention of selling KPFA. That's not true."

HIT AND RUN

On Monday, November 1st, Pacifica launched another attack on freedom of expression, this time not at KPFA alone, but throughout the entire Pacifica network, along with a quarter of its affiliates. While many KPFA supporters and producers were busy arguing against Pacifica's draconian policies at a national board meeting in Houston, Chadwick was preparing to "reassign" Dan Coughlin, the network's national news director for playing a 30-second story on October 27th. This segment, little more than a soundbite in the 30-minute news broadcast, concerned a one-day boycott staged by 16 Pacifica affiliates to protest management's handling of the KPFA crisis. According to Coughlin, he had been blasted by Chadwick for reporting on the boycott of Pacifica, which she labeled as "bullshit news."

The story was mild compared to the outrage it provoked among affilates. Dozens of producers at community stations from Seattle to Maine expressed shock at the use of censorship and armed guards, as well as at the cut-off of programming services when the KPFA staff was locked out. Subsequently, some of Pacifica's best known voices spoke out against Coughlin's removal from the national news. Among them were *Democracy Now!* co-hosts Amy Goodman and Juan Gonzalez. *Pacifica Network News* (PNN) national daily news anchor Vera Avery Brown staged a sick-out in protest of Coughlin's silencing.

The national producers stated in a November 3rd memo to Berry that they agreed with Coughlin's decision to air the story about Pacifica. They pointed out that, "If a quarter of CBS affiliates did not run the *CBS Evening News*, we see that as newsworthy. If a quarter of NPR affiliates did not run *All Things Considered*, it is newsworthy. A quarter of Pacifica's affiliates did not run *Pacifica Network News* or *Democracy Now!* We think that is newsworthy."

The national producers went on record with an eloquent statement: "We strongly believe that Dan Coughlin's ouster can only undermine the editorial content and direction of Pacifica. It is a violation of the most basic journalistic standards at a time when those standards are being increasingly corrupted and debased within the commercial broadcast media.... We cannot stand idly by while this network becomes a pale version of what it was intended to be."

The producers expressed futher outrage at Chadwick's selection of PNN reporter Marc Bevis as Coughlin's replacement. They asserted that Bevis had been a consistent critic of KPFA and shown little sympathy for progressive politics. The attempt to elevate Bevis "sends a chilling message to the entire Pacifica staff—that individual judgments on whether to air a story about the ongoing crisis should not be based solely on whether we consider the issue newsworthy, but also on whether we will be ousted or summarily transferred for that decision.... In addition, his [Coughlin's] replacement by Mark Bevis sends yet another discouraging message: side with management and you'll be promoted; maintain independent professional coverage of the crisis and you will be pushed aside."

Having perhaps learned a lesson from the firestorm that her firings at KPFA had ignited, Chadwick made a transparent attempt to disguise Coughlin's sacking as a "promotion." According to the national producers, "Dan received an e-mail from Chadwick saying he 'did not understand' their brief conversation and that 'appreciation is the only basis for your reassignment, not a disagreement over news content.' Chadwick explained that Coughlin had been named "Development Specialist for News Operations for Pacifica" and would consult on a newly-created Task Force on Programming and Governance. Minutes later, Dan received a news release announcing his new appointment. "Chadwick had never discussed this with him," the national producers charge. "It is clear that Dan was punished for his decision to air the Pacifica story, and that we are now witnessing Chadwick's shoddy attempts at covering up his ouster."

Laura Flanders is a former acting director of the PNN news and former co-host of *CounterSpin*, the media show from Fairness and Accuracy in Reporting (FAIR), and a columnist for *In these Times*. Flanders wrote, "The censorship carried out by Pacifica has been nothing short of extraordinary. As for accountability, national programmers—of which I am one—have seen their work arbitrarily censored and edited by Pacifica management and station staff. In Washington, WPFW's staff cut headlines and stories about Pacifica from PNN, and aired shortened shows complete with credits, leaving the impression that producers were ignoring the story (even as management was talking to commercial media). "WPFW pulled *CounterSpin* without notice because it addressed Pacifica affairs." Program director Lou Hankins told me, "We're not putting that garbage on our air."

In a December 9th press release, FAIR complained about the continuing censorship of its *CounterSpin* show. "Without notice to producers or listeners, the Washington, DC–based Pacifica affiliate WPFW has cancelled FAIR's radio show, *CounterSpin*.... *CounterSpin*—a media criticism show—has been censored by Pacifica stations five times this year for covering the ongoing crisis at the network. It's hard to conclude this is anything but a final act of censorship by WPFW," commented *CounterSpin* co-host Steve Rendall. "For years, WPFW has run our analysis of fear and favor at other news outlets— but when we turned our attention to Pacifica, WPFW repeatedly interfered with and finally cancelled our show." The final show, which regrettably never made it to the air at WPFW, was of course about the removal of Dan Coughlin as director of PNN.

On July 14, *Democracy Now!* was pulled for the same reason at Pacifica's Washington and Los Angeles stations. Listeners in Washington heard WPFW switch to music mid-show, but Hankins told the *Washington Post*'s Frank Ahrens that he'd aired *Democracy Now!* in full, "front to back."

THE POWER AND IMPORTANCE OF PACIFICA

It's hard to comprehend what Berry, Chadwick, and Palmer were thinking when they initiated their frontal assault on KPFA. Perhaps, convinced of their own righteousness and hypnotized by a kind of Beltway tunnel-vision, they thought they could simply roll over this radio station. The staff could be disciplined, or if all else failed, simply kicked out. The rest of the community would adopt a "So what?" attitude and ignore the takeover.

If they thought this, they were badly mistaken. The community had been listening, and they cared deeply about progressive, alternative radio. Even people who said that they disagreed with KPFA's politics or didn't listen to the station at all, rose to its defense. Pacifica's action had touched some very raw nerve. It involved not just one radio station, but the new world of corporate control and the relentless logic of the market. As the national producers said in their protest memo to Berry, this battle was about the future, not reliving the 1960s.

Those who pay attention to media issues—including many in mainstream organizations—were shocked at the news that a radio journalist was forcibly removed from his radio station and put on "administrative leave" for covering a public press conference. Or that broadcasters would be fired for discussing the overall direction of a listener-sponsored station. Or that armed guards would be hired to seize a station founded by pacifists.

There were inquiries from journalists and activists from across the country and around the world. My phone rang off the hook with queries from sympathetic mainstream and alternative journalists from Tokyo to Toronto. The mayors of Berkeley, Oakland, and San Francisco threw their support behind the staff and its supporters. Willie Brown, the recently re-elected Mayor of San Francisco, and perhaps the most influential present-day African-American politician, called for the resignation of Pacifica's leadership. The state legislature Joint Audit Committee commenced hearings to investigate what one legislator referred to as the "ethnic cleansing" of community radio. Pulitzer Prize–winning author Alice Walker and Oscar-winning filmmaker Michael Moore spoke up strongly on behalf of KPFA.

At the height of the crisis, on July 19, a benefit concert was held in support of KPFA. The program was headlined by progressive icon Joan Baez. The 3,400 seat Berkeley Community Theater sold out on just four days notice. On July 31 the KPFA staff led a March of 15,000 people from the University of California campus, the birthplace of the Free Speech Movement, past the boarded-up, locked-down quarters of KPFA.

Pacifica claimed it is simply trying to modernize, expand, and diversify. Pacifica envisioned "modernization" along corporate lines—more top-down control, greater reliance on foundation money, and programming based on ratings. It characterized those who oppose these moves as holdovers from a bygone era.

Management's censorship and my subsequent arrest by Pacifica violated everything that free-speech radio stands for. In fact, enhancing diversity was precisely the goal of Nicole Sawaya, KPFA's fired station manager. Sawaya had been the first manager to unify the contentious KPFA staff, she had hired KPFA's first African-American program director and diversified KPFA's programming.

In contrast, Pacifica's executive director, Lynn Chadwick, has been firing or alienating people into quitting since she arrived. KPFA's African-American program director quit to protest the summary firing of reporter Larry Bensky after more than 30 years at Pacifica. The African-American morning show host quit, saying Chadwick and the new board had created a "toxic atmosphere." African-American producers at KPFA wrote to Berry, saying they refused to be "complicit in any Pacifica-driven purge of KPFA staffers under the guise of diversity." Other minority producers have delivered similar messages of solidarity and are still waiting for a reply.

Pacifica's tactics mirror those used in corporate takeovers. Of course all radio stations want to attract more listeners, but robbing KPFA of its independence will rob it of its uniqueness, its loyal listener-base, and its reason for existence. KPFA at its best has been about conscience and truth, not about audience-share. A station like KPFA, differing much of the time from conventional positions and accommodating to minority views on controversial issues, is unlikely to achieve the numbers of, for instance, an all-music station or one committed to lowest-common-denominator news and opinion.

We have seen what happens when market-driven solutions are implemented. They lead to less, not more, diversity—racially and politically.

The corporate market-driven approach has particularly troubling features when applied to the media. Will everything we see and hear be filtered through corporate public relations departments and market-share accountants? Will sensationalism, celebrity, and homogenized coverage rule everywhere?

In this era of U.S. triumph, is even one alternative, sometimes radical, voice too many?

THE PAST INTO THE FUTURE

KPFA's founders certainly considered war a poor solution to global problems. They apparently knew the power of information and the inherent dangers if the media were controlled by the needs and desires of the burgeoning military-industrial complex. Lewis Hill certainly understood that media domination by companies directly linked to the military establishment did not bode well for common good. Pacifica's founders and early pioneers knew that democracy was about an informed populace with the knowledge to hold the state and the powers that be accountable. And they realized early on the state's quest for secrecy posed a direct threat to free expression: and freedom of expression was at the center of it all.

Throughout the period of its dispute with KPFA, Pacifica has striven mightily to portray the controversy as a conventional labor/management contest. This, of course, is utterly untrue. For one thing, the staff of KPFA has been united in standing up to Pacifica's steamroller—station management, unionized staff, and unpaid volunteers alike. On a more profound level, it is obvious that the issues are not the usual ones of pay scales, working hours, medical benefits, and so forth. They are issues of local autonomy versus centralized, authoritarian control, and of freedom of expression versus the requirement to parrot a dictated party line or remain silent.

At the beginning of the year 2000, a listener to KPFA or a visitor to the station in Berkeley would encounter a seemingly normal operation. But while the explosive sense of crisis has quieted, the underlying issues remain unresolved. Sawaya and Bensky remain fired although both have appeared on KPFA without pay; Dan Coughlin is off the national news and Verna Avery Brown, PNN's signature voice, has been pushed out of the network after many years of dedicated service, because she took a bold stand against Pacifica's new censors. Meanwhile, the same network bureaucrats and board chair who attempted to undermine Pacifica's radical edge and abandoned its alternative vision, still hold sway over the network, and the situation remains dangerous.

On July 31, 1999, 15,000 marched from Sproul Plaza, UC Campus—birth of the 1964 Free Speech Movement—to Caesar Chavez Park. Brenda Prager

Robbin Henderson, director of the Berkeley Art Center, recently curated an exhibition documenting the free speech battle between Pacifica and KPFA. "Stay Tuned the Revolution will be Broadcast" offered an amazing array of wire and paper mache sculptures, poster art, and T–shirts.

In a recent interview, Henderson described to me what was going on outside within minutes of our sit-down inside the station. She had heard the shouting over the air and rushed over to the station. Within a half-hour, she said, there were over 600 people chanting in front of the station. And several protestors had already crawled under a police

The night KPFA was closed down, hundreds of supporters came to the station and packed the hallways. In foreground, J. Imani, local KPFA board member, with his daughter. Scott Braley

wagon that was trying to leave the scene with the first batch of support-ers who had already committed civil disobedience by sitting down inside KPFA.

"It was scary and it was very exciting," said Henderson. "I hadn't seen that kind of militancy in a crowd in a really long time. When we got there,

it was just getting dark [and] there were so many police in riot gear there I couldn't believe it. And so many people and the crowd just kept growing and growing. It was thrilling to see the people. And people did not want that van to move. It was kind of reminiscent of 1964, and the free speech movement. People decided they were going to

In police wagon the night the station was closed—Mark Mericle, KPFA news; Dennis Bernstein; Robbie Osman, 30-year programmer at KPFA. Scott Braley

get under the wheels of the police van, and surround it so that it couldn't move. They were really challenging the police directly."

Ann Fagan Ginger, Bay Area civil rights activist, upbraids Lynn Chadwick for her role at KPFA while Dennis Bernstein tapes. This happened on June 21, the day after Chadwick terminated veteran music producer Robbie Osman. Later that morning, Chadwick made a citizen's arrest of 14 KPFA listeners who were blocking the Pacifica door in an attempt to get a meeting with her. Scott Braley

Van Jones, director of the Ella Baker center for civil rights, Board member of Media Alliance, and key organizer in the fight to get KPFA back on the air after Pacifica locked out the staff and the community. Scott Braley

Henderson said people were in shock and they were determined to take back their station. "There was just incredible electric energy, amazing tension. People were outraged, absolutely outraged. They kept saying how could they do this to our station. It was a great loss and an important community battle to fight and win," said Henderson, scanning the sea of posters, and huge sculptors, including a 15-foot expandable free speech fist, that adorned the Berkeley Art Center, transformed into a recreation of a KPFA protest for the exhibition. "As you can see, artists came out to document the battle in every way possible." Henderson said for her and many of the artists in the exhibition, it was very personal. "When I'm in my studio working, I have KPFA on all day long," she said. "And I really count on it. So when they changed it and started broadcasting from Houston, I felt lost. KPFA is an anchor in my life."

CHAPTER 11

Falun Gong: Demonized in China, Downplayed in America

BY DANNY SCHECHTER

"Inscrutable" is one of those words that often insinuates itself into Western media coverage of China. Sometimes it seems especially pejorative, even racist, when reporters resort to vague references to cultural factors or Asiatic proclivities to explain puzzling developments.

Yet some stories are objectively challenging to decipher—and only a media that is up to the task can possible do them justice. China, and in particular Washington's relationship with Beijing, was frequently in the news in 1999. Acres of print were lavished on unproven red menace–type spy scandals, exaggerated threats of war over Taiwan, and the battles involving Beijing's on-again off-again on-again entry into the World Trade Organization.

More significant than them all was China's ongoing crackdown on a spiritual practice virtually unknown in the West, Falun Dafa or Falun Gong. The world media missed and frequently misinterpreted this ongoing development. It was distorted and downplayed in mainstream and progressive media alike. When it was covered, it was often covered with a sense of incomprehension. "Has it come to this?" asked the *New York Times* front page on November 4, 1999, "that the Chinese Communist Party is terrified of retirees who follow a spiritual master in Queens?"

Yes, it has come to "this": "This" being a story involving as many as 100 million people with deep roots in the traditions and contradictions of the

People's Republic of China. It pits one of the most powerful and most repressive regimes on Earth against a nonviolent anti-materialist spiritual practice drawing on Buddhist and Taoist traditions. While Falun Gong is Gandhian in its nonviolent approach, the government has committed pervasive human rights abuses including killings, jailings, torture, and massive book burnings to suppress it.

Inside China, since July 20, 1999, news about Falun Gong has been censored, twisted, and massaged to reinforce a political decision to ban and "smash" what President Jiang Zemin had proclaimed his country's number one domestic enemy. The Chinese called Falun Gong a "cult," accused it of killing people, disrupting social order, and menacing the state. They issued banning orders, rounded up practitioners, and sentenced individuals they labeled leaders to longer prison sentences than those earlier meted out to pro-democracy activists.

The Chinese leadership launched a media war, deploying its state-owned newspapers, radio, and TV stations as if they were instruments in an official orchestra. National newscasts were lengthened by a half-hour to disseminate daily diatribes on the issue. Dramatic "investigative exposes," using hidden cameras and informants, were plastered all over prime-time TV to convince the public that Falun Gong was a serious threat to China and its people. In all of these accounts, Falun Gong's point of view was left out. The views of its supporters, defenders, and practitioners were, quite simply, missing from these government-sponsored accounts.

Balance and fairness, never prized in Chinese state-controlled journalism, was conspicuous in this case by a total absence. That was not surprising, given the role that media pays in China as an appendage of, and cheerleader for, Communist Party policy.

Western media, on the other hand, claims to be free of all restraints, unencumbered by censors or government oversight. And, yet, on this issue, China's controlled media and the West's ostensibly "free" media dealt with this story in not dissimilar ways. When China's propaganda turned into a steady drum beat of denigration, with Falun Gong's founder Li Hongzhi dubbed a "sorcerer," much of the Western media echoed the refrain. In wire stories and press reports, when the story was covered at all, negative terminology was prominent. The group was branded a "sect," "a mishmash." Both mainstream and alternative media were culpable. In the words of one amused writer for *In These Times*, Falun Gong were a "handful of religious oddballs."

Getting a grip on what's happening in China has never been on one of Western media's strong points. Developments there have often been reduced to a single, simplistic news frame. As James Mann of the *Los Angeles Times* reflected in *Media Studies Journal*, "In the 1950s the 'frame' was of China as little blue ants or automatons. In the 1970's, the frame was of the virtuous (entertaining, cute) Chinese displaying their timeless qualities even under Communism. In the 1980s, the frame was that of China 'going capitalist.' And for most of the 1990s, the frame was of a 'repressive China.'"

Mann's injunction to journalists best captures the challenge of covering the recent rise of Falun Gong. "Above all," he concludes, "American media coverage of China needs to challenge existing assumptions and be ready for the unexpected."

Falun Gong is the unexpected—and most journalists missed its emergence and rapid spread. The press today always appears more interested in what's happening in the higher reaches of politics than what may be stirring in the parks. Its eye is on the suites, rarely the streets. It looks up at leaders, not down to people at eye level. For seven years, as this spiritual practice was mushrooming in popularity, it was barely acknowledged in the media or reported on outside of China.

The Falun Gong story does challenge many assumptions. Many us first heard about it because of an event on April 22, 1999. Suddenly, seemingly out of nowhere, a new force dramatically burst on the world scene. Ten to fifteen thousand Falun Gong practitioners quietly surrounded Zhongnanhai, the government leadership compound in the heart of Beijing. They lined the streets, sometimes eight deep, quietly, and without placards. They shouted no slogans, just stood there, or sat there—for 12 hours—with great dignity but little expressiveness. Some meditated. Others read books.

When asked, they explained that they were there to file an appeal with the government against what they considered a slanderous attack on Falun Gong published in a state-sponsored magazine in Tianjin, a nearby city. They explained that some of their fellow practitioners, who had challenged the article had been jailed and beaten by local police. When the complaints to the headquarters of the magazine went unheeded, they decided to take their case to the central government. They insisted that as Chinese citizens they had a right to appeal to their own government.

They came, seemingly out of nowhere and vanished quickly after some of their number met with government officials and presented them with a letter seeking official recognition and legal protection of their rights to free speech and assembly.

The international media was perplexed: Who were they? Where did they come from? What was this about? It was covered internationally only because it happened in the center of the capital. At first, it was pictured as a political protest perhaps because most journalists there were not really familiar with Falun Gong. *Time* magazine, like most of the foreign press, put it in a predictable anti-regime context: "The silent sit-in was by far the boldest protest in Beijing since the butchering of the pro-democracy movement almost exactly a decade ago "

There had been similar Falun Gong vigils earlier in other provincial cities (the government later cited over 300 "sieges"), but most went uncovered because they occurred outside of media view. This one raised eyebrows, and then the hackles of the Chinese authorities. The international press virtually assured a negative government reaction when they played it as a political challenge to the system.

Later, veteran China watcher John Gittings would rationalize China's crackdown in the *Guardian* suggesting that the protest was so large that it was a provocation that the government had to take seriously. Falun Gong activists told me that they didn't understand why the media kept stressing the size of the protest. "We could have mobilized millions if we wanted to. That wasn't the point." In fact, China only singled out Falun Gong because, by that time, its less visible roots had sunk much deeper, across China and even in the Chinese Communist party, and state military and intelligence agencies. The figure that kept being bandied about was 100 million practitioners. Compare that to the Chinese Communist Party, which claims 56 million members.

The English journalist Gittings also put the development in a context one rarely found explained in the American press: "The Falun Gong reflects a grassroots mood in China of greater assertiveness: interest groups, whether they be peasants complaining of corruption or laid-off workers seeking benefits they've been denied, are more prepared to protest. As Chinese society becomes more differentiated and more vocal, this is a growing trend with which the Communist Party has to come to terms."

Falun Gong's "coming out party" in Beijing was mostly a one-day story. There was little follow-up or background offered. Falun Gong's founder, Li Hongzhi, a one time granary clerk and soldier, was then living in New York. He had moved first to Houston and then New York after China banned one of his books in 1996. He insists that he only spent two years personally teaching in China, and the movement's spread was not the result of an underground conspiratorial apparatus, as claimed by China, but through word of mouth. When I interviewed him in July, he also stressed that contrary to many media accounts, his movement was not political and not against the government.

"We are not against the government now nor will we be in the future," he said matter of factly. "Other people may treat us badly but we do not treat others badly, nor do we treat people as enemies." He told me he wanted to dialogue with the government, not overthrow it.

When the crackdown thrust Falun Gong back into the news, a few outlets interviewed Li but his inability to speak English made him an undesirable media guest. *60 Minutes* looked into and then dropped the story partly for this reason. "Mike Wallace was calling me every day from his vacation home on Martha's Vineyard," recalled Gail Rachlin, an American practitioner of Falun Gong who became a volunteer publicist because of her background in professional PR, "but then after we arranged a meeting, he never called back." I can understand why: it would be difficult for Mike Wallace to stage one of his showy confrontational interviews with someone he had to talk to through an interpreter. That always slows things down and makes it hard to spring surprise questions. Dan Rather was another prominent CBS journalist who lobbied for the story but then didn't do it.

"What the Chinese government has taken on is a very vicious campaign—and so unnecessary," said Rachlin early on. "But the American media is playing the story their way."

CNN did take the story seriously, covering the crackdown, but often with what appeared to be Chinese TV–supplied footage. "In Beijing, Saturday, the government crackdown continued on members of the now-outlawed Falun Gong meditation group banned on Thursday after several days of silent protest," said one report. "The police have also detained Falun Gong leaders and members." They did show practitioners in detention in stadiums, but of course could not cover subsequent torture sessions that invariably occur out of public view.

ABC's *Nightline* offered a half-hour report, probably the longest single program about Falun Gong on American TV. Spokesperson Erping Zhang was invited on the show along with a Chinese official who refused to be interviewed in the same segment. Koppel seemed peeved that Li Hongzhi, then in hiding after rumors circulated that hit men were on the way from China to track him down, was not available. Zhang thought he would get a chance to appeal for help for those detained in China, but host Koppel aggressively went after him on other issues. He focused on whether or not Zhang would go to the hospital if he was sick, obviously seeking to discredit the movement or unmask him as a fanatic. When Zhang tried to bring the conversation back around to the repression, Koppel told him curtly that he would decide what subjects could be discussed.

The Chinese official was treated far kinder, with Koppel pressing him to allow ABC News more access to the story. (As a Washington embassy official, he, of course, had nothing to do with media access in China.) The official seemed most upset with Falun Gong's alleged threat to social order. "They have mobilized so-called demonstrations throughout the country in all 30 cities. They are interrupting traffic, blocking traffic, and social order," he steamed.

At other outlets, producers and editors had little appreciation of the story's context of the content or Li's teachings. He was perceived as a weirdo and Falun Gong a fringe group of fanatics akin to the Moonies. Falun Gong had a video news release produced, which was satellited to all U.S. news programs. Only a very few carried any footage or interviews from it. There was far more coverage in Canada and abroad than in the United States, even though the U.S. is China's largest trade partner—or put another way, perhaps because the U.S. is China's largest trade partner.

Under-covered major stories like these point to key structural and ideological problems in the American media itself. Most international coverage for U.S. news organizations—what there is of it—relies on correspondents based overseas. They are presumed to have the best access and background even though, in this case, most were uninformed about Falun Gong and limited in covering the story. (Most practitioners in China were terrified of talking with them.) U.S.-based journalists are rarely assigned to cover or seek out background or comments for China-based stories, and team coverage with both overseas and U.S. components is a rarity.

Also, Falun Gong was considered in most newsrooms falsely to be only a Chinese phenomenon. Many journalists did not notice—or chose not to

THIS MODERN WORLD   by TOM TOMORROW

ACROSS THIS NATION, FROM THE FARMLANDS TO THE SUBURBS, AMERICANS IN SEARCH OF GUIDANCE AND INSIGHT DEPEND ON THE CEASELESS TOIL OF THE EAST COAST MEDIA ELITE!

THE PROBING POLITICAL COMMENTARY OF HOWARD FINEMAN IS LIKE A SHINING BEACON IN THE FOG OF MY DREARY EXISTENCE!

IF NOT FOR THE CONDÉ NAST PUBLISHING EMPIRE, I WOULDN'T EVEN KNOW WHAT COLOR NAIL POLISH TO WEAR!

THROUGHOUT MIDTOWN MANHATTAN, SELFLESS SCRIBES LABOR TIRELESSLY TO KEEP THEIR GEOGRAPHICALLY DISADVANTAGED COUNTRYMEN UP TO DATE ON THE LATEST NEW YORK CITY STYLE DICTATES...

HEY, JOE-BOB, I FORGET--ARE SUNGLASSES WITH YELLOW LENSES STILL A DARINGLY OUTRÉ FASHION STATEMENT?

OH FOR HEAVEN'S SAKE, ELMER--DON'T YOU PAY ANY ATTENTION TO DETAILS MAGAZINE? THOSE GLASSES ARE SO 1998!

notice—that the practice had actually become internationalized with groups now in 30 countries and 104 cities in 38 states in the United States. Despite its spread, practitioners outside of China somehow lacked "standing" with their local media, who wanted to hear only from practitioners in China or the wire services. Many media outlets wanted Li Hongzhi or no one, an indication of the celebrity orientation that drives most interviewers. They like personalities, not issues. Before long the story was driven by the wires with the British agency Reuters and the French Agence France-Presse (AFP) filing most of the stories, with the Associated Press far behind. American newspapers tend to lean more on AP than the others and so the story did not rate regular play.

Another factor: Journalism tends to operate as if politics is the driving force in the lives and interests of most people. Political leaders and their agendas dominate coverage. Spiritual and religious issues are treated marginally, when they are treated at all. Few media professionals have the sensibility or curiosity to explore people's beliefs and convictions. It is not usually considered newsworthy unless they are dramatic, strange, or perceived to fuel conflict. Moreover, in the case of critical coverage of China, there seems to be another and perhaps more significant factor: a decision by media executives in America to downplay human rights abuses there. While the American government is trying to get more access for our corporations to the lucrative China market, media corporations have interests of their own.

A few years ago, Rupert Murdoch dropped BBC from one of his satellites over China for that very reason. (He is now married to someone from Mainland China.) This year, on September 28, 1999, Sumner Redstone, who had just merged the giant Viacom corporation with CBS, was in Shanghai, China

for a conference organized by a leading U.S. media outlet, *Fortune* magazine, and keynoted by President Jiang Zemin. He called for American press restraint in the coverage of China, to the delight of the Beijing government. The media, he said, should report the truth but avoid being "unnecessarily offensive" to foreign governments. "As they expand their global reach, media companies must be aware of the politics and attitudes of the governments where we operate.

"Journalistic integrity must prevail in the final analysis. But that doesn't mean that journalistic integrity should be exercised in a way that is unnecessarily offensive to the countries in which you operate," he said.

Remarks like this by leaders of the American media industry set the tone for news coverage. Redstone was predictably silent on human rights abuses in China. Earlier, human rights advocates, including the Tiananmen Square veterans who publish *Human Rights in China*, had urged the business leaders at the *Fortune* conference to speak out on the issue.

Falun Gong's practitioners were then in detention, but their plight was not discussed or reported upon at this media-organized event. Ironically, the Chinese then censored a *Time* magazine special on China. As one news report explained, "The edition, whose masthead was emblazoned with the headline 'China's Amazing Half-Century,' fell foul of Chinese censors by including articles written by exiled dissidents Wei Jingsheng and Wang Dan, and Tibet's Dalai Lama."

Falun Gong grew out of Chinese *qigong* practices with a history stretching back thousands of years. It has a context and a framework that requires background research that is usually not allowed by deadline-driven, headline-oriented, dumbed-down ("let's keep it simple") news operations.

Qigong is a traditional Chinese exercise system with a variety of practices that seek to tap internal energy forces, or our *qi* (or *chi*). Many practitioners turn to it for their physical well being as well as moral elevation. Li Hongzhi's contribution within the *qigong* world was to reconnect the physical exercises with their historic spiritual base.

Falun Gong draws on *qigong* but also brings in its own philosophy and characteristics based on both Buddhist and Taoist thought. Falun Gong, also known as Falun Dafa, incorporates some Buddhist principles like the Law Wheel and the yin-yang of Taoism, while retaining its own distinctive system of thought—neither strictly Buddhist or Taoist. Falun Gong promotes physical and mental balance, bringing together mind, spirit, and reality to achieve a closer harmony with nature and the universe. It concerns itself with what the practitioners say is the law of the universe, moral values, and cultivation principles they call the "Fa."

Li says he modified the original practice to make it more accessible to the public at large. That's why there seems to be two names. Falun Dafa stands for the "Great Way of the Law Wheel," while Falun Gong means "*Qigong* of the Law Wheel." It is a distinction with a difference in China because of *qigong*'s popularity. In essence, it is a "rebranding" calculated to give the practice a broader appeal.

To the casual eye, this exercise system may look like tai chi or some martial art featuring distinctive slow-motion exercises. Yet Falun Gong aspires to a deeper approach to human development, seeking to guide people to a higher understanding of spiritual values and moral consciousness. They call it a "cultivation practice." As one practitioner explained to me, "As a form of self-cultivation, Falun Gong is intended to help an individual develop or cultivate his/her mind-body-spirit principles. As a person's practice deepens, they gradually learn to take more lightly the desires and ambitions that ordinarily rule human life."

Falun Gong stresses that it is not a religion, a cult, or a sect. There is no organization to join. There are no priests, temples, or churches. There are no rituals or worship services. Practitioners insist no one is making money off of it, and most of all, that it is not "political." "We are not interested in politics," insists 27-year-old Feng Keran, "We do not have political intentions. We are also not against the government. We just try to live for ourselves, cultivate our hearts. Try to be good people." While they have not been "political," the Chinese government is in effect politicizing them through its continuing assaults.

Falun Gong's insistence that it is not a political organization may be understandable given China's overheated political environment and the reaction that set in after the excesses of the Cultural Revolution. Orville Schell blames the Party for encouraging people to abandon politics by its emphasis on getting rich and becoming self-centered. Falun Gong's anti-political stance represents a rejection of both political correctness from above and the spread of materialism below.

In addition, as people began living longer in China, the country's health care system was proving inadequate. Older people in particular searched out alternative health care regimes. They flocked to traditional Chinese *qigong* practices when they began to become popular again, after the reform era started in 1979. (In the 1950s, many Communist leaders practiced *qigong*.) Many of these retired people soon discovered Falun Gong's special appeal, in large part because the teachings were free or at a lower cost than competing *qigong* practices.

Former *New York Times* Beijing bureau staffer, W. Huang, offers his mother's case as an example. She turned to Falun Gong because she was both physically sick, and sick at heart about what was happening to China. "Society is deteriorating," she told her son, "—rampant corruption within the Communist Party, rising crime rates, drug abuse among young people. People don't have any goal except to earn money."

Remarkably, her practice of Falun Gong led to what her son calls a "miraculous recovery." "As more and more people like my mother become disillusioned, they search for something to fill the ideological and spiritual void," he wrote in the *Christian Science Monitor*. "Falun Gong meets the spiritual needs of ordinary Chinese because it has familiar Buddhist and Taoist roots." Many in Falun Gong also embrace the original spirit of Communism that once was, but no longer is, promoted by the Party. Their key principles are "truthfulness, compassion, and forbearance."

Falun Gong's moral appeal and anti-materialist orientation—as something pure and anchored in traditional values—is also reflected itself in an almost Puritan attitude toward money. China says Li Hongzhi is getting rich off of Falun Gong and are busy "investigating" the sale of books and videos. Li says, "I make a comfortable living off my books." He certainly has received royalties from his writing, but so do most authors. American practitioners like Noah Parker deny that greed is a factor. "If anyone tries to make money or personal gain from the practice, that's an incorrect approach. You're not a practitioner. You're not doing Falun Gong if that's your attitude toward it. It's not a money thing at all."

Falun Gong had many media obstacles to overcome in the West. It was foreign. Its first language was not English. It was complicated and, perhaps more important, it was amorphous and unstructured—without the full-time big-time PR operation that most journalists rely on for handouts and statements.

Li Hongzhi, while charismatic to his followers, was not comfortable as a media celebrity. Most of his propaganda was oriented toward spreading Falun Gong, not promoting himself or an organization. Falun Gong's New York–based press office had a lot of heart but few resources, perhaps because their members were more focused on their internal growth than their external operation.

Falun Gong may have been newsworthy but it was not news-oriented. Gail Rachlin's media "operation" was based in her West Side apartment. It was run with two computers, a fax machine, and a cell phone. It was hardly a match for the Chinese State. And yet the Internet and e-mail enabled it to get reporters to cover the story even if it wasn't always played prominently.

Specifically, Rachlin was able to encourage the use of less pejorative and more neutral language in coverage. In one instance, the early edition of the Sunday *New York Times* made a front-page reference to Falun Gong as a cult. A timely phone call explanation to an attentive editor led to the phrase being changed to "spiritual practice" for the late edition. It took months, but Falun Gong's persistence in lobbying the press and the U.S. government resulted in more coverage and statements by President Clinton and many members of Congress. The U.N. was less outspoken but "appeals" by Falun Gong supporters to Secretary General Kofi Annan did get into the press even if he seemed to think they were aimed at him rather than China's policy. Nonetheless, overall, there was shameful silence from opinion leaders and even human rights groups on the issue for months.

High profile writers and publishers did not even condemn the widespread burning of millions of Falun Gong books in China. While other movements criticizing China like the Tibetans have inspired active solidarity movements, Falun Gong remains isolated and alone in large part because of the poor job the media has done in explaining who they are and what China is doing to them.

When the Western media covered the story, the frame was primarily one of repression, not resistance. Few news organizations followed it with any regularity. Reporting was spotty. Most of the alternative media seemed uninterested, too. The United Nations Correspondents Association did invite Falun Gong supporters to present their views, over the objection of Chinese diplomats. The *New York Times* sent a photographer and a correspondent to the event, but nothing appeared in the paper.

By late October 1999, this began to change when Falun Gong practitioners in China, reacting to an imminent decision by the Chinese Parliament to officially brand Falun Gong a cult, took a more aggressive course of action. They mounted daily protests in Tiananmen Square, and even dramatically called a secret press conference, a daring move in China. The story broke onto the front page of the *New York Times*, which reported, "A far wider and more profound confrontation appears to be building between clearly unnerved authorities and an uncrushed movement that with astonishing speed drew in millions of ordinary, seemingly nonpolitical Chinese, creating an unexpected challenge to Communist authority."

In response to the press conference, the police mounted a massive manhunt, tracked down the location and ultimately arrested some of the principals. They didn't stop there. Five western reporters who covered the unprecedented October 28th event had their press accreditation cards seized and were warned against covering illegal events. None were ejected but the intimidating message was sent to their news organizations. No major media outlets want to be barred from China.

Falun Gong practitioners have shown the world they may be peaceful but they are not passive. In many ways their campaign is comparable to Gandhi's civil disobedience movement in India and the nonviolent civil rights activism of Martin Luther King, Jr., in the American South. Falun Gong may represent as many as 100 million people, but apparently for many Western governments and much of the media, they are the wrong people. You don't have to believe what they believe to support their right to believe it. This story will not go away. In mid-January 2000, after criticisms of U.S.–China policy started appearing in the *Washington Post* and on NBC's *Meet the Press,* the White House announced that it would push for a U.N. resolution critical of China's deteriorating human rights record. After seven months, the Falun Gong issue had moved from the margins to the mainstream and even occasionally from the back of the book to the front page. Credit must be given to some reporters like the *Washington Post*'s John Pomfret and vigilant Chinese journalists in Beijing who stayed with the story, refusing to be intimidated. The rest of the media has yet to catch up. Falun Gong practitioners have continued to press for more and fairer coverage, patiently reaching out week after week to educate a media that sometimes seems allergic to being educated, and won't even take the trouble to visit their Web site.

Look closely at the media coverage of Falun Gong and you realize that the American media and the Chinese media are not as different as they think or perhaps as they should be. All too often the world of news and the world of newsmakers are far apart.

DANNY SCHECHTER, author of *The More You Watch, The Less You Know*, is the executive editor of Globalvision's media channel (www.mediachannel.org), which reports on global media trends.

Most Censored News Stories for 1999 Publication Source List

COMPILED BY KATIE SIMS

Subscription information for U.S. only / * indicates multiple stories in top 25

AMERICAN JOURNALISM
REVIEW
Tel: (800) 827-0771
(301) 405-8803
Fax: (301) 405-8323
E-mail: ajr@ajr.umd.edu
Web site: www.ajr.org
$24.00/1 year (10 issues)

THE ANIMAL'S AGENDA
Publication of the Animal
Rights Network
P.O. Box 3083
Langhorne, PA 19047-9294
Tel: (800) 426-6884
(410) 675-4566
Fax: (410) 675-0066
E-mail: office@animalsagenda.org
Web site: www.animalsagenda.org
$24.00/1 year (6 issues)
$42.00/2 years (12 issues)

BECAUSE PEOPLE MATTER
403 21st Street
Sacramento, CA 95814-1116
Tel: (916)444-3203
E-mail: bpmnews@aol.com
$15.00/1 year (6 issues)

BULLETIN OF THE
ATOMIC SCIENTISTS
6042 South Kimbark Avenue
Chicago, IL 60637
Tel: (773) 702-2555
Fax: (773) 702-0725
E-mail: bulletin@bullatomsci.org
Web site: www.bullatomsci.org
$28.00/1 year (6 issues)
Free trial issue

CLEVELAND FREE TIMES
1846 Coventry Road, PMB 100
Cleveland, OH 44118
Tel: (216) 321-2300

Fax: (216) 321-4456
E-mail: letters@freetimes.com
Web site: www.freetimes.com
$80.00/1 year
$40.00/6 months, weekly

COUNTERPUNCH*
3220 N Street, NW, PMB 346
Washington, DC 20007-2829
Tel: (800) 840-3683
Fax: (202) 967-3620
E-mail:
counterpunch@counterpunch.org
Web site: www.counterpunch.org
$40.00/1 year (23 issues)
$30.00/1 year (low-income student
discount)

COVERTACTION QUARTERLY *
1500 Massachusetts Avenue, NW, #732
Washington, DC 20005
Tel: (202) 331-9763
Fax: (202) 331-9751
E-mail: info@covertaction.org
Web site: www.caq.com
$22.00/1 year (4 issues)
$38.00/2 years (8 issues)

DOLLARS AND SENSE
1 Summer Street
Somerville, MA 02143
Tel: (617) 628-8411
Fax: (617) 628-2025
E-mail: dollars@igc.apc.org
Web site: www.igc.org/dollars
$18.95/1 year (6 issues)
$29.95/2 years (12 issues)

EARTH ISLAND JOURNAL
Publication of the
Earth Island Institute
300 Broadway, Suite 28
San Francisco, CA 94133
Tel: (415)788-3666 ext.123
Fax: (415) 788-7324
E-mail: earthisland@earthisland.org
Web site: www.earthisland.org
$25.00/1 year
Free trial issue and on-line newsletter

ENVIRONMENTAL HEALTH
MONTHLY
Center for Health, Environment and
Justice
150 S. Washington Street, #300
Falls Church, VA 22040
Tel: (703) 237-2249

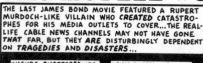

Fax: (703) 237-8389
E-mail: cchw@essential.org
Web site: essential.org/cchw
 $24.00/1 year (4 issues)

EXTRA!
130 West 25th Street
New York, NY 10001
Tel: (212) 633-6700
Fax: (212) 727-7668
E-mail: info@fair.org
Web site: www.fair.org
$19.00/1 year
(6 issues + 6 *Extra!* Updates)
$29.00/2 years
(12 issues + 12 *Extra!* Updates)

IN THESE TIMES*
2040 North Milwaukee, 2nd Floor
Chicago, IL 60647-4002
Tel: (800) 827-0270
(773) 772-0100
Fax: (773) 772-4180
E-mail: itt@inthesetimes.com
Web site: www.inthesetimes.com
$19.95/1 year (24 issues)
$34.95/2 years (48 issues)

INTERNATIONAL JOURNAL
OF HEALTH SERVICES
P.O. Box 337
Amityville, NY 11701
Tel: (516) 691-1270
Fax: (516) 691-1770
E-mail: baywood@baywood.com
Web site: www.baywood.com
$48.00/ 1 year (4 issues)
Free sample copy

MOTHER JONES*
731 Market Street, Suite 600
San Francisco, CA 94103
Tel: (800) GET-MOJO
(415) 665-6637
Fax: (415) 665-6696
E-mail: query@motherjones.com
Web site: www.motherjones.com
$18.00/1 year (6 issues)
$31.00/2 years (12 issues)

MS.
20 Exchange Place, 22nd Floor
New York, NY 10005
Tel: (800) 234-4486
(212) 509-2092
Fax: (212) 509-2407
E-mail: info@msmagazine.com

Web site: www.msmagazine.com
$35.00/1 year (6 issues)

THE NATION
33 Irving Place
New York, NY 10003
Tel: (212) 209-5400
Fax: (212) 463-9712
E-mail: info@thenation.com
Web site: www.thenation.com
$18.00/6 months (24 issues)
$36.00/1 year (47 issues)

NEWS WATCH
Center for the Integration and
Improvement of Journalism
San Francisco State University
924 Market Street, #309
San Francisco, CA 94102
Tel: (415) 398-8305
Fax: (415) 398-8706
E-mail: newsproj@sirius.com
Web site: www.newswatch.sfsu.edu
$12.00/1 year (4 issues)

PEACE REVIEW:
A TRANSNATIONAL
QUARTERLY
A publication of CarFax
Publishing Ltd.
875-81 Massachusetts Avenue
Cambridge, MA 02139
Tel: (800) 354-1420
Fax: (617) 354-6875
E-mail: sales@carFax.co.uk
Web site: www.carFax.co.uk
$60.00/1 year (4 issues)

THE PROGRESSIVE
409 East Main Street
Madison, WI 53703
Tel: (800) 827-0555
(608) 257-4626

Fax: (608) 257-3373
E-mail: circ@progressive.org
Web site: www.progressive.org
$12.00/1 year (12 issues)
Free sample copy

THE PROGRESSIVE REVIEW
1312 18th Street NW
Washington, DC 20036
Tel: (202) 835-0770
Fax: (202) 835-0779
E-mail: info@prorev.com
Web site: www.prorev.com
$18.00/1 year (6 issues)
$32.00/2 years (12 issues)

THE SAN FRANCISCO BAY
GUARDIAN*
520 Hampshire Street
San Francisco, CA 94110
Tel: (415) 255-3100
Fax: (415) 255-8762
E-mail: sfguardian@aol.com
Web site: www.sfbg.com
$17.00/6 Months (26 issues),
$32.00/1year (52 issues)

SONOMA COUNTY
PEACE PRESS
Published by Sonoma County Center
for Peace and Justice
540 Pacific Avenue
Santa Rosa, CA 95404
Tel: (707) 575-8902
Fax: (707) 575-8903
E-mail: peacentr@sonic.net
Circulated with membership
nationwide
Minimum membership
$30.00 per year or
$15.00 Low Income

SOUTHERN EXPOSURE
A publication of the Insititute
for Southern Studies
P.O. Box 531
Durham, NC 27702
Tel: (919) 419-8311
Fax: (919) 419-8315
E-mail: southern_exposure@i4south.org
Subscription comes with membership
at $24.00 a year

THIS MAGAZINE
401 W. Richmond Street
Toronto, ON M5V 3A8
Canada
Tel: (877) 999-8447
(416) 979-9429
Fax: (416) 979-1143
E-mail: thismag@web.net
Web site: www.thismag.org
$34.00/1 year
$57.00/2 years
$77.00/3 years

TOWARD FREEDOM*
Box 468
Burlington, VT 05402-0468
Tel: (802) 658-2523
Fax: (802) 658-3738
E-mail: Tfmag@aol.com
Web site: www.towardfreedom.com
$22.50/1 year (8 issues)

THE VILLAGE VOICE
36 Cooper Square
New York, NY 10003
Tel: (800) 875-2997
(212) 475-3300
Fax: (212) 475-8944
E-mail: editor@villagevoice.com
Web site: www.villagevoice.com
$79.00/1 year
$158.00/2 years

WOMEN AGAINST
MILITARY MADNESS
310 East 38th Street, Suite 225
Minneapolis, Minnesota 55409
Tel: (612) 827-5364
Fax (612) 827-6433
E-mail: wamm@mtn.org
Subscription included with
membership: $40.00 per year

WORKERS WORLD
Workers World Party
55 W. 17th Street
New York, NY 10011
Tel: (212) 627-2994
Fax (212) 675-7869
E-mail: wwp@workers.org
Web site: www.workers.org
$25.00/1 year

WORLD RIVERS REVIEW
Publication of International Rivers
Network
1847 Berkeley Way
Berkeley, CA 94703
Tel: (510) 848-1155
Fax: (510) 848-1008
E-mail: irn@irn.org
Web site: www.irn.org
$35.00 regular membership/1 year
(6 issues)
$20.00 low income/student
membership/1 year (6 issues)
Free on-line publication

Media Activist Resource Guide

RESEARCH AND EDITING BY TAYNA ALEXANDER,
KAREN TORRES-VALLE, KATIE SIMS, & MELISSA BONHAM.

ACTIVIST MEDIA PROJECT
Rocky Mountain Peace
& Justice Center
1520 Euclid Avenue
Boulder, CO 80302
Tel: (303) 444-6981
Fax: (303) 444-6523
E-mail: Amproject@colorado.edu

AFRICA NEWS SERVICE
P.O. Box 3851
Durham, NC 27702
Tel: (919) 286-0747
Fax: (919) 286-2614
E-mail: newsdesk@africanews.org
Website: www.africanews.org

News releases, information sources,
and links on Africa

ALTERNATIVE MEDIA, INC.
733 St. Antoine
Detroit, MI 48226
Tel: (313) 961-4060
Email: rwilliams@amnic.com

ALTERNATIVE PRESS CENTER
P.O. Box 33109
1443 Gorsuch Avenue
Baltimore, MD 21218
Tel: (410) 243-2471
Fax: (410) 235-5325
E-mail: Altpress@altpress.org
Web site: www.altpress.org

Publishes the quarterly *Alternative
Press Index*, a database which covers
300 periodicals with central focus on
socialism, liberation struggles, labor,
indigenous peoples, gays/lesbians,
feminism, ecology, antiracism, and
anarchism. Co-publishes with the
Independent Press Association.

ALTERNATIVE RADIO
Contact: David Barsamian
2129 Mapleton
Boulder, CO 80304
Tel: (303) 444-8788
Email: ar@orci.com
Web site: www.alternativeradio.org

Cassettes and transcripts of programs with movement activists and scholars like Noam Chomsky, Helen Caldicott, Ralph Nader, Angela Davis, Howard Zinn, Winona LaDuke, Manning Marable, and many others. Free catalog.

ALTERNATIVES IN PRINT TASK FORCE OF THE AMERICAN LIBRARY ASSOCIATION'S SOCIAL RESPONSIBILITIES ROUND TABLE
Contact: Rory Litwin
P.O. Box 72051
San Jose, CA 95172
Tel: (408) 286-6409
E-mail: rlitwin@earthlink.net

Advocates local selection and cataloging of materials from small and alternative presses and independent producers by sponsoring programs and Internet discussions; grassroots groups; and producing reviews, articles, exhibits, on-line resources, the biennial directory Alternative Publishers of Books in North America (CRISES Press), etc. Publishes quarterly review journal, *Counterpoise*.

ALTERNET
Tate Hausman, Managing Editor
77 Federal Street
San Francisco, CA 94107
Tel: (415) 284-1420
Fax: (415) 284-1414
E-mail: Info@alternet.org
Web site: www.alternet.org

An on-line news and syndication service for the independent press. A project of the Independent Media Institute, AlterNet offers about 30 new stories a week.

AMERICAN LIBRARY ASSOCIATION
Office for Intellectual Freedom
50 East Huron Street
Chicago, IL 60611
Tel: (312) 280-4223
Fax: (800) 545-2433
E-mail: Oif@ala.org
Web site: www.ala.org/oif.html

AMERICAN SOCIETY OF JOURNALISTS AND AUTHORS
1501 Broadway, Suite 302
New York, NY 10036
Tel: (212) 997-0947
E-mail: asja@compuserve.com
Web site: www.asja.org

Produces a membership directory, including a list of 1,000 non-fiction freelance writers, with their phone, fax, and writing specialty.

ARIZONA MEDIA ACTION
P.O.Box 80496
Phoenix, AZ 85060-0496
Tel: (602) 996-5823
E-mail: mediamaven@home.com

ASSOCIATION FOR EDUCATION JOURNALISM AND MASS COMMUNICATION
71 Fifth Avenue
New York, NY 10003-3004
Tel: (212) 255-0200
Fax: (212) 255-7007
Web site: www.publishers.org

A national trade association dedicated to the protection of intellectual property rights and defense of free expression.

ASSOCIATION OF ALTERNATIVE NEWSWEEKLIES
1660 L Street, NW, Suite 316
Washington, DC 20036
Tel: (202) 822-1955
Fax: (202) 822-0929
E-mail: Aan@aan.org
Web site: www.aan.org

The trade group that represents 119 alternative newsweeklies in the United States and Canada, including papers like the *Village Voice*, *Boston Phoenix*, *Chicago Reader* and *San Francisco Bay Guardian*.

ASSOCIATION OF AMERICAN PUBLISHERS
71 Fifth Avenue
New York, NY 10003-3004
Tel: (212) 255-0200
Fax: (212) 255-7007
Web site: www.publishers.org

A national trade association dedicated to protection of intellectual property rights and defense of free expression.

BALANCE & ACCURACY IN JOURNALISM
P.O. Box 824
Carrboro, NC 27510
Tel: (919) 968-4062
E-mail: mediashun@mindspring.com

THE BEAT (92.3, KKBT-FM)
Community Action Department
Dominique DiPrima, Community Action Director
5900 Wilshire Boulevard, Suite 1900
Los Angeles, CA 90036
Tel: (323) 692-5434
Fax: (323) 931-4710
Web site: www.thebeatla.com

Dominique DiPrima, 92.3 The Beat's Community Action Director, hosts *Street Science with Dominique DiPrima*, a live call-in show. Listeners aggressively explore the many levels of an issue with in-studio guests including politicians, celebrities, and experts. The show strives to empower listeners and give the community access to the airwaves. All discussions focus on positive alternatives which add to the understanding and knowledge of a topic, while making sure the listeners have fun.

BENTON FOUNDATION
1800 K Street, NW
Washington, DC 20006
Tel: (202) 638-5770
Fax: (202) 638-5771
E-mail: Benton@benton.org
Web site: www.benton.org

A private foundation that works to shape the emerging communications environments to realize the social benefits made possible by the public interest use of communications.

BERKELEY MEDIA STUDIES GROUP
2140 Shattuck Avenue, Suite 804
Berkeley, CA 94704
Tel: (510) 204-9700
Fax: (510) 204-9710
E-mail: Bmsg@bmsg.org

BETWEEN THE LINES
c/o WPKN Radio
Contact: Scott Harris
244 University Avenue
Bridgeport, CT 06604-5700
Tel: (203) 331-9756
Fax: (203) 331-1314

E-mail: Betweenthelines@snet.net
Web site:
www.wpkn.org/betweenthelines

BLACK WOMEN
IN PUBLISHING
P.O. Box 6275, FDR Station
New York, NY 10150
Tel: (212) 772-5951
E-mail: bwip@hotmail.com
Web site: http://www.bwip.org

An employee-based trade association
dedicated to increasing the presence
and supporting the efforts of African
Heritage women and men in the
publishing industry.

CALIFORNIA FIRST
AMENDMENT COALITION
2701 Cottage Way, Suite 12
Sacramento, CA 95825-1226
Tel: (916) 974-8888
E-mail: wzlotlow@cfac.org or
tfrancke@cfac.org
Web site: www.cfac.org

California journalist's legal notebook
and annual conference, the California
First Amendment Assembly.

CENTER FOR CAMPUS
ORGANIZING
165 Friend Street, M/S #1
Boston, MA 02114-2025
Main Office: (617) 725-2886
FAX: (617) 725-2873
E-mail:cco@igc.org
Web site: www.cco.org

Supports progressive on-campus
publishing.

CENTER FOR INTEGRATION AND
IMPROVEMENT OF JOURNALISM
Journalism Department
San Francisco State University
1600 Holloway Avenue
San Francisco, CA 94132
Tel: (415) 338-2083
E-mail: emartine@sfsu.edu
Web site: www.journalism.sfsu.edu or
www.newswatch.sfsu.edu

A series of model programs designed to
bring ethnic diversity to the country's
newsrooms and promote a fair and
balanced coverage of our multicultural
society.

CENTER FOR INVESTIGATIVE
REPORTING
500 Howard Street, Suite 206
San Francisco, CA 94105
Tel: (415) 543-1200
Fax: (415) 543-8311
E-mail: Center@cironline.org
Web site: www.muckraker.org

Exposes abuse of power in bureaucracy
by working with local and national
media focusing on public
accountability.

CENTER FOR MEDIA AND
DEMOCRACY
Publisher of *PR Watch Quarterly*
520 University Avenue #310
Madison, WI 53703
Tel: (608) 260-9713
Fax: (608) 260-9714
E-mail: Stauber@compuserve.com
Web site: www.prwatch.org

Specializes in blowing the lid off
today's multi-billion dollar
propaganda-for-hire industry.

CENTER FOR MEDIA
AND PUBLIC AFFAIRS
2100 L Street NW, Suite 300
Washington, DC 20037
Tel: (202) 223-2942
Fax: (202) 872-4014
E-mail: Cmpamm@aol.com
Web site: www.cmpa.com

Conducts scientific studies of news
and entertainment content.

CENTER FOR MEDIA CULTURE
AND HISTORY
25 Waverly Place, #501
New York, NY 10003
Tel: (212) 998-3759
E-mail: ba2@is.nyu.edu
Web site:
www.nyu.edu/gsas/program/media

Focuses on the role that media play
in shaping our perceptions of history
and culture; in forging individual,
collective, national, and transnational
identities; and in mediating the
direction and character of social
change.

THE CENTER FOR MEDIA
EDUCATION
2120 L Street NW, Suite 200
Washington, DC 20037
Tel: (202) 331-7833
Fax: (202) 331-7841
E-mail: cme@cme.org
Web site: www.cme.org/cme

The Center for Media Education is a
non-profit research and advocacy
organization founded in 1991 to
educate the public and policymakers
about critical media policy issues.

CENTER FOR WAR, PEACE,
AND THE NEWS MEDIA
1418 Lafayette Street, Suite 554
New York, NY 10003
Tel: (212) 998-7960
Fax: (212) 995-4143
E-mail: War.peace.news@nyu.edu
Web site: www.nyu.edu/cwpnn

Dedicated to supporting journalists and
news organizations in their efforts to
sustain an informed citizenry.

CENTER ON BLACKS
AND THE MEDIA
P.O. Box 4689
Atlanta, GA 30302
Tel: (404) 526-5470
Monitors the black image in the media.

CHIAPAS MEDIA PROJECT
4834 N. Springfield
Chicago, IL 60625
Tel: (773) 583-7728
Fax: (773) 583-7738
E-mail: Cmp@vida.com
Web site:
www.chiapasmediaproject.org

A bi-national partnership that provides
tools and training so that marginalized
indigenous communities can establish
their own informational outlets. The
project provides video cameras, editing
equipment, computers, and appropriate
training so that communities in
Chiapas can tell their own stories in
their own words.

CHICAGO MEDIA WATCH
P.O. Box 268737
Chicago, IL 60626
Tel: (773) 604-1910
E-mail: cmw@mediawatch.org

Web site: www.mediawatch.org/chicago

Chicago-based media activist group that publishes a quarterly newsletter on grassroots media activism and vital public information that the mainstream press chooses to omit, distort, or ignore.

CITIZENS' COUNCIL ON CORPORATE ISSUES
P.O. Box 74513 Kitsilano
Vancouver, B.C. V6K 4P4
Tel: (604) 734-1815
Fax: (604) 734-1815
E-mail: ccci@corporateissues.org

CCCI's purpose is to increase public awareness about the corporation through research and public education within media sources, to foster greater corporate accountability, and to promote and explore alternative institutional structures necessary to bring about change in civil society.

CITIZENS FOR INDEPENDENT PUBLIC BROADCASTING
1029 Vermont Avenue NW, Suite 800
Washington, DC 20005
Tel: (202) 638-6880
Fax: (202) 638-6885
E-mail: jmstarr@cais.com

Coordinates a national educational campaign to reform public broadcasting as a public trust, independent of government and corporate control, and to organize community groups to democratize their local public broadcasting stations.

CITIZENS FOR MEDIA LITERACY
34 Wall Street, Suite 407
Asheville, NC 28801
Tel: (704) 255-0182
Fax: (704) 254-2286
E-mail: Cml@main.nc.us
Web site: www.main.nc.us/cml

CITIZENS' MEDIA CORPS
c/o Steve Provizer
23 Winslow Road
Brookline, MA 02446
Tel: (617) 232-3174
Web site: www.radfrall.org

Seeks out the most politically and culturally disenfranchised citizens and community groups and provides them with the tools necessary to both access mainstream media and to create alternative media outlets.

THE CIVIC MEDIA CENTER & LIBRARY, INC.
1021 W University Avenue
Gainesville, FL 32601
Tel: (352) 373-0010
Web site: www.gator.net

A non-profit library and reading room of alternative press publications. Contains books, periodicals, reference materials (including the Alternative Press Index), Î-zine library, and an audio and video collection.

CLEIS PRESS, INC.
P.O. Box 14684
San Francisco, CA 94114
Tel: (415) 575-4700
(800) 780-2279
Fax: (415) 575-4705
E-mail: cleis@aol.com

Publishes literature by women; books on lesbian and gay studies, sexuality, and travel; and writer's reference books.

COLLEGE OF NOTRE DAME
Department of Communication
Dr. Miriam Zimmerman, Chair
Belmont, CA 94002
Tel: (650) 508-3736
Fax: (650) 508-3736
E-mail: Miriam@cnd.edu
Web site: www.cnd.edu/commdept/

Media activism is an ongoing assignment in the Introduction to Communication course required of all department majors. Students become critical consumers of media by learning how to be media responsive to social issues, in keeping with the college mission to promote a just society.

COLLISION COURSE VIDEO PRODUCTIONS
Contact: Doug Norgerg
P.O. Box 347383
San Francisco, CA 94134-7383
Tel: (415) 587-0818
Fax: (415) 587-0818
E-mail: video@collissioncourse.com
Web site: www.collisioncourse.com

Creates and distributes activist videos on anti-interventionism, police abuse, abortion rights, and indigenous issues; also the educational video *Viva La Casa! 500 Years of Chicano History*. Produces two youth-oriented cable TV shows each month in San Francisco.

COMMITTEE TO PROTECT JOURNALISTS
330 Seventh Avenue, 12th Floor
New York, NY 10001
Tel: (212) 465-1004
Fax: (212) 465-9568
E-mail: Info@cpj.org
Web site: www.cpj.org

The Committee to Protect Journalists is dedicated to safeguarding journalists and freedom of expression worldwide is a non-profit, non-partisan organization that monitors abuses of the press and promotes press freedom internationally.

COMMON COURAGE PRESS
One Red Barn Road
Monroe, ME 04951
Tel: (207) 525-0900; (800) 497-3207
Fax: (207) 525-3068
E-mail: info@commoncouragepress.com
Web site: commoncouragepress.com

Publishes books on race, feminism, gender issues, class, media, economics, ecology, and foreign policy to help readers in the struggle for social justice.

COMMUNITY MEDIA WORKSHOP
600 South Michigan Avenue
Chicago, IL 60605-1996
Tel: (312) 344-6400
Fax: (312) 344-6404
E-mail: Cmw@newstips.org
Web site: www.newstips.org

Trains community organizations and civic groups to use media more effectively and helps journalists learn of their stories. Publishers of *Getting on the Air & Into Print*, a 200-page citizen's guide to media in the Chicago area.

CULTURAL ENVIRONMENT
MOVEMENT (CEM)
3508 Market Street, Suite 3-030
Phildelphia, PA 19104
Tel: (215) 204-6434
Fax (215) 387-1560
E-mail: ggerbner@nimbus.Temple.edu

A broad-based international coalition
of citizens, scholars, activists, and
media professionals who promote
democratic principles in the cultural
environment.

CURBSTONE PRESS
321 Jackson Street
Willimantic, CT 06226
Tel: (860) 423-5110; (860) 423-9190
Fax: (860) 423-9242
E-mail: info@curbstone.org
Web site: www.curbstone.org

Publishes translations of Vietnamese,
Latin American, Puerto Rican, and
Chicano literature; poetry; U.S. fiction;
and photography.

DEMOCRACY NOW!
Web site: www.webactive.com/pacifica/
demnow.html

Launched by Pacifica Radio in 1996
to open the airwaves on a daily basis
to alternative voices traditionally
excluded from the political process.
Programs with Amy Goodman are now
available on-line.

DIRECT ACTION
MEDIA NETWORK
(DAMN)
Web site: www.damn.tao.ca

An on-line multi-media news service
that covers direct actions that

progressive organizations and
individuals take to attain a peaceful,
open, and enlightened society.

DISABILITY MEDIA PROJECT
Contact: Suzanne Levine
P.O. Box 22115
San Francisco, CA 94122-0115
Tel: (415) 387-0617
Fax: (415) 387-0583
Web site: www.dmedia.org

Disability Media Project was founded
to challenge and assist media
educators, the news media, and
creative media in fostering fair
representation of people with
disabilities.

DOWNTOWN COMMUNITY TV
(DCTV) CENTER
87 Lafayette Street
New York, NY 10013
Tel: (212) 966-4510
Fax: (212) 219-0248
E-mail: Wed@dctvny.org
Web site: www.dctvny.org

Founded in 1972, DCTV believes that
expanding public access to the
electronic media arts invigorates our
democracy. DCTV pursues a grassroots
mission to teach people, particularly
members of low-income and minority
communities, how to use media.

ELECTRONIC FRONTIER
FOUNDATION
1550 Bryant Street, Suite 725
San Francisco, CA 94103
Tel: (415) 436-9333
Fax: (415) 436-9993
E-mail: Eff@eff.org
Web site: www.eff.org

A leading civil liberties organization devoted to maintaining the Internet as a global vehicle for free speech.

FAIRNESS AND ACCURACY IN REPORTING (FAIR)
130 West 25th Street
New York, NY 10001
Tel: (212) 633-6700
Fax: (212) 727-7668
E-mail: Fair@fair.org
Web site: www.fair.org

A national media watchdog group that focuses public awareness on "the narrow corporate ownership of the press," FAIR seeks to invigorate the First Amendment by advocating for greater media pluralism and the inclusion of public interest voices in national debate.

FAIR's Local Activist Contacts:
Chicago: Dan Kaplan (312) 828-0350
Denver: Paul Klite (303) 832-7558
Ithaca (NY): Will Burbank
(607) 272-7555
Phoenix: Dave Winkler (602) 996-5823

FEMINISTS FOR FREE EXPRESSION
2525 Times Square Station
New York, NY 10108
Tel: (212) 702-6292
Fax: (212) 702-6277
E-mail: Freedom@well.com
Web site: www.well.com/user/lfreedom

A national not-for-profit organization of feminist women and men who share a commitment both to gender equality and to preserving the individual's right to read, view, rent, or purchase media materials of their choice, free from government intervention.

FOUNDATION AGAINST ORGANIZED SUPPRESSION
Contact: Baldor Svalbard (Coordinator)
E-mail: mowry@lycosmail.com
Web site: www.homestead.com/faos

FREE SPEECH TV
P.O. Box 6060
Boulder, CO 80306
Tel: (303) 442-8445
Fax: (303) 442-6472
E-mail: Programming@sftv.org
Web site: www.freespeech.org

Progressive voice in the media revolution bringing activist & alternative media into seven million homes each week.

FREEDOM FORUM WORLD CENTER
1101 Wilson Boulevard
Arlington, VA 22209
Tel: (703) 528-0800
Fax: (703) 522-4831
E-mail: News@freedomforumu.org
Web site: www.freedomforum.org

A non-partisan, international foundation dedicated to free press, free speech, and free spirit for all people.

FREEDOM OF INFORMATION CENTER
University of Missouri
127 Neff Annex
Columbia, MO 65211
Tel: (573) 882-4856
Fax: (573) 884-4963
E-mail: Kathleen_edwards@jmail.jour.missouri.edu
Web site: www.missouri.edu/~foiwww

Collects and indexes materials relating to controls on the flow and content of information to research free-press issues.

FREEDOM TO READ FOUNDATION
Judith Krug,
Executive Director and Secretary
50 East Huron Street
Chicago, IL 60611
Tel: (312) 280-4226
Fax: (312) 280-4227
E-mail: Ftrf@ala.org
Web site: www.ftrf.org

Promotes and protects freedom of speech and freedom of the press; protects the public's right of access to libraries, supplies legal counsel; and otherwise supports libraries and librarians suffering injustices due to their defense of freedom of speech and of the press (run by ALA, but a separate organization does First Amendment litigation).

FRIENDS OF FREE SPEECH RADIO
905 Parker Street
Berkeley, CA 94710
Tel: (510) 548-0542
E-mail: savepacifica@peacenet.org
Web site: www.savepacifica.net

Founded in April 1999, working to preserve community radio stations owned by Pacifica, and to institute democratic practices in their governance.

FUND FOR INVESTIGATIVE JOURNALISM
5540 32nd Street NW
Washington, DC 20015
Tel: (202) 362-0260
E-mail: fundfij@aol.com
Web site: www.fij.org

Gives grants to journalists seeking help for investigative pieces involving environmental issues, corruption, malfeasance, incompetence, and societal ills in general as well as for media criticism.

GLOBAL CINEMA CAFÉ
Central Jersey Branch of Women's International League For Peace and Freedom Charlotte Hussey
125 Jefferson Road
Princeton, NJ 08540
Tel: (609) 497-3998

Offers free monthly video programs addressing peace, justice, and human rights by screening videos followed by activist-oriented discussions lead by community organizers, filmmakers, academics, and experts on the issues. All served with coffee, tea, and cookies at the Third World Center of Princeton University—usually the first or second Sunday afternoon of the month at 4 P.M.

GLOBAL EXCHANGE
2017 Mission Street, Suite 303
San Francisco, CA 94110
Tel: (415) 255-7296
Fax: (415) 255-7498
E-mail: Info@globalexchange.org
Web site: www.globalexchange.org

Publishes books and pamphlets on various social and economic topics; promotes alternative trade for the benefit of low-income producers; helps build public awareness about human rights abuses; and sponsors Reality Tours to foreign lands, giving participants a feel for the people of a country.

GLOBALVISION, INC.
1600 Broadway, Suite 700
New York, NY 10019
Tel: (212) 246-0202
Fax: (212) 246-2677
Web site: www.globalvision.org and
http://mediachannel.org

An independent international media company specializing in an inside-out style of journalism. It has produced *Rights & Wrongs: Human Rights Television* and *South Africa Now* along with many highly acclaimed investigative documentaries; and has recently launched an Internet supersite focusing on global media issues.

GRASSROOTS MEDIA NETWORK
1602 Chatham
Austin, TX 78723
Tel: (512) 459-1619
E-mail: gnn@grassrootsnews.org
Web site: www.onr.com/user/gnn

Grassroots News Network, Queer News Network, Pueblos-Unidos. Grassroots film and video collective.

HISPANIC EDUCATION AND MEDIA GROUP, INC.
P.O. Box 221
Sausalito, CA 94966
Tel: (415) 331-8560
Fax (415) 331-2636
E-mail: margotsegura@yahoo.com

Dedicated to improving the quality of life of the Latino community with a main focus on high school dropout prevention and health issues

HUCK BOYD NATIONAL CENTER FOR COMMUNITY MEDIA (HBNC)
Kansas State University
105 Kedzie Hall
Manhattan, KS 66506
Tel: (913) 532-6890
Fax: (913) 532-5484
E-mail: Huckboyd@ksu.edu

The mission of HBNC is to strengthen local media in order to help create better, stronger communities in America.

HUMANIST MOVEMENT, THE
197 Harbord Street
Toronto ON M55 1H6
Canada
Tel: (416) 535-2094
E-mail: roberto@ilap.com
Web site: www.cynaptica.com/hm

Produces a wide range of media outlets at the grassroots level through neighborhood newspapers, neighborhood radio, and neighborhood TV stations all over the world. These are completely non-profit, volunteer projects which focus on raising (and organizing around) issues ignored by the forces of Big Media.

INDEPENDENT PRESS ASSOCIATION (IPA)
2390 Mission Street, #201
San Francisco, CA 94110
Tel: (415) 643-4401
E-mail: indypress@indypress.org
Web site: www.indypress.org

A membership-based association providing nuts-and-bolts technical assistance, loans, and networking to over 175 independent, progressive magazines, and newspapers. Formed during the first Media & Democracy Congress in San Francisco (1996), the IPA promotes a diversity of voices of the newsstand.

INSTITUTE FOR
MEDIA POLICY AND
CIVIL SOCIETY
207 W, Hastings Street, Suite 910
Vancouver, BC V6B 1H6
Canada
Tel: (604) 682-1953
Fax: (604) 683-4353
E-mail: Media@impacs.org
Web site: www.impacs.bc.ca

The society's mission is to build strong communities by training and educating Canadian civil society organizations.

INSTITUTE FOR POLICY STUDIES
(IPA)
733 15th Street NW, Suite 1020
Washington, DC 20005
Tel: (202) 234-9382
Fax: (202) 387-7915
E-mail: Ipsps@igc.apc.org
Web site: http://www.ips.dc.org

Since 1963, IPS has been the nation's leading center of progressive research link to activism.

INSTITUTE FOR PUBLIC
ACCURACY
65 Ninth Street, Suite 3
San Francisco, CA 94103
Tel: (415) 552-5378
Fax: (415) 552-6787

E-mail: Institute@igc.org
Web site: http://www.accuracy.org

Serves as a nationwide consortium of progressive policy researchers, scholars, and activists providing the media with timely information and perspectives on a wide range of issues.

INTERNATIONAL
ACTION CENTER
(IAC)
39 West 14th Street, # 206
New York, NY 10011
Tel: (212) 633-6646
Fax: (212) 633-2889
E-mail: Iacenter@iacenter.org
Web site: www.iacenter.org

Initiated in 1992 by former Attorney General Ramsey Clark and other anti-war activists, IAC coordinates international meetings, teach-ins, massive demonstrations, publishes news releases and produces video documentaries.

INTERNATIONAL
MEDIA PROJECT
National Radio Project
1714 Franklin, #100-251
Oakland, CA 94612
Tel: (510) 251-1332
Fax: (510) 251-1342
Web site: www.radioproject.org

Produces a half-hour, weekly, public affairs radio program called *Making Contact*, which is heard on 150 stations nationally, in Canada and South Africa. Shows also heard on the Internet as Radio for Peace International. Their mission is to air the voices of those not often heard in the mass media.

JAM RAG
P.O. Box 20076
Ferndale, MI 48220
Tel: (248) 542-8090
Fax: (248) 542-9826
E-mail: jamrag@genie.com

A local activist publication in the Detroit area. *Jam Rag* has been very active with community radio issues, Green issues, and the Alliance of Democracy.

THE KONFORMIST
P.O. Box 24825
Los Angeles, CA 90024-0825
Tel: (310) 737-1081
Fax: (310) 737-1081
Contact: Robert Sterling
E-mail: robalini@aol.com
Web site: www.konformist.com

Promotes media activism and has an Internet magazine dedicated to "rebellion, conspiracy, and subversion."

LONG ISLAND ALTERNATIVE MEDIA
120 Orleans Lane
Jericho, NY 11753
Tel: (516) 822-2582
E-mail: robmgold@spec.net

Focuses on the production and distribution of progressive educational material. Members currently have and/or participate in a number of radio and public access cable projects.

LOS ANGELES ALTERNATIVE MEDIA NETWORK
8124 West Third Street, Suite 208
Los Angeles, CA 90048
E-mail: Sekler@labridge.com

Listserve: la-amn@igc.org
Web site:
www.home.labridge.com/~laamn

A network of journalists in print, radio, video and on the Internet, dedicated to creating a democratic media by increasing the coverage of those whom the media would otherwise ignore. Through media outlets, they provide a voice for the voiceless, and produce the stories that remain untold.

LOS ANGELES
NEWSPAPER GUILD
Local 69 of The Newspaper Guild
114 E. 7th Street
Long Beach, CA 90801
Tel: (562) 432-3888

MEDIA ACCESS PROJECT
950 18th Street NW, Suite 220
Washington, DC 20006
Tel: (202) 232-4300
Fax: (202) 223-5302
Web site: www.mediaaccess.org

Promotes the public's First Amendment right to hear and be heard on electronic media. Advocates a pro-commercial model of microradio legalization.

MEDIA ALLIANCE
814 Mission Street, Suite 205
San Francisco, CA 94103
Tel: (415) 546-6334
Fax: (415) 546-6218
E-mail: Info@media-alliance.org
Web site: www.media-alliance.org

Review and analysis of San Francisco Bay Area media issues; Activism and Media Advocacy Training.

MEDIA CHANNEL, THE
The Global Center
Produced by Globalvision
New Media, Inc.
1600 Broadway, #700
New York, NY 10019
Web site: www.mediachannel.org

An on-line global media supersite.

MEDIA COALITION
139 Fulton Street, Suite 302
New York, NY 10038
Tel: (212) 587-4025
Fax: (212) 587-2436
E-mail:
Mediacoalition@mediacoalition.org
Web site: www.mediacoalition.org

Defends the American public's First
Amendment right to have access to the
broadest possible range of opinion and
entertainment.

THE MEDIA CONSORTIUM
2200 Wilson Boulevard, Suite 102-231
Arlington, VA 22201
Tel: (703) 920-1580
Fax: (703) 920-0946
E-mail: Rparry@ix.netcom.com
Web site: www.consortiumnews.com

An independent investigative news
company.

MEDIA EDUCATION
FOUNDATION
(MEF)
26 Center Street
Northampton, MA 01060
Tel: (413) 584-8500
Fax: (413) 586-8398
E-mail: Mediaed@mediaed.org
Web site: www.mediaed.org

Media research and production
fostering analytical media literacy.
MEF produces and distributes a
number of educational videos including
The Myth of the Liberal Media (with
Noam Chomsky and Ed Herman),
Reviving Ophelia (with Mary Pipher),
Killing Us Softly III (with Jean
Kilbourne), and *Tough Guise: Violence,
Media & the Crisis* in Masculinity (with
Jackson Katz).

MEDIA ISLAND INTERNATIONAL
P.O. Box 7204
Olympia, WA 98507
Tel: (360) 352-8526
E-mail: mii@olywa.net
Web site: www.mediaisland.org

Works to popularize social,
environmental, and political justice
frontline issues by helping coordinate
issue-focused organizations with media
organizations and mapping allies for
change internationally.

MEDIA NETWORK
Alternative Media Information Center
2565 Broadway, #101
New York, NY 10025
Tel: (212) 501-3841

MEDIAVISION
P.O. Box 1045
Boston, MA 02130
Tel: (617) 522-2923
Fax: (617) 522-1872
E-mail: Mediavi@aol.com

Works for wider exposure of
progressive views through mass media.
Provides strategic media consulting,
training, and other services for
organizations and individuals.

MISC. ACTIVISM PROGRESSIVE

Contact: Richard Winkel
E-mail: Rch@math.Missouri.edu
Posting address:
map@pencil.math.missouri.edu

A moderate Internet net-news group concerned with human rights, empowerment, and democracy, with a worldwide readership.

MOSAIC TV

P.O. Box 7740
Chicago, IL 60680
Tel: (888) 667-2423
Fax: (773) 933-9776
Web site: www.mosaictv.com

The global truth perspective for Black people. Featuring video lectures, research and coverage of news that is ignored or purposefully hidden by mainstream media.

NATIONAL ASIAN AMERICAN TELECOMMUNICATION ASSOCIATION

346 9th Street, 2nd Floor
San Francisco, CA 94103
Tel: (415) 863-0814
Fax: (415) 863-7428
Web site: www.naatanet.org

Organization seeking to increase Asian and Pacific Islanders participation in the media and the promotion of fair and accurate coverage of these communities.

NATIONAL ASSOCIATION OF BLACK JOURNALISTS

8701A Adelphi Road
Adelphi, MD 20783-1716
Tel: (301) 445-7100
Fax: (301) 445-7101
E-mail: nabj@nabj.org
Web site: www.nabj.org

Our mission is to strengthen ties among African-American journalists, promote diversity in newsrooms, and expand job opportunities and recruiting activities for established African-American journalists and students.

NATIONAL ASSOCIATION OF HISPANIC JOURNALISTS (NAHJ)

1193 National Press Building
Washington, DC 20045
Tel: (202) 662-7145; (888) 346-NAHJ
Fax (202) 662-7144
E-mail: najh@nahj.org
Web site: www.nahj.org

NAHJ is dedicated to the recognition and professional advancement of Hispanics in the news industry.

NATIONAL CAMPAIGN FOR FREEDOM OF EXPRESSION (NCFE)

1429 G Street, NW, PMB. #416
Washington, DC 20005-2009
Phone: (202) 393-2787
E-mail: ncfe@ncfe.net
Web site: www.artswire.org/~ncfe/

The NCFE is an educational and advocacy network of artists, arts organizations, audience members, and concerned citizens formed to protect and extend freedom of artistic expression and fight censorship throughout the United States.

NATIONAL COALITION AGAINST CENSORSHIP (NCAC)

275 7th Avenue, 20th Floor
New York, NY 10001
Tel: (212) 807-6222
Fax: (212) 807-6245

E-mail: ncac@ncac.org
Web site: www.ncac.org

NCAC works to educate members and the public at large about the dangers of censorship and how to oppose it.

NATIONAL COALITION TO PROTECT POLITICAL FREEDOM (NCPPF)
3321 12th Street, NE
Washington, DC 20017
E-mail: Kgage@igc.org
Web site: www.ifconews.org/ncppf.html

National membership organization dedicated to protecting the First Amendment and due process rights of all Americans. The NCPPF defends the right of people to give humanitarian and political support to causes in the U.S. and abroad. They connect individuals under attack with lawyers working on the issues nationally, they provide legal support and briefs, and also educate individuals on strategic media communication.

NATIONAL CONFERENCE OF EDITORIAL WRITERS
6223 Executive Boulevard
Rockville, MD 20852
Tel: (301) 984-3015
Fax: (301) 231-0026
E-mail: Ncewhqs@erols.com
Web site: www.ncew.org

Dedicated to the purpose of stimulating the conscience and quality of the editorial.

NATIONAL LAWYERS GUILD COMMITTEE ON DEMOCRATIC COMMUNICATIONS
558 Capp Street
San Francisco, CA 94110
Tel: (415) 522-9814
E-mail: aakorn@igc.apc.org
Web site: www.nlgcdc.org

Focuses on the right of all peoples to have access to a worldwide system of media and communications with the principles of cultural and informational self-determination. This committee is an important force in microradio advocacy and activism.

NATIONAL LESBIAN & GAY JOURNALISTS ASSOCIATION
2120 L Street, NW, Suite 840
Washington, DC 20037
Tel: (202) 588.9888
Fax: (202) 588.1818
E-mail: nlgja@aol.com
Web site: www.nlgja.org

Works form within the news industry to foster fair and accurate coverage of lesbian and gay issues.

NATIONAL WRITERS UNION (NWU)
337 17th Street, #101
Oakland, CA 94612
Tel: (510) 839-0110
Fax: (510) 839-6097
E-mail: Nwu@nwu.org
Web site: www.nwu.org/nwu

NWU's national quarterly *American Writer* tracks developments in the media/information industry and the labor movement that concern working writers and reports on union activities.

NATIVE NEWS

E-mail: Nativenews@mlists.net

Provides both mediums for Native American–specific news and action alerts permitting dissemination of action alerts pertinent to our various nations and to provide a news feed for newspapers and radio stations.

NET ACTION

601 Van Ness Avenue, #631
San Francisco, CA 94102
Tel: (415) 775-8674
Fax: (415) 673-3813
E-mail: audrie@netaction.org
Web site: www.netaction.org

Educates the public, policy-makers, and media about technology policy issues; trains Internet users in how to use technology for organizing, outreach, and advocacy; promotes universal accessibility and affordability of information technology.

NEW DAY FILMS

22-D Hollywood Avenue
Hohokus, NJ 07423
Tel: (888) 367-9154
Fax: (201) 652-1973
E-mail: orders@newday.com
Web site: www.newday.com

New Day Films is a film/video distribution cooperative. New Day's films focus on multiculturalism and diversity; physical and mental health; social and political history; global politics; media, art, and culture; gender and socialization; community politics; and young adult and family issues. New Day filmmakers are available for speaking engagements.

NEW MEXICO MEDIA LITERACY PROJECT

6400 Wyoming Boulevard, NE
Albuquerque, NM 87109
Tel: (505) 828-3129
Fax: (505) 828-3320
E-mail: mccannon@aa.edu or lacko@aa.edu
Web site: www.nmmlp.org

Their goal is to make New Mexico the most media literate state in the U.S.

NEW PARADIGM MEDIA (NPM)

Contact: Groode
1655 Halama Street
Kihei-Maui, HI 96753
Tel: (808) 243-0336
E-mail: edelkin@aol.com

NPMN is a private network, promoting individual, community and/or planetary evolution via print, Internet, radio, TV, music, theater, etc.

THE NEW PRESS

450 W. 41st Street
New York, NY 10036
Tel: (212) 629-8802; (800) 233-4830
Fax: (212) 268-6349; (212) 629-8617; (800) 458-6515

Publishes international fiction, general nonfiction, and foreign translations.

NEW YORK FREE MEDIA ALLIANCE

Tel: (212) 989-8636
Web site:
artcon.rutgers.edu/papertiger/nyfma

A NYC–based activist group dedicated to increasing democracy and public space in local and national media.

Maintains an active listserve and Web site; organizes free workshops, forums, screenings, and demonstrations.

NEWSWATCH CANADA
Simon Fraser University
8888 University Drive
Burnaby, BC V5A 1S6
Canada
Tel: (604) 291-4905
Fax: (604) 291-4024
E-mail: newswtch@sfu.ca
Web site:
http://newswatch.cprost.sfu.ca

Canadian media watch organization and freedom of information advocacy group.

NATIONAL INSTITUTE FOR COMPUTER-ASSISTED REPORTING (NICAR)
138 Neff Annex
Missouri School of Journalism
Columbia, MO 65211
Tel: (573) 882-2042
Fax: (573) 882-5431
Resource Center: (573) 882-3364
E-mail: info@ire.org
Web site: www.nicar.org

National Institute for Computer-Assisted Reporting (NICAR) is a program of Investigative Reporters and Editors, Inc., and the Missouri School of Journalism. Founded in 1989, NICAR has trained thousands of journalists in the practical skills of finding, prying loose, and analyzing electronic information.

OFFLINE
Tel: (206) 781-2044
E-mail: snoegel@u.washington.edu
Web site: www.lightlink.com/offline

A national arts organization that screens cable television and distributes independently produced films and videos. Serves as a creative conduit to numerous national and international screenings, arts organizations, microcinemas, festivals, netcast providers, and artists.

PACIFIC NEW SERVICE
450 Mission Street, Room #204
San Francisco CA 94105
Tel: (415) 438-4755; (415) 243-4364
Fax: (415) 438-4935
E-mail: pacificnews@pacificnews.org
Web site: www.ncmonline.com

Produces a daily article for reprint in a variety of newspapers worldwide.

PAPER TIGER TELEVISION
339 Lafayette Street
New York, NY 10012
Tel: (212) 420-9045
Fax: (212) 420-8223
E-mail: tigertv@bway.net
Web site: www.papertiger.org

A non-profit volunteer collective that has been pioneering media criticism through video since 1981, conducting workshops, creating installations, and producing videotapes. Their programs address issues of democratic communication media representation and the economics of the information industry.

THE PAUL ROBESON FUND FOR INDEPENDENT MEDIA

The Funding Exchange
666 Broadway, #500
New York, NY 10012
Tel: (212) 529-5300
Fax: (212) 982-9272
E-mail: Viviana.bianchi@FEX.org
Web site: www.fex.org/robeson

Supports local, state, national and international media activism; grassroots organizing; and funds media producers (radio, video, and film).

PEOPLES VIDEO NETWORK

39 West 14th Street, #206
New York, NY 10011
Tel: (212) 633-6646
Fax: (212) 633-2889
E-mail: pvnnyc@peoplesvideo.org
Web site: www.peoplesvideo.org

A group of video activists committed to publicizing stories that the corporate media won't cover on the struggles of poor and oppressed people. They reach 50 cities every week and have many special editions.

PIRATE TELEVISION

6057 3rd Avenue, NW
Seattle, WA 98107
Tel: (206) 782-7605
E-mail: edmays@scn.org

Produces a weekly public access program called *Crack the CIA*, which uses talks, documentaries, interviews, and rare archival news clips to expose the link between the drug trade and U.S. foreign policy.

PROGRESSIVE MEDIA PROJECT

409 E Main Street
Madison, WI 53703
Tel: (608) 257-4626
Fax: (608) 257-3373
E-mail: pmproj@progressive.org
Web site: www.progressive.org

An affiliate of *The Progressive* magazine: edits and distributes commentaries to mainstream newspapers throughout the country.

PROJECT CENSORED

Sonoma State University
1801 E. Cotati Avenue
Rohnert Park, CA 94928
Tel: (707) 664-2500
Fax: (707) 664-2108
E-mail: censored@sonoma.edu
Web site:
www.sonoma.edu/projectcensored

A faculty/student media research project dedicated to building free democratic news systems. Produces an annual yearbook that discusses the year's top 25 most censored stories.

PUBLIC ACCESS OF INDIANAPOLIS (PAI)

P.O. Box 30269
Indianapolis, IN 46230-0269
Tel: (317) 335-5272
Fax: (317) 466-8386
E-mail: nhess@indyaccess.org
Web site: www.indyaccess.org

Public Access of Indianapolis (PAI) is a 501(c) 3 organization dedicated to promoting access to the tools of electronic communication. PAI provides video cameras and support equipment as well as nonlinear editing facilities to producers of non-commercial videos in central Indiana.

PUBLIC MEDIA CENTER
446 Green Street
San Francisco, CA 94133
Tel: (415) 434-1403
Fax: (415) 986-6779
Web site: www.publicmediacenter.org

A non-profit, public interest advertising agency focused on social, political, and environmental issues.

RADIO FOR ALL
Web site: www.radio4all.org

The hub Web site for the U.S. microradio movement, with links to clandestine stations, support groups, news and announcements, policy updates, activist alters, legal information, and detailed primers on how to start a new station.

REAL NEWS NETWORK
Providing Vital Human Information
35 Green Valley Drive, Unit 1204
Kitchener, ON N2P 2A5
Canada
Tel: (519) 893-5321
Fax: (519) 893-0735
E-mail: pboini@realnewsnetwork.com
Web site: www.realnewsnetwork.com

Publishes public interest journalism and *Real Society* magazine, "Canada's Real News Magazine."

REPORTER'S COMMITTEE FOR FREEDOM OF THE PRESS
1815 N. Ft. Myer Drive, Suite 900
Arlington, VA 22209
Tel: (800) 336-4243
Fax: (703) 807-2109

E-mail: rcfp@rcfp.org
Web site: www.rcfp.org

Serves as a major national and international resource in free speech issues, disseminating information in a variety of forms, including a quarterly legal review, a bi-weekly newsletter, a 24-hour hotline, and various handbooks on media law issues.

ROCKY MOUNTAIN MEDIA WATCH
Box 18858
Denver, CO 80218
Tel: (303) 832-7558
Web site: www.bigmedia.org

SATAN MACNUGGIT POPULAR ARTS
3584 John Street
Vineland Station, ON L0R 2E0
Canada
Tel: (905) 562-7267
Fax: (905) 562-5138
E-mail: satanmacnuggit@tao.ca

An independently run media outlet devoted to the production and distribution of radical, subversive, and grassroots music, video, literature, and collage art.

SEAL PRESS
3131 Western Avenue, Suite 410
Seattle, WA 98121-1028
Tel: (206) 283-7844; (800) 754-0271
Fax: (206) 285-9410
E-mail: sealprss@scn.org
Web site: www.sealpress.com

Publishes fiction and nonfiction by women writers.

SEATTLE INDEPENDENT FILM
AND VIDEO CONSORTIUM
2318 Second Ave, PMB. #313-A
Seattle, WA 98121
Tel: (206) 568-6051
E-mail: joel@blackchair.com
Web site: www.sifvc.org

Maintains press and public awareness
of independent media-makers to
increase dialogue between regional,
national, and international
organizations via micro-cinema
screenings, television, netcasting, salon
activity, and art events.

SEVEN STORIES PRESS
140 Watts Street
New York, NY 10013
Tel: (212) 226-8760
Fax: (212) 226-1411
E-mail: info@sevenstories.com
Web site: www.sevenstories.com

Publishes books for the general reader
in the area of literature, literature in
translation, popular culture,
journalism, and alternative health and
nutrition.

SOCIETY OF PROFESSIONAL
JOURNALISTS (SPJ)
16 South Jackson Street
Greencastle, IN 46135-1514
Tel: (765) 653-3333
Fax (765) 653-4631 fax
E-mail:spj@spjhq.org e-mail
Web site: www.spj.org

The Society of Professional Journalists
is the nation's largest and most broad-
based journalism organization. SPJ is a
not-for-profit organization made up of
13,500 members dedicated to
encouraging the free practice of

journalism; stimulating high standards
of ethical behavior; and perpetuating a
free press.

SOUTH END PRESS
7 Brookline Street, No. 1
Cambridge, MA 02139-4146
Tel: (617) 547-4002; (800) 533-8478
Fax: (617) 547-1333
E-mail: southend@igc.org
Web site: www.lbbs.org/sep.htm

An affiliate of the Institute for Social
and Cultural Change, SEP is a
collectively managed non-profit
publisher of original trade paperbacks,
offering nonfiction analyses of politics,
culture, ecology, feminism, race, and
sexuality from a progressive
perspective.

SOUTHWEST ALTERNATE MEDIA
PROJECT
1519 West Main Street
Houston, TX 77006
Tel: (713) 522-8592
Fax: (713) 522-0953
Web site: www.swamp.org

A non-profit media center promoting
the creation and appreciation of film
and video as art forms for a
multicultural public.

TAO COMMUNICATIONS
Web site: www.tao.ca

A Canada-based federation comprised
of local autonomous collectives and
individuals. Tao organizes networks
in order to defend and expand
public space and the right to self-
determination. Host to an array of
on-line movement networks and Web
sites.

THE TELEVISION PROJECT
2311 Kimball Place
Silver Springs, MD 20910
Tel: (301) 588-4001
Fax: (301) 588-4001
E-mail: apluhar@tvp.org
Web site: www.tvp.org

An organization to help parents understand how television affects their families and community, and propose alternatives that foster positive emotional, cognitive and spiritual development within families and communities.

THIS ALTERNATIVE
A-Infos Radio Project
E-mail: radio4al@radio4all
Web site: www.radio4all.org

Global Links to alternative free radio. This alternative to satellite downlinking provides microbroadcasters with a means to distribute and archive broadcast quality radio programming via the Internet.

THE THOMAS JEFFERSON
CENTER FOR THE
PROTECTION OF
FREE EXPRESSION
400 Peter Jefferson Place
Charlottesville, VA 22911
Tel: (804) 295-4784
Fax: (804) 296-3621
E-mail: freespeech@tjcenter.org
Web site: www.tjcenter.org

An organization devoted to the defense of free expression in all its forms.

TORONTO VIDEO ACTIVIST
COLLECTIVE
Contact: David Hermolin
P.O. Box 108, Station P
Toronto, ON M5S 2S8
Canada
E-mail: Hermolin@pathcom.com or tvac@tao.ca

Focused on documenting and promoting social and environmental justice movements by taping events, organizing screenings, and conducting workshops on video activism.

UNION PRODUCERS AND
PROGRAMMERS NETWORK
(UPPNET)
c/o Labor Education Service Union Producers and Programmers Network
437 Mgmt. & Econ. Bldg.
271 19th Avenue South
University of Minnesota
Minneapolis, MN 55455
Tel: (612) 624-4326
E-mail: uppnet@labornet.org
Web site:
www.mtn.org/jsee/uppnet.html

Organized to promote production and use of TV and radio shows pertinent to the cause of organized labor and working people. Publishes UPPNET *News*.

VANGUARD COMMUNICATIONS
1019 19th Street, NW, Suite 1200
Washington, DC 20036
Tel: (202) 331-4323
Fax: (202) 331-9420
Web site: www.vancomm.com

A full-service strategic communications company that develops and implements advocacy communications campaigns on critical environmental, health and social justice issues. Vanguard also conducts media training, produces award-winning publications, stages national and local media events, and creates innovative partnerships for the many diverse organizations it works with.

VERSO
180 Varick Street
New York, NY 10014
Tel: (212) 807-9680
Fax: (212) 807-9152
E-mail: versoinc@aol.com
Web site: www.verso-nlr.com

Publishes nonfiction titles.

VIDEAZIMUT
3680, rue Jeanne-Mance, Bureau 430
Montreal, Quebec H2X 2K5
Canada
Tel: (514) 982-6660
Fax: (514) 982-6122
E-mail: videaz@web.net
Web site: www.tao.ca/videazimut

An international non-governmental coalition promoting audiovisual communication for development and democracy.

WE INTERRUPT THIS MESSAGE
965 Mission Street, Suite 220
San Francisco, CA 94103
Tel: (415) 537-9437
Fax: (415) 537-9439
E-mail: Interrupt@igc.org
Web site: www.interrupt.org

Builds capacity in public interest groups across the country to do traditional media work, reframe public debate, and interrupt media stereotypes through training, technical assistance,

and joint campaigns to document and challenge distorted news reporting.

WHISPERED MEDIA
P.O. Box 40130
San Francisco, CA 94140
Tel: (415) 789-8484
E-mail: whisper@energy-net.org
Web site: www.videoactivism.org

Provides video witnessing, video post-production, and media resources for grassroots activist groups. Facilitates Bay Area Video Activist Network (VAN). Specializes in direct action campaigns.

WOMEN FOR MUTUAL
SECURITY (WMS)
5110 West Penfield Road
Columbia, MD 21045
Tel: (410) 730-7483
Fax (410) 964-9248
E-mail: foerstel@aol.com
Web site: www.iacenter.org/wms/

WMS is a network of women's organizations and individuals committed to making a paradigm shift in the world from a heirarchical and violent mode of society to a new cooperative and peaceful model.

WOMEN'S INSTITUTE FOR
FREEDOM OF THE PRESS
8306 Ross Place, NW
Washington, DC 20008-3332
Tel: (202) 966-7783
Fax: (202) 966-7783
E-mail: wifponline@igc.org
Web site: www.igc.org/wifp

Explores ways to assure that everyone has equal access to the public and that all information is taken into account when decision-making.

WORKING GROUP
1611 Telegraph Avenue, Suite 1550
Oakland, CA 94612
Tel: (510) 268-9675
Fax: (510) 268-3606
E-mail: info@theworkinggroup.org
Web site: www.pbs.org/livelyhood or
www.pbs.org/noit

Non-profit media production company
focused on ordinary, hard-working
Americans. The group has produced
the *We Do the Work* series, the *Not In
Our Town* specials, which gained
national recognition for showcasing
positive community response and
intolerance of hate violence.

WORLD PRESS FREEDOM
COMMITTEE (WPFC)
11690-C Sunrise Valley Drive
Reston, VA 20191
Tel: (703) 715-9811
Fax: (703) 620-6790
E-mail: freepress@wpfc.org
Web site: www.wpfc.org

A coordination group of national and
international news media organization,
WPFC is an umbrella organization that
includes 44 journalistic organizations
united in the defense and promotion of
freedom.

Top 5 Censored Reprints

1 CENSORED

Multinational Corporations Profit from International Brutality

"CORPORATION CRACK-DOWNS: BUSINESS BACKS BRUTALITY"
by Arvind Ganesan
Dollars and Sense, May/June 1999

In the sleepy fishing village of Veldur in India, Sadhana Bhalekar, a young woman in her mid-twenties, was taking a bath on the morning of June 3, 1997, when police broke down her door, beat her retarded nephew, and mercilessly dragged her naked out of her house. They beat and then arrested her. She was three months pregnant at the time. The police officer in charge reportedly said, "This is Baba Bhalekar's wife, bash her head on the road." Why? Vithal "Baba" Bhalekar, is a leading opponent of the Houston-based Enron Corporation's Dabhol Power project—the largest power plant in the world—in the state of Maharashtra, India. The brutal police raid on Veldur village was clearly an act of terror to silence critics of the project.

Police assaults against opponents of Enron's project are a regular occurrence in Ratnagiri district, where the power plant is located. Authorities threw in jail a high profile critic of the project, Sadanand Pawar, an economics professor from Bombay, because he had "spread false information to the public which is against Enron."

The police—in what is often viewed as the world's largest democracy—

criminalized demonstrations against Enron in December 1996, by banning all "public utterance of cries, singing of songs, playing of music" and the "delivery of harangues, the use of gestures or mimetic representations, and the preparation, exhibition, or dissemination of pictures, symbols, placards, or any other object or thing which may in the opinion of such authority offend against decency or morality...." The orders squashing free speech expire every 15 days, but police routinely renew them to maintain the semblance of rule of law. By March 1998, more than 3,000 people had been jailed, and some beaten, simply for demonstrating against the project.

The Indian state government did everything it could to ensure that Enron's project would move forward. What about the company? Enron paid the police who arrested and beat the protesters and continues to pay them to this day, a relationship legal under state law. Enron also loaned police a helicopter to survey the demonstrators.

But the actions of the company go beyond material and financial support for abusive police. On at least four occasions, contractors for the company directly threatened, harassed, and attacked individuals who opposed the project. When the victims tried to press charges, they found the rule of law did not operate for them. The police looked the other way in some cases. In others, the police arrested the victims.

The corporation denies any culpability. Instead, the multinational criticizes human rights organizations for documenting its abuses.

Since the East India Company first embarked on colonial ventures centuries ago, corporations have been complicit in human rights abuses. Because energy companies like Enron invariably displace residents from their land, or make it unlivable by polluting it, they are involved in some of the worst human rights abuses today. They have received more attention since November 1995, when the Nigerian government executed human rights activist Ken Saro-Wiwa and eight others who opposed the environmental devastation wrought by Royal Dutch Shell in the Ogoniland region. An international campaign against Shell continues to this day even as the corporation, the largest foreign investor in Nigeria, has endorsed United Nations human rights guidelines and says it will devise policies to follow them.

Since Saro-Wiwa's death, human rights and environmental organizations have stepped up their scrutiny of corporate abuses and ugly corporate partnerships with repressive governments. Local and national governments increasingly vie for lucrative business deals with multinationals and are more than willing to sideline human rights in favor of commerce. Similarly, the United States and other home governments of corporations are only too happy to support these multibillion-dollar energy or infrastructure projects by taking human rights off their foreign policy agenda.

Companies and governments often argue that these investments will improve human rights, but a cursory look at operations throughout the world in the 1990s paints a very different picture.

➤ Mobil Oil's natural gas subsidiary provided the bulldozers used by the Indonesian military to dig mass graves during its murderous campaign to crush an insurgency on the island of Aceh in the early 1990s, according to allegations that only recently surfaced. Indonesia is the world's largest exporter of liquefied natural gas.

➤ Since 1993, when they began construction on the Yadana natural gas field and pipeline in Burma, the French oil company TOTAL and the U.S.-based Unocal partnered with the brutal Burmese junta. The Burmese military providing security for the project killed, tortured, raped, and conscripted the labor of villagers along the pipeline's route, according to press accounts. These charges will soon be judged in a California federal court, where a lawsuit filed by the Center for Constitutional Rights and Earth Rights International alleges that Unocal benefited from the use of forced labor and the Burmese military's human rights abuses.

➤ In 1996, the human rights world learned of British Petroleum's multimillion-dollar contracts with the Colombian military—among the world's most brutal—to provide security for BP's exploitation of the massive Cusiana-Cupiagua oil fields. These fields were the largest discovered in the Western Hemisphere since 1967.

➤ Exxon is under fire after the slaughter of 20 citizens living near the oil company's proposed pipeline through Chad and Cameroon. The German parliament and African and European groups predict further human rights violations, forced relocations, and environmental damage once construction begins. Environmental organizations from the North and South are calling on the World Bank to suspend funding for the project until Exxon addresses these issues. The pipeline would make Chad one of Africa's top five oil exporters.

Burma, Colombia, Indonesia, and Nigeria. All are countries with a history of rule by repressive governments even without the collusion of multinationals. In this context, corporations often argue that their presence and investment will improve human rights. Superficially, "constructive engagement," as this argument is called, has merit: If economic activity increases, so will the possibility of international dialogue with abusive governments and an improvement of living standards that gives citizens the power to raise their voices in protest.

Human rights violations become framed as a "necessary evil" that insures improvement in the long term. Essentially this view serves to justify million or even billion-dollar investments in abusive countries.

Mobil—soon to merge with Exxon—is the most vocal on the issue. Its "editorial advertisements" lambast government sanctions to punish abusive governments. In one 1997 ad Mobil wrote: "Rather than taking action that merely makes us feel virtuous, government should clarify its objectives and weigh the full costs before imposing sanctions. It should seek ways to engage, not retreat..." Joining Mobil in attacking sanctions is the American Petroleum Institute, an industry-funded advocacy organization and think tank. Its August 1998 report—titled "Oil and Natural Gas Industry Promotes Human Rights Abroad"—proclaimed that the use of "sanctions to punish regimes that abridge their peoples' human rights" denies local people the "rights enhancements" that oil companies "confer." This report was written in conjunction with USA*ENGAGE, another industry-funded lobbying organization whose purpose is to severely limit or curtail the use of sanctions by the U.S. government.

The reality is that "constructive engagement" with undemocratic governments is a myth. Instead, engagement has the opposite impact as a look at only the last five years reveals. Consider Burma, where Unocal claims its Yadana gas project—the largest single foreign investment in the country—"is bringing sustainable, long-term, economic and social benefits to the 35,000 villagers living in the immediate pipeline region and lasting benefits to the people of Myanmar [Burma]." The IMF reports that Burma's economy is collapsing, there is virtually no social spending by the military junta, and there is no short-term prospect for reforms, despite foreign investment. Throughout this process, the military junta tightened its grip over the country.

Similarly, in Kazakhstan, President Nursultan Nazarbaev signed a deal with Chevron in 1993 to develop the nine-billion barrel Tengiz field—the world's largest single oil discovery since 1967, worth at least $78 billion. Five years after the deal was inked, Nazarbaev has shut down the independent media, announced snap elections, and arrested and harassed his leading political opponent to insure that no credible opposition can challenge his increasingly autocratic rule. He also appointed his son-in-law to manage the state oil company.

The most compelling evidence, not just of constructive engagement's failure, but of its role in undermining progress on human rights, comes from a seemingly unlikely source—the final report of South Africa's Truth and Reconciliation Commission. The commission found that corporations were "willing collaborators" with the apartheid regime since the early 1960s with "a direct interest in maintaining the status quo." They bypassed attempts to impose sanctions by "forming partnerships with South African parastatal organizations." The apartheid regime "depended on five major oil companies to break the oil ban: Shell, British Petroleum (BP), Mobil, Caltex, and Total."

"Foreign investment prevented governments from taking any real action against apartheid" because of the pressure exerted by these companies to maintain the system, said the commission—a pattern we see today. Some examples of government-corporate complicity in abuses:

Just this year, the Dutch government reversed its long criticism of China's human rights record and refused to sponsor a United Nations Human Rights

Commission resolution condemning China. In February, the Chinese government awarded Royal Dutch Shell the largest single foreign investment in Chinese history—a $4.5 billion contract to build an ethylene plant with a government oil company.

In March 1998, the U.S. State Department ignored its own report on human rights abuses in Turkmenistan to okay a $96 million award from the Export-Import Bank to four U.S. companies selling natural gas and other equipment to the country. Any Ex-Im Bank loan over $10 million requires the State Department to conduct a human rights impact assessment "to determine if it may give rise to significant human rights concerns." Its 1997 human rights report began with the statement, "Turkmenistan, a one-party state dominated by its President and his closest advisers, made little progress in moving from a Soviet-era authoritarian style of government to a democratic system." Its state security forces "operate with relative impunity and have been responsible for abusing the rights of individuals as well as enforcing the Government's policy of repressing political opposition."

Turkmenistan possesses some of the largest oil and gas reserves in Central Asia and companies such as Mobil, Exxon, and Royal Dutch Shell operate there. So the State Department okayed the deal that gives Bateman Engineering, Dresser Rand, Corning, and General Electric $96 million in public funds.

While Turkmenistan's president Saparmurad Niyazov was visiting President Clinton a month later, the U.S. government's Trade and Development Administration awarded Enron a $750,000 grant to conduct a pipeline feasibility study for a proposed $2.8 billion pipeline in Turkmenistan. (General Electric and Bechtel, both U.S. companies, eventually won the pipeline project in February 1999.) After the Enron deal was signed, the White House issued a press release stating, "Turkmenistan is committed to strengthening the rule of law and political pluralism, including free and fair elections for Parliament and the presidency in accordance with international standards...." But when reporters asked Niyazov about the government's attitude toward opposition parties, he said, "We do not have any opposition parties—you are ill-informed. We have none."

U.S. officials said they raised human rights issues privately with Niyazov during his April 1998 visit. The U.S. and Turkmen governments played the game of "hostage politik"—where repressive governments release political prisoners to gain political and commercial favor with Washington—during the visit. The State Department lobbied for and secured the release of 10 political prisoners which the U.S. government then cited as an example of improvement in human rights, in justification of its commercial interests.

Behind the political smokescreens, undemocratic governments further consolidate their stranglehold over resources and revenues once partnered with international corporations. A dictatorship or one-party state has no incentive to distribute its gains to a population it does not pretend to represent. Agreements between a company and a repressive government are essentially deals between two private parties—they are a profit-making enterprise for the company and for those in power. When a resource brings in hard currency, like oil, an autocratic government often becomes a kleptocratic one, enabling a few to steal the wealth of the nation. Then there is Enron. If increased investment necessarily leads to improvements in human rights and respect for the rule of law, then how to explain the human rights violations surrounding the company's power project in India? India is considered the world's largest democracy, governing under the banner of human rights, the rule of law, and an active judiciary. It largely accepts free expression and peaceful assembly. The conflict in the Ratnagiri district flows directly from the conduct of Enron's subsidiary and the state after villagers opposed the seizure of their lands, and the polluting and diversion of their water. The abuses visited upon dissenting villagers are traceable to the supposedly beneficial investment by Enron.

Despite cheerleading that promotes foreign investment as the key to improving human rights, the reality is human rights are not safeguarded—even in countries considered democratic—without forceful action on the scale that defeated apartheid in South Africa. Financial institutions must enact human rights guidelines in their loans. Campaigns sanctioning corporate investors must enlist the support of those suffering under corporate/government collusion. Corporate codes on human rights—such as those enacted by Unocal and Shell after their operations in Burma and Nigeria were exposed—are only one piece of a project that requires action by governments, financial institutions, and the citizenry of the world.

NIGERIA'S "PROGRESS" Nowhere is the need for concerted action more urgent than in Nigeria, the largest oil producer in Africa, and the fifth largest in the Organization of Petroleum Exporting Countries (OPEC). Instead of this rich resource transforming Nigeria into one of the most prosperous states on the African continent and a model of human rights and democracy, these natural resources have enriched a small minority and multinationals at the expense of human rights.

Ironically, in August 1998, Mobil called on governments to "Seize the Day"—not to tie increased investment to real improvements in human rights by corporations and the government—but to promote foreign investment in Nigeria as a way to engage the repressive regime.

It is true that the military government led by General Abdusalami Abubakar released many political prisoners and relaxed restrictions on freedom of expression, assembly, and association. It allowed elections so that now Olusegun Obasanjo is Nigeria's civilian president.

But the situation in the oil-producing Niger Delta is worsening, contrary to oil companies' claims that they improve human rights.

In the Niger Delta, protests directed at oil companies and the lack of development are increasing. Many of the projects built by oil company money in areas largely ignored by the Nigerian government are inappropriate for the needs of the communities or shoddily carried out, exacerbating conflicts within and among the oil-producing communities. Protesters regularly occupy flow stations, stop production, or take oil workers hostage.

The Nigerian government set up special task forces to handle security issues in the region, including the protests of Saro-Wiwa and his allies. They crack down on anyone deemed a threat to oil production. In virtually every community in the oil regions, the paramilitary Mobile Police, the regular police, or the army continue to beat, detain, or even kill those involved in protests, peaceful or otherwise. They target whistleblowers for arrest, including a coordinator of the African section of the international watchdog group Oil Watch.

In a particularly brutal series of incidents on December 30, Ijaw youths protesting against multinational oil companies throughout Bayelsa State were met with an influx of several thousand military personnel. Two days later, in the town of Yenagoa, security forces killed 25 youths over three days. The government detained at least a dozen more.

Five days later, 100 armed soldiers, using boats and a helicopter owned by Chevron, attacked Opia and Ikenyan, two small communities of perhaps 500 people each in the north part of Delta State. Community members told Human Rights Watch later that they were used to seeing Chevron's helicopter flying low over the community since two Chevron wells are within 100 metres of Opia. At first they thought nothing of it, but as the helicopter approached the village this time it started firing down at them. It then flew to nearby Ikenyan and opened fire. Soldiers then sped to shore in what appeared to be Chevron's boats and opened fire, killing at least two people in each village, including the traditional leader of Ikenyan who was approaching them to negotiate. Fifteen people from Opia and 47 from Ikenyan are still missing. The soldiers torched each village before they left, destroying virtually all the houses and sinking the canoes.

Chevron defended the soldiers, who claimed to be "counterattacking" youths who threatened them as they were guarding a Chevron drilling rig. Villagers said they knew of no such altercation. Chevron expresses no regret for what happened. In this environment, companies cannot claim human rights have improved.

2 CENSORED

Pharmaceutical Companies put Profit before Need

"MILLIONS FOR VIAGRA, PENNIES FOR DISEASES OF THE POOR"

by Ken Silverstein
The Nation, July 19, 1999

Almost three times as many people, most of them in tropical countries of the Third World, die of preventable, curable diseases as die of AIDS. Malaria, tuberculosis, acute lower-respiratory infections; in 1998, these claimed 6.1 million lives. People died because the drugs to treat those illnesses are nonexistent or are no longer effective. They died because it doesn't pay to keep them alive. Only 1 percent of all new medicines brought to market by multinational pharmaceutical companies between 1975 and 1997 were designed specifically to treat tropical diseases plaguing the Third World. In numbers, that means 13 out of 1,223 medications. Only four of those thirteen resulted from research by the industry that was designed specifically to combat tropical ailments. The others, according to a study by the French group Doctors Without Borders, were either updated versions of existing drugs, products of military research, accidental discoveries made during veterinary research or, in one case, a medical breakthrough in China. Certainly, the majority of the other 1,210 new drugs help relieve suffering and prevent premature death, but some of the hottest preparations, the ones that, as the *New York Times* put it, drug companies "can't seem to roll out fast enough," have absolutely nothing to do with matters of life and death. They are what have come to be called lifestyle drugs—remedies that may one day free the world from the scourge of toenail fungus, obesity, baldness, face wrinkles, and impotence. The market for such drugs is worth billions of dollars a year and is one of the fastest-growing product lines in the industry. The drug industry's calculus in apportioning its resources is cold-blooded, but there's no disputing that one old, fat, bald, fungus-ridden rich man who can't get it up counts for more than half a billion people who are vulnerable to malaria but too poor to buy the remedies they need.

Western interest in tropical diseases was historically linked to colonization and war, specifically the desire to protect settlers and soldiers. Yellow fever became a target of biomedical research only after it began interfering with European attempts to control parts of Africa. "So obvious was this deterrence, that it was celebrated in song and verse by people from Sudan to Senegal," Laurie Garrett recounts in her extraordinary book *The Coming Plague*. "Well into the 1980s schoolchildren in Ibo areas of Nigeria still sang the praises of mosquitoes and the diseases they gave to French and British colonialists." U.S. military researchers have discovered virtually all important malaria drugs. Chloroquine was synthesized in 1941 after quinine, until then the primary drug to treat the disease, became scarce following Japan's occupation of Indonesia. The discovery of Mefloquine, the next advance, came about during the Vietnam War, in which malaria was second only to combat wounds in sending U.S. troops to the hospital. With the end of a ground-based U.S. military strategy came the end of innovation in malaria medicine.

The Pharmaceutical Research and Manufacturers of America (PhRMA) claimed in newspaper ads early this year that its goal is to "set every last disease on the path to extinction." Jeff Trewhitt, a PhRMA spokesman, says U.S. drug companies will spend $24 billion on research this year and that a number of firms are looking for cures for tropical diseases. Some companies also provide existing drugs free to poor countries, he says. "Our members are involved. There's not an absolute void." The void is certainly at hand. Neither PhRMA nor individual firms will reveal how much money the companies spend on any given disease—that's proprietary information, they say—but on malaria alone, a recent survey of the 24 biggest drug companies found that not a single one maintains an in-house research program, and only two expressed even minimal interest in primary research on the disease. "The pipeline of available drugs is almost empty," says Dyann Wirth of the Harvard School of Public Health, who conducted the study. "It takes five to ten years to develop a new drug, so we could soon face [a strain of] malaria resistant to every drug in the world." A 1996 study presented in *Cahiers Santé*, a French scientific journal, found that of 41 important medicines used to treat major tropical diseases, none were discovered in the '90s and all but six were discovered before 1985.

Contributing to this trend is the wave of mergers that has swept the industry over the past decade. Merck alone now controls almost 10 percent of the world market. "The bigger they grow, the more they decide that their research should be focused on the most profitable diseases and conditions," one industry watcher says. "The only thing the companies think about on a daily basis is the price of their stocks; and announcing that you've discovered a drug [for a tropical disease] won't do much for your share price." That comment came from a public health advocate, but it's essentially seconded by industry. "A corporation with stockholders can't stoke up a laboratory that will focus on Third World diseases, because it will go broke," says Roy Vagelos, the former head of Merck. "That's a social problem, and industry shouldn't be expected to solve it." Drug companies, however, are hardly struggling to beat back the wolves of bankruptcy. The pharmaceutical sector racks up the largest legal profits of any industry, and it is expected to grow by an average of 16 to 18 percent over the next four years, about three times more than the average for the Fortune 500. Profits are especially high in the United States, which alone among First World nations does not control drug prices. As a result, prices here are about twice as high as they are in the European Union and nearly four times higher than in Japan.

"It's obvious that some of the industry's surplus profits could be going into research for tropical diseases," says a retired drug company executive, who wishes to remain anonymous. "Instead, it's going to stockholders." Also to promotion: In 1998, the industry unbuckled $10.8 billion on advertising. And to politics: In 1997, American drug companies spent $74.8 million to lobby the federal government, more than any other industry; last year they spent nearly $12 million on campaign contributions.

Just 45 years ago, the discovery of new drugs and pesticides led the World Health Organization (WHO) to predict that malaria would soon be eradicated. By 1959, Garrett writes in *The Coming Plague*, the Harvard School of Public Health was so certain that the disease was passé that its curriculum didn't offer a single course on the subject. Resistance to existing medicines—along with cutbacks in health care budgets, civil war, and the breakdown of the state—has led to a revival of malaria in Africa, Latin America, Southeast Asia and, most recently, Armenia and Tajikistan. The WHO describes the disease as a leading cause of global suffering and says that by "undermining the health and capacity to work of hundreds of millions of people, it is closely linked to poverty and contributes significantly to stunting social and economic development."

Total global expenditures for malaria research in 1993, including government programs, came to $84 million. That's paltry when you consider that one B-2 bomber costs $2 billion, the equivalent of what, at current levels, will be spent on all malaria research over 20 years. In that period, some 40 million Africans alone will die from the disease. In the United States, the Pentagon budgets $9 million per year for malaria programs, about one-fifth the amount it set aside this year to supply the troops with Viagra. For the drug companies, the meager screen. As Neil Sweig, an industry analyst at Southeast Research Partners, puts it wearily, "It's not worth the effort or the while of the large pharmaceutical companies to get involved in enormously expensive research to conquer the Anopheles mosquito."

The same companies that are indifferent to malaria are enormously troubled by the plight of dysfunctional First World pets. John Keeling, a spokesman for the Washington, DC–based Animal Health Institute, says the "companion animal" drug market is exploding, with U.S. sales for 1998 estimated at about $1 billion. On January 5, the FDA approved the use of Clomicalm, produced by Novartis, to treat dogs that suffer from separation anxiety (warning signs: barking or whining, "excessive greeting," and chewing on furniture). "At Last, Hope For Millions of Suffering Canines Worldwide," reads the company's press release announcing the drug's rollout. "I can't emphasize enough how dogs are suffering and that their behavior is not tolerable to owners," says

Guy Tebbitt, vice president for research and development for Novartis Animal Health. Also on January 5, the FDA gave the thumbs up to Pfizer's Anipryl, the first drug approved for doggie Alzheimer's. Pfizer sells a canine pain reliever and arthritis treatment as well, and late last year it announced an R&D program for medications that help pets with anxiety and dementia.

Another big player in the companion-animal field is Heska, a biotechnology firm based in Colorado that strives to increase the "quality of life" for cats and dogs. Its products include medicines for allergies and anxiety, as well as an antibiotic that fights periodontal disease. The company's Web site features a "spokes-dog" named Perio Pooch and, like old "shock" movies from high school driver's-ed classes, a photograph of a diseased doggie mouth to demonstrate what can happen if teeth and gums are not treated carefully. No one wants pets to be in pain, and Heska also makes drugs for animal cancer, but it is a measure of priorities that U.S. companies and their subsidiaries spend almost nothing on tropical diseases while, according to an industry source, they spend about half a billion dollars for R&D on animal health.

Although "companion animal" treatments are an extreme case—that half-billion-dollar figure covers "food animals" as well, and most veterinary drugs emerge from research on human medications—consider a few examples from the brave new world of human lifestyle drugs. Here, the pharmaceutical companies are scrambling to eradicate:

➤ Impotence. Pfizer invested vast sums to find a cure for what Bob Dole and other industry spokesmen delicately refer to as "erectile dysfunction." The company hit the jackpot with Viagra, which racked up more than $1 billion in sales in its first year on the market. Two other companies, Schering-Plough and Abbott Laboratories, are already rushing out competing drugs.

➤ Baldness. The top two drugs in the field, Merck's Propecia and Pharmacia & Upjohn's Rogaine (the latter sold over the counter), had combined sales of about $180 million in 1998. "Some lifestyle drugs are used for relatively serious problems, but even in the best cases we're talking about very different products from penicillin," says the retired drug company executive. "In cases like baldness therapy, we're not even talking about health care."

➤ Toenail fungus. With the slogan "Let your feet get naked!" as its battle cry, pharmaceutical giant Novartis recently unveiled a lavish advertising campaign for Lamisil, a drug that promises relief for sufferers of this unsightly malady. It's a hot one, the war against fungus, pitting Lamisil against Janssen Pharmaceutical's Sporanox and Pfizer's Diflucan for shares in a market estimated to be worth hundreds of millions of dollars a year.

➤ Face wrinkles. Allergan earned $90 million in 1997 from sales of its "miracle" drug Botox. Injected between the eyebrows at a cost of about $1,000 for three annual treatments, Botox makes crow's feet and wrinkles disappear.

"Every 7 1/2 seconds someone is turning 50," a wrinkle expert told the *Dallas Morning News* in an article about Botox last year. "You're looking at this vast population that doesn't want frown lines."

Meanwhile, acute lower respiratory infections go untreated, claiming about 3.5 million victims per year, overwhelmingly children in poor nations. Such infections are third on the chart of the biggest killers in the world; the number of lives they take is almost half the total reaped by the number-one killer, heart disease, which usually strikes the elderly. "The development of new antibiotics," wrote drug company researcher A.J. Slater in a 1989 paper published in the *Royal Society of Tropical Medicine and Hygiene's Transactions*, "is very costly and their provision to Third World countries alone can never be financially rewarding."

In some cases, older medications thought to be unnecessary in the First World and commercially unviable in the Third have simply been pulled from the market. This created a crisis recently when TB re-emerged with a vengeance in U.S. inner cities, since not a single company was still manufacturing Streptomycin after mid-1991. The FDA set up a task force to deal with the situation, but it was two years before it prodded Pfizer back into the field.

In 1990 Marion Merrell Dow (which was bought by German giant Hoechst in 1995) announced that it would manufacture Ornidyl, the first new medicine in 40 years that was effective in treating African sleeping sickness. Despite the benign sounding name, the disease leads to coma and death, and kills about 40,000 people a year. Unlike earlier remedies for sleeping sickness, Ornidyl had few side effects. In field trials, it saved the lives of more than 600 patients, most of whom were near death. Yet Ornidyl was pulled from production; apparently company bean-counters determined that saving lives offered no return.

Because AIDS also plagues the First World, it is the one disease ravaging Third World countries that is the object of substantial drug company research. In many African countries, AIDS has wiped out a half-century of gains in child survival rates. In Botswana—a country that is not at war and has a relatively stable society—life expectancy rates fell by twenty years over a period of just five. In South Africa, the Health Ministry recently issued a report saying that 1,500 of the country's people are infected with HIV every day and predicting that the annual death rate will climb to 500,000 within the next decade. Yet available treatments and research initiatives offer little hope for poor people. A year's supply of the highly recommended multidrug cocktail of three AIDS medicines costs about $15,000 a year. That's exorbitant in any part of the world, but prohibitive in countries like Uganda, where per capita income stands at $330. Moreover, different viral "families" of AIDS, with distinct immunological properties, appear in different parts of the world. About 85 percent of people with HIV live in the Third World, but industry research to develop an AIDS vaccine focuses only on the First World. "Without research dedicated to the specific viral strains that are prevalent in developing countries, vaccines for those countries will be very slow in coming," says Dr. Amir Attaran, an international expert who directs the Washington-based Malaria Project.

All the blame for the neglect of tropical diseases can't be laid at the feet of industry. Many Third World governments invest little in health care, and First World countries have slashed both foreign aid and domestic research programs. Meanwhile, the U.S. government aggressively champions the interests of the drug industry abroad, a stance that often undermines health care needs in developing countries.

In one case where a drug company put Third World health before profit—Merck's manufacture of Ivermectin—governmental inertia nearly scuttled the good deed. It was the early '80s, and a Pakistani researcher at Merck discovered that the drug, until then used only in veterinary medicine, performed miracles in combating river blindness disease. With one dose per year of Ivermectin, people were fully protected from river blindness, which is carried by flies and, at the time, threatened hundreds of millions of people in West Africa. Merck soon found that it would be impossible to market Ivermectin profitably, so in an unprecedented action the company decided to provide it free of charge to the WHO. (Vagelos, then chairman of Merck, said

the company was worried about taking the step, "as we feared it would discourage companies from doing research relevant to the Third World, since they might be expected to follow suit.") Even then, the program nearly failed. The WHO claimed it didn't have the money needed to cover distribution costs, and Vagelos was unable to win financial support from the Reagan Administration. A decade after Ivermectin's discovery, only 3 million of 120 million people at risk of river blindness had received the drug. During the past few years, the WHO, the World Bank, and private philanthropists have finally put up the money for the program, and it now appears that river blindness will become the second disease, after smallpox, to be eradicated. Given the industry's profitability, it's clear that the companies could do far more. It's equally clear that they won't unless they are forced to.

The success of ACT UP in pushing drug companies to respond to the AIDS crisis in America is emblematic of how crucial but also how difficult it is to get the industry to budge. In late 1997, a coalition of public health organizations approached a group of major drug companies, including Glaxo-Wellcome and Roche, and asked them to fund a project that would dedicate itself to developing new treatments for major tropical diseases. Although the companies would have been required to put up no more than $2 million a year, they walked away from the table. Since there's no organized pressure—either from the grassroots or from governments—they haven't come back. "There [were] a number of problems at the business level," Harvey Bale, director of the Geneva-based International Federation of Pharmaceutical Manufacturers Association, told *Science* magazine. "The cost of the project is high for some companies."

While the industry's political clout currently insures against any radical government action, even minor reforms could go a long way. The retired drug company executive points to public hospitals, which historically were guaranteed relatively high profit margins but were obligated to provide free care to the poor in return. There's also the example of phone companies, which charge businesses higher rates in order to subsidize universal service. "Society has tolerated high profit levels up until now, but society has the right to expect something back," he says. "Right now, it's not getting it." The U.S. government already lavishly subsidizes industry research and allows companies to market discoveries made by the National Institutes of Health and other federal agencies. "All the government needs to do is start attaching some strings," says the Malaria Project's Attaran. "If a company wants to market another billion-dollar blockbuster, fine, but in exchange it will have to push through a new malaria drug. It will cost them some money, but it's not going to bankrupt them."

Another type of "string" would be a "reasonable pricing" provision for drugs developed at federal laboratories. By way of explanation, Attaran recounted that the vaccine for hepatitis A was largely developed by researchers at the Walter Reed Army Institute. At the end of the day, the government gave the marketing rights to SmithKline Beecham and Merck. The current market for the vaccine, which sells for about $60 per person, is $300 million a year. The only thing Walter Reed's researchers got in exchange for their efforts was a plaque that hangs in their offices. "I'll say one thing for the companies," says Attaran. "They didn't skimp on the plaque; it's a nice one. But either the companies should have paid for part of the government's research, or they should have been required to sell the vaccine at a much lower price."

At the beginning of this year, Doctors Without Borders unveiled a campaign calling for increased access to drugs needed in Third World countries. The group is exploring ideas ranging from tax breaks for smaller firms engaged in research in the field, to creative use of international trade agreements, to increased donations of drugs from the multinational companies. Dr. Bernard Pécoul, an organizer of the campaign, says that different approaches are required for different diseases. In the case of those plaguing only the Southern Hemisphere—sleeping sickness, for example—market mechanisms won't work because there simply is no market to speak of. Hence, he suggests that if multinational firms are not willing to manufacture a given drug, they transfer the relevant technology to a Third World producer that is.

Drugs already exist for diseases that ravage the North as well as the South —

AIDS and TB, for example— but they are often too expensive for people in the Third World. For 25 years, the WHO has used funding from member governments to purchase and distribute vaccines to poor countries; Pécoul proposes a similar model for drugs for tropical diseases. Another solution he points to: In the event of a major health emergency, state or private producers in the South would be allowed to produce generic versions of needed medications in exchange for a small royalty paid to the multinational license holder. "If we can't change the markets, we have to humanize them," Pécoul says. "Drugs save lives. They can't be treated as normal products."

3 CENSORED

Financially Bloated American Cancer Society Fails to Prevent Cancer

AMERICAN CANCER SOCIETY: THE WORLD'S WEALTHIEST "NONPROFIT" INSTITUTION

by Samuel S. Epstein
International Journal of Health Services,
Vol.29, #3, 1999

The American Cancer Society is fixated on damage control—diagnosis and treatment—and basic molecular biology, with indifference or even hostility to cancer prevention. This myopic mindset is compounded by interlocking conflicts of interest with the cancer drug, mammography, and other industries. The "nonprofit" status of the Society is in sharp conflict with its high overhead and expenses, excessive reserves of assets, and contributions to political parties. All attempts to reform the Society over the past two decades have failed; a national economic boycott of the Society is long overdue.

The American Cancer Society (ACS) is accumulating great wealth in its role as a "charity." According to James Bennett, professor of economics at George Mason University and recognized authority on charitable organizations, in 1988 the ACS held a fund balance of over $400 million with about $69 million of holdings in land, buildings, and equipment [1]. Of that money, the ACS spent only $90 million—26 percent of its budget on medical research and programs. The rest covered "operating expenses," including about 60 percent for generous salaries, pensions, executive benefits, and overhead. By 1989, the cash reserves of the ACS were worth more than $700 million [2]. In 1991, Americans, believing they were contributing to fighting cancer, gave nearly $350 million to the ACS, 6 percent more than the previous year. Most of this money comes from public donations averaging $3,500, and high-profile fundraising campaigns such as the springtime daffodil sale and the May relay races. However, over the last two decades, an increasing proportion of the ACS budget comes from large corporations, including the pharmaceutical, cancer drug, telecommunications, and entertainment industries.

In 1992, the American Cancer Society Foundation was created to allow the ACS to actively solicit contributions of more than $100,000. However, a close look at the heavy hitters on the Foundation's board will give an idea of which interests are at play and where the Foundation expects its big contributions to come from. The Foundation's board of trustees included corporate executives from the pharmaceutical, investment, banking, and media industries. Among them:

➤ David R. Bethune, president of Lederle Laboratories, a multinational pharmaceutical company and a division of American Cyanamid Company. Bethune is also vice president of American Cyanamid, which makes chemical fertilizers and herbicides while transforming itself into a full-fledged pharmaceutical company. In 1988, American Cyanamid introduced Novatrone, an anticancer drug. And in 1992, it announced that it would buy a majority of shares of Immunex, a cancer drug maker.

➤ Multimillionaire Irwin Beck, whose father, William Henry Beck, founded the nation's largest family-owned retail chain, Beck Stores, which analysts estimate brought in revenues of $1.7 billion in 1993.

➤ Gordon Binder, CEO of Amgen, the world's foremost biotechnology company, with over $1 billion in product sales in 1992. Amgen's success rests almost exclusively on one product, Neupogen, which is administered to chemotherapy patients to stimulate their production of white blood cells. As the cancer epidemic grows, sales for Neupogen continue to skyrocket.

➤ Diane Disney Miller, daughter of the conservative multimillionaire Walt Disney, who died of lung cancer in 1966, and wife of Ron Miller, former president of the Walt Disney Company from 1980 to 1984.

➤ George Dessert, famous in media circles for his former role as censor on the subject of "family values" during the 1970s and 1980s as CEO of CBS, and now chairman of the ACS board.

➤ Alan Gevertzen, chairman of the board of Boeing, the world's number one commercial aircraft maker with net sales of $30 billion in 1992.

➤ Sumner M. Redstone, chairman of the board, Viacom Inc. and Viacom International Inc., a broadcasting, telecommunications, entertainment, and cable television corporation.

➤ The results of this board's efforts have been very successful. A million here, a million there much of it coming from the very industries instrumental in shaping ACS policy, or profiting from it.

In 1992, The Chronicle of Philanthropy reported that the ACS was "more interested in accumulating wealth than in saving lives." Fund-raising appeals routinely stated that the ACS needed more funds to support its cancer programs, all the while holding more than $750 million in cash and real estate assets.[3]

A 1992 article in the Wall Street Jour-

nal, by Thomas DiLorenzo, professor of economics at Loyola College and veteran investigator of non-profit organizations, revealed that the Texas affiliate of the ACS owned more than $11 million worth of assets in land and real estate, as well as more than 56 vehicles, including 11 Ford Crown Victorias for senior executives and 45 other cars assigned to staff members. Arizona's ACS chapter spent less than 10 percent of its funds on direct community cancer services. In California, the figure was 11 percent, and under 9 percent in Missouri.[4]

Thus for every $1 spent on direct service, approximately $6.40 is spent on compensation and overhead. In all 10 states, salaries and fringe benefits are by far the largest single budget items, a surprising fact in light of the characterization of the appeals, which stress an urgent and critical need for donations to provide cancer services. Nationally, only 16 percent or less of all money raised is spent on direct services to cancer victims, like driving cancer patients from the hospital after chemotherapy and providing pain medication.

Most of the funds raised by the ACS go to pay overhead, salaries, fringe benefits, and travel expenses of its national executives in Atlanta. They also go to pay chief executive officers, who earn six-figure salaries in several states, and the hundreds of other employees who work out of some 3,000 regional offices nationwide. The typical ACS affiliate, which helps raise the money for the national office, spends more than 52 percent of its budget on salaries, pensions, fringe benefits, and overhead for its own employees. Salaries and overhead for most ACS affiliates also exceeded 50 percent, although most direct community services are handled by unpaid volunteers. DiLorenzo summed up his findings by emphasizing the hoarding of funds by the ACS.[5]

If current needs are not being met because of insufficient funds, as fundraising appeals suggest, why is so much cash being hoarded? Most contributors believe their donations are being used to fight cancer, not to accumulate financial reserves. More progress in the war against cancer would be made if they would divest some of their real estate holdings and use the proceeds—as well as a portion of their cash reserves—to provide more cancer services. Aside from high salaries and overhead, most of what is left of the ACS budget goes to basic research and research into profitable patented cancer drugs.

The current budget of the ACS is $380 million and its cash reserves approach $1 billion. Yet its aggressive fund-raising campaign continues to plead poverty and lament the lack of available money for cancer research, while ignoring efforts to prevent cancer by phasing out avoidable exposures to environmental and occupational carcinogens. Meanwhile, the ACS is silent about its intricate relationships with the wealthy cancer drug, chemical, and other industries.

A March 30, 1998, Associated Press release shed unexpected light on questionable ACS expenditures on lobbying.[6] National vice president for federal and state governmental relations Linda Hay Crawford admitted that the ACS was spending "less than $1 million a year on direct lobbying." She also admitted that over the last year, the society used 10 of its own employees to lobby. "For legal and other help, it hired the lobbying firm of Hogan & Hartson, whose roster includes former House Minority Leader Robert H. Michel (R–IL)." The ACS lobbying also included $30,000 donations to Democratic and Republican governors' associations. "We wanted to look like players and be players," explained Crawford. This practice, however, has been sharply challenged. The Associated Press release quotes the national Charities Information Bureau as stating that it "does not know of any other charity that makes contributions to political parties."

Tax experts have warned that these contributions may be illegal, as charities are not allowed to make political donations. Marcus Owens, director of the IRS Exempt Organization Division, also warned that "The bottom line is campaign contributions will jeopardize a charity's exempt status."

TRACK RECORD ON PREVENTION Marching in lockstep with the National Cancer Institute (NCI) in its "war" on cancer is its "ministry of information," the ACS.[7] With powerful media control and public relations resources, the ACS is the tail that wags the dog of the policies and priorities of the NCI.[8,9] In addition, the approach of the ACS to cancer prevention reflects a virtually exclusive "blame-the-victim" philosophy. It emphasizes faulty lifestyles rather than unknowing and avoidable exposure to workplace or environmental carcinogens. Giant corporations, which profit handsomely while they pollute the air, water, and food with a wide range of carcinogens, are greatly comforted by the silence of the ACS. This silence reflects a complex of mindsets fixated on diagnosis, treatment, and basic genetic research together with ignorance, indifference, and even hostility to prevention, coupled with conflicts of interest.

Indeed, despite promises to the public to do everything to "wipe out cancer in your lifetime," the ACS fails to make its voice heard in Congress and the regulatory arena. Instead, the ACS repeatedly rejects or ignores opportunities and requests from Congressional committees, regulatory agencies, unions, and environmental organizations to provide scientific testimony critical to efforts to legislate and regulate a wide range of occupational and environmental carcinogens. This history of ACS unresponsiveness is a long and damning one, as shown by the following examples:[10]

1. In 1971, when studies unequivocally proved that diethylstilbestrol (DES) caused vaginal cancers in teenaged daughters of women administered the drug during pregnancy, the ACS refused an invitation to testify at Congressional hearings to require the FDA (U.S. Food and Drug Administration) to ban its use as an animal feed additive. It gave no reason for its refusal.

2. In 1977 and 1978, the ACS opposed regulations proposed for hair

coloring products that contained dyes known to cause breast and liver cancer in rodents. In so doing, the ACS ignored virtually every tenet of responsible public health as these chemicals were clear-cut liver and breast carcinogens.

3. In 1977, the ACS called for a Congressional moratorium on the FDA's proposed ban on saccharin and even advocated its use by nursing mothers and babies in "moderation" despite clear-cut evidence of its carcinogenicity in rodents. This reflects the consistent rejection by the ACS of the importance of animal evidence as predictive of human cancer risk.

4. In 1978, Tony Mazzocchi, then senior representative of the Oil, Chemical, and Atomic Workers International Union, stated at a Washington, DC, roundtable between public interest groups and high-ranking ACS officials: "Occupational safety standards have received no support from the ACS."

5. In 1978, Congressman Paul Rogers censured the ACS for doing "too little, too late" in failing to support the Clean Air Act.

6. In 1982, the ACS adopted a highly restrictive cancer policy that insisted on unequivocal human evidence of carcinogenicity before taking any position on public health hazards. Accordingly, the ACS still trivializes or rejects evidence of carcinogenicity in experimental animals, and has actively campaigned against laws (the 1958 Delaney Law, for instance) that ban deliberate addition to food of any amount of any additive shown to cause cancer in either ani-

mals or humans. The ACS still persists in an anti-Delaney policy, in spite of the overwhelming support for the Delaney Law by the independent scientific community.

7. In 1983, the ACS refused to join a coalition of the March of Dimes, American Heart Association, and the American Lung Association to support the Clean Air Act. 8. In 1992, the ACS issued a joint statement with the Chlorine Institute in support of the continued global use of organochlorine pesticides—despite clear evidence that some were known to cause breast cancer. In this statement, Society vice president Clark Heath, M.D., dismissed evidence of this risk as "preliminary and mostly based on weak and indirect association." Heath then went on to explain away the blame for increasing breast cancer rates as due to better detection: "Speculation that such exposures account for observed geographic differences in breast cancer incidence or for recent rises in breast cancer occurrence should be received with caution; more likely, much of the recent rise in incidence in the United States... reflects increased utilization of mammography over the past decade."

9. In 1992, in conjunction with the NCI, the ACS aggressively launched a "chemoprevention" program aimed at recruiting 16,000 healthy women at supposedly "high risk" of breast cancer into a five-year clinical trial with a highly profitable drug called tamoxifen. This drug is manufactured by one of the world's most powerful cancer drug industries, Zeneca, an offshoot of the Imperial

Chemical Industries. The women were told that the drug was essentially harmless, and that it could reduce their risk of breast cancer. What the women were not told was that tamoxifen had already been shown to be a highly potent liver carcinogen in rodent tests, and also that it was well-known to induce human uterine cancer.[11]

10. In 1993, just before PBS *Frontline* aired the special entitled "In Our Children's Food," the ACS came out in support of the pesticide industry. In a damage- control memorandum sent to some 48 regional divisions, the ACS trivialized pesticides as a cause of childhood cancer, and reassured the public that carcinogenic pesticide residues in food are safe, even for babies. When the media and concerned citizens called local ACS chapters, they received reassurances from an ACS memorandum by its vice president for Public Relations:[12] The primary health hazards of pesticides are from direct contact with the chemicals at potentially high doses, for example, farm workers who apply the chemicals and work in the fields after the pesticides have been applied, and people living near aerially sprayed fields.... The American Cancer Society believes that the benefits of a balanced diet rich in fruits and vegetables far outweigh the largely theoretical risks posed by occasional, very low pesticide residue levels in foods.

11. In September 1996, the ACS together with a diverse group of patient and physician organizations filed a "citizen's petition" to pressure the FDA to ease restrictions on access to silicone gel breast implants. What the ACS did not disclose was that the gel in these implants had clearly been shown to induce cancer in several industry rodent studies, and that these implants were also contaminated with other potent carcinogens such as ethylene oxide and crystalline silica.

This abysmal track record on prevention has been the subject of periodic protests by both independent scientists and public interest groups. A well-publicized example was a New York City, January 23, 1994, press conference, sponsored by the author and the Center for Science in the Public Interest. The press release stated: "A group of 24 scientists charged that the ACS was doing little to protect the public from cancer-causing chemicals in the environment and workplace. The scientists urged ACS to revamp its policies and to emphasize prevention in its lobbying and educational campaigns." The scientists—who included Matthew Meselson and Nobel laureate George Wald, both of Harvard University; former OSHA director Eula Bingham; Samuel Epstein, author of *The Politics of Cancer*; and Anthony Robbins, past president of the American Public Health Association—criticized the ACS for insisting on unequivocal human proof that a substance is carcinogenic before it will recommend its regulation.

This public criticism by a broad representation of highly credible scientists reflects the growing conviction that a substantial proportion of cancer deaths are caused by exposure to chemical carcinogens in the air, water, food supply, and workplace, and thus can be prevented by legislative and regulatory action. Calling the ACS guidelines an "unrealistically high-action threshold," a letter to ACS executive vice president Lane Adams states that "we would like to express our hope that ACS will take strong public positions and become a more active force to protect the public and the work force from exposure to carcinogens."

ACS's policy is retrogressive and contrary to authoritative and scientific tenets established by international and national scientific committees, and is in conflict with long-established policies of federal regulatory agencies. Speakers at the conference warned that unless the ACS became more supportive of cancer prevention, it would face the risk of an economic boycott. Reacting promptly, the ACS issued a statement claiming that cancer prevention would become a major priority. However, ACS policies have remained unchanged. More recently, the author has issued this warning again, a warning echoed by activist women's breast cancer groups.

In *Cancer Facts & Figures—1998*, the latest annual ACS publication designed to provide the public and medical profession with "Basic Facts" on cancer—other than information on incidence, mortality, signs and symptoms, and treatment—there is little or no mention of prevention.[13] Examples include: no mention of dusting the genital area with talc as a known cause of ovarian cancer; no mention of parental exposure to occupational carcinogens as a major cause of childhood cancer; and no mention of prolonged use of oral contraceptives and hormone replacement therapy as major causes of breast cancer. For breast cancer, ACS states: "Since women may not be able to alter their personal risk factors, the best opportunity for reducing morality is through early detection." In other words, breast cancer is not preventable in spite of clear evidence that its incidence has escalated over recent decades, and in spite of an overwhelming literature on avoidable causes of this cancer.[14] In the section on "Nutrition and Diet," no mention at all is made of the heavy contamination of animal and dairy fats and produce with a wide range of carcinogenic pesticide residues, and on the need to switch to safer organic foods.

CONFLICTS OF INTEREST Of the members of the ACS board, about half are clinicians, oncologists, surgeons, radiologists, and basic molecular scientists—and most are closely tied in with the NCI. Many board members and their institutional colleagues apply for and obtain funding from both the ACS and the NCI. Substantial NCI funds go to ACS directors who sit on key NCI committees. Although the ACS asks board members to leave the room when the rest of the board discusses their funding proposals, this is just a token formality. In this private club, easy access to funding is one of the "perks," and the board routinely rubber-stamps approvals. A significant amount of ACS research funding goes to this extended membership. Such conflicts of interest are evident in many ACS priorities, including their policy on mammography and their National Breast Cancer Awareness campaign.[15]

MAMMOGRAPHY The ACS has close connections to the mammography industry. Five radiologists have served as ACS presidents, and in its every move, the ACS reflects the interests of the major manufacturers of mammogram machines and films, including Siemens, DuPont, General Electric, Eastman Kodak, and Piker. In fact, if every woman were to follow ACS and NCI mammography guidelines, the annual revenue to health care facilities would be a staggering $5 billion, including at least $2.5 billion for premenopausal women. Promotions of the ACS continue to lure women of all ages into mammography centers, leading them to believe that mammography is their best hope against breast cancer. A leading Massachusetts newspaper featured a photograph of two women in their twenties in an ACS advertisement that promised early detection results in a cure "nearly 100 percent of the time." An ACS communications director, questioned by journalist Kate Dempsey, responded in an article published by the *Massachusetts Women's Community's Journal on Cancer*: "The ad isn't based on a study. When you make an advertisement, you just say what you can to get women in the door. You exaggerate a point.... Mammography today is a lucrative [and] highly competitive business."

In addition, the mammography industry conducts research for the ACS and its grantees, serves on advisory boards, and donates considerable funds. DuPont also is a substantial backer of the ACS Breast Health Awareness Program; sponsors television shows and other media productions touting mammography; produces advertising, promotional, and information literature for hospitals, clinics, medical organizations, and doctors; produces educational films; and, of course, lobbies Congress for legislation promoting availability of mammography services. In virtually all of its important actions, the ACS has been strongly linked with the mammography industry, ignoring the development of viable alternatives to mammography.

The ACS exposes premenopausal women to radiation hazards from mammography with little or no evidence of benefits. The ACS also fails to tell them that their breasts will change so much over time that the "baseline" images have little or no future relevance. This is truly an American Cancer Society crusade. But against whom, or rather, for whom?

NATIONAL BREAST CANCER AWARENESS MONTH The highly publicized National Breast Cancer Awareness Month campaign further illustrates these institutionalized conflicts of interest. Every October, ACS and NCI representatives help sponsor promotional events, hold interviews, and stress the need for mammography. The flagship of this month-long series of events is National Mammography Day, on October 17 in 1997.

Conspicuously absent from the public relations campaign of the National Breast Cancer Awareness Month is any information on environmental and other avoidable causes of breast cancer. This is no accident. Zeneca Pharmaceuticals—a spin-off of Imperial Chemical Industries, one of the world's largest manufacturers of chlorinated and other industrial chemicals, including those incriminated as causes of breast cancer—has been the sole multimillion-dollar funder of National Breast Cancer Awareness Month since its inception in 1984. Zeneca is also the sole manufacturer of tamoxifen, the world's top-selling anticancer and breast cancer "prevention" drug, with $400 million in annual sales. Furthermore, Zeneca recently assumed direct management of 11 cancer centers in U.S. hospitals. Zeneca owns a 50 percent stake in these centers known collectively as Salick Health Care.

The link between the ACS and NCI and Zeneca is especially strong when it comes to tamoxifen. The ACS and NCI continue aggressively to promote the tamoxifen trial, which is the cornerstone of its minimal prevention program. On March 7, 1997, the NCI Press Office released a four-page document entitled "For Response to Inquiries on Breast Cancer." The brief section on prevention reads:

> Researchers are looking for a way to prevent breast cancer in women at high risk.... A large study [is underway] to see if the drug tamoxifen will reduce cancer risk

in women age 60 or older and in women 35 to 59 who have a pattern of risk factors for breast cancer. This study is also a model for future studies of cancer prevention. Studies of diet and nutrition could also lead to preventive strategies. Since Zeneca influences every leaflet, poster, publication, and commercial produced by National Breast Cancer Awareness Month, it is no wonder these publications make no mention of carcinogenic industrial chemicals and their relation to breast cancer. Imperial Chemical Industries, Zeneca's parent company, profits by manufacturing breast cancer–causing chemicals. Zeneca profits from treatment of breast cancer, and hopes to profit still more from the prospects of large-scale national use of tamoxifen for breast cancer prevention. National Breast Cancer Awareness Month is a masterful public relations coup for Zeneca, providing the company with valuable, if ill-placed, good will from millions of American women.

THE PESTICIDE INDUSTRY Just how inbred the relations between the ACS and the chemical industry are became clear in the spring of 1993 to Marty Koughan, a public television producer. Koughan was about to broadcast a documentary on the dangers of pesticides to children for the Public Broadcasting Service's hour-long show, *Frontline*. Koughan's investigation relied heavily on an embargoed, ground-breaking report issued by the National Academy of Sciences in June of 1993 entitled "Pesticides in the Diet of Children." This report declared the nation's food supply "inadequately protected" from cancer-causing pesticides and a significant threat to the health of children.

An earlier report, issued by the Natural Resources Defense Council in 1989, "Intolerable Risk: Pesticides in our Children's Food," had also given pesticide manufacturers failing marks. The report was released in high profile testimony to Congress by movie actress Meryl Streep. A mother of young children, Streep explained to a packed House chamber the report's findings, namely, that children were most at risk from cancer-causing pesticides on our food because they consume a disproportionate amount of fruits, fruit juices, and vegetables relative to their size, and because their bodies are still forming. Shortly before Koughan's program was due to air, a draft of the script was mysteriously leaked to Porter-Novelli, a powerful public relations firm for produce growers and the agrichemical industry. In true Washington fashion, Porter-Novelli plays both sides of the fence, representing both government agencies and the industries they regulate. Its client list in 1993 included Ciba-Geigy, DuPont, Monsanto, Burroughs Wellcome, American Petroleum Institute, Bristol-Meyers-Squibb, Hoffman-LaRoche, Hoechst Celanese, Hoechst Roussel Pharmaceutical, Janssen Pharmaceutical, Johnson & Johnson, the Center for Produce Quality, as well as the U.S. Department of Agriculture, the NCI, plus other National Institutes of Health.

Porter-Novelli first crafted a rebuttal to help the manufacturers quell public fears about pesticide-contaminated food. Next, Porter-Novelli called up another client, the American Cancer Society, for whom Porter-Novelli had done pro bono work for years. The rebuttal that Porter-Novelli had just sent off to its industry clients was faxed to ACS Atlanta headquarters. It was then circulated by e-mail on March 22, 1993, internally—virtually verbatim from the memo Porter-Novelli had crafted for a backgrounder for 3,000 regional ACS offices to have in hand to help field calls from the public after the show aired.

"The program makes unfounded suggestions... that pesticide residue in food may be at hazardous levels," the ACS memo read. "Its use of `cancer cluster' leukemia case reports and non-specific community illnesses as alleged evidence of pesticide effects in people is unfortunate. We know of no community cancer clusters which have been shown to be anything other than chance grouping of cases and none in which pesticide use was confirmed as the cause."

This bold, unabashed defense of the pesticide industry, crafted by Porter-Novelli, was then rehashed a third time, this time by the right-wing group, Accuracy in Media (AIM). AIM's newsletter gleefully published quotes from the ACS memo in an article with the banner headline: "Junk Science on PBS." The article opened with "Can we afford the Public

Broadcasting Service?" and went on to disparage Koughan's documentary on pesticides and children: 'In Our Children's Food'... exemplified what the media have done to produce these 'popular panics' and the enormously costly waste [at PBS] cited by the *New York Times*."

When Koughan saw the AIM article he was initially outraged that the ACS was being used to defend the pesticide industry. "At first, I assumed complete ignorance on the part of the ACS," said Koughan. But after repeatedly trying, without success, to get the national office to rebut the AIM article, Koughan began to see what was really going on. "When I realized Porter-Novelli represented five agrichemical companies, and that the ACS had been a client for years, it became obvious that the ACS had not been fooled at all," said Koughan. "They were willing partners in the deception, and were in fact doing a favor for a friend—by flakking for the agrichemical industry."

Charles Benbrook, former director of the National Academy of Sciences Board of Agriculture, worked on the pesticide report by the Academy of Sciences that the PBS special would preview. He charged that the role of the ACS as a source of information for the media representing the pesticide and produce industry was "unconscionable."[16] Investigative reporter Sheila Kaplan, in a 1993 *Legal Times* article, went further: "What they did was clearly and unequivocally over the line, and constitutes a major conflict of interest." [17]

CANCER DRUG INDUSTRY The intimate association between the ACS and the cancer drug industry, with current annual sales of about $12 billion, is further illustrated by the unbridled aggression which the Society has directed at potential competitors of the industry.[18]

Just as Senator Joseph McCarthy had his "black list" of suspected communists and Richard Nixon his environmental activist "enemies list," so too the ACS maintains a "Committee on Unproven Methods of Cancer Management" which periodically "reviews" unorthodox or alternative therapies. This Committee is comprised of "volunteer health care professionals," carefully selected proponents of orthodox, expensive, and usually toxic drugs patented by major pharmaceutical companies, and opponents of alternative or "unproven" therapies which are generally cheap, non-patentable, and minimally toxic.[19]

Periodically, the Committee updates its statements on "unproven methods," which are then widely disseminated to clinicians, cheerleader science writers, and the public. Once a clinician or oncologist becomes associated with "unproven methods," he or she is blackballed by the cancer establishment. Funding for the accused "quack" becomes inaccessible, followed by systematic harassment.

The highly biased ACS witchhunts against alternative practitioners is in striking contrast to its extravagant and uncritical endorsement of conventional toxic chemotherapy. This in spite of the absence of any objective evidence of improved survival rates or reduced mortality following chemotherapy for all but some relatively rare cancers.

In response to pressure from People Against Cancer, a grassroots group of cancer patients disillusioned with conventional cancer therapy, in 1986 some 40 members of Congress requested the Office of Technology Assessment (OTA), a Congressional think tank, to evaluate available information on alternative innovative therapies. While initially resistant, OTA eventually published a September 1990 report that identified some 200 promising studies on alternative therapies. OTA concluded that the NCI had "a mandated responsibility to pursue this information and facilitate examination of widely used `unconventional cancer treatments' for therapeutic potential"[20]

Yet the ACS and NCI remain resistant, if not frankly hostile, to OTA's recommendations. In the January 1991 issue of its *Cancer Journal for Clinicians* ACS referred to the Hoxsey therapy, a nontoxic combination of herb extracts developed in the 1940s by populist Harry Hoxsey, as a "worthless tonic for cancer." However, a detailed critique of Hoxsey's treatment by Dr. Patricia Spain Ward, a leading contributor to the OTA report, concluded just the opposite: "More recent literature leaves no doubt that Hoxsey's formula does indeed contain many plant substances of marked therapeutic activity."[21]

Nor is this the first time that the Society's claims of quackery have been called into question or discredited. A growing number of other innovative ther-

apies originally attacked by the ACS have recently found less disfavor and even acceptance. These include hyperthermia, tumor necrosis factor (originally called Coley's toxin), hydrazine sulfate, and Burzynski's antineoplastons. Well over 100 promising alternative nonpatented and nontoxic therapies have already been identified.[22] Clearly, such treatments merit clinical testing and evaluation by the NCI using similar statistical techniques and criteria as established for conventional chemotherapy. However, while the FDA has approved approximately 40 patented drugs for cancer treatment, it has still not approved a single nonpatented alternative drug.

Subsequent events have further isolated the ACS in its fixation on orthodox treatments. Bypassing the ACS and NCI, the National Institutes of Health in June 1992 opened a new Office of Alternative Medicine for the investigation of unconventional treatment of cancer and other diseases. Leading proponents of conventional therapy were invited to participate. The ACS refused and still refuses. The NCI grudgingly and nominally participates while actively attacking alternative therapy with its widely circulated Cancer Information Services. Meanwhile, the NCI's police partner, the FDA, uses its enforcement authority against distributors and practitioners of innovative and nontoxic therapies.

In an interesting recent development, the Center for Mind-Body Medicine in Washington, DC, held a two-day conference on "Comprehensive Cancer Care: Integrating Complementary and

Alternative Medicine." According to Dr. James Gordon, president of the Center and chair of the Program Advisory Council of the NIH Office of Alternative Medicine, the object of the conference was to bring together practitioners of mainstream and alternative medicine, together with cancer patients and high-ranking officials of the ACS and NCI. Dr. Gordon warned alternative practitioners that "they're going to need to get more rigorous with their work—to be accepted by the mainstream community."[23] However, no such warning was directed at the highly questionable claims by the NCI and ACS for the efficacy of conventional cancer chemotherapy. As significantly, criticism of the establishment's minimalistic priority for cancer prevention was effectively discouraged.

THE ROLE OF ACS IN THE WAR AGAINST CANCER The launching of the 1971 War Against Cancer provided the ACS with a well-exploited opportunity to pursue it own myopic and self-interested agenda. Its strategies remain based on two myths—that there has been dramatic progress in the treatment and cure of cancer, and that any increase in the incidence and mortality of cancer is due to aging of the population and smoking, while denying any significant role for involuntary exposures to industrial carcinogens in air, water, consumer products, and the workplace.

As the world's largest nonreligious "charity," with powerful allies in the private and public sectors, ACS policies and priorities remain unchanged. Despite periodic protests, threats of boycotts, and questions on its finances, the Society leadership responds with powerful public relations campaigns reflecting denial and manipulated information and pillorying its opponents with scientific McCarthyism.

The verdict is unassailable. The ACS bears a major responsibility for losing the winnable war against cancer. Reforming the ACS is, in principle, relatively easy and directly achievable. Boycott the ACS. Instead, give your charitable contributions to public interest and environmental groups involved in cancer prevention. Such a boycott is well overdue and will send the only message this "charity" can no longer ignore. The Cancer Prevention Coalition (chaired by the author) in April 1999 formally announced a nationwide campaign for an economic boycott of the ACS (www.preventcancer.com).

Note—This article is modified from Chapters 16 and 18 of *The Politics of Cancer Revisited*, East Ridge Press, Fremont Center, New York, NY 12736.

REFERENCES

1. J. T. Bennett, "Health research charities: Doing Little Research but Emphasizing Politics," *Union Leader* (Manchester, NH), September 20, 1990.

2. J. T. Bennett, and T. J. DiLorenzo, Unhealthy Charities: Hazardous to Your *Health and Wealth* (New York: Basic Books, 1994).

3. H. Hall and G. Williams, "Professor vs. Cancer Society." *The Chronicle of Philanthropy*, January 28, 1992: 26.

4. T. J. DiLorenzo, "One Charity's Uneconomic War on Cancer," *Wall Street Journal*, March 15, 1992: A10.

5. T. J. DiLorenzo, A10.

6. J. D. Salant, "Cancer Society Gives to Governors," Associated Press release, March 30, 1998.

7. S. S. Epstein, D. Steinman, and S. LeVert, *The Breast Cancer Prevention Program* (New York: Macmillan, 1997).

8. S. S. Epstein, "Losing the War against Cancer: Who's to Blame and What to Do about it," *Int. Jnl. Health Serv.* 20: 53–71, 1990.

9. S. S. Epstein, "Evaluation of the National Cancer Program and Proposed Reforms," *Int. Jnl. Health Serv.* 23(1): 15–44, 1993.

10. Epstein, Steinman, and LeVert, 304-314.

11. Epstein, Steinman, and LeVert, 145-151.

12. American Cancer Society, "Upcoming television special on pesticides in food," Memorandum from S. Dickinson, Vice-President, Public Relations and Health, to C. W. Heath, Jr., M.D., Vice-President. Epidemiology and Statistics, March 22, 1993.

13. American Cancer Society, *Cancer Facts & Figures—1998* (Atlanta, 1998): 1-32.

14. Epstein, Steinman, and LeVert, Chpater 6.

15. Epstein, Steinman, and LeVert, 311-314.

16. S. Kaplan, "PR Giant makes Hay from Client Cross-pollination: Porter/Novelli Plays All Sides," *PR Watch*, First quarter, 1994: 4.

17. S. Kaplan, "Porter-Novelli Plays All Sides," *Legal Times* 16(27), November 23, 1993: 1.

18. R. W. Moss, *Questioning Chemotherapy* (Brooklyn, NY: Equinox Press, 1995).

19. R. W. Moss, *Questioning Chemotherapy* (Brooklyn, NY: Equinox Press, 1995).

20. U.S. Congress Office of Technology Assessment, *Unconventional Cancer Treatments*, (Washington, DC: U.S. Government Printing Office, 1990.)

21. R. W. Moss, *Questioning Chemotherapy* (Brooklyn, NY: Equinox Press, 1995).

22. R. W. Moss, *Cancer Therapy: The Independent Consumer's Guide to Non-toxic Treatment and Prevention* (Brooklyn, NY: Equinox Press, 1992).

23. Castellucci, L. Practitioners seek common ground in unconventional forum. J. Natl. Cancer Inst. 90: 1036–1037, 1998.

DIRECT REPRINT REQUESTS TO: Dr. Samuel S. Epstein School of Public Health, University of Illinois at Chicago, (M/C 922) 2121 W. Taylor Street, Chicago, IL 60612-7260

4 CENSORED
American Sweatshops Sew U.S. Military Uniforms

"AN AMERICAN SWEATSHOP"
by Mark Boal
The MoJo Wire May/June 1999

The women at the Lion Apparel factory in Beattyville, Kentucky, are part of a largely female workforce of 15,000 nationwide that sews U.S. military uniforms. The Defense Department keeps costs as low as possible, and these workers ultimately pay the price. by Mark Boal May/June 1999 (This is a corrected version of this article. It was last updated August 19, 1999. Lion Apparel has responded to this story. You can read a summary of the company's reaction here and a special Editor's note here.)

The two-lane road into Beattyville, Kentucky, winds through breathtaking Appalachian foothills, past rusty machinery and heaps of broken coal left over from the last strip-mining boom. Little handmade signs offer acreage for sale. But there is no demand for land like this—too rocky for commercial farming and too remote for development. Beattyville (population 1,800) is less a town than a three-light strip bordered by aluminum shacks and a pine forest.

These days, the chief economic activity in town can be found in the parking lot of the local garage, where teenagers offer a visitor deals on moonshine by the gallon and homegrown marijuana at $2,500 a pound, about half what it would cost in an urban area. Legitimate work opportunities, after all, remain limited. There's a private prison and a data processing center, but both require a high school education, and since half the population never graduates, most seek jobs elsewhere. Inevitably, many of the women turn to Lion Apparel, which operates a sewing factory on the edge of town.

Lion, meanwhile, takes full advantage of its labor pool. Carol Shelton, 48, friendly but blunt, says that every day for the nine years she worked at Lion she would come home exhausted, her hands swollen from pushing stiff fabric past a moving needle. She had to work fast to meet quotas kept by a timekeeper, and if she slowed down or had to redo a seam, her hourly income dropped to the base rate, which usually hovered around minimum wage. Besides the low pay, the job gave her back pain from hunching over old sewing machines held together with spare parts and electrical tape. Fumes from formaldehyde, a suspected carcinogen used to keep fabric stiff, would cling to her clothes, make her short of breath, give her headaches, and cause rashes on her arms. During the sweltering summers, the plant had no air conditioning. One winter, Shelton says, the water in the toilets froze.

In May 1998, Shelton was fired after refusing to perform a job she feared would hurt her back, and she says she has spoken to a lawyer about filing a workers' compensation claim. Meanwhile, five former and two current employees corroborate her description of work conditions at Lion. According to their accounts, the factory fits the definition of a sweatshop as specified by the laws of more than a dozen U.S. cities and counties that ban using public funds to buy from such places. Those criteria include wages so low that workers can't meet basic needs, dangerous working conditions, and intimidation when workers try to unionize. Lion, in a written response to questions from *Mother Jones*, categorically denies these conditions exist.

The responsibility for the environment these women endure doesn't rest solely with Lion, but also with its main client: the U.S. government. The 650 employees at Lion's facilities are among an estimated 15,000 apparel workers nationwide who produce uniforms for the military, which spends more than $800 million annually on clothing for its 1.4 million personnel. (Lion, based in Dayton, Ohio, is among the top three private suppliers, with a $51 million contract.)

These factories are located in some of the most rural and impoverished communities in America: isolated hamlets in the Appalachian mountains of Kentucky and Tennessee, and small towns in Louisiana. In many of these communities, the stories are similar to Shelton's. Joyce Bennett, a 58-year-old mother of five, says that in the four years she stitched collars on Navy uniforms at Doyle Shirt Manufacturing in Spencer, Tennessee, she never made more than minimum wage and had to supplement her income with food stamps.

In Beattyville, the drive to Shelton's faded-blue clapboard house (the last home on a gravel road with no sign) follows the route Lyndon Johnson took 35 years ago when he toured the area to announce the War on Poverty, his plan for helping the nation's poor join the Great Society. While the resulting social programs managed to reduce the most extreme poverty in Appalachia, the government's role has since changed dramatically. Even though the women of Beattyville work for a large Department of Defense contractor, their dismal workplace conditions remain virtually unregulated by the government. And instead of trying to assist them, the U.S. government trades on their labor for the highest possible return.

When Kathie Lee Gifford's face was splashed across the tabloids in 1996 after her line of Wal-Mart clothing was exposed as the work of underpaid laborers in New York City's Chinatown, the Department of Labor and the White House teamed up to denounce such practices. With much fanfare, the Clinton Administration launched the "No Sweat" campaign, which pressured retailers and manufacturers to submit to periodic independent audits of their workplace conditions.

This campaign urged manufacturers to sign the Workplace Code of Conduct, a promise to self-regulate that has since been adopted by a handful of retailers and many of the nation's largest manufacturers, including Liz Claiborne,

Nicole Miller, Nike, Patagonia, and L.L. Bean. Absent, however, is the Department of Defense, which has a $1 billion garment business that would make it the country's 14th-largest retail apparel outlet, right behind Talbots and just ahead of Charming Shoppes, whose stores include the Fashion Bug chain.

Without the Defense Department's voluntary adherence to the code, the job of stopping public-sector sweatshops falls to the Department of Labor. Federal contractors that violate wage laws or safety and health codes can lose their lucrative taxpayer-financed contracts. But Suzanne Seiden, a deputy administrator at the department, says that to her knowledge the agency has never applied that rule to government apparel manufacturers. "I just assume that they are adhering to safety and health [requirements]," she says. According to records obtained by *Mother Jones* through a Freedom of Information Act request, the Occupational Safety and Health Administration (OSHA) has cited Lion 32 times for safety and health violations in the past 12 years. Furthermore, a 1996 General Accounting Office report estimated that 22 percent of all federal contractors had been cited by OSHA for violating safety standards.

In 1997, Arleenna Lawson, a worker at Lion's plant in West Liberty, about a half-hour drive from Beattyville, began waking up with small bumps on her face. At first she thought it was nothing, but in two weeks the bumps grew into large lumps. When she showed a manager at work, she was told not to worry about it.

An allergist later determined she was suffering a reaction to the formaldehyde in the permanent-press fabrics she sewed at work, and recommended that Lawson be given an assignment away from the offending chemical. "But they just moved me to another line for a few days, and then I was back doing collars," she remembers. "It got so bad I had to quit."

Before she did, Lawson wrote a letter to OSHA. The agency performed an inspection, concluding that "several women had rashes and were complaining about formaldehyde exposure." OSHA also ruled that Lion should have sent Lawson to the doctor when she complained of illness, and that by not doing so had failed to behave appropriately when "a substantial probability that death or serious physical harm could result." Lion's punishment? A $975 fine. (Lawson eventually won an unemployment benefits claim against Lion.)

Lawson's case was the most recent in a history of violations. In 1987, Lion was cited for failing to give employees proper face protection. In 1990, it was fined for not training employees how to handle hazardous chemicals. It was cited seven times in 1993 for a variety of violations, and nine times in 1996 for, among other reasons, failing to train employees how to use portable fire extinguishers in a plant loaded with flammable materials.

In the absence of effective enforcement, union leaders have pushed for legislative protection for all workers employed through federal contracts. In February 1997, Vice President Al Gore championed the cause, proposing an executive order that would require companies that do business with the government to maintain clean OSHA records and permit union activity. "If you want to do business with the federal government, you had better maintain a safe workplace and respect civil, human, and union rights," Gore told an appreciative AFL-CIO audience. But the proposal caused an outcry among Republicans and has remained on the back burner ever since. Chris Lehane, a Gore spokesman, says, "You have to realize these things don't happen overnight."

When *Mother Jones* asked Lion if it had ever threatened to close the Beattyville plant if workers unionized, the company's president, Richard Lapedes, wrote back: "No, and we have been happy to state clearly and openly that we would never do such a thing." The Union of Needletrades, Industrial, and Textile Employees (UNITE) tried to organize Lion in 1997 but failed, union leaders claim, because of the management's swift and unyielding opposition. Several memos circulated by Lion to its workers, and obtained by *Mother Jones*, would appear to support UNITE's interpretation; in one case, the company seems to narrowly evade federal labor laws that prohibit employers from threatening plant closings. The memo reads: "Why [is UNITE] trying to get information which they may want to use to hurt Lion's business? If that happens, that could hurt all of our jobs."

The memos did manage to instill fear in some of the workers. "We had to hide this one girl down in the floorboards of the car whenever we went out to talk about the union," says Tamara Sparks, 23, who is Carol Shelton's daughter. Sparks and her mother are very close, celebrating their weddings (Tamara's first, Carol's third) together in 1991, and working side by side at the Lion factory for three years. Sparks was a union supporter at Lion, and signed a letter, along with seven other employees, that requested outside oversight to prevent the company from retaliating against pro-union workers.

Written with UNITE's help, the letter was sent to Gore, as well as to eight Kentucky congressmen and the state's U.S. senators, telling them: "Some of us have been told point-blank that if we get a union, the plant will close. They've spied on people to see who took union leaflets, and they've told individuals who work here that if we talk to the union we will be fired. Up 'til now, people here have been too afraid to file any official charges, but we'd like to talk to you or someone from your staff about what can be done."

It's not clear how, but shortly thereafter, the letter was forwarded to Lion's management, which then posted it on the company's bulletin board. Soon after that, the union drive sputtered out.

The drive does appear to have had some benefits. Lion's payroll administrator, Tina Ward, says that last year, when Lion raised the hourly pay 30 cents to $5.80—65 cents more than the minimum wage—it was in response to the unionizing efforts.

In Lion's written response, Lapedes told *Mother Jones*: "We believe we are one of the most progressive companies, certainly in our industry, if not any industry in the United States." Lapedes conceded that the plant had no air conditioning, but stated that "investment capital has become available, so that air conditioning all of our facilities has become a viable option." The same day *Mother Jones* received Lapedes's statement, according to current Lion employees, the company began installing air-conditioning systems at the Beattyville plant.

Meanwhile, the government is impressed by Lion's efficiency. "We are obviously pleased with them as a vendor," says Lynford Morton, a spokesman for the Defense Logistics Agency (DLA), the Defense Department office responsible for most outside contracts. A recent DLA annual report even goes so far as to highlight Lion as a success story, attributing annual savings of $4.5 million to the company's finesse.

The DLA has, in turn, received the admiration of Gore, who has honored the agency's efficiency with 51 Hammer Awards, one of the highest honors his office can bestow. The DLA's job is to secure the lowest bid it can for a contract. The agency's officials, proud of their private-sector partners, say they have no desire to revisit the days before Ronald Reagan and, more recently, Bill Clinton, both of whom eased regulations covering government contracts. "We're getting out of the big daddy thing," explains Morton. "We have no right to tell our suppliers how to do their business."

In 1997, the DLA spent $811.8 million on uniforms and textiles for the

Defense Department, and ultimately sold them for $996.9 million, a 22.8 percent markup. Of these uniforms, 97 percent were sold to the U.S. armed services, though the DLA also sells uniforms to foreign governments, including El Salvador ($1 million from 1995 to 1999 in coveralls, flight boots, flight jackets, signal flags, and camouflage cloth), and Saudi Arabia ($17.9 million from 1995 to 1999 in jackets, tents, boots, tarpaulins, helmets, and assorted clothing).

The DLA says that it does not profit from uniform sales, and that the markup is used to cover bureaucratic overhead. But the numbers don't add up. In 1997, the DLA's overhead amounted to 9.3 percent of the cost of purchasing the uniforms, which left an additional $109.6 million unaccounted for. When an internal Defense Department task force reviewed the DLA's 1997 budget, it reported that profits were slated to fund other Defense Department programs, specifically referring to $20 million that was budgeted for the military's operations in Bosnia. The Defense Department has since claimed that the transfer was incorrectly labeled. Members of the task force, meanwhile, are tight-lipped, but stand by their report. "We reported accurately based on the facts we had at the time," says Navy Captain Barbara Brehm. The Coast Guard's Robert Gitschier says task force members maintain "a level of doubt" about the military's denials.

There are other, more direct ways the military profits from uniform sales. Military clothing stores, for example, which are run by the Army and Air Force Exchange Service (AAFES), sell what they describe as "optional uniform" clothing to its troops. Usually of better quality than the standard uniforms issued to recruits—thicker fabric, better tailoring—optional uniforms are purchased from other outside vendors. A survey of these 40 manufacturers shows that 12 of them have received a total of 207 OSHA violations in the past 10 years.

In 1998, $3.4 million in profits from these stores was allocated to the Army's Morale Welfare and Recreation fund, described by a Defense Department official as a network of programs to improve "productivity, mental and physical fitness, individual growth, positive values, *esprit de corps*, and family well-being." Among the projects underwritten by the fund are Shades of Green, an Army hotel in Florida that features heated swimming pools and free transportation to Disney World; a beachside resort in Hawaii; and an 18-hole golf course at Fort Knox, Kentucky, not more than 120 miles west of Beattyville.

Golf isn't the recreation of choice in Beattyville. I drove Tamara Sparks and her husband, Cecil (with whom she no longer lives), around one night in my rented car, and we talked about what they do for fun. "We party hard, son," Cecil says. That, according to the couple and their friends, means Xanax trips that last for days and moonshine that'll make you want to walk naked down Main Street. There's also racing old Buicks along the back roads, with pit stops in the woods for a little of what Sparks elusively refers to as "scroggin' and scotchin'."

Sparks is vivacious and talkative, but her insecurity comes out in offhand comments, such as when she refers to herself as "just a hillbilly redneck." She doesn't delude herself about life in Beattyville, and becomes anxious when talk turns to the future of her family. She tells Cecil that a cousin told her that "there's lots of work in Texas and I could find a job, no problem." But Cecil, the father of her children, is hesitant to go. While work remains scarce in Appalachia (unemployment estimates reach 24 percent), outside opportunities are hard to imagine in an area where only 5 percent of the population has college degrees.

Besides, Beattyville is home, and those who live here have grown to rely heavily on one another. One of Sparks' brothers-in-law grows and distributes tomatoes and beans; Carol Shelton's husband, Herbert, hunts rabbit and deer, which she then makes into sausage; people trade labor for building supplies and staples; and every month, the church hands out 50-pound sacks of potatoes.

At her current job working at a gas station, Sparks doesn't have health insurance, so her mother lends her money for a doctor when one of the children gets sick. Sparks says she prefers the gas station to Lion, except that the pay's not very good. Unemployment, she says, proved more lucrative. During the time she stayed home after leaving Lion, she explains, she could save the $50 a week she now spends for a babysitter. Her lower earnings also forced her to give up an apartment with lots of space in a big cement dwelling—low-income housing built with government aid. For now, she has moved back to her mother's little blue house.

THE MOJO WIRE and *Mother Jones* are projects of the Foundation for National Progress, a non-profit 501(c)3 organization, founded in 1975 to educate and empower people to work toward progressive change. All Rights Reserved.

5 CENSORED

Turkey Destroys Kurdish Villages with U.S. Weapons

"TURKEY'S WAR ON THE KURDS"
by Kevin McKiernan
Bulletin of Atomic Scientists, March/April 1999

Behind army lines in the Turkish province of Siirt, scores of frightened refugees were on the run. They were Kurdish families, fleeing a village that had recently been burned by the Turkish army. When I caught up to them, they were fording the Tigris River, guiding a long line of donkeys laden with refrigerators and other goods.

In the village, most of the houses were in ashes. Only a handful of residents had returned to scavenge some of their belongings. The local mayor told me that an army commander, accompanied by a group of government-armed village guards, had arrived and given residents 24 hours to get out of town. Some quickly dug holes in the outlying fields to bury valuables; others just gathered up what they could carry and abandoned the rest.

I walked through the rubble, taking pictures. The destruction was fresh, maybe a couple of days old, and some of it was still smoldering. I heard an army helicopter overhead. It was American-made, a Sikorsky Black Hawk, the type the Turkish army uses to land troops in the villages. But it was high in the air, on a different mission. I finished my work and moved on.

ROOTS RUN DEEP At 25 million, the Kurds are the largest ethnic group in the world without their own state. With a similar language, religion, and culture, the Kurds have lived for thousands of years in an area that is now part of Turkey, Iraq, Iran, Syria, and the former Soviet Union. Today, the 15 million Kurds who live in Turkey constitute about 25 percent of that country's population.

After World War I, Kurds hoped to create a homeland from the wreckage of the Ottoman Empire, but those dreams vanished with the birth of the Turkish Republic in 1923. Riding a wave of nationalism, Mustafa Kemal, known as Ataturk, "the Father of the Turks," imposed a single identity on the multi-cultural population of Turkmans, Armenians, Assyrians, Kurds, and others. Most minorities were forcibly assimilated; everyone became a Turk. (The Kurds were called "Mountain Turks" until after the Gulf War in 1991.)

In the first 25 years of the Turkish Republic there were dozens of Kurdish uprisings. All were crushed, but discontent continued. In 1984, a Marxist-led group called the PKK, the Kurdistan Workers Party, began an armed struggle against the government.

The war in Turkey represents the single largest use of U.S. weapons anywhere in the world by non-U.S. forces, according to Bill Hartung of the World Policy Institute. "I can think of no instance since the Israeli invasion of Lebanon in 1982,' he said, "where American weaponry has been put to this concentrated a use." In 15 years of fighting in Turkey nearly 40,000 lives have been lost, more than in the conflicts on the West Bank and in Northern Ireland combined. The two million refugees produced by the war in Kurdistan are roughly the number of homeless created by the widely reported war in Bosnia, where U.S. weapons were not a factor. In contrast, 75 percent of the Turkish arsenal was made in the United States, according to estimates.

Despite these statistics, the civil strife in Turkey has received comparatively little coverage in the U.S. media. Television news rarely mentions the Kurds, unless the story relates to the Iraqi Kurds. It is almost as though there are two sets of Kurds: the Kurds in Iraq, who seem to be viewed as the "good" Kurds because they oppose Saddam, and the Kurds in Turkey, who are "bad" because they oppose a U.S. ally. It doesn't seem to matter that there are four times as many Kurds in Turkey, or that both populations have suffered repression from their respective governments.

Until 1991, Kurdish music and language, dress, associations, and newspapers were banned by the Turkish government. After the Gulf War, Kurdish printing was legalized, but in the intervening years numerous Kurdish newspaper offices have been bombed and closed. More than a dozen Kurdish journalists, as well as numerous politicians and activists, have been killed by death squads (human rights groups list more that 4,000 extrajudicial killings during the period). Despite 15 years of fighting the PKK, Turkey today has no POWs; most rebels, according to the government, have been "captured dead." But there are large numbers of civilian Kurds in Turkish prisons where, according to organizations like Amnesty International, the use of torture is routine.

Kurdish TV and radio are still illegal in Turkey, although the government has promised to soften the ban. The Kurdish language still may not be taught in schools or used by merchants on storefronts or in advertising. It is illegal in Turkey for parents to give their child a Kurdish name.

SHEPHERDS AND SOLDIERS In June 1995, the army commander from the city of Mardin informed residents of the village of Alimlikoy, called Bilalya by the Kurds, that they would have to go on the payroll of the state as village guards. The villagers were reluctant to become guards because that would put them in the middle of the war with the PKK rebels. They were shepherds who spent long, isolated hours in the mountains with their flocks; they feared that if they accepted weapons from the government, they would become targets for the guerrillas. The Turkish officer gave them two weeks to think about it. When no answer was forthcoming, he arrested the *muhtar*, or village elder. The shepherd who walked me into Alimlikoy overland, around the blockaded road told me the *muhtar* had been kept in jail for several days. He had been beaten, according to the shepherd, "but not badly."

On the day the *muhtar* was released, which was shortly before my arrival, the villagers hired trucks to haul away household goods and as much of the ripening harvest of lentils and barley as they could carry. I arrived in time to see some of the harvests, piled in heaps by the side of the road. The Kurds were pouring salvaged grain into plastic bags, which they hoped to sell at the market. On a hillside, a giant sign read: "Happy is He Who Can Call Himself a Turk."

Back in Alimlikoy, I asked the shepherd why he hadn't just agreed to become a guard. "Why would we?" he asked. "We have our fields and our animals. We have an income.

"Besides," he said with some emphasis, "why should we try to do a job that not even the state can accomplish?"

U.S. ARMS AND HUMAN RIGHTS Since 1980 the United States has sold or given Turkey, a NATO ally, $15 billion worth of weapons. In the last decade the Turkish army has leveled, burned, or forcibly evacuated more than 3,000 Kurdish villages. That is roughly three-quarters the number of Kurdish settlements destroyed in Iraq in the 1980s during Saddam Hussein's infamous "Anfal" campaign, when the West was arming Iraq and turning a blind eye to widespread human rights violations.

Most of the destruction in Turkey took place between 1992 and 1995, during the Clinton Administration's first term. In 1995 the administration acknowledged that American arms had been used by the Turkish government in domestic military operations "during which human rights abuses have occurred. In a report ordered by Congress, the State Department admitted that the abuses included the use of U.S. Cobra helicopters, armored personnel carriers, and F-16 fighter bombers. In some instances, critics say, entire Kurdish villages were obliterated from the air.

The administration conceded that the Turkish policy had forced more than two million Kurds from their homes. Some of the villages were evacuated and burned, bombed, or shelled by government forces to deprive the PKK of a "logistical base of operations," according to the State Department report, while others were targeted because their inhabitants refused to join the "village guards," a brutal military tactic patterned on the Vietnam-era "model villages" program that requires civilian Kurds to fight Kurdish guerrillas.

Human Rights Watch, the New York-based watchdog group, said the State Department had issued only "half conclusions" in its report, so as to avoid offending the Turkish government. Human Rights Watch, which has also criticized the PKK rebels for serious rights violations, said the U.S.-supplied Turkish army was "responsible for the majority of forced evacuation and destruction of villages.'

In a 1998 interview, John Shattuck, the Assistant Secretary of State for Human Rights, defended U.S. arms deliveries to Turkey. Shattuck, a one-time professor at Harvard and a former member of the advisory board at Amnesty International, said that although abuses against Kurds were "a matter of grave concern" to the United States, Turkey's human rights record was improving. And in any case, he added, "I don't think the United States is responsible for Turkey's internal policies.'

Some members of Congress strongly disagree. Congresswoman Cynthia McKinney, a Democrat from Georgia, believes that human rights, democracy, and nonaggression criteria should be applied before American weapons are sold or given to countries like Turkey. "If they are going to be our ally and they are also going to receive our weapons," McKinney said, "the least that we can do is to suggest to them that they not use the weapons against their own people." McKinney led the fight in 1997 for a code of conduct, which would have mandated congressional review of such transfers. The code, which was opposed by the White House, passed in the House but did not receive adequate support in the

Senate, where it died in conference committee.

Last September the code was reintroduced with 80 co-sponsors in the House, but the session adjourned before a vote could be taken. Congress did pass a less comprehensive measure, an amendment introduced by Senator Patrick Leahy, a Vermont Democrat, which prohibits U.S. military aid to foreign security units that the State Department has found to have "committed gross violations of human rights." The so-called "Leahy Amendment" also bars funding for military training programs if a member of a unit has been found to have committed "gross human rights violations."

Many Europeans are also uneasy with Turkey's current policies. Turkey has been angling for admission to the European Union (EU) for years, but the EU, citing the lack of freedom of expression, the jailing and torture of dissidents, and the state of emergency in Kurdish areas, has locked the door. The Kurdish problem, according to Hugo Paeman, the EU's ambassador to the United States, "is only a reflection of the fact that we don't have the type of government [in Turkey] which we would feel comfortable with within the European Union."

Paeman, a Belgian, said it was difficult for the EU to negotiate in good faith with the civilian government in Ankara when the army generals behind the scenes held the real power. "Do you feel that you are actually not talking to the people who are running Turkey?" I asked him. "Up to a certain point, yes," he responded.

In view of that, I asked, is Turkish democracy merely a facade? Ambassador Paeman paused to make eye contact with his aide, a Danish official, before answering. "One can say that," he replied.

FEEDING THE SPIRIT When I met Ali in 1996, he was drinking tea and playing cards in Midyat, one of dozens of Kurdish towns overflowing with refugees. Ali and his wife and nine kids had all fled Shehkir, a farming village known for its sweet cherries. Long ago the Turks had changed the name of the place to Kocasirt, which is how it appeared on the map. But Ali, like others who had lived there, still called it Shekhir.

Having agreed to take me to the village, Ali drove gingerly down a hill toward his old home, carefully scanning the rock-studded road for signs of surface digging. He said the army often mines access to abandoned Kurdish villages. The week before, on the road to another vacated settlement, a man and a woman were badly injured when a land mine exploded under their donkey. "I have seen President Clinton on television," he told me in a trusting tone. "I don't think he would permit these bad things to happen if he knew about them."

Ali said that in the summer of 1994, 16 army tanks rolled through his village searching for Kurdish guerrillas. Some of the tanks had rubber wheels, like the kind the Germans sell to Turkey; the others were track vehicles, like the M-48 and M-60 tanks made in the United States.

Even though no rebels were found, the soldiers returned a few months later and delivered an ultimatum to the people: Become village guards or abandon your homes. The 70-year-old *muhtar* insisted the villagers had never fed or otherwise assisted the rebels; they just wanted to grow their crops. He told the soldiers that the people chose to be left alone. It was the wrong choice.

A few nights later, the *muhtar* was dragged from his home and shot. The townspeople still refused to take arms from the government. Instead, they gathered their furniture and household belongings and moved away.

Whatever Kocasirt had been before, it was now a collection of deserted, burned, and dynamited houses. It was a ghost town, except for the cemetery. There we encountered an old woman who had just returned to the village by foot. She was wailing softly and sprinkling red cherries on a tombstone. She said she was "feeding the spirit" of her dead brother. My guide recognized her: She was the sister of the *muhtar*. Reaching for a weed in the overgrown graveyard, the woman made a sweeping motion with one hand. "They just plucked him like a flower," she said.

THE WASHINGTON-ANKARA ALLIANCE

Because of its strategic location in the Middle East, between the Balkans and the southern republics of the former Soviet Union, Turkey has served as a major U.S. ally for more than 50 years. The low point in the alliance came in 1974, when in response to the invasion of northern Cyprus by Turkey's U.S.-equipped armed forces, Congress placed a total embargo on U.S. arms transfers to Turkey. The invasion, which has been condemned by numerous U.N. resolutions, might have permanently altered the U.S.-Turkish relationship had it not been for the fall of the U.S.-backed regime in Iran in 1979.

For the United States, a decades-old strategy in the Gulf collapsed with the demise of the Shah. Not only was its Cold War containment strategy threatened, the United States now regarded Islam, stretching from North Africa through the Gulf to southwest Asia, as the single biggest threat to U.S. interests in the region. Turkey, like Israel and Egypt, would form the cornerstone of the new policy to contain Iran and the further spread of Islamic fundamentalism.

Good relations between the United States and Turkey weathered a 1980 coup, in which Turkish army generals overthrew the country's democratically elected leaders. (Almost 20 years later the army's power over the constitution and other Turkish laws is unquestioned.) Within months of the coup, the United States and Turkey signed the Defense and Economic Cooperation Agreement, a treaty which gave the United States the right to locate military bases in Turkey, which borders both Iran and Iraq, in exchange for a promise to modernize Turkey's armed forces.

The agreement proved vital to U.S. strategy against Saddam Hussein in the Gulf War. The Allies flew hundreds of bombing missions against Iraqi targets from Turkish air space. The Turks also agreed to shut down the Iraqi pipeline where it entered Turkey's southeast border. That decision, made at considerable cost to Turkish interests, was key to the post-war embargo of Iraq.

Turkey's value to U.S. policy-makers today is more than just its proximity to Iran and Iraq or the perceived need to contain the spread of Islam. There is also the issue of petroleum. The Caspian Sea to the east is thought to contain more than 100 billion barrels of oil. Capturing the deposits is a mammoth project, the stakes are high, and the parties play hardball. The agreement signed by a consortium of global companies to recover the oil represents the most lucrative contract of any kind in the twentieth century.

No one yet knows how the crude oil will be transported to the West, but the United States is pushing for a pipeline to be built through Turkey to the Mediterranean Sea. Amoco and British Petroleum, the largest companies in the consortium, want to build a shorter pipeline through Georgia and then ship the oil by tanker through the Black Sea. But both companies are currently involved in other projects in Turkey, and Turkey has threatened to revoke their operating permits if they fail to support the Turkish route for Caspian oil. As it turns out, such a route would pass through the center of Kurdistan. Kurdish guerrillas, who already have blown up sections of the Iraqi pipeline and Turkish oil fields in the southeast, have vowed to block the project.

KURDS v. KURDS In 1994, when I last visited Gorumlu, a settlement tucked into the base of a mountain on the Turkish side of the Iraqi border, the village showed signs of support for the rebels, and the area was often the scene of firefights with the army. But today the local Kurds are on the government payroll. The village guards in Gorumlu had joined the widespread program of rural pacification, the army strategy introduced in 1985. In this area the guards were especially valuable because they knew the PKK trails along the border; they had served as scouts for soldiers in several incursions into Iraq in search of rebel base camps.

Because of their decision, the villagers were able to keep their homes. The state was giving them weapons, bullets, U.S.-made Motorola radios, and a salary of $250 a month far more than they could make as farmers. With their help, the Turkish army had driven the guerrillas deep into the mountains, and clashes in the village had become less frequent. But Gorumlu's switchover was not without cost.

The PKK, many of whose local members had been recruited from Gorumlu, views both the guards and their families as Turkish collaborators, and claims that both are legitimate military targets. Soon after one army incursion into nearby Iraq, the guerrillas launched a coordinated attack against the village and the nearby army garrison, resulting in civilian deaths.

During the battle, the army commander told me he had intercepted a radio transmission, which he said came from a PKK superior, urging his fighters to "hit the little mice as well as the big mice."

According to the Turkish officer and several villagers, four children were killed and several adults were injured when the PKK threw a grenade through a window of one of the houses. For its part, the PKK has denied responsibility for the attack, blaming instead the Kontra Gerilla death squads they say are linked to the Turkish security forces.

BUYERS AND SUPPLIERS Today, the United States has several intelligence-gathering posts in Turkey, including a radar installation in Mardin, a largely Kurdish city. The Mardin facility was built by GM Hughes of El Segundo, California, the parent company of Delco Systems. The radar site is said to be capable of "seeing" deep into Iraq, Iran, and south central Asia.

NATO has major installations in Turkey, the most prominent of which is at Incirlik, near the city of Adana. U.S. intelligence planes, including the giant AWACs, take off daily from Incirlik for flights over northern Iraq, monitoring traffic both in Iraq and Iran. U.S. F-15s and F-16s, as well as British aircraft, make regular sorties into northern Iraq, patrolling the "no-fly" zone for violations by Saddam Hussein's air force.

Turkey's war with the Kurds draws on weaponry from dozens of American companies, including McDonnell Douglas, General Dynamics, Hughes, Boeing, Raytheon, and Bell Textron. Kurdish refugees driven into northern Iraq from destroyed villages in Turkey rarely know any English, but in recounting the rocketing of their settlements, they regularly use the words "Cobra" and "Sikorsky," the U.S.-made helicopters used to clear Kurdish villages.

The "King Cobra," the gunship produced by Bell Textron in Texas, is a strong contender for a new Turkish arms contract worth almost $4 billion. In 1997 the State Department granted market licenses to Bell and to Boeing Aircraft for attack helicopters (Boeing makes the "Apache" gunship), but future sales by either company could be delayed if human rights concerns are raised again in Congress. In 1996 Turkey canceled the purchase of 10 Super Cobra helicopters when Congress delayed that deal to consider whether Turkey was using the Cobra against Kurdish civilians. If that happens again, Turkey could buy attack helicopters from France or could turn to a version of the weapon built jointly by Russia and Israel, without strings attached. In fact, the burgeoning relationship between Ankara and Jerusalem which includes Israeli upgrades of Turkey's F-4, F-5, and F-16 fighters; the development of medium-range missiles; and the conduct of joint military exercises has increasingly allowed Turkey to circumvent U.S. and European embargoes.

The giant helicopter sale is one of two prospective U.S. arms transfers that have generated strong opposition from human rights groups. The other is a $45-million sale by AV Technologies in Michigan for 140 armored personnel carriers (APCs) to Turkey. Turkey already has an estimated 2,800 U.S.–made APCs (most of which were made in California by FMC the Food Machinery Corporation).

The new APCs are intended for use by Turkey's "anti-terror" police units. Amnesty International USA conducted a three-year study on these police groups, which it sent to Secretary of State Madeleine Albright in an effort to block the transfer. The report provides examples of identified "anti-terror" units torturing children, sexually assaulting prisoners, using electric shock torture, beating, burning, and the near-drowning of suspects, as well as other gross violations. Among 280 victims of the "anti-terror" units mentioned in the report were "infants, children, and the elderly." But last December, despite such evidence, the State Department okayed the arms deal. Because of the recently enacted Leahy Amendment, some restrictions were placed on the use of U.S. loans for APCs destined for areas of conflict, but the export license for all 140 vehicles to the "anti-terror" police was approved.

That was consistent with past practices, in which arms deals involving Turkey have moved along expeditiously. In 1992 and 1993 the Pentagon quietly facilitated a mammoth military shipment to Turkey at no cost. According to the U.N. arms registry, the U.S. government turned over 1,509 tanks, 54 fighter planes, and 28 heavily armed attack helicopters to Turkey. The weapons were slated for reduction after the Cold War under a 1990 treaty on conventional forces in Europe. Instead of scrapping them, the United States simply gave them away. There was no congressional oversight or public debate about the transfer,

nor was there much question about the purpose of the unprecedented arms shipment. As *Jane's Defense Weekly* revealed as early as 1993, "a high proportion of defense equipment supplied to Turkey is being used in operations against the PKK."

Military assistance to Turkey has even included the use of American soldiers. Last year, according to the *Washington Post*, a special operations team authorized by the Joint Combined Exchange Training Act, a little-known law passed by Congress, conducted its first mission to Turkey. The U.S. team was sent to train the Turkish Mountain Commandos, "a unit whose chief function is to fight Kurdish guerrillas."

Turkey also benefits from the International Military Education and Training program, a Pentagon program funded through the foreign aid budget. From 1984, when the PKK's uprising began, to 1997, about 2,500 Turkish officers received training. Bill Hartung of the World Policy Institute says that much of the training of the Turkish military focuses on how to use weapons already purchased from American companies. Hartung estimates U.S. taxpayers have already paid "tens of millions of dollars' to train Turkish forces to fight the Kurds.

CLEANING UP Cizre has been "cleaned," the Turkish policeman said proudly. And in one sense he was right. The largely Kurdish town of 25,000, located about 50 miles north of the Iraqi border, was firmly under the control of the Turkish security forces.

When I was there in 1994, Cizre was a hotbed of PKK resistance. That memory was still fresh as I rented my old room at the ratty Kadioglu, where an intermittently lit sign said "Turistik Hotel." The room had an outdoor balcony, which overlooked the sign, and from there I used to watch the exchange of tracer fire after dark, the surreal streams of yellow lighting up the intersection below. In 1992, during *Newroz*, the Kurdish new year, the Turkish army shot and killed a photojournalist near the Kadioglu. Since my last visit, someone had repaired the concrete balcony by my room, patching over the bullet-pocked walls.

The reception clerk told me he was getting tired of it all, tired of the war and tired of all the unpaid tasks he was forced to perform. He was still cooperative with the police, and he had no use for the rebels. But, like many accommodating Kurds, he was growing progressively alienated. It was true that the guerrillas had been driven into the tops of the mountains, their logistical base disrupted by deforestation and the widespread destruction of villages. But the government seemed to be losing the battle for the hearts and minds of ordinary Kurds.

The hotel clerk complained that he had to inform the police of all movements by reporters: "When you get up, when you go out, and when you return. It's incredible," he said. "We have to telephone three different places each time: the Army, mit [military intelligence], and the regular police. Why can't we just call one place, and let them handle the rest?"

What he really wanted was a sort of clearinghouse for the surveillance of the press, and we got to joking about it. In jest, I asked him to notify the police that I had used a hotel toilet at 6 A.M. that day, and again at 7:30.

He smiled, shrugging his shoulders and rolling his eyes. "What can we do?" he said.

INTERNATIONALIZING THE CONFLICT The case of PKK leader Abdullah Ocalan has raised the profile of the Kurds in recent months. Ocalan, widely known as Apo was arrested in November 1998 in the Rome airport after arriving from Moscow. After a decade of directing PKK activities from Damascus, Ocalan and other PKK officials had been expelled from Syria a month earlier when Turkish troops began massing on the border, threatening to escalate a long-running political feud between Turkey and Syria.

Turkish officials were jubilant when Ocalan was detained, but their euphoria soon turned to outrage. The Kurdish leader, whom the government charged with "tens of thousands of murders" in the 15-year-old uprising, would have faced execution if returned to Turkey. But the Italian constitution bars extradition to countries where the death penalty is in force. Within days Italy announced it would not extradite, and Ocalan was released.

Turkish politicians unleashed a firestorm of protest. Across Turkey the police reacted by staging raids on the offices of Hadep, the legal Kurdish party. More than 3,000 Hadep members were jailed within a few days. According to human rights groups, a number of party members were subjected to torture; two died in custody.

In Istanbul, the nation's top business lobbies urged a total boycott of Italian goods (Italy ranks as the world's second largest exporter to Turkey). But the European Union immediately threatened Turkey with economic sanctions if it followed through with the boycott.

Turkey's harsh attacks on EU-member Italy seemed especially inflammatory, considering Turkey's persistent efforts to be accepted for membership in the EU. But the Ocalan affair was shaping up to be the nastiest row in memory between NATO members, and the dispute was widening.

Massimo D'Alema, Italy's prime minister, called on the Kurdish leader to renounce violence, a minimum requirement to be considered for political asylum. Ocalan responded by saying: "I am ready to do my part to halt terrorism." He called for a political solution to the war, a demand that Turkey had repeatedly rejected. The disavowal of violence was welcomed by D'Alema, but the Italian leader further angered Turkey by declaring that the struggle of the Kurdish people was an ancient and complex problem that could not be regarded solely in the context of terrorism.

The PKK leader likened his cause to that of the PLO, the IRA, and Basque separatists, movements that sought to make a transition from warfare to diplomacy. He asserted that he had come to Italy to launch the political phase of the Kurdish struggle. Meanwhile, 40,000 Kurds from across Europe gathered in Germany to demonstrate on Ocalan's behalf.

Others condemned the Kurdish leader. Human Rights Watch, which had repeatedly attacked Turkey for abuses against the Kurds, sent a letter to D'Alema charging Ocalan's PKK with massacres in Turkey's southeast, primarily in the early 1990s. The majority of the victims were village guards and their families and Turkish teachers who were targeted by the guerrillas as state collaborators. Opposing extradition to Turkey, Human Rights Watch called instead for Ocalan to be tried under international law in Italy or another EU country.

In January, Ocalan left Italy of his own accord, reportedly aboard an Italian secret service airplane to Moscow, from which he transited to an undisclosed location. His brief appearance on the European stage and the diplomatic tornado it whipped up had received more publicity in two months than he or the PKK had generated in 15 years of guerrilla warfare. But it was increasingly clear that he would not be awarded political asylum and, with relations deteriorating with Turkey, Italy warned Ocalan that if he stayed in the country, he might be brought to trial on terror charges. Ironically, such a trial could also have been Turkey's worst nightmare if it had exposed state terror as well as rebel terror and if it had sparked an international review of the long-standing civil war in that country.

Until now, Turkey has been able to ignore Western demands for dialogue with the Kurds. The brutal scorched earth campaign in the southeast has been a military success. The deforestation and village burnings have been accomplished with little press attention, a minimum of public debate, and no censure from the United Nations. And the PKK, though still a force to be reckoned with, recently has been beset by internal conflicts and beleaguered by defections. Ocalan's arrest, in Turkey's eyes, could have finished the rebels once and for all. But now his fate, the "Kurdish question," and Turkey's suitability as a member of the European Union have once again been postponed.

In early February, two months in advance of the increasingly important national elections, Turkey took steps to ban the Hadep party. Officials said that some members of hadep, which has more than 3,000 registered members, had shown sympathy for the guerrillas by participating in hunger strikes and other non-violent activity following Ocalan's arrest in Rome.

Hadep represents the Kurds' only potential interlocutor with the government other than the rebels. The bid to outlaw the party, which would deny the Kurds any representation in the Turkish parliament, startled the United States and its allies, alienated moderate Kurds, and further undermined the country's fragile democracy.

For all the military assistance the United States has provided its ally over the years, Turkey remains politically unstable. The ruling coalition in Ankara recently collapsed in a corruption-related scandal, and the Islamic party, the scourge of the Turkish army, is stronger today than at any time in history. While still a minority party, it is widely expected to win the national elections this spring. The country is unstable economically as well, and inflation is rampant, a reflection of the fact that $100 billion has been spent, just since 1991, to defeat the rebels.

On the surface, very little seems to have changed. The government still has 300,000 security forces in the southeast, and Apo is underground once again. Notwithstanding recent events, the battleground has yet to shift from the Turkish-Iraqi mountains to the political salons of the Continent. Turkey still boasts the largest army in nato (after the United States), but the path to diplomatic acceptance in Europe despite dogged U.S. efforts will be clouded by the Kurds for some time to come.

KEVIN McKIERNAN, a photojournalist, has visited Turkey and northern Iraq a dozen times since the Gulf War. His work has appeared in *Time*, *Newsweek*, and the *New York Times*, and on ABC, CBS, and NBC.

Reprinted by permission of *The Bulletin of the Atomic Scientists*, © 1998 by the Educational Foundation for Nuclear Science, 6042 South Kimbark, Chicago, Illinois 60637, USA. A one-year subscription is $28.

About the Editor/Director

Peter Phillips is an associate professor of Sociology at Sonoma State University and director of Project Censored. He teaches classes in Media Censorship, Power, Class Stratification, and Social Welfare. This is his fourth edition of *Censored* from Seven Stories Press. Also from Seven Stories Press is Project Censored's *Progressive Guide to Alternative Media and Activism 1999*.

Phillips writes op-ed pieces in the alternative press and independent newspapers nationwide, having published in *Z Magazine*, *Social Policy*, and numerous independents. He frequently speaks on media censorship, and various socio-political issues on radio and TV talk shows including, *Talk of the Nation*, *Public Interest*, *Talk America*, *World Radio Network*, *Democracy Now!*, and the *Jim Hightower Show*.

Phillips had a long career in human service administration. His experiences include two and a half decades of community service and social activism, including serving as a War on Poverty administrator, Head Start director, and refugee assistance consultant.

Phillips earned a B.A. in Social Science in 1970 from Santa Clara University, and an M.A. in Social Science from California State University at Sacramento in 1974. He earned a second M.A. in Sociology in 1991 and a Ph.D. in Sociology in 1994. His doctoral dissertation was entitled, *A Relative Advantage: Sociology of the San Francisco Bohemian Club*.

Phillips is a fifth generation Californian, who grew up on a family-owned farm west of the Central Valley town of Lodi. Phillips lives today in rural Sonoma County with his wife Mary Lia-Phillips and their four pet chickens: Millie, Silly, Dilly, and Booster.

PROJECT CENSORED MISSION STATEMENT Project Censored, founded in 1976, is a non-profit project within the Sonoma State University Foundation, a 501(c)3 organization. Its principle objective is the advocacy for and protection of First Amendment rights and freedom of information in the United States. Through a faculty, student, community partnership, Project Censored serves as a national media ombudsman by identifying and researching important news stories that are underreported, ignored, misrepresented, or censored by media corporations in the United States. It also encourages and supports journalists, faculty, and student investigations into First Amendment and freedom of information issues through its Project Censored Yearbook, Censored Alert Newsletter, and nationwide advocacy.

Index

342 CENSORED

chemicals, 67-69, 101, 115, 122, 134, 313-314, 317, 325
Chevron, 41, 51, 146-147, 149, 298, 301
Chiapas, 142-145, 275
Chiapas Media Project, 275
Chicago Media Watch, 275
Chicago Reader, 273
Chicago Sun-Times, 132, 134, 145
Chicago Tribune, 188
child death rates, 132
Children's Internet Protection Act, 225
Chile, 111, 128
China, 110-111, 129, 135, 168, 253-264, 298-299, 302
Chinese Communist Party, 253, 256
Chiquita, 152
chlorinated chemicals, 122
Chlorine Chemistry Council, 122
chloroquine, 303
cholera, 137
Chomsky, Noam, 176, 185, 208, 220, 272, 284
Christian Aid, 153
Christian Science Monitor, 132-134, 262
Chronicle of Higher Education, The, 112
Chronicle of Philanthropy, 34, 310, 321
CIA, 63, 86, 89, 108, 177, 192, 289
Ciba-Geigy, 318
Citizens' Council on Corporate Issues (CCCI), 276
Citizens for Independent Public Broadcasting, 276
Citizens for Media Literacy, 276
Citizens for Overt Action, 154-155
Citizens for Tax Justice, 105
Citizens' Media Corps, 276
Civic Media Center & Library, Inc., The, 276
civil rights, 72-73, 91, 93, 105, 151, 197, 242, 250-251, 264
civil war, 26, 39, 55, 81, 116, 201, 208, 304, 338
Clark, Ramsey, 42, 44, 107, 282
Clayton and Sherman Acts, 196
Clean Air Act, 213, 313
clean air standards, 120
Clinton Administration, 38, 54-55, 58, 64, 66, 87, 109, 142, 178, 212-213, 324, 331
Clinton, Bill, 12, 29, 38-39, 42, 44, 50-51, 73, 99, 105, 107, 109, 116-117, 160, 169, 174, 204, 263, 299, 326, 332
Clinton, Hillary, 160
CNN, 49, 51, 71, 148, 178, 190, 193, 217, 219, 257
coal, 41, 83, 322
Coast Guard, 60, 327
Coca-Cola, 181
cocaine, 108, 157, 160
Cockburn, Alexander, 57, 63, 209
Cold War, 41, 66, 133, 135, 152, 333, 336
Collections of Information Antipiracy Act, 224
College of Notre Dame, 277
Collision Course Video Productions, 277
Colombia, 30, 88-89, 116, 127, 297
ColorLines Magazine, 73
Columbia School of Journalism, 46, 288
Columbine, 157-159
Commission on Human Rights, 74
Committee to Protect Journalists, 277
Communications Decency Act, 225
Communications Act of 1934, 194
communism, 65, 80, 168, 253-256, 261-263
Communist Party, 168, 253-254, 256, 262
Community Media Workshop, 277
Comprehensive Test Ban Treaty (CTBT), 126, 134-136
concentration camp, 200
Congress, 34, 38, 47, 79, 90, 92, 99, 105, 108, 114, 130, 144, 152, 155, 169, 176, 179, 188, 204, 213, 223-225, 263, 282, 312, 316, 318, 320, 322, 331-333, 335-336

Congressional Budget Office, 175
Connections, 100, 105, 316, 350
Constitution, the, 105, 141, 227, 229, 333
Contra-cocaine smuggling, 108
Contras, 108
Consumer Price Index, 105
contraception, 84-86, 140
Convention on Biological Diversity, 127
corn, 127
corporate media, 11-12, 26, 55, 99, 168, 172, 175, 191, 215-216, 229-230, 289
cosmetics, 34, 69
Costa Rica, 89
Coughlin, Dan, 244-245, 248
Counterpoise, 272
CounterPunch, 57, 63, 266
CounterSpin, 182, 245
CovertAction Quarterly, 52, 58, 62, 86, 106-107, 111, 153, 185, 266
cow's milk, 26, 77-79
creditors, 83
crime, 43, 45, 63, 76-77, 86, 90-92, 96, 99, 107, 149-150, 165-166, 171, 192-193, 199-203, 205, 207-208, 262
criminal justice system, 16, 76, 149, 179
Croatia, 44, 81, 90-92
Crohn's disease, 26, 77-80, 100
Cronkite, Walter, 45, 231
C-SPAN *Washington Journal,* 53
Cuba, 178
Cuban missile crisis, 177
Cultural Environment Movement (CEM), 20, 278
Cyprus, 333
Dabhol Power project, 29, 295
dairy industry, 78-79
Dalai Lama, 260
D'Alema, Massimo, 338
Dallas Morning News, 145, 306
dam sites, 73-74
Dark Night Field Notes, 143-144, 146
Davis, Angela, 272
Dayton Agreement, 82
DDT, 68
DEA. *See* Drug Enforcement Agency.
Defense and Economic Cooperation Agreement, 333
Defense Department. *See* Department of Defense.
Defense Logistics Agency (DLA), 35, 326-327
Defentech, 113-114
Delta and Pine Land Company, 125
Democracy Now, 53, 147-148, 244, 246, 278, 349
Democratic People's Republic of Korea (DPRK), 66
Denver Post, 97, 124
Department of Agriculture, 79, 125, 318
Department of Corrections, 117
Department of Defense, 35, 57, 98, 178, 322, 324, 326-327
Department of Energy, 48, 57-58, 103, 128-130, 135, 137
Department of Interior, 104
Department of Labor, 35, 324
depleted uranium (DU), 43, 107, 131, 133-134
diabetes, 181
Digital Millennium Copyright Act, 224
dioxin, 68
Direct Action Media Network (DAMN), 278
Disability Media Project, 278
Disney, 166-168, 171, 183-184, 187, 189-190, 192-194, 243, 310, 327
Disney World, 166-167, 192, 327
Disneyland, 183
Dissent, 111
Djukanovic, Milo, 81, 88

Communications Decency Act, 225
Communications Act of 1934, 194
communism, 255, 262
Communist, 65, 80, 168, 253-254, 256, 261-263
Communist governments, 80
Communist Party, 168, 253-254, 256, 262
Community Media Workshop, 277
Comprehensive Test Ban Treaty, 126, 134-135
concentration camp, 200
Congress, 34, 38, 47, 79, 90, 92, 99, 105, 108, 114, 130, 144, 152, 155, 169, 176, 179, 188, 204, 213, 223-225, 263, 282, 312, 316, 318, 320, 322, 331-333, 335-336
Congressional Budget Office, 175
Connections, 100, 105, 316, 350
Constitution, the, 105, 141, 227, 229, 333
Content, 102, 105, 130, 161, 167, 170-171, 177, 180-181, 183, 185, 189, 196, 221, 225, 227, 233, 244-245, 258, 275, 280
Contra-cocaine smuggling, 108
Contras, 108
Consumer Price Index, 105
contraception, 84-86, 140
Convention on Biological Diversity, 127
convicts, 8, 26, 75, 161
copyright, 4, 222, 224, 228
corn, 127
corporate media, 11-12, 26, 55, 99, 168, 172, 175, 191, 215-216, 229-230, 289
corporations, 7, 28-30, 33, 37, 41, 47, 50, 94, 120, 122, 125-126, 128-129, 142, 144, 150, 154, 172, 177, 179, 182, 184, 192-195, 214, 218, 227, 259, 295-300, 310, 312, 349
cosmetics, 34, 69
Costa Rica, 89
Coughlin, Dan, 244-245, 248
Counterpoise, 272
CounterPunch, 57, 63, 266
CounterSpin, 182, 245
Courier-Journal, The*****
CovertAction Quarterly, 52, 58, 62, 86, 106-107, 111, 153, 185, 266
cow's milk, 8, 26, 77-79
creditors, 83
crime, 7, 43, 45, 63, 76-77, 86, 92, 149-150, 165-166, 171, 193, 202, 205, 208, 262
crime rates, 77, 262
crimes, 43-44, 76, 90-91, 96, 99, 107, 192, 199-201, 203, 207-208
criminal justice system, 16, 76, 149, 179
Croatia, 44, 81, 90-92
Crohn's disease, 8, 26, 77-80, 100
Cronkite, Walter, 45, 231
C-Span Washington Journal, 53
Cuba, 178
Cuban missile crisis, 177
CTBT
    see Comprehensive Test Ban Treaty.*****
Cultural Environment Movement, 20, 278
Cyprus, 333
Dabhol Power project, 29, 295
dairy industry, 78-79
Dalai Lama, 260
D'Alema, 338
D'Alema, Massimo, 338
Dallas Morning News, 145, 306
dam projects, 73
dam sites, 74
DAMN

see Direct Action Media Network.*****
Dark Night Field Notes, 143-144, 146
Davis, Angela, 272
Dayton Agreement, 82
DCTV
    see Downtown Community TV.*****
DDT, 68
DEA
    see Drug Enforcement Agency.*****
Defense and Economic Cooperation Agreement, 333
Defense Department, 35, 57, 178, 322, 324, 326-327
Defense Logistics Agency, 35, 326
Defentech, 113-114
Delta and Pine Land Company, 125
democracy, 11, 20-21, 38, 42, 53, 89, 92, 95, 147-148, 154, 171, 176-177, 182, 187, 191, 194-197, 208, 216, 218, 221, 244, 246, 248, 274, 278, 282-283, 285, 287, 293, 295, 300, 331-332, 339, 349
Democracy Now, 53, 147-148, 244, 246, 278, 349
Democratic Left, 121
Democratic People's Republic of Korea, 66
Denver Post, 97, 124
Department of Agriculture, 79, 125, 318
Department of Corrections, 117
Department of Defense
    see Defense Department.*****
Department of Energy, 48, 57, 128, 135, 137
Department of Interior, 104
Department of Labor, 35, 324
depleted uranium, 43, 107, 131, 133-134
diabetes, 181
Digital Millennium Copyright Act, 224
Digital Technical Information Service*****
dioxin, 68
Direct Action Media Network, 278
Disability Media Project, 278
Disney, 166-168, 171, 183-184, 187, 189-190, 192-194, 243, 310, 327
Disney World, 166-167, 192, 327
Disneyland, 183
Dissent, 12, 111, 237
Djukanovic, Milo, 81, 88
DLA
    see Defense Logistics Agency.*****
DNA, 78, 137
Doctors Without Borders, 32, 91, 205, 302, 308
DOD
    see Defense Department.*****
DOE
    see Department of Energy.*****
Dole, Bob, 54, 305
Dollars and Sense, 28-29, 266, 295
Dow, 51-52, 162, 306
Dow Jones, 162
Downing, Kathryn, 181
Downs, Hugh, 185
Downtown Community TV, 278
DPRK
    see Democratic People's Republic of Korea.*****
Drillbits & Tailings, 42, 148
Drug Enforcement Agency, 116, 145
drug industry, 32, 302, 307, 319
drug money, 83, 87
drug trade, 83, 289
drugs
    lifestyle drugs, 31, 302, 305
DU
    see depleted uranium.*****
Dugway Proving Ground, 97

350 CENSORED

How to Nominate a Censored Story

Some of the most interesting stories Project Censored evaluates are sent to us as nominations from people all over the world. These stories are clipped from small-circulation magazines or the back pages of local newspapers. If you see a story and wonder why it hasn't been covered in the mainstream media, we encourage you to send it to us as a Project Censored nomination. To nominate a *Censored* story send us a copy of the article and include the name of the source publication, the date that the article appeared, and page number.

CRITERIA FOR PROJECT CENSORED NEWS STORY NOMINATIONS

1. A censored news story is one which contains information that the general United States population has a right and need to know, but to which it has had limited access.

2. The news story is timely, ongoing, and has implications for a significant number of residents in the United States.

3. The story has clearly defined concepts and is backed up with solid, verifiable documentation.

4. The news story has been publicly published, either electronically or in print, in a circulated newspaper, journal, magazine, newsletter, or similar publication from either a foreign or domestic source.

5. The news story has direct connections to and implications for people in the United States, which can include activities that U.S. citizens are engaged in abroad.

We evaluate stories year-round and each week post important under-published stories on our Web site at www.sonoma.edu/projectcensored. The final deadline for nominating a Most *Censored* Story of the year is October 15th. Please send regular mail nominations to the address below or e-mail nominations to: censored@sonoma. edu. Our phone number for more information on Project Censored is (707) 664-2500.

Project Censored Nominations
Sociology Department
Sonoma State University
1801 East Cotati Avenue
Rohnert Park, CA 94928

Thank you for your support.

Peter Phillips
Director, Project Censored